# MELTDOWN

## ALSO BY MIKE CHINOY

*China Live:*
*People Power and the Television Revolution*

# MELT

# DOWN

## THE INSIDE STORY

## OF THE

## NORTH KOREAN

## NUCLEAR CRISIS

# MIKE CHINOY

ST. MARTIN'S PRESS
NEW YORK

MELTDOWN. Copyright © 2008 by Mike Chinoy. All rights reserved. Printed in the United States of America. For information, address St. Martin's Press, 175 Fifth Avenue, New York, N.Y. 10010.

www.stmartins.com

Design by Susan Walsh

Library of Congress Cataloging-in-Publication Data

Chinoy, Mike.
    Meltdown: the inside story of the North Korean nuclear crisis/Mike Chinoy. —1st ed.
            p.   cm.
    Includes bibliographical references and index.
    ISBN-13: 978-0-312-37153-1
    ISBN-10: 0-312-37153-5
    1. United States—Foreign relations—Korea (North)   2. Korea (North)—Foreign relations—United States   3. Nuclear nonproliferation—Korea (North)   4. Nuclear weapons—Korea (North)   5. United States—Foreign relations—2001–   6. United States—Foreign relations—2001—Philosophy   7. National security—United States   8. United States—Politics and government—2001–   I. Title
    E183.8.K6 C455 2008
    327.7305193—dc22

                                                                        2009812746

First Edition: August 2008

10   9   8   7   6   5   4   3   2   1

*To All My Family*

# CONTENTS

# ACKNOWLEDGMENTS

THIS BOOK IS THE PRODUCT OF NEARLY TWO DECADES OF COVering North Korea and its often difficult relations with the United States and the rest of the world. As a journalist, I had the opportunity to visit North Korea on many occasions and to cover many of the key events and talk to the leading players, not only in Pyongyang but in Washington, Seoul, Beijing, and elsewhere. But the great frustration of the working journalist—chained to breaking news and constant deadlines—is the difficulty of getting beyond the headlines. This is especially true when it comes to the diplomatic maneuvering, intelligence judgments, and policy battles over a country as secretive as North Korea.

The support of the Edgerton Foundation and the Pacific Council on International Policy gave me the opportunity to devote eighteen months to unraveling the story of North Korea's nuclear breakout. Without the backing of Brad Edgerton, Pacific Council President Geoffrey Garrett and Chairman Warren Christopher, this project would have remained nothing more than the idle fantasy of a frustrated TV correspondent. The Pacific Council gave me a base to conduct research and an exceptionally genial group of colleagues. Special thanks to David Karl, computer genius Poul-Erik Norgaard, Dawn Nakagawa, Nicole McAllister, Chaka Jones, Jennifer Faust, Betty Feille, Raynon McKee, and Yanisa Jacobs. Michael Parks, director of the Annenberg School of Journalism at the University of Southern California, and Dean Geoffrey Cowan also played a crucial role in bringing me to Los Angeles. Jonathan Aronson and his colleagues at the Annenberg Center for Communication provided office space and other invaluable support. Special thanks as well to the Korea Foundation.

My former employer, CNN, sent to me Pyongyang for the first time in 1989, gave me the opportunity to return on more than a dozen occasions, and graciously allowed me to use material collected during my newsgathering activities in this book. Special thanks to Chris Cramer, Eason Jordan, and my comrades on numerous reporting trips to North Korea, especially Tim Schwarz, Neil Bennett, Scott Clotworthy, and Chris Goacher.

Over the years that I have tried to understand North Korea, I have talked to hundreds of people, but have come to especially value the insights of a small group of North Korea hands to whom I have repeatedly turned for their wise analysis: Balbina Hwang, L. Gordon Flake, Jon Wolfsthal, John Merrill, and Leon Sigal. The hours I spent talking with them not only deepened my understanding of the issues, but also allowed me to turn the idea of this book into reality. Leon Sigal in particular, whose own book, *Disarming Strangers,* is the definitive account of the 1994 nuclear crisis, was unstinting in his support. He generously shared not only his deep knowledge but the transcripts of his own research interviews, as well as the extraordinarily detailed chronology of North Korea–related events he compiled over many years. It became my essential reference point as I tried to piece this exceptionally complicated story together. He, along with David Straub, read the entire manuscript and offered valuable criticisms and suggestions. So did Nick Street, whose editorial insights and help were invaluable, as were those from Bradley Martin.

The research for *Meltdown* took me around the world, and people in many cities offered hospitality, contacts, and support. Particular thanks to Ira, Gail, and Molly Chinoy, Zain Verjee, Joe and Mei-chou Donovan, Peter Beck, Michael Breen, Evans Revere, Inez Ho, and the staff of the West Naomi St. Starbucks and Roaster Family Coffee in Arcadia, California, where much of the book was written.

I was lucky to have a group of extremely capable students, both at the University of Southern California and elsewhere, who helped with gathering information, transcribing interviews, and other time-consuming but essential tasks. My thanks to Tate Rider, Rebecca Johnson, Teresa Cheng, Stephen Duval, Peter Sotiropolis, Spencer Trujillo, Leanne Joyce, Brittany Hayes, Chris Jones, Joseph Popiolkowski, Mark Arteaga, Edward Moreno, David DeSola, Rohan Malhotra, Pradyumna Kejirwal, Shridevi Bajaj, Nicole Hummel, Jeenho Hahn, Karl Yoder, Thomas Klotz, Gavin Yerxa, Andrew Morris, Nancy Wu, Juliette Rousselot, Nur Zulkephli, Sara Chung, Kiran Thakur, Kate Vizza, Jenna Stoeltje, Shanel Melamed, Ashlee Holmes, Stephanie Farrell, Andy Bunting, Melanie Sugarbroad, and Arabella Arcuragi.

A special note of appreciation to Alyson Slack, whose energy and commitment was crucially important.

My agent, Mel Berger, never wavered in his support, and helped to find this book a home at St. Martin's Press. At St. Martin's, I am grateful for the wise counsel of my editor, Phil Revzin, and for the help of Jenness Crawford.

My sister, Clara Mora Chinoy, and my cousin, the writer John Krich, provided moral support and encouragement. My wife, Lynne, and sons, Dan and Ben, all helped with the book—Ben by compiling lists of interviewees, Dan and Lynne by reading the manuscript and offering valuable suggestions—and all of them by tolerating my long absences from home and obsessive preoccupation with North Korea with understanding and good humor. Without them, the book would not have been possible.

When I wrote my last book a decade ago, my mother, Helen Krich Chinoy, read every word and offered wise advice. She was too ill to be able to do so this time—but she was with me in spirit.

—Arcadia, California
March 2008

# CAST OF CHARACTERS

## WASHINGTON

President Bill Clinton, 1993–2001

Sandy Berger—National Security Adviser, 1997–2001

Madeleine Albright—Secretary of State, 1996–2001

Wendy Sherman—North Korea Policy Coordinator, 1997–2001

President George W. Bush, 2001–

Vice President Dick Cheney, 2001–

Colin Powell—Secretary of State, 2001–2005

Donald Rumsfeld—Secretary of Defense, 2001–2006

John McLaughlin—Deputy Director, CIA, 2000–2004

Condoleezza Rice—National Security Adviser, 2001–2004, Secretary of
State, 2005–

Stephen Hadley—Deputy National Security Adviser, 2001–2004,
National Security Adviser, 2005–

Richard Armitage—Deputy Secretary of State, 2001–2004

James Kelly—Assistant Secretary of State for East Asia, 2001–2004

Christopher Hill—Assistant Secretary of State for East Asia, 2005–

John Bolton—Under Secretary of State for Arms Control, 2001–2005,
U.S. Ambassador to the UN, 2005–2006

Robert Joseph—National Security Council, Senior Director for Counterproliferation, 2001–2005, Under Secretary of State for Arms Control, 2005–2007

Michael Green—National Security Council, Director for Asian Affairs, 2001–2004, Senior Director for Asian Affairs, 2004–2005

Victor Cha—National Security Council, Director of Asian Affairs, 2004–2007

Charles "Chuck" Kartman—State Department Special Envoy for Peace Talks with North Korea, 1998–2001, Executive Director, Korean Peninsula Energy Development Organization (KEDO), 2001–2005

Charles "Jack" Pritchard—National Security Council, Senior Director for Asian Affairs, 2000, State Department Special Envoy for Negotiations with North Korea, 2001–2003

Robert Carlin—North Korea Analyst, Bureau of Intelligence and Research, State Department, 1992–2002, Senior Policy Adviser, Korean Peninsula Energy Development Organization (KEDO), 2003–2006

Thomas Hubbard—Principal Deputy Assistant Secretary of State for East Asia, 2000–2001, Ambassador to South Korea, 2001–2004

Evans Revere—State Department Korea Desk Director, 1998–2000, Deputy Chief of Mission, U.S. Embassy, Seoul 2000–2003

David Straub—State Department Korea Desk Director, 2002–2004

James Foster—State Department Korea Desk Director, 2004–2006

David Asher—Senior Adviser for East Asian and Pacific Affairs, State Department, 2001–2005

Sung Kim—State Department Korea Desk Director, 2006–

Richard Boucher—State Department Spokesman, 2000–2005

Lawrence Wilkerson—Colin Powell's Chief of Staff, 2002–2004

Mark Groombridge—Chief Asian Adviser to John Bolton, 2001–2006

John Rood—National Security Council, Director for Counterproliferation, 2001–2003, Senior Director for Counterproliferation, 2005–2006

Aaron Friedberg—Deputy National Security Adviser, Office of the Vice President, 2003–2005

Stephen Yates—Deputy National Security Adviser, Office of the Vice President, 2001–2005

Daniel Glaser—Deputy Assistant Treasury Secretary for Terrorist Financing and Financial Crimes, 2004–

Stuart Levey—Under Secretary of the Treasury for Terrorism and Financial Intelligence, 2004–

## PYONGYANG

Kim Il Sung—North Korean leader, died 1994

Kim Jong Il—Kim Il Sung's son and successor, 1994–

Jo Myong Rok—Vice Marshal, North Korean Armed Forces, 1995–

Kang Sok Ju—First Vice Foreign Minister, 1987–

Kim Gye Gwan—Deputy Foreign Minister, 1995–

Li Gun—Deputy Permanent Representatives to the UN, 1997–2001, Deputy Director-General for North American Affairs, North Korean Foreign Ministry, 2001–2006

Li Hyong Chol—Permanent Representative to the UN, 1997–2001

Han Song Ryol—Deputy Permanent Representative to the UN, 2001–2006

Pak Gil Yon—Permanent Representative to the UN, 2001–

Paek Nam Sun—Foreign Minister, 1998–2007

Pak Ui Chun—Foreign Minister, 2007–

Kim Yong Nam—President of Supreme People's Assembly, 1998–

## SEOUL

Kim Dae-jung—President of South Korea, 1998–2003

Roh Moo-hyun—President of South Korea, 2003–2008

Yoon Young-kwan—South Korean Foreign Minister, 2003–2004

Lee Jong-seok—South Korean Deputy National Security Adviser, 2003–2006, Minister of Unification, 2006

Chun Yung-woo—South Korean envoy to six-party talks, 2006–

## BEIJING

Hu Jintao—President of China, 2003–

Li Zhaoxing—Foreign Minister, 2003–2007

Wu Dawei—Vice Minister of Foreign Affairs, 2004–

Cui Tiankai—Director, Asian Department, Foreign Ministry, 2003–2006, Assistant Minister of Foreign Affairs, 2006–

Tang Jiaxuan—Minister of Foreign Affairs, 2000–2003, State Councilor, 2003–

## TOKYO

Junichiro Koizumi—Prime Minister, 2001–2006

Shinzo Abe—Prime Minister, 2006–2007

Hitoshi Tanaka—Director General, Asia and Oceanian Affairs Bureau, Foreign Ministry, 2001–2002, Deputy Foreign Minister, 2003–2005

## MOSCOW

Vladimir Putin—President of Russia, 1999–2008, Prime Minister, 2008–

# PREFACE

I̴T WAS BITTERLY COLD IN PYONGYANG, AND THERE WAS NO HEAT at the forbidding North Korean Foreign Ministry building off Kim Il Sung Square. On December 5, 2007, a shivering Christopher Hill, the U.S. assistant secretary of state for East Asia, trudged up four flights of dimly lit stairs to the office of North Korean foreign minister Pak Ui Chun. The large but sparsely furnished room was warmed only slightly by a space heater.

Hill took out an envelope. Pak stood up and, with some ceremony, held out both hands to accept it. Speaking with deliberate formality after Hill placed the envelope in his hands, Pak said, "I have received a letter for our General Kim Jong Il from His Excellency George W. Bush, President of the United States, and I will endeavor to faithfully convey this letter to General Kim Jong Il."

The tone of the letter was polite and respectful. It began, "Dear Mr. Chairman," and ended with the simple, handwritten signature, "George W. Bush." In the letter—to which Hill had added a U.S.-drafted translation, as he didn't trust the North Koreans to give Kim an accurate version—the president offered North Korea fully normalized relations with the United States. In effect, Bush was accepting Kim Jong Il as a legitimate partner in international relations, acknowledging the nation over which he ruled with an iron fist as a sovereign state. In return, the president told Kim, the North must fully disclose and abandon the nuclear program that had locked the United States and North Korea in a dangerous mode of confrontation throughout the Bush presidency.

That frigid day in Pyongyang marked a historic turning point in one of the last simmering disputes of the Cold War. But it came only after six years of needless brinksmanship, missed opportunities, and the disasterous elevation of North Korea and Kim Jong Il to the club of nuclear powers. And even then, there were no assurances of a lasting solution. How did this happen?

By his own admission, George W. Bush "loathed" Kim Jong Il. The feeling was personal, visceral, and beyond political calculation. Bush at various times had used the words "pygmy," "tyrant," "dangerous person," and "spoiled child" to describe the man known in North Korea as the "Dear Leader." Most memorably, Bush had included North Korea, along with Iran and Iraq, in the "Axis of Evil."

Throughout his tenure, the president had often aligned himself with neoconservative hard-liners who believed that to negotiate with someone like Kim was immoral because it meant legitimizing and perhaps prolonging the existence of one of the world's most dangerous and inhumane regimes. Efforts by the Clinton administration to forge a rapprochement—which had produced a deal in 1994 under which the North froze its nascent nuclear program in return for economic and diplomatic benefits and that almost led to a Clinton visit to Pyongyang for a summit with Kim—were dismissed as "appeasement."

Instead, under the Bush administration's post-9/11 doctrine of preemption to promote regime change in "rogue states," the United States sought to undermine Kim Jong Il through severe economic and diplomatic pressure while keeping the ultimate threat of military action on the table. Despite repeated North Korean appeals for talks, the administration for more than five years refused to engage in meaningful bilateral negotiations. What diplomatic contacts did occur were marked by threats, acrimony, and calculated rudeness on both sides. American diplomats were ordered by senior officials in Washington not to host meals for their North Korean counterparts, not to be in the same room alone with them, and not to engage in any give-and-take discussions.

As this drama was unfolding, the United States invaded Iraq, toppled Saddam Hussein, and trumpeted his fate as an object lesson in what could happen to a hostile regime that sought to produce weapons of mass destruction.

"Rogue states such as Iran, North Korea, Syria, Libya and Cuba, whose pursuit of weapons of mass destruction makes them hostile to U.S. interests," declared then–Under Secretary of State for Arms Control John Bolton, "will learn that their covert programs will not escape either detection or consequences."

But Kim Jong Il—who, contrary to the conventional stereotype, is neither crazy nor irrational, and whose main goal in a strategically realigned post–Cold War world has always been regime survival—drew the opposite conclusion. In his view, going nuclear was the best and perhaps the only way to ensure he wouldn't share Saddam Hussein's fate. In the face of intense American pressure, Kim staged a nuclear breakout, ending the nuclear freeze, expelling international inspectors from the Yongbyon nuclear facility, restarting the reactor there, and producing enough weapons-grade plutonium to make, by some estimates, from six to ten nuclear bombs.

The North consistently warned that unless the Bush administration ended what Pyongyang called Washington's "hostile policy," North Korea would continue to strengthen its nuclear "deterrent." In October 2006, Kim Jong Il made good on his threat. Defying economic pressure and diplomatic appeals from the United States, China, Japan, South Korea, Russia, the UN Security Council, and the international community, the North—despite acute food shortages, economic collapse, and international isolation—conducted an underground nuclear test and became the world's eighth declared nuclear power. The Bush administration's worst fear—a "rogue state" acquiring nuclear weapons—had become a reality.

How the Bush administration, with a foreign policy built around preventing countries like North Korea from acquiring weapons of mass destruction, was unable to deter a secretive, isolated regime from developing nuclear weapons and the capability of delivering them is the subject of *Meltdown*. It is the story of an American foreign policy failure whose themes resonate well beyond North Korea: the breakdown of the global system of nonproliferation, the challenge of dealing with the nuclear ambitions of so-called rogue states, the fraying of American relations with key allies like South Korea and Japan, the erosion of the U.S. position in Asia, the emergence of China as a major player on the international stage, and the political manipulation of intelligence.

Above all, it is the story of an administration whose North Korea policy making was marked by infighting, incoherence, and diplomatic incompetence. For much of the president's tenure, Korea policy was paralyzed by the bitter struggle between hard-line conservatives—among them Vice President Cheney, counterproliferation policy makers Robert Joseph and John Bolton, Defense Secretary Donald Rumsfeld, and their allies—and those who supported continued engagement with Pyongyang, most notably Secretary of State Colin Powell, his deputy, Richard Armitage, and, later, Condoleezza Rice and her chief negotiator, Christopher Hill. Advocates of engagement also included the Asia/Korea specialists in the State Department. At various times, each side was convinced that it had the support of the president.

In part this confusion and conflict were a reflection of the struggle between President Bush's head and his heart over the issue of North Korea. By instinct, the president—with his black-and-white worldview, empathy for the suffering of the North Korean people, and preference for wielding a big stick—sided with the hard-liners. When they were dominant, however, U.S. decision making on North Korea was a combination of moral outrage, confrontational rhetoric, military muscle-flexing, and a disdain for the subtleties of diplomacy and anything the Clinton administration had tried to accomplish.

In this respect, the echoes of the U.S. disaster in Iraq are clearly evident—with some twists. Bush justified the toppling of Saddam Hussein because he believed the Iraqi dictator's pursuit of weapons of mass destruction—especially a nuclear bomb—threatened U.S. interests. It turned out, of course, that Saddam had no such weapons and that U.S. intelligence agencies had produced assessments under political pressure from administration hard-liners who were seeking to justify the invasion.

In the case of North Korea, the existence of a nuclear program was well-known, and Kim Jong Il had made little effort to disguise his attempts to build a bomb. Moreover, there is little question of the accuracy of U.S. intelligence showing that the North was seeking to acquire components for a program to make weapons from highly enriched uranium. Yet, even in the aftermath of the Iraqi intelligence debacle, the intelligence on North Korea was also politicized, with those seeking confrontation blurring the distinction between procurement efforts and the actual manufacturing of weapons and warning of a shorter—and thus more threatening—time frame for the North's completion of a uranium bomb.

In sharp contrast to Iraq, however—as Kim Jong Il pursued his nuclear breakout—the Bush administration, for all its bluster, did nothing. The North Koreans repeatedly crossed "red lines"—reprocessing spent fuel rods into weapons-grade plutonium, declaring themselves a nuclear power, actually testing a bomb—that, during the Clinton administration, would have likely triggered military action. Having ruled out the direct negotiations Pyongyang was demanding, the Bush administration found itself unable to back up its harsh rhetoric with action.

One cynic dubbed Bush's policy toward Pyongyang, "no talks, no carrots and no sticks."

The administration's all-consuming focus on Iraq provides one explanation for this combination of tough talk and no action. Another is that, however strong his emotional reaction to North Korea's plight, George W. Bush also eventually recognized that the continuing confrontation with North Korea was adversely affecting relations with key allies like South Korea and Japan, as well as an increasingly influential China. Moreover, despite American saber rattling, the military option—already fraught with risk during the Clinton years—had become even more unpalatable with the growth of the North's nuclear arsenal.

The United States did not know where the North was hiding the new bombs it had manufactured. Any preemptive American attack would risk provoking a massive North Korean retaliatory strike on Seoul, missile launches against Japan, and intense opposition from all the nations in the region.

"You can have a very visceral reaction to the way Kim Jong Il treats his people," said one former senior Bush adviser, "but the other half of his [the president's] brain says, 'We have to solve this problem. If we have to try diplomacy to solve the problem, we will.'"

With sanctions and threats of coercion proving ineffective and the military option raising the possibility of a second Korean War at a time when the United States was already bogged down in Iraq and Afghanistan, the Bush administration was left with no real alternatives to negotiation. Reluctantly, the president was forced to heed the advice of Christopher Hill and Condoleezza Rice, who argued that diplomatic give-and-take—which would require uncomfortable compromises with one of the most despotic regimes on the face of the earth—was the only way forward. This about-face culminated in Hill's December 2007 mission to Pyongyang.

When George W. Bush took office, North Korea's nuclear program was on ice and Kim Jong Il was believed to have, at most, enough weapons-grade plutonium for one or two nuclear bombs. By the time Bush wrote his letter to Kim Jong Il, however, North Korea had become a full-fledged nuclear power, with enough fissile material to stage an underground test, manufacture perhaps as many as ten more warheads, and—in the worst-case scenario—provide nuclear know-how or fissile material to terrorist groups. While the North insisted that in principle it was prepared to negotiate full denuclearization—for the right price—it remained far from clear whether the Pyongyang regime was in fact ready to trade its nuclear weapons for a nuclear deal.

Without the bomb, North Korea was just another impoverished third-world dictatorship. With nuclear weapons, Kim Jong Il had successfully defied the world's leading superpower and—nearly two decades after the collapse of Communism almost everywhere else—managed to keep his despotic system afloat.

As 2008 began, the challenge for American diplomacy was whether George Bush's assurances of future diplomatic relations would be enough to prompt the North to make a fundamental strategic change. The same question had existed during the final months of the Clinton administration. But the abrupt change to a more confrontational U.S. policy early in the Bush administration meant that North Korea's oft-stated willingness to denuclearize had never been tested in meaningful, ongoing negotiations. Now, finally, George W. Bush was ready to test Kim Jong Il's intentions. After the harrowing roller-coaster ride of events chronicled in this book, it remains unclear whether the change in U.S. policy has come too late to roll back a nuclear program far more extensive and dangerous than the one that North Korea had when George W. Bush took office.

# MELTDOWN

# 1

# "WITHOUT YOU THERE IS NO US"

O N THE EVENING OF OCTOBER 12, 2000, I STOOD IN THE vast Mayday Stadium in Pyongyang, the capital of North Korea, watching an impassioned crowd of more than 100,000 declare their allegiance to the world's most bizarre and enigmatic leader, Kim Jong Il. On one side of the stadium hung the image of two giant red flowers, representing the "Kimjongilia," a hybrid begonia created by an admiring botanist to honor the man the North Koreans called the "Dear Leader." The stadium floor was packed with thousands of people—marching bands featuring cheerleaders in short skirts and white calf-length boots who would not have been out of place at a Dallas Cowboys halftime show, acrobats fired from cannons, gymnasts dressed in army uniforms, and rows and rows of young men and women waving banners in what seemed like an endless North Korean version of the Mexican wave. In the stands behind them, 35,000 people were flipping colored cards with extraordinary precision, creating images of patriotic heroism, economic achievement, and military triumph aimed at stoking the ardor of the already frenzied throng.

Moments later, with fireworks illuminating the chilly autumn sky, Kim Jong Il entered the VIP area just fifty yards from where I watched with a CNN camera crew and two North Korean government minders. Short, pudgy, wearing his traditional boilersuit, surrounded by other senior officials, the Dear Leader walked confidently with what seemed to be a satisfied smirk on his face, waving somewhat mechanically to the masses below. Children presented him with bunches of flowers as the card flippers spelled out "Highest Glory to the Great Leader Comrade Kim Jong Il" and a band blared out "The Song of General Kim Jong Il." "Without you, there is no country," the crowd sang in unison. "Without you there is no us."

The son of Kim Il Sung, the dictator who had started the Korean War and ruled North Korea for almost fifty years until his death in 1994, the younger Kim was a figure of mystery. Long mocked in the West for his bouffant hairdo and platform shoes, taste for fast cars and Hollywood movies (his personal film collection was said to number 20,000), Kim and his late father were the object of a personality cult that they had spent decades cultivating. In many respects, they had turned North Korea into a secretive and militant quasi-religious sect, a society nominally Communist but devoted primarily to worshipping the father, known as the Great Leader, and the Dear Leader who succeeded him. Statues and giant portraits of the two men dominated the North Korean landscape, including a giant bronze replica of the elder Kim, arm outstretched, which still towers over the skyline of Pyongyang. The country's 22 million citizens all wore small lapel pins bearing the likeness of one or both Kims. The state-run media described Kim Il Sung as a "peerless patriot" and "iron-willed commander," and the son as a "great revolutionary, a great statesman and a great people's father."

This was not my first glimpse of the Dear Leader. I had been to similar events before; in fact, this was my twelfth trip to North Korea in eleven years. This unusual access was in large part an accident. My first trip had come in July 1989, when I was CNN's bureau chief in Beijing. The government in Pyongyang invited a small group of China-based Western reporters to cover the activities of a young South Korean student who had defied her country's laws to travel to the then-forbidden North. Like almost all visitors, I had been both astounded and appalled by the regimentation and brainwashing of the North Korean cult of personality. I also had the feeling that what we were allowed to see amounted to little more than a series of Potemkin villages. Pyongyang, a surprisingly attractive city with manicured parks, vast boulevards, and tall buildings, appeared almost empty. I saw virtually no shops, restaurants, or advertisements, and apart form our official convoy of Mercedes-Benzes, virtually no vehicles.

Three years later, in April 1992, the North Koreans invited the Rev. Billy Graham to visit and agreed to let him bring one American news organization of his choice to cover the trip. He picked CNN. We flew into Pyongyang on a shuddery Russian-built Air Koryo TU-134 that was specially sent to Beijing to fetch Graham and his party.

Since my first visit, the world had changed profoundly: the Berlin Wall had fallen; the Soviet Union and the rest of North Korea's allies in the socialist world had collapsed; and Kim Il Sung's Cold War peers, such as Erich Honecker of East Germany, and Romania's Nicolae Ceaușescu, had been toppled (in Ceaușescu's case, murdered, along with his wife). The Warsaw Pact no longer existed, and both Moscow and Beijing had opened diplomatic relations with North Korea's longtime rival, South Korea. China, which had saved North Korea from defeat in the Korean War and remained its closest friend, had embraced market-style economic reforms.

In addition, the U.S. military's rapid triumph over Saddam Hussein in the first Gulf War highlighted America's high-tech military prowess and the corresponding weakness of North Korea's armed forces, with their outdated Soviet-designed weapons and equipment. More isolated than ever, the regime in Pyongyang was increasingly anxious about its ability to survive in the post–Cold War world. Kim Il Sung's concerns were heightened by growing evidence of internal economic decline. There were reports of growing shortages of food and fuel, and of factories standing idle. The North Korean press had recently issued a call for all citizens to limit themselves to two meals a day.

A number of consequences flowed from this dramatically changed strategic situation. Kim Il Sung and Kim Jong Il apparently reached the conclusion that only an accommodation with the world's sole superpower, the United States, could ensure the continued viability of the regime. But such an accommodation had to be based on a projection of strength, not weakness. The result, which became clearer in the coming years, was a dual-track strategy. Its central elements: seeking to establish a long-term strategic relationship with the United States while building up an arsenal of ballistic missiles and nuclear weapons, to use either as a deterrent or in self-defense, if necessary, or to trade away—if relations fundamentally improved and the price was right.

On the third day of Graham's visit, after he had been allowed to preach at the capital's only Protestant church (I had wondered whether the entire congregation had been assembled just for his benefit), the evangelist received a summons to meet the Great Leader, Kim Il Sung. My cameraman and I drove with Graham to a lavish residence in the countryside outside Pyongyang, where I was allowed to shake Kim's hand, show him pictures of my family, and have a photograph taken with him. During their meeting, Graham conveyed an oral message to Kim from President George H. W. Bush. In the presence of our cameras, Kim said, "We are having sunny spring weather today. I hope this means a spring will come in relations between my country and the U.S." It was a theme other North Korean officials returned to repeatedly during my stay.

The Great Leader was an imposing figure: stocky, broad-shouldered, with a deep voice and a pronounced potbelly. He also had an enormous lump the size of an orange on the right-hand side of his neck, reportedly a benign tumor that

Kim chose not to have removed. His aides and courtiers were clearly both in awe and fear of him. Even the North Korean photographers bowed obsequiously when Kim entered the room, before they turned on their antiquated film cameras—a sharp contrast to the state-of-the-art Sony video camera used by my CNN shooter—to record the handshake with Graham.

Observing Kim, I struggled to understand the dynamics of the society he ruled. In an earlier book, I made the following observations, which, many years later, still make sense to me.

> I came to realize it was not productive to view North Korea as merely just another, slightly more eccentric communist state. The best analogy seemed to be a religious camp grafted onto a very conservative, inward-looking society steeped in Confucian tradition, where the purpose of life was to glorify the reigning deity, namely the Great Leader.[1]

I also noted some "striking parallels—not with the substance but with the trappings—to primitive Christianity. Kim's birthplace resembled the nativity scene, to the point that members of Graham's entourage jokingly called it Bethlehem. There was a father (Kim Il Sung), a son (Kim Jong Il), and a holy ideology (*juche,* or self-reliance). People displayed their faith by wearing not crucifixes, but the ubiquitous Kim Il Sung buttons. And, as in medieval societies, heretics were condemned to terrible punishments."[2]

Kim's persona as an all-powerful leader, the often inflammatory rhetoric in North Korean propaganda, and the regime's state of permanent political and military mobilization produced the overwhelming sensation of a society and leadership that felt under perpetual siege, struggling to survive in an increasingly inhospitable world. From the outside, North Korea appeared menacing and bellicose. Inside, its truculent posture appeared defensive rather than offensive in nature.

Two years after Graham's visit, on April 16, 1994, I met Kim Il Sung again. Since my last encounter, tensions had risen dramatically because of North Korea's nuclear program. The shadow of nuclear weapons had hung over the Korean peninsula since the Korean War, when the United States threatened to use its nuclear arsenal to bring the conflict to a rapid and victorious conclusion. Kim Il Sung's interest in acquiring his own bomb is widely believed to date from this time. In the late 1950s, a nuclear research complex was established at Yongbyon north of Pyongyang, and by the mid-1980s, a five-megawatt reactor was in full operation. Although Pyongyang signed the Non-Proliferation Treaty

(NPT) in 1985, the International Atomic Energy Agency (IAEA) in 1992 had uncovered discrepancies in data provided by the North Koreans. The questionable data raised suspicions that the North had produced, and was concealing, weapons-grade plutonium from fuel previously extracted from the reactor at Yongbyon. The IAEA demanded special inspections.

In response, in early 1993, the North announced plans to withdraw from the NPT. Following this threat, Pyongyang had test-fired a Rodong-1 missile, potentially capable of carrying a nuclear warhead, into the Sea of Japan; limited the access of IAEA inspectors; and threatened to remove more spent fuel rods from Yongbyon and reprocess them into weapons-grade plutonium. The Clinton administration, fearing that the North was on the brink of expanding its nuclear capability, threatened to bring a sanctions resolution to the United Nations. Pyongyang declared that it would regard such a step as an "act of war."

In a meeting at the Demilitarized Zone in March 1994, a North Korean official warned that if conflict broke out, the North would turn Seoul into "a sea of fire."

With my coverage of Billy Graham's visit having apparently impressed the North Koreans with CNN's global reach, I was invited to bring a CNN team to Pyongyang to cover a visit by a small group of foreign dignitaries participating in celebrations to mark Kim Il Sung's eighty-second birthday on April 15. The following morning, we spent two and a half hours with the Great Leader at the lavish marble-clad Kumsusan Palace on the outskirts of the capital. Kim appeared confident, relaxed, and in robust health. Over a lunch of roast goose and quail egg soup, he went out of his way to emphasize his desire for a peaceful resolution of the nuclear crisis.

"The world is now calling on our country to show nuclear weapons we don't have," Kim said emphatically. "I have had just about enough. What's the use to have them? We don't want war . . . We have done a lot of construction in our country and we don't want to destroy it. Those who want war are out of their minds."

I interpreted Kim's statement as a signal that he wanted to negotiate a way out of the looming crisis. Yet, for reasons of national pride and negotiating leverage, Pyongyang followed Kim's statement with another signature act of brinksmanship, unloading nearly 8,000 spent fuel rods from the reactor at Yongbyon. During the process, according to nuclear proliferation experts, the North refused "to allow the IAEA to record the location of the individual fuel rods in the core, thus destroying one of the key technical means for measuring the operational history of the reactor and determining total plutonium production."[3] The result was to make the task of determining whether Pyongyang had already produced more weapons-grade plutonium much more difficult, if not impossible. Moreover, if the fuel rods were processed, experts said North Korea would be able to build five or six new nuclear weapons.

The prospect that North Korea—impoverished, isolated, anxious about its own survival, and with a long track record of selling missiles and military technology to nations hostile to the United States—might soon possess a half-dozen nuclear weapons set off alarm bells in Washington. As spring moved toward summer in 1994, the Clinton administration began serious preparations for a military option. Plans were drawn up for the evacuation of American civilians from South Korea and for a preemptive air strike to destroy the Yongbyon nuclear facility with precision-guided bombs. U.S. commanders were convinced that North Korea would respond to such a strike by attacking South Korea. In a country long victimized by its larger, more powerful neighbors, now organized under a system whose guiding ideology, devised by Kim Il Sung, *juche*—loosely translated as "self-reliance"—there was no way that Kim would bow to external pressure, especially from the hated Americans. The U.S. military calculated that a full-scale war would kill as many as one million people, including nearly 100,000 Americans residing in South Korea.[4]

Alarmed at what seemed to be an inexorable slide toward disaster, former U.S. president Jimmy Carter decided to intervene, traveling to Pyongyang in mid-June for talks with Kim Il Sung. The report I had broadcast on CNN of my meeting with Kim in April had impressed North Korean authorities with the network's global reach. At the last minute, I received permission to travel with Carter, and was the only journalist allowed by the North Koreans to accompany him. In an atmosphere of extreme tension, I followed the former president on the almost deserted four-lane highway from the DMZ to Pyongyang and watched as he met Kim Il Sung at the palace, where I'd enjoyed lunch with the Great Leader two months before. At Kim's side was Deputy Foreign Minister Kang Sok Ju, a tough, plain-spoken veteran of earlier diplomatic encounters with the United States. Given North Korea's preoccupation with "dignity," the presence of such a distinguished foreign visitor provided an opportunity for Kim Il Sung to compromise without appearing to lose face. On June 16, Carter brokered the outlines of a deal, under which the North Korean leader agreed to freeze his nuclear program in return for an end to the U.S. push for sanctions and the resumption of talks with Washington. The former president announced the breakthrough in a live interview on CNN as senior Clinton administration officials were finalizing their war plans; they halted their meeting to gather around a TV set in the White House to hear Carter's news.

A dangerous confrontation had been averted. North Korean officials were so relieved they took Carter for a cruise on Kim Il Sung's luxurious yacht and gave me and my CNN colleagues the most precious possible gift—our very own Kim Il Sung buttons.

Four months later, in Geneva on October 21, 1994, after intensive and difficult negotiations, Assistant Secretary of State Robert Gallucci and Kang Sok Ju signed a three-page document called the Agreed Framework. The talks had been complicated by Kim Il Sung's sudden death from a heart attack in July and uncertainties surrounding the succession of Kim Jong Il. But the North appeared politically stable, and Kim was apparently eager to build on the commitments his father made to Jimmy Carter.

The Agreed Framework was for all practical purposes a treaty, but given the likelihood of resistance in Washington from Republicans who were opposed to any deal benefiting the Kim regime, the Clinton administration preferred to structure the accord so that no formal congressional ratification was required. Under the Agreed Framework, Pyongyang pledged to freeze its one operating reactor, the five-megawatt facility at Yongbyon that had produced the weapons-grade plutonium at the heart of the crisis. Construction on two other reactors would be halted, and North Korean nuclear facilities would be opened to international inspection.

For its part, the United States promised to back the creation of an international consortium to build, by 2003, two light-water reactors, which were considered "proliferation-resistant" because they produced less material that could be used to make bombs. Washington also agreed to help meet North Korea's energy needs in the interim by supplying 500,000 tons of heavy fuel oil annually, and to move toward a broader diplomatic engagement, including, eventually, the full normalization of relations. Before the completion of the light-water reactors, the North would come into full compliance with the IAEA, including allowing intrusive "special inspections," and would eventually dismantle altogether both its existing five-megawatt reactor and two others under construction.

Soon after the agreement was signed, the North Koreans shut down the reactor and permitted inspectors, including some Americans, to return to Yongbyon. Pyongyang worked with teams of U.S. government experts to safely store in cooling ponds the 8,000 spent fuel rods that had been unloaded from the five-megawatt reactor, thus ensuring continuous international monitoring of plutonium which could otherwise have been turned into nuclear bombs. In March 1995, the United States, Japan, and South Korea established a consortium to oversee the construction of the light-water reactors. Despite haggling over who would pay the estimated $5 billion cost, and who would build the reactors (South Korea wanted its own firms to supply them while Pyongyang initially insisted on a non–South Korean company), agreement was reached on the fundamentals, and the Korean Peninsula Energy Development Association, or KEDO, came into full operation.

From the moment the Agreed Framework was signed, however, it received a skeptical reaction in the United States. Instead of focusing on stopping the North's production of plutonium for nuclear weapons, the headline in the *New York Times* read: "Clinton Approves Plan to Give Aid to North Korea." The *Washington Post* headline was: "North Korea Pact Contains U.S. Concessions: Agreement Would Allow Presence of Key Plutonium-Making Facilities for Seven Years." Clinton's critics in the Republican Party were even harsher, denouncing the administration for giving too much to North Korea and not getting enough in return. Words like "appeasement" and "surrender" filled the airwaves.

Just seventeen days after the accord was signed, the Republicans took control of both the Senate and the House of Representatives in midterm elections. In the following years, besieged by the Republicans on many fronts, the administration struggled to secure Congressional authorization for even the modest amounts of money needed to cover the shipments of heavy fuel oil promised by the Agreed Framework. Funding for KEDO became equally contentious, with the result that fuel shipments were frequently delayed. In addition, construction of the light-water reactors was slow to start, making the target date of 2003 an increasingly distant prospect. Washington did little to ease sanctions against North Korea. Neither Washington nor Pyongyang moved to abrogate the accord, but the prospect of a broader thaw in the long-running conflict on the Korean peninsula faded.

With the Congress against him and his standing undermined by the Monica Lewinsky scandal, President Clinton had little political capital to expend to sell the idea of engaging with a regime as unsavory as North Korea's. Meanwhile, for its part, North Korea's frustration at what it saw as the Clinton administration's failure to deliver on its promises continued to mount. On my visits to Pyongyang in 1995 and 1996, North Korean officials hinted at differences between "moderates" in the Foreign Ministry who supported the deal and wanted to improve ties with Washington, and "hard-liners" in the military who were skeptical that the North was gaining anything from the accord. The state-run media began making periodic threats that North Korea might withdraw from the Agreed Framework and restart the nuclear program if the United States didn't live up to its obligations.

Still, the immediate crisis over the North's nuclear ambitions that had led Washington and Pyongyang to the brink of war in 1994 had eased. And whatever its flaws, the Agreed Framework had unquestionably halted a rapidly expanding nuclear program in its tracks. As the nuclear specialist David Albright noted in 2002, "If the Agreed Framework had not 'frozen' North Korea's nuclear program . . . in total, by about 2000, North Korea could have accumulated 300–400 kilograms of weapons-grade plutonium. Assuming that five kilograms is enough for a nuclear weapon, this amount of plutonium is enough for about 60–80 nuclear weapons."[5]

In the mid-1990s, however, North Korea faced a new crisis. Devastating floods, a catastrophic harvest, and the inefficiency of the country's centrally planned socialist economy triggered massive food shortages. Crippled by a lack of fuel and electrical power, the country's industry and transport ground to a halt, and the economy virtually imploded. By early 1997, North Korea was in the grip of a brutal famine, forcing the regime, for the first time—in stark contrast to the *juche* ideology of self-reliance—to appeal for international help. As the UN and other aid agencies gained access to parts of the country previously off-limits to foreigners, they brought back horrifying reports of starving citizens struggling to survive on grass and tree bark, corpses lying in the streets, even instances of cannibalism. Estimates of the death toll ranged as high as two million people—nearly 10 percent of the population. The situation appeared so grim that in 1997, the CIA predicted that North Korea would collapse within five years. "The current situation in North Korea appears beyond corrective actions that do not fundamentally threaten the regime's viability," the agency reported in a secret analysis declassified in 2006.[6]

At the height of the famine, I had my first glimpse of Kim Jong Il. In April 1997, I was invited with my crew to Pyongyang to cover the anniversary of the founding of the Korean People's Army. As the food crisis intensified, the power of the military had grown: Kim, as the commander in chief and still consolidating his authority three years after his father's death, had made it the cornerstone of his power. On a sparkling spring day, we were taken to Kim Il Sung Square in the heart of Pyongyang for a calculated display of military might. Tens of thousands of goose-stepping troops with razor-sharp bayonets marched in perfect formation past Soviet-style buildings emblazoned with flags and enormous portraits of Kim Il Sung, followed by lines of civilians, each carrying a red or pink paper flower—one, the Kimjongilia, the other, the Kimilsungia, a hybrid orchid also specially developed by scientists as a gesture of political loyalty to the elder Kim.

Suddenly, Kim Jong Il appeared on the rostrum, waving to the marching masses below. It was the first time he had ever been seen and photographed by Western journalists. The reaction of the crowd astonished me—cheering, weeping, frantically waving the paper flowers. It was a display of loyalty bordering on mass hysteria. His face expressionless, Kim calmly walked the length of the rostrum as the band played "The Song of General Kim Jong Il." The muscle flexing, and the invitation to CNN to cover it, had a clear purpose. The North

Koreans wanted to dispel the impression, which the CIA was not alone in holding, that the food shortages and economic crisis had left them militarily weakened, on the brink of collapse, and therefore vulnerable to outside pressure.

In private conversations, senior North Korean officials reinforced this point,
acknowledging the seriousness of the food crisis while also telling me that
Pyongyang was increasingly convinced that the major concessions it had made
in the Agreed Framework were producing few tangible benefits.

In the late 1990s, with relations between the United States and North Korea
still chilly, Pyongyang remained convinced the U.S. goal was to see the collapse
of Kim Jong Il's regime, while in the United States, not only Clinton administration officials but their critics in the Republican Party continued to worry that
Pyongyang had not abandoned its long-term nuclear ambitions. In July 1998, a
Republican-dominated commission headed by Donald Rumsfeld, the once and
future secretary of defense, issued a report claiming that the ballistic missile
threat from North Korea had been underestimated by U.S. intelligence and that
Pyongyang could fire a missile that could hit the United States "with little or no
warning."

The commission had been created under pressure from right-wing
Republicans in Congress who were ideologically committed to building a missile
defense system to protect the United States from attacks by rogue states. This
idea, originally raised by President Ronald Reagan in the 1980s and dubbed Star
Wars after the hit movie series, was one of the main planks of the right-wing re-
vival that would become so influential after George W. Bush was elected in 2000.
Convinced that arms-control agreements were a sign of weakness, deeply opposed to seeking engagement with American adversaries such as North Korea,
and concerned that the United States was not confronting threats aggressively
enough, the neoconservatives and their allies spent the 1990s developing their
ideas and strengthening their influence in the Republican Party. Among the
Rumsfeld commission's members were several figures who would go on to hold
key government positions after George W. Bush became president, including
Paul Wolfowitz, who became Rumsfeld's deputy at the Pentagon.

As the debate over Korea policy raged in Washington, concerns about
North Korea were heightened when a leak to the *New York Times* on August
17, 1998, claimed that U.S. spy satellites had discovered an underground complex at Kumchangri, not far from the Yongbyon nuclear facility. Some experts
believed the tunnels were suspected of being the site of a secret nuclear reactor
or reprocessing facility. As the shock waves from this revelation reverberated
across Washington, some members of Congress demanded the abrogation of
the Agreed Framework and others, including Senator John McCain, called for
military action.

In the midst of this turmoil, I received another invitation to Pyongyang. On August 31, the day my crew and I arrived, North Korea staged the first flight test of a three-stage Taepodong-1 missile. Launched from the eastern part of the country, the solid-fuel missile flew over Japan before landing in the Pacific Ocean and confirmed North Korea's ability to strike U.S. troops in Japan. American officials worried that it would be followed by the test of a long-range Taepodong-2, with the capability of reaching the United States. Although Pyongyang insisted the sole purpose of the launch was to put into orbit a satellite that would transmit "The Song of General Kim Jong Il," critics said the test appeared to confirm the dire warnings of the Rumsfeld commission, although it was equally possible that the launch had a political as well as military purpose—to show that the North would not be intimidated by harsh rhetoric from Washington.

The Kumchangri leak and the missile test badly damaged the already shaky political support in Washington for the Agreed Framework. Under intense pressure, President Clinton appointed a high-level coordinator to review American policy toward North Korea. He gave the job to William Perry, who had served as his secretary of defense from 1994 to 1997, and also in the Pentagon during the Carter administration. An expert on high-tech weapons with a low-key style, Perry was highly respected across the political spectrum. And he had experience on the North Korea issue, since it had been on his watch, in June of 1994, that the United States had come close to mounting a preemptive attack on the Yongbyon facility.

In early 1999, as Perry continued his policy review, Richard Armitage, a former assistant secretary of defense and a Republican Party Asia-policy specialist, issued what was dubbed a "Team B" review calling for a much tougher approach to North Korea. While supporting the concept of engagement, Armitage was sharply critical of the substance and tactics of the Clinton administration's North Korea policy. The report described the Agreed Framework as an insufficient curb against North Korea's nuclear program, and urged that it be renegotiated, especially the sections dealing with energy supplies. It also proposed that the United States bolster its "deterrent military posture" by deploying Patriot missile batteries in Japan. In addition, it suggested exploring the possibility of intercepting North Korean missile shipments, staging preemptive strikes against the North, and drawing "red lines" which, if crossed by Pyongyang, would be met with a tough U.S. response. Together the Armitage report and the Rumsfeld commission laid the groundwork for the subsequent policies of the Bush administration, where Armitage, like Rumsfeld and Wolfowitz, would hold an important position.

In May 1999, two months after the release of the Armitage report—following consultations with Japan, South Korea, and China—Perry and a small delegation visited Pyongyang. Other members of the delegation included Wendy Sherman, special adviser to the president and secretary of state, and the administration's North Korea Policy Coordinator; Kenneth Lieberthal, a distinguished China scholar from the University of Michigan who had left academia to become Director of Asian Affairs at the National Security Council; Evans Revere, a Korean-speaking foreign service officer who was director of the State Department's Korea Desk, and two others. In a series of meetings, Perry bluntly told the North Koreans the current situation was untenable and offered them two paths. One was improved relations and expanded dialogue to get rid of their nuclear and missile programs, which would lead to the lifting of economic sanctions and eventual normalization of ties with Washington. He invited the North to reciprocate by sending a high-level envoy to Washington. At the same time, he spelled out the other path—a downward spiral toward increased tension and confrontation. The North Koreans were belligerent and unyielding. Kenneth Lieberthal was startled by the hostile response of a senior military official.

"This guy sat there, listened to him [Perry], and said, 'Well, thank you very much Mr. Secretary. I know a lot about your background. I know where you're from'—and he named the city where he grew up. And then he proceeded to indicate that as far as he was concerned, if the U.S. were to use military force against North Korea, Perry's home town would be vaporized. It was one of those shocking things. When they used the term 'vaporized,' they made it very clear: 'we will hit your town with nuclear weapons.'"

On the flight out of Pyongyang, Perry and his colleagues debated the significance of what they had heard. Said one participant: "The overall message was typical when you are making a pitch to the North Koreans: accusatory, defensive, it's all your fault, you haven't delivered the light-water reactors, you haven't delivered on your commitments, the entire reason the relationship is so bad is because of you, you've made no efforts to try to improve relations with us—why should we even listen to you? Every line you've ever heard was rolled out."

Another member of the team, Korean-speaking Evans Revere, had a different take. "My own sense was that you need to be careful . . . because sometimes when a North Korean says no he means yes. And that basically was the pitch I made. I described some past instances in which the North Koreans had spoken harshly and hostilely about our initiatives. I reminded Perry that things are not always what you think they are when dealing with North Korea, and obviously the initial reaction will be typical of the North Koreans, which will be defensive and accusatory and hostile. But I drew attention to some of the comments that had been made that gave us some hope. I mentioned that they hadn't outright rejected dialogue, they had just responded to it with some familiar accusatory words and then had focused on raising some questions about our sincerity in this process, etc. And I said it seems to me the door is still a little bit left open here, we ought to give this process time."

Kenneth Lieberthal shared a similar assessment.

"Kim Jong Il knows he plays a very weak hand," Lieberthal said. "And he plays with folks that can squash him on every side: he's weaker than South Korea, he's weaker than Japan, he's weaker than China, Lord knows he's weaker than the U.S. If it ever comes to military confrontation, he's dead. Playing from a weak hand, his strategy is to appear very tough. And when challenged, to escalate rather than compromise in order to demonstrate that he's willing to go farther on this issue than the issue is worth to the U.S. To the U.S. it's a minor thing, and to him it's central. But all of that is always with the objective of selling something, and getting something for the sale. And he'll sell anything."

In the preceding months, as Perry had been preparing for his Pyongyang trip amid a rising chorus of domestic criticism for Clinton's approach, Charles Kartman had been engaged in negotiations with the North Koreans over gaining access to the suspected nuclear site at Kumchangri. Known to all as Chuck, within the State Department, Kartman had earned the nickname "Iron Butt" for his ability to sit patiently and listen to North Korean envoys spew out venom, bombast, and threats across the negotiating table. A longtime Northeast Asia hand, he had served at the U.S. embassies in Tokyo and Seoul and headed the State Department's Korea Desk. In 1998, he had been designated Washington's Special Envoy for Peace Talks with North Korea, the point man in the Clinton administration's effort to improve relations with Pyongyang and reduce tensions on the Korean peninsula. Despite the alarming story in the *New York Times*, the American intelligence community was sharply divided over what the North Koreans were actually doing. The Defense Intelligence Agency (DIA), headed by Lt. General Patrick Hughes, insisted that Kumchangri was a construction site for a secret, underground nuclear reactor and that its existence proved Pyongyang was cheating on the Agreed Framework.

"The DIA was adamant," then-National Security Adviser Sandy Berger recalled. "They said they could see the roads that were characteristic of this kind of facility, they could actually see . . . that this hole was perfectly suited for a nuclear reactor."

Other intelligence agencies, including the CIA, were more skeptical.

"I looked at that evidence," said one senior Clinton administration official, "and I could easily see innocent explanations for virtually everything they pointed to. And others in the intel community looked at exactly the same stuff and heard the DIA's arguments about it, and said essentially, this is really flimsy stuff."

Still, the allegation had created major problems. In Washington, the administration was again under attack for Pyongyang's alleged violation of the framework. And, unless the issue was handled with great skill, the already strained and fragile dialogue between the United States and North Korea would face certain collapse.

Kartman's style of avoiding direct accusations and threats and framing the issue in terms of how *both* sides could work through a vexing problem was based on several years and hundreds of hours of interaction with North Koreans, in which he had concluded that Pyongyang tended to lash out when it felt backed into a corner, even if such a strategy was not in its own long-term interest. His approach produced results. In May 1999, the North agreed to permit U.S. inspectors to visit Kumchangri. After initially demanding a payment of $300 million for a onetime visit, the North eventually accepted a shipment of 100,000 tons of potatoes as the "price" of permitting the inspection.

To the Americans' surprise and embarrassment, they found a large, empty underground cave. There was no evidence of a secret nuclear site. The crisis passed. According to Gary Samore, then the National Security Council's Senior Director for Nonproliferation, "The conclusion was that Kumchangri was not configured in a way that could be used either for plutonium or for enrichment. So, whatever we thought Kunchangri was, it wasn't. It was not nuclear-related."

A decade later, the purpose of the construction site at Kumchangri remains unknown. But the episode left lingering doubts about how to assess intelligence on North Korea. The rush to judgment, driven by the DIA's aggressive briefings and the deliberate leak of the story to the media, left many officials cautious, if not downright skeptical about subsequent intelligence findings.

"DIA hyped their findings unbelievably," noted one former senior official. "They misstated their level of certainty, and the further up the food chain they went, the more they dropped the caveats, and ended up putting us in a terrible position."

Gary Samore had accepted the DIA's analysis and lobbied strongly for the administration to make Kumchangri a major issue. "Sandy Berger depended pretty heavily on my judgment," he said, "and I feel that my recommendation to him that it was a serious issue led the administration to deal with it more seriously than it ever turns out is justified. I would say that was the biggest mistake I made in my career as a civil servant."

During the summer of 1999, there was renewed concern in Washington about the possibility of a second missile test, and in August, I received yet another invitation to visit Pyongyang. In keeping with North Korea's traditional pattern of exacerbating tensions and then offering to negotiate, Pyongyang used my visit to signal its readiness to observe a moratorium on future missile tests if the United States would agree to renewed talks. In an interview just outside the Magnolia Room—a lavish, mirror-lined banquet hall with a mechanical stage that rose from the floor to display an all-female music troupe playing electric guitars—Kim Yong Sun, Secretary of the ruling Korean Workers' Party and a close confidante of Kim Jong Il, told me in response to a question about missiles: "If things are discussed in a reasonable manner, they will turn out well. I am optimistic about it."

"If a visitor brings us cake," Kim explained, "we will also give cake. But if they bring a sword, we will respond with a sword."

It was a pithy summation of a tit-for-tat attitude that North Korea had repeatedly displayed over the years. Within weeks, at a meeting in Berlin, North Korean diplomats confirmed to Chuck Kartman that Pyongyang would observe a moratorium on testing long-range missiles as long as the talks continued. The United States in turn committed itself to a partial lifting of economic sanctions. At last, the tension began to ease.

In October 1999, Perry issued his long-awaited report. The former defense secretary rejected the view that the Pyongyang regime was on the verge of collapse. "While logic would suggest that the DPRK's evident problems would ultimately lead its regime to change," the report said, "there is no evidence that change is imminent. United States policy must, therefore, deal with the North Korean government as it is, not as we might wish it to be." Under the circumstances, Perry argued that the most important U.S. interest was the "complete and verifiable cessation" of North Korea's missile and nuclear program. The report endorsed the Agreed Framework because it had led to the freezing of the Yongbyon facility and concluded that the best way to achieve Washington's long-term goals was to engage Pyongyang in high-level talks and, "in a step-by-step and reciprocal fashion, move to reduce pressures on North Korea that it perceives as threatening" by offering an end to sanctions and eventual normalization of economic and political relations. At the same time, Perry made clear that North Korea's failure to cooperate would produce a much tougher set of American policies.[7]

One analyst dubbed the Perry approach "bigger carrots, and bigger sticks."

As relations between the United States and North Korea alternated between accusations of bad faith and often strained diplomatic dialogue, the political landscape on the Korean peninsula had been dramatically altered by the election of Kim Dae-jung as South Korea's president at the end of 1997. A longtime dissident, Kim had survived several attempts on his life by government agents. In 1981, he had been tried and condemned to death on sedition charges by military dictator Chun Doo-hwan; his execution was prevented only by the last-minute intervention of the Reagan administration.

Kim proposed a radical shift in South Korea's previously hard-line approach to the North. Instead, he advocated what became known as the "Sunshine Policy." Underpinned by the belief that South Korea would not be able to handle the influx of refugees and possible internal instability that would follow the collapse of North Korea, Kim sought to engage Pyongyang through expanded trade and economic ties and increased people-to-people contact. Kim loosened restrictions on South Korean investment in the North and boosted humanitarian aid. In late 1998, South Korea's Hyundai Corporation reached an agreement to develop a tourist center at a famous North Korean scenic spot called Mt. Kumgang and to explore the creation of a Special Economic Zone just beyond the North's side of the Demilitarized Zone.

With South Korea's leader joining former Defense Secretary Perry in urging engagement, the Clinton administration embarked on a series of meetings with North Korea to resolve what was then seen as the most pressing issue—Pyongyang's ballistic missile development and exports. In January 2000, Chuck Kartman led an American delegation to meet with the North Koreans in Berlin. When William Perry had visited Pyongyang eight months earlier, he had invited the North to send its own high-level envoy to Washington. In anticipation of such a visit, Kartman had put together the draft of a joint statement to be issued if it did take place. The draft had been coauthored by Robert Carlin, a rumpled, bearded former veteran of eighteen years analyzing North Korea for the CIA who, since 1992, had been doing similar work at the State Department's intelligence arm, the Bureau of Intelligence and Research. As the range of American diplomatic contacts had grown in the '90s, Carlin had become the point man for distilling intelligence into a form that would have practical use to American officials who were involved in negotiations with Pyongyang.

The draft included the statement that "neither government would have hostile intent toward the other" and stressed the desire of both governments to "build a new relationship free from past enmity." Kartman gave the statement to the North Koreans in Berlin. "We were playing off what we had heard from them at every meeting about our hostility being the big impediment to improving relations," he said.

"They knew where we were going," Bob Carlin observed. "They knew what the Americans were aiming at this whole time, there was no question as to where we wanted to go. I always thought that was an important data point in their calculations."

The following month, the longtime North Korea intelligence analyst noted an intriguing sign of a possible shift in Pyongyang's policy. The state-run Korea

Central News Agency announced that a senior vice premier had declared that North Korea was strong enough militarily and that it should now concentrate on economic development. Using skills gained in over two decades spent studying North Korean propaganda, Carlin quickly read the tea leaves.

"The key . . . the trick," Carlin recalled, "was, first, taking it seriously, and second, understanding what was intended to be policy versus what was intended to be simple propaganda. Then utilizing this . . . compare not just two years or five years of statements, but ten years of statements . . . understand what they changed and when . . . understand the economic motivation."

He shared his insights with Kartman. It was clear, the two men agreed, that the famine had so devastated North Korean society that there appeared to be a growing recognition within the North Korean leadership that some kind of reform was crucial to ensure the regime's survival.

"Both Chuck and I said, literally the same morning, *Holy cow!*" Carlin recalled. "This means there's a brand-new front opening up here, which gives us a lot of capital to spend in negotiations. They want to focus on their economy."

This declaration was followed by a series of steps indicating that Kim Jong Il might be serious about changing North Korea's security environment to allow for a greater focus on rebuilding the country's shattered economy. In late May, Kim, who had not made a publicly announced visit to China in two decades, traveled secretly to Beijing. After his departure, the state-run *People's Daily* quoted Kim as praising China's policies of economic reform and opening its doors to the outside world. It was an intriguing sign that the Dear Leader was at least pondering whether and how North Korea could follow suit.

Two weeks later, on June 15, 2000, came an historic turning point. After months of negotiations that he kept secret from the United States, South Korean president Kim Dae-jung flew to Pyongyang for a summit meeting with Kim Jong Il. It was the first meeting between the heads of state of the two Koreas.

"The door of the plane at the North Korean airport opened, and I got out and looked down," President Kim remembered in an interview with me. "And there was Chairman Kim Jong Il, who was quite small, standing there. Only then did I know for sure he was coming out to meet me. It's hard to express what I was feeling then. I thought, 'I am really going to meet the North Korean leader. And he and I will have to achieve something that will dramatically change the joint future, the joint destiny of our people.'"

The two leaders embraced as TV cameras rolled, while hundreds of thousands of people mobilized by the regime lined the streets of Pyongyang to cheer as a motorcade carrying the two men drove into the city center.

"Usually when I am in one of those open cars," Kim said, "I am sitting alone. But suddenly someone plopped down beside me. I turned around, and it was Kim Jong Il. That was most unusual. People keep asking me what we talked about in the fifty-minute ride. But we had just met, and it was still very awkward between us. It was also very loud with all the cheering from the crowd. His only words to me were, 'Those people are out here cheering for you, President Kim Dae-jung.'"

After two days of meetings punctuated by exchanges of toasts and promises of better ties, the two Kims signed a five-point joint declaration in which they pledged to pursue reunification "independently" and accelerate economic co-operation. Kim Jong Il also agreed to make a return visit to Seoul. Still, the summit did not resolve all the tensions that had accumulated over half a century, and memories of earlier, failed attempts at North-South rapprochement remained. But the surprisingly cordial atmosphere reflected a broader shift in the mood on the peninsula. And in his debut on the international stage, Kim Jong Il shed much of his reputation as a dangerous nutcase, a point the Dear Leader himself emphasized in a conversation with a sympathetic Korean-American writer, Moon Myung-ja, soon after the summit.

"I know that my image used to be much more negative among the South Korean people," Kim told her. "After I appeared on TV screens, I'm sure, they came to know that I am not like a man with horns on the head."[8]

Kim was right. While covering the story in South Korea, I was struck by the emotional public response. To many South Koreans the Dear Leader was no longer seen as a dangerous threat, but rather as a wayward relative eager to mend fences after so many years of hostility. It was a sea-change in public attitudes and was followed by a series of tightly controlled reunions between families separated by the Korean War, expanded contact between officials from North and South, and an increase in South Korean aid—especially food and fertilizer—for Pyongyang.

In Washington, too, eyes were opened. "For the most part, our intelligence had told us that he was a recluse and that he was crazy," Madeleine Albright told me in a 2005 interview. On the day after the summit, Robert Carlin drafted a memo which his boss, J. Stapleton Roy, the former U.S. ambassador to China and at that time head of the State Department's Bureau of Intelligence and Research, submitted to Albright. It argued that the Kim-Kim meeting undermined the view widely held in the U.S. intelligence community of the Dear Leader as irrational and illogical. "Rather than being a recluse, Kim has appeared frequently (about twice a week in media-reporter appearances, more than that in public settings not reported by the DPRK media) for the past several years. He has long followed ROK media and has kept himself well-informed on events in South Korea. He may well know more about South Korea than Kim Dae-jung knows about events in the North."

And Carlin and Roy suggested that, for all its overblown rhetoric and propaganda, Kim's regime was capable of showing surprising flexibility. "The North Koreans have survived," the memo noted, "independent and prickly, among their larger neighbors precisely because they have not had an ideologically rigid foreign policy. On the contrary, the policy has reacted to changing circumstances in and around the peninsula."[9]

It was a view the South Korean leader confirmed in discussions with Albright after he returned to Seoul. "Kim Dae-jung told me that he was somebody that I could deal with, that he was rational and informed," Albright said.

In an interview, Kim Dae-jung said, "I got the impression that Chairman Kim Jong Il was a very bright person . . . and he was very well aware of the situations across the world, and in particular about South Korea. He listened to what other people were saying. And if he decides that what he listened to was the right thing, then he would follow what was suggested. But he made his judgment without asking for any others' opinion on the spot. So without consultation with other colleagues or his government, he made his judgment on the spot about what was right and what was wrong."

The South Korean leader said that Kim Jong Il "kept saying that the only option for them to survive is to improve their relations with the United States. Only if the United States guarantees the survival of the North Korean regime, and that North Korea will be introduced to international society, then they will abandon everything, including nuclear weapons, missiles, and weapons of mass destruction, everything."

Shortly afterward, the Clinton administration moved to lift some economic sanctions imposed on North Korea under the Trading With the Enemy Act (TWEA). At the same time, Pyongyang continued its diplomatic offensive by establishing relations with Italy, Australia, the Philippines, Australia, Canada, Britain, and Germany. When Russian president Vladimir Putin visited Pyongyang in July 2000, Kim offered to abandon his missile program if other nations would help his country put satellites into space. Putin, in announcing the proposal, provided few details of what appeared on its face to be a wholly impractical idea, both because North Korea did not have a meaningful satellite capability and because so few nations would likely be interested in cooperating. Yet the move appeared to be a signal of Pyongyang's willingness to use its missile program as a bargaining chip in a process aimed at reaching an accommodation with the United States. In a meeting at the G8 summit in Tokyo in July, the Russian leader gave Clinton additional insights about his just-completed journey to Pyongyang.

"One of the interesting things was how candid [Putin] was with us about his reaction to what he saw in North Korea," said Sandy Berger. "This was a very refreshing kind of, 'This is a strange place that I've just come from' description by Putin. Much more transparent than one would think. And we thought, well that's kind of refreshing that the new Russian president doesn't feel that he has to give the party line with respect to North Korea. And Kim Jong Il had said to Putin he was prepared to make a deal with us with respect to missiles."

The apparent change in Pyongyang's priorities was underscored by the astonishing spectacle at Mayday Stadium on October 12, 2000. The usual martial images were overshadowed by those of tractors, farmers, and factories. The message was reinforced with dancers dressed up as farm animals prancing along the stadium floor. The previous day, I had seen a similar message in a mass rally at Kim Il Sung Square, also attended by the Dear Leader. Resembling a North Korean version of the Rose Bowl parade, the throngs marching in unison had been accompanied by a series of floats. Some were predictable, such as a giant white representation of Kim Il Sung, his arm outstretched, facing bravely forward. Behind home, though, came a float of a giant potato, with a beaming face and moving eyelashes. It seemed so incongruous my colleagues and I could not help laughing. But, like the card-flipping, it conveyed a serious signal aimed not only at the rest of the world, via reporters like me, but at the people of North Korea as well. Kim Jong Il was urging the population to grow potatoes, and, by extension, to concentrate not on preparations for war, but on economic reconstruction. To do so would require a more congenial international environment, one that could be created only by a meaningful thaw in relations with the United States. And almost literally as I strained for a close-up glimpse of the Dear Leader in Kim Il Sung Square, the number two figure in the North Korean hierarchy was making history in Washington.

# 2

# SO CLOSE . . .

I T WAS THE UNIFORM HE WORE THAT EVERYONE WOULD REMEM-
ber. It brought to mind a Soviet general of bygone era—dull green,
gold braid, and epaulettes, a chest covered with medals. The whole
effect was jarringly out of place at the twenty-first-century White House.
Yet on the morning of October 10, 2000, Vice Marshal Jo Myong Rok of
the Korean People's Army, the highest-ranking North Korean official
ever to visit Washington, walked into the Oval Office, saluted sharply,
and extended a hand to President Bill Clinton. As an official photographer snapped away, Clinton, exuding his customary charm, escorted the
tall, dignified Jo to a chair by the Oval Office fireplace, the seat of honor
for foreign dignitaries. In the last months of Bill Clinton's second term,
the unthinkable was happening. Two adversaries in one of the most enduring conflicts of the Cold War were talking about making peace.

Jo's official title was First Vice Chairman of the National Defense
Commission of the Democratic People's Republic of Korea, a title befit-
ting the top military officer in North Korea's equivalent of the politburo
and the top party figure in the army. A veteran of the Korean War, he was
in Washington as the personal envoy of North Korean ruler, Kim Jong Il.

Sitting across from Jo and Clinton were the leading members of the
president's National Security team—Madeleine Albright, former Ambassador to the United Nations and the first female secretary of state;
National Security Adviser Sandy Berger, an associate of Clinton from his
first presidential campaign; and the small group of policy advisers and

North Korea specialists who had spent most of the past few years struggling to deal with the endlessly intractable problem of North Korea.

Catching his first glimpse of Jo's uniform, Chuck Kartman, the lead negotiator in Washington's frequently torturous dealings with Pyongyang, silently sucked in his breath. Kartman had been designated to meet Jo the previous evening. At Washington's Dulles Airport, Jo had been wearing a business suit and had seemed almost grandfatherly to Kartman. Always crafty, the North Koreans had told none of their American interlocutors of Jo's intention to wear his marshal's uniform to the White House.

*Is this really the photo op we want on page one tomorrow?* Kartman wondered to himself.

The same thought occurred to Charles "Jack" Pritchard, a soft-spoken twenty-eight-year army veteran with a background in intelligence. Since 1996, Pritchard had been an Asia expert at the National Security Council and now served as senior director for Asian Affairs, as well as Kartman's deputy negotiator with the North Koreans. In preparing for Jo's visit, Pritchard had explicitly asked North Korean officials whether the vice marshal would wear his uniform and had been told no. Wary of the North Koreans's obsession with winning the psychological upper hand, as the Clinton meeting approached Pritchard worried over how such an image would play in the American media and with the administration's political opponents, who were eager to jump at any chance to criticize efforts to engage North Korea.

The uniform did not surprise Wendy Sherman. Thin, intense, with cropped silver-gray hair, a confidante of the secretary of state, and highly skilled at navigating Washington's treacherous bureaucracy, Sherman had been a key player in pushing the Clinton administration toward engagement with Pyongyang. Her first reaction to Jo's agit-prop was a grudging professional respect. "For everybody who is in diplomacy," she recalled, "you appreciate a good piece of choreography. And that was a good piece of choreography."

The symbolism was indeed powerful. Jo Myong Rok's uniform represented the unity of North Korea's army and ruling party behind Kim Jong Il's engagement with America. His visit to the White House came exactly fifty years after that army, then led by Kim Jong Il's father, Kim Il Sung, launched a surprise attack across the 38th parallel, where the Korean peninsula had been divided by American and Russian officials at the end of World War II. The invasion marked the start of the Korean War, and cost four million lives, including 36,000 American soldiers.

Although the shooting stopped after three years, the 1953 armistice had never been replaced by a permanent peace, and the Korean peninsula remained divided into the Communist-backed North and the American-backed South. The 155-mile-long, two-and-a-half-mile-wide Demilitarized Zone was scarred with barbed wire, dotted with land mines, and guarded by heavily armed troops on both sides. It had also been the site of frequent small-scale clashes over the years, each of which raised the specter of renewed hostilities.

A half century after the armistice, North Korea still maintained a million-strong army, much of it deployed just a few hours' striking distance from the South Korean capital, Seoul. Thirty-seven thousand U.S. troops, the latest to serve in a security commitment dating back to the war itself, were stationed in South Korea. Their mission was to act as a deterrent—regarded by many as a "trip wire"—in the event of a new attack from the North.

And in 1994, the two sides had come frighteningly close to war over Pyongyang's effort to develop nuclear weapons, when the Clinton Pentagon seriously considered a preemptive U.S. attack on North Korea's nuclear reactor at Yongbyon, despite the very real risk it could trigger a broader conflict that could devastate the Korean peninsula.

Despite these continuing tensions, the Clinton administration remained convinced that diplomacy offered the best hope of easing the threat from Pyongyang, and thus pursued a series of contacts with Kim Jong Il's regime over the following half-dozen years. For the Clinton team, Jo's presence at the White House, wearing his KPA uniform in front of photographers, underscored an uncomfortable fact: if the U.S. administration was to make progress on the issues it most cared about, such as keeping the North's nuclear program frozen, rolling back its missile program, and reducing tensions on the Korean peninsula, it had little choice but to hold its nose and offer some respect to the leaders of a system it abhorred. For Jo and Kim Jong Il, the meeting demonstrated that the United States, long Pyongyang's most bitter enemy, had accepted the legitimacy of the Dear Leader and the system the Kims had created.

Clinton and Jo sat in front of the fireplace, with Jo holding a brown leather folder in his hand. As Clinton's gaze kept darting toward the folder, Kartman's thoughts returned to the diplomatic twists and turns that had set the stage for Jo's visit. At the end of September, Kartman had held what he expected to be yet another unproductive meeting with North Korean diplomats at the U.S. mission to the United Nations in New York. On the agenda were the two central issues between the United States and North Korea. One was the status of the Agreed Framework. Six years after the accord had been signed, it remained, in the words of Robert Gallucci, the man who had led the U.S. negotiating team in 1994, little more than a "cold peace." Both sides were unhappy, believing the Framework hadn't delivered all the benefits they had anticipated.[1]

The other issue was scheduling new talks on the North's missile program. With the nuclear facilities at Yongbyon shut down, curbing Pyongyang's production, deployment, testing, and export of ballistic missiles had become the chief goal of the Clinton administration's North Korea diplomacy. The U.S. concern was not just related to the delicate military balance on the Korean peninsula: in the mid-1990s, North Korea had become a major exporter of missiles and missile technology to other U.S. adversaries such as Iran and Syria. In addition, it had become clear that Pakistan's 1,500-kilometer Ghauri intermediate range missile, which Islamabad had tested in 1998, had been produced with North Korean help. Indeed, Pakistan's weapon appeared to be an enhanced copy of North Korea's indigenously produced Rodong missile.

And there was one other factor. The launch of a longer-range missile, the Taepodong, in 1998 had rattled nerves across Northeast Asia and, in Washington, had further undermined support in Congress for the Agreed Framework. A series of meetings with the North Koreans to discuss the missile issue in October 1998, March 1999, and July 2000 had produced no results.

Now, at this session less than two months before the U.S. presidential election, with Clinton's term drawing to an end, Kartman expected little progress. "There was no time to get anything done before the U.S. election," Kartman recalled. "I thought the two sides would just be marking time until a new administration took office in January."

An episode earlier in September had reinforced Kartman's sense that diplomacy was virtually at a standstill. Kim Yong Nam, president of the Supreme People's Assembly, North Korea's legislature, had been due to attend the annual session of the UN General Assembly in New York at the start of the month, and was scheduled to see Secretary of State Madeleine Albright. On previous trips to the United States, North Korean officials had usually flown on United Airlines, whose personnel, aware of the diplomatic sensitivities, ensured the North Koreans were treated respectfully. This time, however, the North Korean Foreign Ministry had booked Kim on American Airlines, apparently in the mistaken belief that because of its name, American was the "official" U.S. air carrier. American Airlines had never dealt with a North Korean before. As the foreign minister changed planes in Frankfurt and prepared to board his flight to New York, airline officials insisted on frisking him and demanded that he take his shoes. Kim, insulted and outraged at being treated "like a criminal," in the words of officials accompanying him, abruptly cancelled his trip, turned around and flew home to Pyongyang.

In Washington, veteran intelligence analyst Robert Carlin feared a major setback in Washington's delicate diplomatic dance with the North Koreans. He and Chuck Kartman, along with Thomas Hubbard, the Deputy Assistant Secre-

tary of State for East Asian Affairs and another veteran of the Agreed Framework and other negotiations with the North Koreans, immediately contacted
Madeleine Albright. "We got to her fairly quickly and said 'We've got to apologize,'" Carlin recalled. "'We have to tell Kim it was a mistake, and we are
sorry.'" Albright agreed, and Hubbard was sent to deliver a letter of apology to
North Korean officials in New York.

Two weeks later, holding a cup of coffee and admiring the view of New
York's East River from the top floor of the American mission to the UN, Chuck
Kartman wasn't expecting much. But before formal discussions began, North
Korea's chief negotiator, Kim Gye Gwan suddenly turned to him and asked for
a private word. "I have something important to tell you," Kim said. "Kim Jong
Il is preparing to send his personal envoy to Washington with an important proposal on missiles." Kartman knew Kim Gye Gwan well. The two men had sat
across from each other on many occasions. From the way Kim spoke, Kartman
concluded that the North Koreans wanted to present the proposal directly to
Bill Clinton. It appeared Kim Jong Il was ready for a dramatic improvement in
relations with the United States. Albright's apology had in fact produced the
desired effect.

N ow, as Bill Clinton and Jo Myong Rok sat next to each other, the president
glanced at the mysterious brown folder and asked, "Is that a letter for
me?" With a flourish, Jo stood up, as did Clinton, and formally handed over the
leather folder, which Clinton accepted graciously and immediately opened. Inside was a letter from Kim Jong Il, in Korean, along with an English translation
provided by the North Koreans. While everyone else in the room waited in silence, Clinton read the document.

The president turned to Jo and said, "This is a good letter." In the document, Kim Jong Il had indicated North Korea was prepared to cease the
production, sale, and use of long-range ballistic missiles—the central concern
of American policy in recent years. Vice Marshal Jo followed that moment with
another bombshell. On behalf of Kim Jong Il, he said, he was inviting the American president to visit Pyongyang for a summit meeting to seal a missile deal. "If
you come to Pyongyang," Jo said, "Kim Jong Il will guarantee that he will satisfy
all your security concerns."

Then Jo said something that appeared strikingly out of character for a North
Korean general. In what Jack Pritchard recalled as almost a "pleading" tone, Jo
said to Clinton: "I need to secure your agreement to come to Pyongyang. I really
need to take back a positive answer." To some observers in the room, the plea
reinforced a sense that Jo, for all his clout, was desperate not to displease Kim

Jong Il by returning with bad news, with the potentially grave personal consequences that might ensue in North Korea's harsh system.

Clinton, of course, was noncommittal. But in Chuck Kartman's view, the
president "intuited that it was important that the North Koreans come away
with the belief, deep down, that he stood behind the premise that we could normalize relations if we could get the [missile] deal." Furthermore, Kartman recalled, "his relaxed and friendly body language didn't need translation. Clinton
understood, in a way that perhaps most of us would not have, that this was all
about establishing your personal rapport, this wasn't about the language, the
substance of making a deal. This was about carrying back a feeling that 'okay
here is somebody that we can trust and whose word will be good.' So he had
turned on the charm." It was a radical departure from decades of hostility—a
signal to Jo and, by extension, to Kim Jong Il—that the United States was not
irrevocably committed to being North Korea's enemy.

As Clinton spoke, the other Americans were struck by how visibly the
North Korean general relaxed. "Jo's mission, in retrospect," said one U.S. official, "was to get Clinton to take Kim Jong Il seriously. That was his charge. As
soon as the president spoke, you could see and feel that something in that room
had occurred on the North Korean side that was extremely important." The
meeting had gone well. As Wendy Sherman noted, by the time the two men exchanged farewell handshakes, "We all knew there was something real here. Kim
Jong Il was ready to do a deal."


Since the early 1990s, Pyongyang's goal had been to achieve a fundamental
change in the adversarial relationship with the United States, to ensure that
Washington would no longer view—and treat—North Korea as an enemy. The
communiqué following Jo's visit committed the United States to just such a position and marked a historic milestone in the tense relationship between the two
longtime Cold War adversaries. The communiqué's most important declaration
emphasized that both sides were "prepared to undertake a new direction in
their relations." As a crucial first step, the two sides stated that "neither government would have hostile intent toward the other and confirmed the commitment of both governments to make every effort in the future to build a new
relationship free from past enmity."[2] As to the issue of whether Clinton would
go to Pyongyang, the two sides fudged the question by announcing that, "Secretary of State Madeleine Albright will visit the D.P.R.K. in the near future to
convey the views of U.S. President William Clinton directly to Chairman Kim
Jong Il of the D.P.R.K. National Defense Commission and to prepare for a possible visit by the President of the United States."[3]

On October 23, 2000, Madeleine Albright stood in an ornate, high-ceilinged reception room at the Paekhawan Guest House in Pyongyang, on what she described in her memoirs as "a bilious green carpet in front of a large mural of a storm at sea."[4] A beaming Kim, dressed in his trademark green-brown boilersuit and platform shoes, walked into the room, clasped Albright's hand firmly, and welcomed her to Pyongyang.

"It is really for the first time for the Secretary of State of the United States to come to our country like this," he declared in a deep, confident voice, as reporters, photographers, and TV crews looked on. "And this is a new one from a historical point of view, and I am very happy."

"Mr. Chairman," Albright replied. "It's a pleasure. I am very glad to be here."

In an interview, Albright said, "What was the most interesting was obviously, we have all seen pictures of Kim, but none of us has seen him in person. So when he walked in wearing his brown leisure suit and stood next to me during our opening press conference, I have to say that I was just surprised that it has really happened and I thought about the things that we needed to get down in the meeting but mostly, it was just strange to actually be there with him at a press conference, where we noticed the kind of 1950s vintage camera. And I'm standing there next to him with the same height and I know that I've got on high heels and I looked down and so does he."

Kim escorted Albright to a meeting room with a highly polished wooden table. Kim was accompanied by Kang Sok Ju and two interpreters, one an older man who had been his father's interpreter, the other a young man introduced as the Dear Leader's personal interpreter. Watching the TV images, I was startled to recognize the younger man. He was Kim Chol, who had been my interpreter on several previous visits and spoke impeccable, Oxford-accented English. With Albright were Wendy Sherman, Chuck Kartman, Jack Pritchard, and Assistant Secretary of State for East Asian Affairs Stanley Roth.

Kim was friendly and conciliatory. He thanked Albright for a message of condolence sent by President Clinton when Kim Il Sung died in 1994, and for her own visit earlier that day to the mausoleum containing his father's embalmed remains. The decision to visit the mausoleum had been a source of sharp debate within the Clinton administration. The North Koreans had told Thomas Hubbard, the principal deputy assistant secretary of state for East Asian affairs who was handling advance planning for the trip, that such a gesture was crucial to a successful outcome. Albright had been uneasy.

"Ordinarily, this would have been a simple enough courtesy," she noted in her memoirs. "But Kim Il Sung had started the Korean War. He had then instituted a cradle-to-grave propaganda system that blamed America for the war and brainwashed his countrymen into worshipping him as a god."[5]

However, Hubbard, a veteran of the Agreed Framework negotiations, had worked out a compromise under which Albright would pay her respects, but with no reporters or cameras in attendance. And while she would pause in front of Kim's bier, she would not bow her head. The North Koreans were mollified.

"If both sides are genuine and serious," Kim Jong Il said to her, "there is nothing we will not be able to do."

For Albright and her team, the central issue was missiles.

"We were most concerned about long-range missiles because that's what—with a nuclear warhead attached—is an existential threat to the United States," said Wendy Sherman. "But we also understood that if we didn't deal with medium-range missiles we wouldn't be able to hold the Japanese on board with us. So getting them to end all of their missile sales and sales of missile-related technology and all of their service contracts was part of the deal—that they would stop any development, testing, or deployment of long-range missiles, and that they would begin discussions on the already deployed Rodong missile. And in return for that—for those three things—they wanted a path to the normalization of the relationship—no hostile intent between our countries, which we had already put in the communiqué. And they expected some recognition, as they made good on this, in the fullness of the normalization relationship that they would see the benefits of that normalization."

Once the pleasantries finished, Albright handed Kim the letter from President Clinton, which State Department Press Secretary Richard Boucher described to reporters as "outlining the expectation of further developing relations." Then she turned the discussion to the missile issue. "I told Kim that I hadn't yet decided what to tell President Clinton," Albright recalled, "but that I couldn't recommend a summit without a satisfactory agreement on missiles."[6]

Kim said North Korea was selling missiles to Iran and Syria to earn badly needed foreign currency. "So it's clear," he said, "since we export to get money, if you guarantee compensation, it will be suspended."[7]

"Mr. Chairman," Albright replied, "we've been concerned about your intentions for fifty years, and so we have been concerned about your production of missiles. And now you say it is just to earn foreign currency."

"Well, it's not just foreign currency," Kim answered. "We also arm our own military as part of our self-reliance program."

Expressing concern over South Korea's military, Kim added, "If there is an assurance that South Korea will not develop 500-kilometer-range missiles, we won't either. As for the missiles already deployed, I don't think we can do much about them. You can't go inside the units and inspect them, but it's possible to stop production. It's been ten years since the collapse of the USSR, the opening of China, and the disappearance of our military alliance with either country.

The military wants to update its equipment, but we won't give them new equipment. If there's no confrontation, there's no significance to weapons. Missiles are now insignificant."[8]

As the conversation drew to an end after more than three hours, Kim indicated he would meet with Albright again the following day. For the U.S. team, it had been a chance to take the measure of this still mysterious and inscrutable figure. All of them were, somewhat to their surprise, impressed.

"I found him as somebody who was very well-bred, who did not have to turn to his advisers for answers and somebody that was there as a negotiator," Albright recalled. "I did find him as somebody who clearly understood what he was talking about."

In the summer of 2001, Kim would spend twenty-four days traveling by train across Russia. In extended conversations with President Vladimir Putin's envoy Konstantin Pulikovsky, who published a book on his experiences accompanying the North Korean leader on the trip, Kim offered his own take on the Albright meeting, which suggests he was well aware of the way the Americans were observing him and was anxious to win her approval.

"First, Albright interrogated me like a prosecutor," Pulikovsky quoted Kim as saying. "I answered all her questions, and she was watching whether I was using notes or speaking offhand. I expressed myself simply, in my own words. She seemed to like my personality."[9]

Meanwhile, with the first meeting over, Kim informed Albright he had a special surprise for that evening. "I have changed the entertainment," he announced.

In the dark, Albright's delegation was driven through the now empty and night-shrouded streets of Pyongyang to the Mayday Stadium. Inside the stadium, it was dark as well. Kim walked in with Albright. "There was a huge crowd. And they just burst into wild applause," she recalled.

It was clear to the secretary and her advisers that, as Wendy Sherman put it, "This stadium performance was to impress us with the discipline and the power of Kim Jong Il. When he entered the stadium people called his name for a full ten minutes before things settled down. We well understood that this was all staged in a very careful way to show the power and the presence of North Korea and it was part of North Korea's sense of dignity and pride that they were really going to have an equal kind of negotiation with the powerful United States."

At one point, Sherman said to Kim, "Mr. Chairman, I have this feeling that in another life you were a great director." Kim replied, "Oh yes, I have watched every Academy Award movie, I know all the great directors of the world." Sherman thought it was a revealing moment. "You get a sense that in some way he sees himself as the great director on the stage of his country's life, pulling the strings and directing the play."

The emphasis of the performance was heavily on economic construction, with many images of factories, tractors, electrical transformers, and farms, apparently reflecting Kim's desire to focus more on development. There was, however, one particularly militaristic display—the placards moving in unison to show the launch of a Taepodong missile—the very one the Secretary had come to Pyongyang to convince Kim to give up. As the crowd roared, Kim turned to Albright and said, "That was our first missile launch—and our last." Kim then turned and, just to make sure his point was clear, repeated the remark to Wendy Sherman. To the secretary and her advisers, it was an important and positive gesture.

"As that was what we were there to talk about," Albright noted later, "we took it as fairly significant." Kim, Albright was convinced, appeared serious about reaching a missile deal.


The next morning, U.S. arms control expert Robert Einhorn met with North Korean officials to discuss the missile issue in detail. The Americans had a host of questions, but the North Korean negotiator was blunt. According to Einhorn, all he would say was, "Look, I can't give you any response on your questions. The only way you're going to get a response is for you to put this to our Dear General." So Einhorn drafted a set of fourteen detailed and highly technical questions. Among them: Was Kim prepared to give up not just exporting complete missiles but exporting missile components and technologies? What range of missile was he prepared to include in any deal? Would an export ban apply to existing as well as new contracts? Would North Korea accede to the Missile Technology Control Regime (MTCR), the voluntary association of countries set up in 1987 to prevent the proliferation of missile systems that could deliver weapons of mass destruction?

In the afternoon, Albright, Kim, and their aides met for a second time. "As you know," she began, "our experts met in the morning on the missile issues, and we've presented you a number of questions. I hope you've had a chance to go over them."[10]

According to Einhorn, "Kim looked puzzled, turned to Kang Sok Ju and they had a little discussion. Kang goes through his papers and takes out the translated questions, and after more discussion with Kim, gives it to him. And Kim turns to the secretary and says, 'Well actually, this is the first time I'm taking a look at these questions, but I'm happy to answer them.' And then what was interesting at that point was, he gave precise and very positive responses to about two-thirds of them."

"Kim Jong Il was on top of his brief," noted Wendy Sherman. "He said, 'well let me go through them.' He started walking down the list of fourteen questions. He didn't answer every single one of them thoroughly, but he had an answer for all fourteen. Some of it was at a fairly technical level, and I dare say that few presidents or prime ministers would have tried what he did. He did it quite clearly to say there is only one decision-maker in this country and it's me, and one of the things that he always tries to impress upon people is as he often is heard saying, only leaders can make the final decisions."

Einhorn was equally impressed by how Kim handled questions where he clearly did not know the answer.

"What was interesting about it, he knew what he didn't know," Einhorn said. "You see in the North Korean newspapers Kim giving 'on-the-spot guidance.' You know, he's driving through the countryside, a peasant is having a difficult time planting a tree. He gets out of his car, gives him a few hints, and the next day, the tree is ten feet tall. So here's the guy who can give on-the-spot guidance about anything, knowing that he didn't know certain answers to questions. And that sort of impressed us all, that despite this aura of omniscience, he knew what he didn't know. By the end of the meeting, we had actually achieved a good amount of clarity, and it was clarity in a direction that was fairly reassuring to us."

Kim told Albright the export ban would apply not just to missiles but to components and technologies, that it would apply to existing contracts, and that he was ready to accede to the MTCR. On other issues—whether a ban would apply to further production, testing, and deployment or would mean eliminating all existing missiles, the range of missiles subject to the ban, and, above all, on verification—differences remained. But Kim adopted a positive tone, and agreed that North Korean and U.S. experts would meet the following week in Kuala Lumpur, Malaysia, for further discussions.

Kim was also conciliatory on one of the most contentious matters in the United States' long history of conflict with North Korea—the role of American troops in South Korea. Kim said that since the end of the Cold War, his position on American troops had changed, and that he now felt American troops played a stabilizing role. For a regime that had made the withdrawal of U.S. forces a central demand for decades, it was a striking shift, although Kim acknowledged to Albright that the leadership of his armed forces were evenly divided between supporters and opponents of improving relations with the United States, and that some officials in his Foreign Ministry had argued against talking to Washington. According to Albright, "Kim said the solution rested with the normalization of relations."

That night, at a farewell banquet, there was no mistaking the dramatic improvement in the atmosphere between such longtime adversaries. In her toast, Albright noted the improbability of their entire encounter, holding her wineglass and declaring, "I never expected to play the role of host for such a gathering as this." At that moment, she gave the Dear Leader, a well-known basketball fan, a special gift—a basketball signed by Michael Jordan. "Pick up the phone any time," she told him.

Kim, leader of a country with few computers, Internet access limited to a tiny segment of the elite, and no cell phones, replied: "Please give me your e-mail address."

The next day, Bob Carlin drove south along the deserted highway to the DMZ in order to cross into South Korea. He was exhausted but elated. The prospect of a Clinton-Kim summit and an end to over fifty years of hostility and danger on the Korean peninsula seemed tantalizingly close. Back in Seoul, Carlin put together a draft of a possible joint communiqué for consideration by Albright and Clinton in the event the president did decide to travel to Pyongyang. "The development of more normal relations between the US and the DPRK conforms to the interests of the two peoples and will contribute to long-term peace and stability on the Korean Peninsula and throughout the Asia-Pacific region," Carlin wrote. "The two leaders . . . reaffirm their commitment to building non-hostile relations free from past enmity."

Albright had come back from North Korea convinced that Kim Jong Il was "someone who is practical, decisive, and seemingly non-ideological."[11]

"We're under no illusions," she said at a dinner of North Korea experts she hosted in Washington following her return. "We're not there yet. But this guy is not a nutcase. A presidential trip could seal a deal."

"The president was powerfully tempted to go," National Security Adviser Sandy Berger acknowledged. "I think he felt that this could represent a significant development in the security of Asia and the world, and that he should not miss this opportunity."

For Clinton, nearing the end of his term and increasingly contemplating his legacy, the possibility of a dramatic visit to Pyongyang that would bring half a century of Cold War hostility to an end must have seemed extraordinarily appealing.

But without nailing down the details in advance, Berger and others argued that it would be dangerous for Clinton to take North Korean assurances on faith, and unseemly for a U.S. president to get involved in negotiating with Kim Jong Il about the technical issues of missile size or the mechanics of verification.

"I thought that was just too risky, that we would show up in Pyongyang, that there would not be an agreement on, for example, verification, which is tricky," said Berger. "We would be in the awkward position of either leaving without an agreement or signing something that was unsatisfactory. I was worried about political fallout if we wound up in Pyongyang without an agreement. And I was worried about the pressure that the president would be under to accept something that was not ironclad. We'd be standing there in Pyongyang with ourselves very exposed."

In the White House, the discussions, as one participant recalled, went "round and round," with the president "a little like a bridled horse" eager to bolt. Clinton's instinct was that, with his personal involvement, he could still pull off a deal. His advisers continued to rein him in.

To a large degree, the debate came down to the difference between the American and North Korean political systems. In Pyongyang, Kim Jong Il made virtually all the decisions. Officials below him had little or no independence or flexibility. What to the Americans seemed like an outrageous North Korean demand to take a leap of faith and simply accept assurances that Kim Jong Il would "satisfy" U.S. concerns was in fact a reflection of the way the North Korean system worked.

From Seoul, South Korean president Kim Dae-jung weighed in, urging Clinton to take the risk of visiting Pyongyang. According to a former senior South Korean diplomat, "That's what Kim was saying. That it's a Communist system where Kim Jong Il ultimately makes the decisions . . . so you have to deal with him. And it's not like there is a process to make a final outcome or decision. Kim Jong Il can change. He makes a decision just like snapping your fingers."

After years of dealing with the North Koreans, Chuck Kartman and Bob Carlin were cautiously hopeful that if Clinton did go, Kim Jong Il was prepared to deliver an acceptable deal.

"There's no way that the North Koreans wouldn't have agreed to something if an American president went to Pyongyang," Kartman said. "The North Korean style is to hold something back for the final moment. So the notion that there would be favorable movement in the end game—that, to me, is pretty certain. I don't think it was a trick."

"Most times when Kim Jung Il sits down with another head of state, things pop out of it," added Carlin. "Good things. So it was always possible to get some things, and Clinton was such a good communicator maybe we could have gotten something."

But as the debate raged inside the White House, Kartman and Carlin began to feel uneasy, concerned that the fixation on swift resolution of the details of a missile deal was causing the president's team to lose sight of the bigger strategic picture—Kim Jong Il's clearly expressed desire for a fundamental shift in North Korea's relationship with the United States.

"They had given us clear indications that this was how they saw their future, and all we had to do was continue on this path and we were going to get there, and the decades of danger and crises were about to end," Kartman said. "We had this sense that not only a page but an entire chapter of history was turning. And it wasn't going to rise or fall on the details of a missile agreement."

With the debate still raging in the White House, on November 7 Americans went to the polls to elect Bill Clinton's successor.

The man with the sandy hair, wire-rimmed glasses, and walrus mustache strode into the library in Tallahassee, Florida. "I'm with the Bush-Cheney team," John Bolton declared, "and I'm here to stop the count."[12]

This scene was one of the most dramatic moments in an election that had become the most controversial in American history. With Democrat Al Gore and Republican George W. Bush virtually deadlocked, a recount in the disputed state of Florida would determine who would become the next president. John Bolton—a lifelong Republican who'd been active in the party's ultra-conservative wing ever since he campaigned for Senator Barry Goldwater's ill-fated presidential campaign as a high school student in 1964—was one of many lawyers and political operatives who descended on Florida to help the Bush camp. Blunt, combative, close to the extreme right-wing Republican senator Jesse Helms, Bolton had held a series of positions in the administrations of Ronald Reagan and George H. W. Bush. During the Clinton years, he had based himself at the conservative American Enterprise Institute in Washington, writing articles and making speeches denouncing Clinton's policies. The Agreed Framework and the president's conciliatory approach to North Korea were particular targets. Bolton viewed both strategies as forms of "appeasement."

Bolton's bold intervention in Tallahassee was part of a determined effort by the Bush camp to shut down the recount before it showed that Gore had in fact gained more votes than Bush—which would have given the Democratic candidate the state's electoral votes and the presidency. The Bush team's goal was to delay any recount until the issue got to the U.S. Supreme Court, where five of the nine judges had been appointed by Republican presidents. In mid-December, the court, in a controversial decision, ruled in Bush's favor and further recounts were halted. With a margin of victory in Florida of 537 votes, George W. Bush was elected the nation's forty-third president.

John Bolton was only one of several prominent Republicans whose efforts in Florida would be rewarded by high-level appointments in the new administration. "People ask what [job] John should get," Vice President-elect Dick Cheney was quoted as saying at the time. "My answer is—anything he wants."[13] With strong backing from Cheney, Bolton would be made Under Secretary of State for Arms Control, putting him in charge of all nonproliferation efforts, including those dealing with North Korea.

As Americans went to the polls, the North Koreans signaled their desire for continuing rapprochement with Washington. A commentary on election day in Pyongyang's official *Rodong Sinmun* newspaper praised the "multi-faceted contacts and dialogues" between the United States and North Korea. "The improved relations between the two countries are in line with the desire and interests of the two peoples," the commentary said. "The improved DPRK-U.S. relations are not only good for both countries but will greatly help preserve peace and security on the Korean peninsula and in the Asia-Pacific region and the rest of the world. The DPRK will do its best to develop the DPRK-U.S. relations."[14] The message was clear: whoever became president, North Korea wanted to do business with him.

But the five-week stalemate over the outcome of the election vastly complicated the debate in Clinton administration over whether the president should visit North Korea. Despite Pyongyang's conciliatory signals and Clinton's evident desire to go, the president's advisers concluded that another high-level meeting with the North Koreans would be necessary before they could reach a final decision.

Behind the scenes, unbeknownst to most of the players, Sandy Berger, conscious of the president's desire to go, proposed making a commitment for Clinton to go to Pyongyang and trying to work out key details of the deal in the administration's remaining time in office. If the North did not budge, the president could always find an excuse not to go. Track II discussions with North Korean diplomats in New York suggested that the North might be willing to negotiate further once they had a commitment from Clinton.

Plans were drawn up for Wendy Sherman to lead a team to the North Korean capital in the hope that she could nail down the final details. But with the election results in doubt as the recount controversy dragged on, Sandy Berger and the president were reluctant to send her.

"He [Clinton] ultimately decided that we needed one more round with them," Berger recalled, "in which we determined that Wendy would go and say, 'I have in my pocket the date of the president's trip. If we can reach agreement here with respect to verification and definitions, I will give you this piece of paper; if not, the president is not prepared to come.' What then happened was the extraordinary election of 2000 and the recount. And it was not only unclear how the recount would be resolved, but also how long it would take, whether it would be thrown to the House of Representatives, whether there would be a constitutional confrontation. And we were very unwilling to commit the president to be in Pyongyang in the midst of an enormously difficult moment for the United States."

"I couldn't go to Pyongyang until we could make the decision whether the president really could come," said Sherman. "And we couldn't make the decision the president could come until we knew who was going to be president. Because we thought it would be appropriate to brief whoever was going to be president."

"The administration was paralyzed in terms of pursuing a North Korea missile deal and summit," said Bob Einhorn. "We waited, waited, and waited."

In his book *State of Denial*, journalist Bob Woodward recounts an episode in June 2000, when George W. Bush's presidential campaign was gathering steam. Concerned about his son's lack of knowledge of foreign policy, the candidate's father, former president George H. W. Bush, arranged for Saudi Arabia's ambassador to the United States, Prince Bandar, a longtime family friend, to brief the younger Bush. In one discussion, Bush asked, "Why should I care about North Korea?"[15]

When he won the disputed 2000 election, George W. Bush's views on many foreign policy issues were still vague and ill-defined. "In over his head" was the view of Colin Powell, who would become the new president's secretary of state.[16] Yet his lack of experience and knowledge had not hurt Bush politically. Foreign policy played virtually no role in the 2000 campaign, where the focus was on domestic issues like taxes, health care, and social security reform. To compensate for his weakness, Bush had surrounded himself with a group of advisers, who, between them, had decades of experience in the Republican administrations of Richard Nixon, Gerald Ford, Ronald Reagan, and George H. W. Bush. They would hold the key foreign and defense policy positions in the new administration.

Dick Cheney, Bush's vice president, had served as White House chief of staff in the Ford administration, where he became a harsh critic of détente with the Soviet Union. He then spent many years in the House of Representatives before becoming secretary of defense under George H. W. Bush in 1989. His low-key manner disguised views so robustly conservative that Colin Powell, who was chairman of the Joint Chiefs of Staff at the same time, considered them "just short of the loony fringes of the Republican Party."[17] As James Mann observed in his landmark study of Bush's advisers, Cheney "preferred to operate in the shadows. His stock-in-trade was not persuasion but discretion."[18]

Donald Rumsfeld, who would become secretary of defense in the new administration, had long been Cheney's patron and political ally. During the Nixon presidency, when Rumsfeld headed the Office of Economic Opportunity, Cheney had been his administrative assistant. After Gerald Ford succeeded Nixon, Rumsfeld became White House chief of staff; and when he was subsequently appointed secretary of defense, Cheney took his place. Like Cheney, Rumsfeld advocated a tough line toward the Soviet Union and a more muscular assertion of American power abroad and executive power at home. He was also a vicious bureaucratic infighter. In the 1970s, he had maneuvered to deprive Secretary of State Henry Kissinger, a key architect of the policy of détente toward the Soviet Union, of his second post of national security adviser (Kissinger had held both jobs under Nixon), and then working to impede progress in strategic arms talks with Moscow.

Abrasive and outspoken, Rumsfeld came to the new Bush White House with strong views on North Korea, having led a commission which in 1998 identified North Korea's missiles as a dangerous threat, giving new ammunition to supporters of a missile defense system.

The number two job at Defense was given to Paul Wolfowitz, who had been a top aide to Cheney at the Pentagon under the first president Bush. During the 1990s, he was a member of Rumsfeld's missile-threat commission. Like many Bush advisers, Wolfowitz had been publicly skeptical of the Agreed Framework and Clinton's conciliatory policies.

As an academic specialist on the Soviet Union, with views on the need to exercise American power shaped by the Cold War, Condoleezza Rice had been drawn to Republican foreign policy ideas by what she saw as the Carter administration's weak response to the Soviet invasion of Afghanistan. She worked on Soviet affairs as a junior member of the National Security Council staff in the first Bush administration before returning to Stanford University in the 1990s, eventually becoming the university's provost. She too saw North Korea as a growing threat to American security and disparaged Clinton's efforts to engage Pyongyang. She enlisted in George W. Bush's presidential campaign in 1998, during its earliest days, and had bonded with the younger Bush, sharing a common passion for sports; they even worked out together.[19] As his campaign gathered momentum, she became his principal foreign affairs adviser, able to explain complex issues in a way the candidate, largely untutored in foreign policy, felt comfortable with—so comfortable that he treated her like a member of the family, a kid sister. After Bush's election, she was appointed national security adviser.

Richard Armitage was a colorful figure, balding and barrel-chested—the result of a passion for weight lifting—with a reputation for bluntness tempered by a deep knowledge of the Far East. A Vietnam veteran who left Saigon during the final American evacuation in 1975 and then spent several years working in Asia as businessman, Armitage had taken from that experience the need both to restore American power and to maintain America's Asian alliances. As assistant secretary of defense under Reagan, he met Colin Powell, another Vietnam vet. The two became close friends.

As a black immigrant from Jamaica who had made it to the highest levels of the military and had helped orchestrate the U.S. victory in the first Gulf War, Colin Powell's life story had made him a hugely popular figure. As a key aide to Reagan's secretary of defense, and then as his national security adviser, Powell was a consummate Washington insider, skilled at navigating the bureaucracy. Under the administration of George H. W. Bush, Dick Cheney, then Bush's secretary of defense, picked Powell to be chairman of the Joint Chiefs of Staff, where he played a key role in the war to drive Saddam Hussein's forces from Kuwait.

This group, which also included a number of other prominent conservative foreign policy hands, was dubbed the "Vulcans," in honor of the Roman god of fire whose statue was a prominent landmark in Birmingham, Alabama, Rice's home town. Their views had been shaped during the tumultuous period that began with the nation's humiliating defeat in Vietnam and ended a decade and a half later with America's victory in the Cold War. Eager to cast aside the shadow of Vietnam, they were comfortable with the idea of using military power to advance American interests. Some of them were deeply skeptical of alliances, treaties, and international institutions and reluctant to negotiate with adversaries. But others, most notably Powell and Armitage, "were mistrustful of people with strong views or ideologies."[20]

In January 2000, Rice had published a long article in *Foreign Affairs* outlining the approach to foreign policy a Bush administration would take. One of the top priorities was missile defense. Most of the Vulcans believed the 1972 antiballistic missile treaty signed with the Soviet Union was obsolete, and that its strictures prevented the United States from developing a space defense system that could shoot down incoming missiles. Fear that such an attack might be launched by North Korea was one of the arguments regularly made by proponents of National Missile Defense (NMD).

In the article, Rice called North Korea a "rogue state" with "malign motives" living on "borrowed time" and sharply criticized the Clinton approach to Pyongyang. She described the 1994 Agreed Framework agreement as an attempt "to bribe North Korea into forsaking nuclear weapons. . . . One thing is clear: the United States must approach regimes like North Korea resolutely and decisively. The Clinton administration has failed here."[21]

Rather than seeking a negotiated deal to roll back Pyongyang's missile program, Rice argued that the United States "should accelerate efforts to defend against these weapons. This is the most important reason to deploy national and theater missile defenses as soon as possible."[22]

As for Bush himself, it was clear he knew very little about geopolitics and missile defense and had not given the issue much thought. Apart from the notion of North Korea as a justification for an increase in defense spending, he appears to have had an attitude—the North Koreans were bad guys—rather than any clear vision or policy.

Three days after Al Gore conceded defeat, Bush announced his first cabinet appointment: Colin Powell would be secretary of state. Although he shared the Vulcans' skeptical view of Clinton's foreign and security policies, he was the most moderate of Bush's advisers—a pragmatist rather than an ideologue. He was willing to use military force, but he also believed in the value of engagement, negotiations, and reason to resolve international disputes.

Indeed, Powell's caution had brought him into conflict with Madeleine Albright when he served as chairman of the Joint Chiefs of Staff in the early years of the Clinton administration. Albright was one of the most vocal advocates for using U.S. military might to bring the bloody ethnic war in Bosnia to an end. Powell consistently objected, leading Albright to ask him in exasperation, "What are you saving this superb military for, Colin, if we can't use it?"[23]

Despite the conservative inclinations of Bush's other advisers, it was widely believed that Powell would be the leading voice on foreign policy. And the fact that several other key figures—Rice, Cheney, Armitage—came from the first Bush administration contributed to a sense that, when it came to international affairs, the new team, while perhaps more conservative, would have the qualities Bush's father brought to foreign affairs: vast experience and a careful, cautious internationalism.

For the members of the outgoing Clinton administration, Powell's appointment offered some hope that their diplomacy with North Korea, which had come so close to a historic breakthrough, would be continued, in one form or another.

On a Sunday evening just before Christmas, Wendy Sherman, Chuck

Kartman, Jack Pritchard, and Bob Einhorn drove to Powell's home in subur-
ban Virginia to brief him on North Korea. It was just after dinner. Powell, genial as always, escorted them to his sitting room and personally served drinks.
Pritchard, who had served as a captain in the army's 101st Airborne Division
when Powell was a brigade commander, felt he immediately established some
rapport with the new secretary. Sherman spelled out the state of play—what the
North Koreans had put on the table, how close the Clinton administration had
gotten, what remained to be negotiated. She told Powell that Clinton had not
yet given up hope of going to Pyongyang. In any case, she said, "While there's
no way to know for sure, our sense is that a deal is still possible. We hope the
new administration will pick up the cards on the table." Pritchard, Kartman,
and Einhorn helped fill in details on the status of the negotiations.

Powell listened intently, occasionally interjecting "good, good." Midway
through the meeting, Condoleezza Rice arrived, having been delayed on a flight
from the president-elect's ranch in Crawford, Texas. As she walked in, Powell
turned and said, "Let me bring you up to speed. They've been briefing me on all
the good work they've been doing." But a difference between Rice and Powell
immediately became apparent. While Kartman thought Powell appeared "affirming and positive," Rice was cool and distant, "certainly not affirming what
we were saying, no reinforcement at all." Rice said little other than that Bush
would want to conduct his own policy review on Korea.

For his part, Powell felt it was a "good, solid briefing, very interesting, very
useful. They had done a lot of good work." But he also had questions. How
would any agreement be verified? Could the North Koreans be trusted? And he
sensed that Sherman's team, in sounding out Powell about the new administration's willingness to continue a similar approach with the North, was still trying
to work out a way for Clinton to get to Pyongyang before leaving office. On this
point, Powell told them, "You're on your own. And if he does this, it is because
he has decided to do it based on what he has done, and not with any impri-
matur from the new administration."

Still, as Sherman, Kartman, Einhorn, and Pritchard left, they all felt the
meeting had gone well. Whatever doubts Rice may have had, it was Powell who
appeared very much in charge. Rice seemed clearly in a subordinate position.

"At the end," Kartman recalled, "Powell said words to the effect that this
was all really promising and I think we've got to pick up on these things. Condi
Rice didn't say anything. You could sense that they were not on the same page."

"But this was not bad," Kartman noted. "We had just talked to the new secretary of state and national security adviser, and it sounded like at least the secretary of state was going to pick up on where things were. Maybe there will be
some bumps and adjustments. But this isn't a disaster at all."[24]

In addition to the meeting with Kartman and the others, Madeleine Albright and Sandy Berger provided their own briefing to Powell and Rice and came away with a similar impression. "We all felt that from our perspective, they were going to pick up the ball where we had left it," Albright recalled. "That they thought we had actually moved it quite far, and if there were opportunities here, that this would be continued."

"I was convinced by Powell," observed Sandy Berger. "Remember . . . Powell was an 800-pound gorilla coming into this administration. He was the most popular man in America, he was former chairman of the Joint Chiefs of Staff, former national security adviser, almost a presidential candidate in 2000. And I think the expectation was that Powell would be the major voice in this administration, certainly with respect to foreign policy, rather than someone who was relegated to a supplicant."

Clinton himself raised the idea of going to Pyongyang in a meeting with George Bush, asking the president-elect if he would object to a summit with Kim Jong Il. Bush, however, was unresponsive, saying that it was Clinton's decision, and that the country only had one president at a time. Privately, Bush didn't like the idea at all. During the transition, he was getting regular intelligence briefings from the CIA. One of his briefers was the agency's Associate Deputy Director of Intelligence, Jami Miscik. As she spelled out details of Clinton's efforts and the North Korean situation, Bush raised questions. What is Clinton doing? Is he going to negotiate something I am going to be stuck with? Miscik came away with the impression that Bush didn't care about the intricacies of North Korea. He just didn't want to inherit a deal he didn't agree with.

Clinton and Berger, however, after meeting the president-elect, came away with a very different impression. They concluded that the new administration would continue negotiating with North Korea and try to close the missile deal. Much as Clinton wanted to go to Pyongyang, the two decided it was better to let his successor try to work out the remaining missile issues with the North and make the policy of negotiating with the North their own. It was not the first time that people would misread Bush and his relationship with Powell.

With the president also deeply involved in high-stakes negotiations to reach a final settlement between the Israelis and the Palestinians, it finally became clear that time had run out and that a trip to Pyongyang was no longer possible. On December 28, 2000, Clinton announced that the North Korea trip was off.

"We've made a lot of progress with the North Koreans," he told reporters. "But I concluded that I did not have sufficient time to put the trip together and to execute the trip in an appropriate manner."[25]

What the White House did not announce was that, in the same message advising Pyongyang the president could not make the trip, Clinton had invited Kim Jong Il to Washington. The idea originated with Charles Kartman and his colleagues at the State Department, partly as a way to blunt any negative reaction from the North Koreans, and partly to demonstrate continued good will in the hope of smoothing the transition to a new administration.

"Rather than simply sending them a note saying we are interested in your missile proposal but we are not interested in going to Pyongyang, and since the president wasn't averse to meeting with Kim Jong Il but the logistics, timing, and various downsides of going to Pyongyang were too much, it came out—let's turn it around," Kartman recalled. "Let's take this condition [of a Clinton-Kim meeting] and turn it around. Why not have Clinton meet Kim Jong Il in Washington?"

No one really expected the North Koreans to agree. In her memoirs, Albright attributed Kim's reluctance to accept to "the lateness of the invitation and the importance of face in East Asia diplomacy."[26] But the offer was a way of cushioning the blow to Kim's pride and signaling that Pyongyang should not give up its hopes for better relations with the United States.

It was the Clinton administration's final move on North Korea. Shortly before leaving office, Clinton sent a farewell message to Kim. "We tried to word it to suggest that we were looking ahead," according to Bob Carlin. "So Kim Jung Il sent a reply message, and to me, it was clear that it was not just to Clinton, but a signal to the new administration. It was just positive enough to suggest that, yes, we had accomplished a lot and we would be staying on this course. They indicated that at some point the missile deal they had sketched out was still on the table."

# 3

# REGIME CHANGE

A S GEORGE W. BUSH TOOK OFFICE, NORTH KOREAN DIPLO-
mats were doing their best to signal a desire to resume dialogue
with the new administration. At a meeting organized by the At-
lantic Council on February 8 in Washington, Li Gun, North Korea's
deputy permanent representative to the UN, told a group of American
North Korea specialists, "Now it is time to move onto action. We hope the
Bush administration maintains the U.S. engagement policy toward North
Korea."[1]

Thomas Hubbard—now acting assistant secretary of state for
East Asia pending confirmation of Bush's nominee for the position,
James Kelly—did what he could to reassure the North Koreans.
In early February, he hosted a meeting for Li Gun and North Korea's
permanent representative to the UN, Lee Hyong Chol, in his office
at the State Department. The object of the meeting was to explain
that a new administration was in place, and while Hubbard couldn't
predict what it would do, he urged the North Koreans to stay calm.
The North Koreans indicated that they were not too worried. After
all, they told him, there was the communiqué signed by Clinton and
Jo Myong Rok pledging "no hostile intent." Hubbard recalled that
his guests viewed this as "gospel." As long as it remained so, they appeared confident that engagement with Washington would remain on
course.

*   *   *

Robert Joseph was not interested in rapprochement or engagement. Joseph, director of the Counter-Proliferation Center at the National Defense University and previously deputy assistant secretary of defense in both the Reagan and Bush I administrations, was a longtime defense hawk, skeptical of the value of arms-control agreements and enamored of muscular U.S. policies to deter potential adversaries. He believed North Korea was one of the most brutal and repressive regimes of the twentieth century, and he had watched Madeleine Albright's Pyongyang visit with disgust. Her appearance with Kim Jong Il at a mass rally, in Joseph's eyes, marked the lowest point in 200 years of American diplomacy. He viewed the Agreed Framework as nothing but appeasement—a lifeline to keep one of the world's worst regimes in power while failing to eliminate Pyongyang's nuclear program.

"Bob really hated the Agreed Framework," observed Lawrence Wilkerson, who at the start of the administration was working in the State Department's Office of Policy Planning and would in 2002 become Colin Powell's chief of staff. "He thought it was probably the worst piece of diplomatic trash that had ever been concocted . . . so his objective was first to kill the Agreed Framework and to make sure that nothing like it ever got created again."

Following Bush's victory, Joseph was asked to join the transition team and work on proliferation and defense issues. One of his first jobs was to draft "National Security Presidential Directive One" with recommendations on how the new administration should organize the process of reviewing and adjusting existing policies. He recommended that the National Security Council, not the State Department, chair any review of proliferation issues. When Bush took office, Joseph was appointed the NSC's Senior Director for Nonproliferation—a powerful position from which to influence the new administration's review of North Korea policy.

All administrations conduct such reviews; they are a natural part of any political transition in Washington. But the process of assessing what the Clinton administration had done, and determining what elements of his policy to retain, change, or discard, within days of Mr. Bush taking office brought to surface the bureaucratic and personal rivalries and policy disputes that were to shape—and cripple—the administration's approach to North Korea.

In early February 2001, Tom Hubbard climbed into a limousine with Colin Powell for the short ride from the State Department to the White House. In the Situation Room, they joined Donald Rumsfeld, Paul Wolfowitz, Condoleezza Rice, and Robert Joseph for a "principals meeting" to kick off the administration's North Korea policy review. Hubbard, who had invested much of his time over the past decade in negotiations aimed at rolling back Pyongyang's nuclear and missile programs, had discussed the Korea issue with Powell. The new secretary of state had made clear his view that it would have been wrong for Bill Clinton to go to Pyongyang—a view that Hubbard shared.

But Powell had also indicated that engaging Pyongyang was the right approach, and that there was much in what the Clinton administration had achieved that was worth building on. Still, Hubbard was concerned about the policy review. If the exercise was structured with two separate working groups—one to deal with the "functional" issue of proliferation and the other with "regional" issues—he worried that Powell would have trouble controlling the process and the outcome.

At the meeting it quickly became apparent that Powell was outnumbered by critics of the idea of engaging North Korea. The result, just as Hubbard had feared, was the creation of two working groups. Hubbard would chair the Korea working group, and Bob Joseph would chair the group working on proliferation. Then Deputy National Security Adviser Stephen Hadley issued a directive that the NSC would function as the "secretariat" during the review. Hubbard saw this as primarily an administrative function—taking the minutes at meetings and circulating position papers. But the NSC had other ideas. It soon became clear that the "secretariat" had seized the power to sign off on all documents, ensuring that the hawks would dominate the entire process.

Moreover, Hadley formalized the involvement of the vice president and his staff in North Korea policy. As the process began, Hadley instructed senior officials involved in the policy review to share information and position papers with the vice president's key national security staffers. The arrangement gave Cheney unprecedented clout in shaping the new administration's approach to Pyongyang.[2] "You had the vice president's office playing a far more involved role than any vice president's office had ever played before," observed Colin Powell. "It was almost an alternative NSC."

Joseph and Hubbard clashed from the very beginning. To Hubbard, Joseph appeared to be an ideologue with close ties to the neocons and who was driven by an abhorrence of everything Clintonian. For his part, Joseph was struck by the first conversation between the two men, in which Hubbard expressed frustration with Bush, saying "If only the President understood these issues." In Joseph's mind, it was a display of the kind of arrogance typical of the professional diplomats he so despised.

As the working-level meetings got under way, some new faces appeared. Joseph was assisted by Richard Falkenrath, an arms-control expert who, like Joseph, had worked on the transition team before joining the NSC to work on nonproliferation issues. They were joined by Mary Tighe, who had been made the NSC's "regional expert." An inveterate hard-liner with a background in the CIA, she was deeply distrustful, not only of North Korea, but also of the State

Department, and spent much of her time trying to discredit the department's Asia hands. Two staffers from the office of Vice President Cheney also began attending meetings—Samantha Ravich and Stephen Yates, a fluent Chinese speaker and a onetime Mormon missionary in Taiwan who'd been appointed as Cheney's Asia policy adviser. Yates's own view of Kim Jong Il appeared to reflect that of his boss. "Kim Jong Il is among the most loathsome of beings in the world," Yates said, "and I think the regime has committed crimes against humanity that probably match any of the top-tier purveyors of human rights abuses in the world. I think the world would be a better place if he went to meet his father, whether he's in heaven or hell."

Hubbard and others who had previously dealt with the North Koreans suddenly found their observations and insights falling on deaf ears. Carlin recalled that the staffers from the NSC and the vice president's office "made it clear that the administration was not prepared to do things in the same way, didn't want to use as a basis anything that had been accomplished, didn't trust the State Department at all, thought the State Department had given away too much to the North Koreans, and hadn't been sufficiently protecting U.S. interests." Carlin also commented: "When you came up with the answer that you could negotiate with the North Koreans, that they had abided by agreements, that there were positive paths, that pressure was counterproductive—it was fairly clear that it couldn't be used, because these people would not listen. Their idea of having a meeting was to shout down anybody who disagreed, to imply that they were somehow disloyal, not following orders, not in tune with what the administration wanted." Carlin was shocked. "We never had meetings like that before," he said, "ever."

The policy review group immediately confronted—and disagreed on—two key issues: whether to remain in touch with the North Koreans while the policy review was in process and whether the Bush administration should reaffirm the communiqué signed during Vice Marshal Jo Myong Rok's visit to Washington the previous October in which the two sides pledged "no hostile intent" toward each other.

Hubbard, who had just hosted Pyongyang's UN envoys in an effort to reassure them, argued that the North Koreans might "go off half-cocked" if communications were cut off during the course of the policy review. He urged that U.S. officials to go to New York to meet the UN envoys and brief them. Joseph, however, argued that the mere act of consulting with the North Koreans would suggest a continuation of the Clinton policy. A frustrated Hubbard took his complaint to Powell. But the new secretary of state did not want to pick a fight on what seemed like a minor issue. Hubbard was overruled.

The issue of the communiqué was even more sensitive. Hubbard argued that just as the government of China viewed the Shanghai Communiqué signed by President Richard Nixon on his path-breaking trip in 1972 as the foundation of its relationship with Washington, Kim Jong Il viewed the communiqué signed by Vice Marshal Jo as the basis for Pyongyang's cautious rapprochement with the United States. Failure to reaffirm the communiqué, with its pledge of "no hostile intent," Hubbard warned, would lead to trouble. If North Korea believed the Bush administration was ending dialogue, there was no way to predict what Kim might do.

Joseph, however, was dismissive. "No hostile intent," he argued, was just "one of those North Korean sort of phrases." There was no reason to be sensitive to Pyongyang's feelings.

Looking back afterward, Hubbard concluded, "These people did have hostile intent and they thought it was a mistake to say otherwise."

As the policy review got under way, Powell and Armitage began to put their own team in place. For the post of assistant secretary of state for East Asia—the job Tom Hubbard was temporarily filling—they tapped James Kelly. A graduate of the U.S. Naval Academy with an MBA from Harvard, Kelly had served in the navy for twenty-three years. During the Reagan administration, he had been deputy assistant secretary of defense dealing with Asia, and then senior director for Asian affairs at the National Security Council.

With his vast experience in the region, he was widely respected.

"He was a wise man," observed one person who worked closely with him. "He was a vast source of knowledge on East Asia. He'd visit a country and know more than the CIA guys would know in-country."

Kelly shared the general Republican critique that the Clinton administration had not been tough enough with North Korea. But, like Powell, he felt the Agreed Framework, for all its flaws, was "the best solution to a difficult problem," and he supported engaging Pyongyang, although in a more skeptical way. He was also by nature a cautious man. Throughout the winter and spring, as he waited for congressional confirmation, Kelly worked quietly behind the scenes. In the early days of the administration, Chuck Kartman stopped by Kelly's office to chat. The two men knew each other well, and had worked together before. Kartman had confidently expected to be named as the new ambassador to Seoul—the culmination of years of involvement with Korean issues. He was stunned when Kelly told him the job was no longer his. Instead, Kelly proposed making Kartman ambassador to the Philippines. The tone of the conversation was cordial. Kartman realized that Kelly and Armitage were trying to preserve his career him by placing him in an important post. But it was equally clear that sending him to Manila was a way of deliberately sidelining him from involvement in Korean policy. The new administration, Kartman concluded, was simply not interested in anything he had to say about North Korea.

Kartman told Kelly that even if the Seoul job was out, he would like to continue as the Special Envoy for Korean Peace Talks. Kelly indicated that too was out. Trying to be the loyal trooper, Kartman responded that if he was going to be replaced, the job should go to Jack Pritchard. But Kartman, probably the most experienced North Korea hand in the U.S. government, was disheartened. "I did feel that I was a big resource with a lot of experiences that they should draw on," he said. "The simple fact that there were half a dozen people who spent six hours in a small room in a negotiation with Kim Jong Il . . . that certainly is something that I would have, if I were coming into the administration, I would want to be very certain what had occurred and what the impressions were. That was never drawn on."

In fact, Kartman was not invited to any meetings, never got so much as a phone call. He was just cut off. In an interview, I asked Kartman whether he was tainted by too many hours spent in the presence of North Koreans. "No," he replied dryly. "I was tainted by too many hours in the presence of Madeleine Albright."

A disheartened Kartman submitted his resignation and took a job as director of the Korean Peninsula Energy Development Organization (KEDO), the multinational consortium handling the construction of the light-water reactors being provided to North Korea under the terms of the Agreed Framework.

"It was not yet obvious that the administration would be able to kill off the Agreed Framework," Kartman recalled. "And so I hoped that the Agreed Framework at least could be preserved just by carefully continuing to fulfill its obligations. That in effect would neutralize the nuclear problem."

Kartman was the first of the U.S. government's most experienced North Korea hands to leave the Bush administration. He would not be the last.

Indeed, the new administration's hostility toward Kim Jong Il was matched only by its hostility toward Bill Clinton and his associates. Soon, the term "ABC"—Anyone But Clinton—became a mantra in the new administration.

"It was pervasive throughout," Jack Pritchard remembered. "It really was. Every turn along the way, you know . . . 'No that's too much like Clinton, you can't do that.' "

When Pritchard was offered Kartman's position, which had been known as "Special Envoy for Peace Talks" with the North Koreans, he had name cards made up with that title. White House staffers immediately challenged him.

"They asked, 'Who gave you permission to use that? We don't use that term around here.'" Pritchard said. "I had someone come up and say 'Peace? Peace talks? That's a Democratic term. That's from the Clinton era. We don't use that term here.'" The reference to "peace" in the job title was removed.

For Pritchard, the transition to a new administration was proving awkward. A career military man with a background in intelligence, he had a coldly realistic view of North Korea. Within the Clinton administration, he had been considered one of the more skeptical voices. Under Bush, though, he was viewed with suspicion. "I was the Clinton guy even though I was as a U.S. Army colonel brought into the Clinton administration. Within the Clinton administration internally I was viewed as the hard-line guy. But once I joined the Bush administration," he said, "the hard-line folks viewed me as the Clinton guy, and on the far left of the field. It was a very strange position to be in."

Pritchard was particularly concerned by the total lack of dialogue with the North Koreans. Bob Carlin shared the concern. As the new administration was taking shape, he was furiously writing memos to his boss, Carl Ford, the head of the State Department's Bureau of Intelligence and Research (INR), and to Colin Powell as well. In the memos, he tried to spell out where things stood and offered a series of suggestions on what the United States might do to keep the lines of communication open to the North Koreans. But he got no response.

With formal contact banned while the policy review was under way, Pritchard authorized Carlin to undertake a series of secret meetings. In the early 1990s, Carlin had engaged in similar back-door negotiations. With tensions growing in the run-up to the 1994 nuclear crisis, he had made periodic visits to New York. He would call North Korean diplomat Li Gun and say, "I'm going to be in New York visiting my sister. Would you like to have coffee?"

After the first couple of times, Li knew exactly what Carlin meant. It was a chance, the ex-CIA man noted, to talk "off-line," to trade ideas and to keep some form of communication going.

Now, Pritchard and Carlin believed, politics had created a crisis even though the North Koreans had not done anything different or wrong. So Carlin again began letting officials at North Korea's UN mission know he would be "visiting his sister," and periodic meetings were held.

Once George W. Bush took office, he began holding a series of official phone calls with various world leaders. One of his earliest was with South Korean president Kim Dae-jung. In October 2000, shortly before Madeleine Albright's trip to Pyongyang, Kim had been awarded the Nobel Peace Prize for his summit meeting with Kim Jong Il. The South Korean leader had developed a close relationship with Bill Clinton. The American president treated Kim respectfully, frequently solicited his advice, and embraced Kim's "sunshine policy" of improving relations with North Korea. Kim had been rooting for Vice President Al Gore to defeat Bush, and he was worried about future U.S. policy toward North Korea.

"I wanted Mr. Gore to be the next president," Kim told me, "because if Mr. Bush becomes the next president of the United States, I thought, he will go through many disruptions about the North Korean policy from the Clinton administration. That's why I was very concerned."

In early January, Kim had spelled out his concerns publicly in an interview with David Ignatius of the *Washington Post*. Kim said he was hoping for an early summit with Bush, and that his message would be: "Don't change course; support continued dialogue; don't push the North's leader, Kim Jong Il, back into a corner."[3] Kim emphasized his belief that North Korea really was changing, and pointed to Kim Jong Il's apparent openness to the idea of U.S. forces remaining on the peninsula as one important sign. Kim Dae-jung and his advisers were also anxious about the incoming administration's support for a missile defense system. A senior South Korean Foreign Ministry official expressed concern to Ignatius that in the mind of Defense Secretary-designate Donald Rumsfeld, North Korea was a "poster child" for missile defense. Pyongyang's utility as a rallying point for advocates of the missile shield, officials in Seoul worried, could make the new administration even less receptive to pursuing the missile deal that Bill Clinton had run out of time to complete.

The first Bush-Kim phone call, in early February, did not go well. Kim Dae-jung immediately began to tell Bush how important it was to continue with the Sunshine Policy and to engage North Korea. He mentioned Kim Jong Il's recent visit to China and told Bush he believed Pyongyang was exploring Chinese-style reforms.[4]

As Kim spoke, Bush put his hand over the phone, turned to Pritchard and Hadley, and asked, "Who is this guy?" At 11:00 P.M. that night, Pritchard suddenly received a call from Condoleezza Rice summoning him back to the White House to write a paper for the President explaining who Kim was, spelling out his background and philosophy, and explaining why he had spoken as he did earlier in the evening. To Pritchard, it was the first sign that differences over North Korea were going to cause serious problems in the U.S. alliance with South Korea.

With 37,000 U.S. troops stationed in South Korea, many of them along the Demilitarized Zone, Washington's alliance with Seoul had long been one of America's most important international relationships. Forged in blood during the Korean War, a bulwark in the decades-long struggle against Communism during the Cold War, and providing a key base for the projection of American power in Northeast Asia, the alliance had endured despite the collapse of the Soviet Union and its socialist allies. The reason, of course, was North Korea.

But the election of Kim Dae-jung in 1997 marked a sea-change in South Korea. Until the late 1980s, the country had remained under the thumb of successive military dictatorships that imposed draconian national security laws and crushed dissent in the name of countering the North Korean threat. The United States, viewing Korea through a Cold War lens, accepted and worked with the authoritarian regimes in Seoul, as it did with similar right-wing regimes elsewhere in Asia.

As South Korea began to emerge as an economic power, however, popular demands for democracy and political freedom intensified, fueled by a younger generation with no living memory of the trauma of the war years. This movement was spearheaded by what became known as the "386" generation—people who were born in the 1960s, attended college in the 1980s, and were in their 30s.

Gradually, the generation that had fought the Communists was supplanted by a generation that fought military rule and chafed at the "little brother" relationship that had characterized South Korea's dealings with the United States for so many years. As citizens in the world's eleventh-largest economy, brimming with self-confidence and resentful of a large-scale foreign military presence on their soil, many South Koreans longed to escape from the shadow of Uncle Sam.

The election of Kim, a longtime pro-democracy dissident, reflected this dramatic change. His June 2000 summit in Pyongyang with Kim Jong Il also crystallized an emerging public perception in South Korea that the North Koreans were no longer fearsome enemies that had to be contained at all costs. Instead, public opinion increasingly began to view them as wayward cousins to be coaxed back into the fold through conciliation and engagement. With Kim and Bill Clinton sharing similar views on the value of negotiations and diplomacy in dealing with North Korea, the two governments had been largely in sync.

With the change of administration in Washington, Kim was worried about the intentions of the new president and pushed for an early summit with Bush. Another factor added to Seoul's sense of urgency. The South Koreans had heard that Japan's prime minister Yoshiro Mori was also planning a Washington visit. Given the long-standing rivalry between Seoul and Tokyo, it became a matter of national pride for the South Koreans to have their leader meet with Bush before his Japanese counterpart did. In Washington, South Korean diplomats were given instructions to push for a meeting at the earliest possible date.

Seoul's anxiety about a change in the U.S. position on North Korea was somewhat alleviated when South Korean foreign minister Lee Jeong-binn met with Colin Powell in Washington on February 7 to discuss Kim's upcoming trip. Powell was reassuring, telling Lee the Bush administration was supportive of Kim's approach to Pyongyang and, while it might want to "improve" on some points in the Agreed Framework, was committed to maintaining the accord.

Privately, though, U.S. officials were urging the South Koreans not to push for an early meeting. Hubbard and others told South Korean diplomats that the new administration had barely begun its policy review, and many key officials were awaiting confirmation and were not yet in place. Washington was simply not ready for a summit. A similar message was conveyed directly to Kim by several prominent American academics and former officials who were in Seoul in February, among them, Leon Sigal, a scholar at the Social Science Research Council and author of a widely respected book on the 1994 nuclear crisis, who told Kim that Bush and his top advisers were still in "campaign mode" and it would be better to wait a while for them to face the practicalities of governing.

A former U.S. ambassador to Seoul, Donald Gregg, also appealed to Kim not to rush a summit, as did Michael Green, a Japan specialist at the Council on Foreign Relations who had been tapped to become Director of Asian Affairs at the National Security Council. "Please don't preach to the new president," Green pleaded. "He needs time to get his team ready."

The South Korean embassy in Washington, feeling itself squeezed between pressure from Seoul and reluctance from the new administration, also passed along warnings about the prospects for a meeting, but they did not register. "Kim was determined to go ahead." said one South Korean diplomat. "He was a little bit spoiled by American politicians because everybody—politicians, financiers, businessmen—who came to the Blue House [Seoul's equivalent of the White House] took the opportunity to praise Kim Dae-jung for democracy, for peace, for the Nobel Prize. He was so convinced . . . he could talk to Bush and persuade him."

Just days before Kim Dae-jung's departure for Washington, he hosted Russian president Vladimir Putin in Seoul. On February 27, 2001, the two men issued a joint communiqué praising the 1972 antiballistic missile treaty as "a cornerstone of strategic stability and an important foundation of international efforts on nuclear disarmament and nonproliferation."[5]

The statement, which a *New York Times* headline described as "South Korea Takes Russia's Side in Dispute Over U.S. Missile Defense Plan," was an implicit criticism of Bush administration plans to erect a national missile defense system.

Putin had been waging a campaign to oppose such a move, and enlisting the support of a key U.S. ally marked an important development. From Seoul's perspective, the statement reflected concerns that the antimissile system could torpedo efforts initiated by the Clinton administration to resolve the North Korea missile issue through negotiations. "We just had a summit with the North Koreans," noted one former senior South Korean Foreign Ministry official, "and if we support it we will give a very critical negative signal to North Korea. So we were reluctant."

Kim's statement did not go down well at the White House and served to further accentuate emerging differences between the president and Condoleezza Rice, on the one hand, and Colin Powell on the other. Bush and Rice were angry that, just days before arriving in Washington, one of the president's first foreign visitors should so publicly question one of the new administration's top priorities. Rice in particular was said to be furious, viewing Kim's position as little more than reflecting the views of the hated Bill Clinton. She sent Seoul a sharply worded message expressing displeasure.

Shortly after Putin left Seoul, South Korea issued a carefully worded "clarification," noting that support for the treaty did not mean opposition to NMD.[6] For his part, Powell, who "was agnostic about eliminating the ABM treaty and lacked the missionary zeal with which some Republicans pursued missile defense,"[7] and who favored extensive consultations with Moscow before any decision was made, was less concerned.

Acting on her irritation with Kim, a profound mistrust for North Korea, and support for a tougher line toward Pyongyang, Rice, without informing the State Department, held a background briefing on March 6 for David Sanger of the *New York Times* and other journalists ahead of Kim's meeting with Bush the next day. Speaking as a "senior administration official," Rice said, "The North Korean regime is a problem, and Kim Jong Il is a problem."[8] Sanger's report said the Bush administration viewed "North Korea as a major threat, and they are clearly wary that Mr. Kim's peace initiatives have moved too fast with too few concessions from the North."[9]

The same day, Colin Powell met with reporters at the State Department and delivered a very different message. Praising Kim and his Sunshine Policy, Powell said, "We do plan to engage with North Korea to pick up where President Clinton and his administration left off. Some promising elements were left on the table, and we'll be examining those elements."[10]

The next morning, Powell hosted Kim and his National Security Adviser Lim Dong-won for breakfast at Blair House, the official guest house for presidential visitors, located on Pennsylvania Ave. opposite the West Wing of the White House. Powell was accompanied by Acting Assistant Secretary of

State for East Asia Tom Hubbard, Press Secretary Richard Boucher, and Evans Revere, now Acting U.S. Ambassador to Seoul. It was, in the words of one American participant, a "wonderful meeting."

Powell, who had never met Kim, went out of his way to be respectful. "The dynamics were great," recalled Evans Revere. "People were relaxed and comfortable with each other. They were on basically the same page, in terms of policy approaches. Sunshine Policy, engagement policy, engagement is the way to go. There was no question in my mind that we were indeed picking up the ball where things had been left off. Yes, there was going to be a policy review, as we always do, but there was every reason to think we would come out at a place that was not that dissimilar from where we were."

Kim used the occasion to try out the presentation he intended to make to Bush, putting the Korea issue in the context of history and making the case for engagement as the way to end the last conflict of the Cold War. The Americans were impressed. Hubbard thought the presentation was brilliant.

For his part, Kim left the breakfast with Powell reassured. "Everything seemed so fine that morning," he told me. "The talk was very smooth. The Korean government and the State Department agreed that they would follow the Clinton approach toward North Korea."

Buried on page 20 of the *Washington Post* that same morning was a short article about Powell's comments the previous day. The headline was "Bush to Pick Up Clinton Talks on N. Korean Missiles." As Powell prepared to head to the White House for Bush's meeting with Kim, he received a call from a furious Condoleezza Rice.

"All hell breaks loose," Powell recalled. "The president's very unhappy. Condi conveys his unhappiness to me. And when I got there, it was clear he was unhappy."

Although Powell had mentioned the word "Clinton," he "didn't find this to be shocking or politically inflammable." Others in the administration, however, were incensed, viewing Powell's comments as a deliberate attempt to impose his moderate views about Korea on the president.

"One of the top rules in any administration, particularly this administration, is no surprises," noted Bob Joseph's aide Richard Falkenrath, who was playing a major role in the North Korea policy review. "And what Colin Powell did in that case was to say something to the press that was really a surprise to the president, the secretary of defense, the national security adviser, and the vice president. So that went over really badly. And it occasioned a very quick review of the president's personal preferences for dealing with North Korea. And they were not to continue with the policy that the Clinton administration was negotiating with them. The president looked at North Korea and saw it as an absolutely terrible regime—it brutalized its people, it cheated on its international commitments, and presented a threat to the region and the world, one which he was very reluctant to deal with."

Rice told Powell that he needed to speak to the press and correct the impression left by his comments the previous day, and to do so before Bush and Kim held their own press conference at the conclusion of their summit. As Powell later described it, "I had to go out and in an embarrassing way say to the press, 'Well, you know we'll study it.'"

Even as the two presidents were meeting, Powell slipped out of the Oval Office to address a crowd of surprised and slightly puzzled reporters. "There was some suggestion that imminent negotiations are about to begin," Powell declared. "That is not the case. The president forcefully made the point that we are undertaking a full review of our relationship with North Korea, coming up with policies that build on the past, coming up with policies unique to the administration, the other things that we will want to see on the table. And in due course, when our review is finished, we'll determine at what pace and when we will engage with the North Koreans."[11]

Later, after Kim had returned to Korea, Powell and Armitage discussed the episode. Armitage said the two men had a similar reaction: "Oh man, we're going to have a long ride if they're getting upset about that headline. We have real issues out there."


The meeting between the two presidents was a disaster. At the age of seventy-five, Kim came across, in Colin Powell's words, as a "dignified oriental gentleman." He was formal, walked stiffly (a legacy in part of his mistreatment while in prison, and partly of a traffic accident he claimed the Korean CIA had staged in an attempt to kill him), was prone to long-winded expositions of his views, and was used to being treated with respect, if not deference, by others, including Bill Clinton.

But, as one senior South Korean official observed, Kim had a "core of steel," forged from a lifetime of suffering for his beliefs. He had been kidnapped, beaten, jailed, sentenced to death, and only reprieved at the last minute. His position on North Korea was not at all naïve. The previous year, the South Korean president had hosted Democratic Senator Joseph Biden and his chief Asia policy aide on the Senate Foreign Relations Committee, Frank Jannuzi, for lunch in Seoul. Kim told them some people in the United States misunderstood his "sunshine policy" toward Pyongyang. He knew what Kim Jong Il's regime was like. "North Korea is like a mold," he explained to Biden. "Sunshine is the disinfectant."

Kim, seeking Bush's blessing for his approach to Pyongyang, began to spell out his views on North Korea, telling Bush that Kim Jong Il's overriding goal was regime survival, and that engagement was the best way to deal with the North Korean threat. He noted that the North Korean leader had expressed a willingness to accept a continued U.S. military presence on the Korean peninsula after it was reunified. "I made clear that Chairman Kim Jong Il aspired to make better relations with the United States," Kim Dae-jung recalled. "So therefore, you can resolve the North Korean issues through dialogue."

But Bush, in the words of one official who was there, "really lit into Kim Dae-jung," interrupting the South Korean leader, challenging the premises of his argument, expressing hostility toward North Korea and skepticism about the "sunshine policy." Bush made clear he had no intention of resuming the missile talks pursued by the Clinton administration in the foreseeable future.[12]

Body language alone reflected Bush's perspective. Slouched in his chair, he showed little respect or deference and even less understanding. "Bush didn't understand who Kim Dae-jung was or where he was coming from," recalled one of Powell's State Department colleagues. "He didn't know Kim's personal history." As then-Deputy Secretary of State Richard Armitage bluntly recalled, "There was no sort of respect given an elder diplomat in station, and certainly no respect for his past suffering for his beliefs, and a sort of, 'We hate him' and 'Your sunshine policy sucks.'"

Bush's tone left the South Korean president deeply offended. As Kim said to me, "In terms of his attitude or manners, he was very 'Texas.' And overall, I can say that his manners were not very good. I was very astonished and stunned by his behavior at the time, because I had had such a nice conversation in the morning together with Colin Powell. I believed that everything important is now settled. So I was very embarrassed."

Powell and others were also taken aback by the depth of Bush's antipathy to North Korea and to Kim Jong Il personally. The issue had barely figured in the campaign or in the transition. It did not appear to be high on Bush's list of priorities. Condoleezza Rice had briefed him before the Kim meeting, but that did not appear to account for the intensity of Bush's feelings.

Richard Armitage believed that North Korea had suddenly entered the realm of administration "theology," which brooked no argument. "North Korea wasn't in the theology until President Bush just woke up one morning and decided he hated it," Armitage said. "I'm serious, I'm not joking about that, that's what did it. He hates this guy."

From this point on, Bush did little to disguise his visceral "loathing" for Kim Jong Il, as he subsequently described his feelings to journalist Bob Woodward.[13] Armitage recalled that Bush now "started talking to world leaders in scatological terms about him. He's an asshole, I hate him, he's a son of a bitch—to different foreign leaders. That kind of stuff. Without ever meeting him."

At noon, after the meeting and before the two leaders went to lunch, reporters were allowed into the Oval Office for a brief news conference where the differences in approach were evident. Bush started off by referring to Kim Dae-jung as "this man," a casual reference—possibly indicating he had forgotten Kim's name and chose not to refer to his title—which Kim, and South Korean officials, media, and citizenry found disrespectful and offensive. Years later, when I interviewed Kim, the memory still rankled. "He humiliated me by calling me 'this man,' " Kim said.

Then, referring to Kim Jong Il, Bush told the assembled reporters, "I do have some skepticism about the leader of North Korea. We're not certain they're keeping all terms of all agreements."

"At that joint press conference," Kim recalled, "Mr. Bush started to criticize Chairman Kim Jong Il of North Korea, describing him as a dictator. So what Mr. Bush did at the time was to reverse the statement between two different governments already agreed earlier in the morning," a reference to the meeting of minds he had at the breakfast with Powell before going to the White House.

Nevertheless, Kim continued, "I decided not to be angry or upset about his manners at the time, because I believed I was going to be in this position for several years more, and [Bush] was going to be in that position for several more years, which means we could have more conversations over the coming years, and I thought I could persuade him and make him understand."

Using the cautious language often employed to signal diplomatic disagreements, President Kim simply observed to reporters, "President Bush was very frank and honest in sharing with me his perceptions about the nature of North Korea and the North Korean leader."

Added Bush, "The President was very forthright in describing his vision and I was forthright in describing my support for his vision, as well as my skepticism."[14]

After the meeting, Hubbard and Torkel Patterson, the Senior Director for Asia at the National Security Council, were asked to hold a background briefing for reporters. Before the session, they were given a read-out by Lewis "Scooter" Libby, Vice President Cheney's chief of staff. Hubbard was struck by how much Bush's "total distaste for North Korea" dominated Libby's account of the encounter, and the extent to which Libby seemed elated by Bush's tough line. "You wouldn't believe how strong the president was," Libby gloated.

"I realized that for Bush, North Korea transcended the policy argument," Hubbard recalled. "The visceral distaste for Kim Jong Il did not come out until that meeting."

As he prepared to meet the press, Hubbard was briefly taken aside by Powell. "He grabbed me and told me what a fiasco it had been," Hubbard recalled. "He said he'd been blindsided."

The press briefing was dominated by questions about the negative tone of the meeting. David Sanger of the *New York Times* pressed Patterson on Bush's statement that North Korea was not abiding by agreements signed with the United States. Sanger noted that there was really only one accord—the Agreed Framework. Was the President accusing Kim Jong Il of violating it? Patterson was forced to acknowledge there was no evidence Pyonygyang was violating the terms of the Framework. Other reporters asked whether the Agreed Framework was now dead. Hubbard emphasized that the president had stated a willingness to continue to abide by the accord. But the damage was done. "What came out instead was—we don't like the 'Sunshine Policy,'" he noted. "We hold Kim Jong Il in deep distaste. By implication [we] won't be working with South Korea on this."

Before leaving Washington, Kim Dae-jung met with Madeleine Albright. She was struck by his bleak mood, observing that, "It was evident that the rug had been pulled out from under him."

Two days later, Kim took the initiative to telephone Bush's father, former President George H. W. Bush. The two men were acquaintances from Kim's earlier days as a South Korean opposition leader. Kim recalled telling the older Bush. "I emphasized many times that I would base my North Korea policy on engagement." Bush senior tried to reassure Kim about his son's hard-line opinions. "The father Bush said, 'You don't need to be too concerned. Eventually, the junior Bush will also follow the option of dialogue in resolving the North Korean issue." Within weeks, the new president's father would intervene in a successful effort to moderate the new administration's approach to Pyongyang.

Still, on his flight back to Seoul, Kim told Foreign Minister Lee Jeong-binn that he was deeply worried. Returning home, the South Korean president found public opinion in an uproar over Bush's use of the disrespectful term "this man."

"It gave a very bad impression of Bush, his team, his administration," noted a South Korean diplomat who had been involved in the visit. It offended the national pride of ordinary Koreans as well. "Even neutral South Koreans, who have no sympathy for Kim Dae-jung, felt offended because our leader was treated like that."

More than any other event, the Kim-Bush summit was the crucial turning point, locking the Bush administration and one of Washington's key allies into a pattern of distrust, tension, and hostility that would endure for years. Over the previous decade, the two sides had differed, often sharply, on North Korea, but a pattern of close consultation and recognition of the importance of their security alliance had kept things on track. Now, though, the Americans and South Koreans were out of sync on the issue at the heart of their alliance—how to deal with Pyongyang.

The Kim visit also marked Colin Powell's first real skirmish with the forces he would battle throughout his tenure as secretary of state. And he did not emerge unscathed. His public embarrassment and the president's unexpected hard-line stance had dominated the headlines. The internal tensions were partly a reflection of the fact that the Bush White House viewed Powell as a threat and a competitor to the young, inexperienced president. Powell's comments on the Agreed Framework, which also fed the intense "Anyone But Clinton" sentiment in the administration, offered an opportunity to cut him down to size. The other key factor was the issue of missile defense. Before September 11, NMD was the central feature of the Bush administration's security policy. North Korea, as Kim Dae-jung had feared, had become the "poster child" for missile defense. An untidy and not-easily-verifiable agreement to curb Pyongyang's missile program was much less useful to the administration than a threat from a bizarre and odious regime that could be repeatedly invoked to build political support for an antimissile system. Together, all these factors produced a diplomatic fiasco with far-reaching consequences.

"It was an exercise in naiveté, ignorance, lack of diplomatic skills, and understanding of the country Kim Dae-jung had come from," Richard Armitage noted.

In one conversation with Powell, Armitage had described the meeting as "the cowboy president from Texas, unequipped and arrogant as hell, met the Nobel Peace Prize winner that our allies had tried to kill. And the meeting went downhill from there." Powell nodded his head in agreement.

Whatever his private read on the visit, however, Powell, as he usually did in periods of adversity, remained unfazed and upbeat. "To me, it was just a little blip in passing," he said when I interviewed him for this book.

To his colleagues, Powell exuded confidence that the situation would soon be corrected. "My sense about Powell's feeling was that it was, as usual when anything like that happens, it was kind of okay," observed Richard Boucher, who had been asked by Powell to stay on as State Department spokesman. "We'll work this out. It will come around. It can be brought back around." With their years of experience and unparalleled savvy in negotiating Washington's bureaucratic turf wars, Powell and Armitage were confident they would soon be driving administration policy.

One day that spring, a discouraged Jack Pritchard bumped into Armitage in the halls of the State Department. "Hang in there," Armitage told him. "We're biding our time. Pretty soon, Powell and I will be in control."

Speaking to CNN some weeks after the visit, Powell downplayed the episode. "The only thing that happened that day was that, as I have kidded others in saying, I got a little too far forward on my skis."[15]

In the wake of the disastrous summit, Robert Carlin quietly continued to see North Korean diplomats, with some meetings taking place outside the United States. "We knew we were in big, big trouble," he noted. "I had conversations with North Koreans later in the spring. I could tell they were beginning to wring their hands. They could sense how bad things were getting and they didn't know how to cut into the process to stop the downward slide and convince the new administration that yes, they could do business. They said to me, 'We don't want to meet with you anymore, we know what you think. We need to meet with the new people.' "

Carlin was not offended. The North Korean position made sense to him. But at that stage, there were no Bush administration officials willing to meet them.

In Washington, the debate over the policy review continued. Michael Green, who had been hired by Rice to work on Northeast Asia at the NSC, joined the process shortly after the Kim Dae-jung visit. "None of the options were particularly good," he recalled. "The biggest divide that I saw was between people who tended to see North Korea as just an absolutely horrible, abhorrent regime that they could barely bring themselves to want to talk to or deal with or dignify, versus a more pragmatic group who knew all that about North Korea but were prepared to set it aside to a greater extent to do some business and to get talks going and to see where they would go."

The arguments frequently got nasty. One hard-liner felt Tom Hubbard and the State Department's Korea Desk "were serving up dung . . . you know, serving up what they had been serving before . . . what the Clinton Korea people who had left told him to do." The State Department people felt the hard-liners were blinded by ideology and unreceptive to rational argument.

"You can never have a calm, decent discussion because of the climate of intimidation," Tom Hubbard noted. "The climate was so bad these things could never be talked out." Seeking to buttress their position, officials from State quietly urged the governments of South Korea and Japan to weigh in supporting engagement with North Korea. South Korea's ambassador to the United States, Yang Sung-chul, an academic specializing in North Korea, made repeated private statements to Bush administration officials in favor of a more moderate line. He did the same thing publicly in numerous speeches around the country.

In early May, new players joined the battle. John Bolton was made under secretary of state for arms control. He entered the government determined to kill the Agreed Framework. "I came in feeling it was a bad deal and needed to basically get rid of it," he said. "I thought the whole structure of it was flawed, the whole concept underlying it was flawed."

Bolton was a stridently combative bureaucratic infighter, described by one former senior official as "not only very articulate, but single-minded in a single-issue way. Nothing else matters. There is no balance to be struck. His job was to argue his brief as forcefully and uncompromisingly as possible." Bolton had, in effect, been foisted on Secretary of State Powell under pressure from Vice President Cheney, whose backing immeasurably strengthened what was on paper only a mid-level bureaucratic position.

Before agreeing to accept Bolton, Powell discussed the issue with Richard Armitage, his closest friend.

"Look," Armitage told Powell, "John Bolton—he's smart as shit, but he won't be loyal to you."

"The way I do business," Powell replied, "you've known me twenty-five years. Everybody's on the team until you prove you're not. I will include everybody."

"No," countered Armitage, "Bolton is immune from this." Armitage lost the argument.

"Bolton didn't think he worked for the secretary of state," noted a former official sympathetic to Powell. "He thought he took his marching orders from people with whom he agreed, in Cheney's office and in the Pentagon. He was not someone who felt loyalty to Colin."

Bolton quickly formed an alliance with the NSC's Robert Joseph. The two men shared the view that it was both impossible and morally wrong to talk to the North Koreans, who, they believed, would simply break any agreement they signed. Instead, they advocated isolating and containing Pyongyang, trying to impoverish the regime and to dissuade other countries from dealing with it.

In the same month, Jim Kelly was confirmed as assistant secretary of state for East Asia. Kelly was a tough-minded and careful pragmatist. Deeply skeptical of North Korea, he nonetheless believed in the value of diplomacy in dealing with Pyongyang. He joined the administration with almost universal respect from conservatives for his service in the Pentagon under Ronald Reagan. Almost everyone who dealt with him described Kelly as a "gentlemen," a wise, avuncular figure with a profound knowledge of Asia.

But, as one former aide noted, Kelly "was not a confrontational person" and he faced bureaucratic adversaries spoiling for a fight. Joseph, with Bolton's backing, had "huge fights, complete with yelling and screaming" with Kelly and the NSC's Michael Green, both over the specifics of policy and over who would control the process.

Joseph repeatedly went to National Security Adviser Rice and her deputy Stephen Hadley to accuse the State Department Asian experts of "clientitis"— placing the interests of America's allies, Japan and South Korea, both of whom were skeptical about confronting North Korea, ahead of what they saw as U.S. interests.

In response, Green would argue, "We're not living in outer space here. We have to have the allies or we're not going to be able to contain North Korea." As one participant noted, "There was very bad blood."[16]

As the debate intensified, President Bush's father, former President George H. W. Bush, intervened.[17] Concerned about signs of a more confrontational U.S. policy, the elder Bush passed to his son a memo from a longtime adviser, arguing that Washington should resume negotiations with Pyongyang. The memo was written by Donald Gregg, who had been ambassador to South Korea during the first Bush administration. Gregg was a man of vast knowledge and experience of Korea. He had joined the CIA in 1951 and spent much of the Cold War operating in Asia, at a time when the North Koreans were considered one of the most dangerous adversaries the United States faced. Later, he served as ambassador to Seoul from 1989 to 1993. After Kim Il Sung welcomed Billy Graham and then Jimmy Carter to Pyongyang, he had begun to change his views. Gregg was convinced the North Korean regime was looking for as way to end its isolation, and that it was in the interest of the United States to respond.

Now president of the Korea Society, Gregg had watched with alarm at the way South Korean president Kim had been treated by the new president. In the memo, Gregg warned that failure to reengage with North Korea would damage the government of a key ally and undermine the U.S. position in the region. The *New York Times* reported that the memo had originally been sent by Gregg to Bush senior, who passed it to his son. It is not known how much the episode influenced the president's thinking. On June 6, however, when the result of the policy review was made public, the president announced that the United States was prepared to resume "serious negotiations" with North Korea.

But the review was a messy compromise, in which a stated willingness to negotiate was accompanied by a series of tough new conditions demanded by the hard-liners. The administration sought "improved implementation of the Agreed Framework relating to North Korea's nuclear activities and IAEA [International Atomic Energy Agency] compliance"—meaning, in effect, that the United States would insist on more thorough and accelerated inspections of the North's nuclear facilities than it had so far without offering anything in return.

In addition, Washington demanded a "verifiable ban" on missile exports, "constraints on indigenous missile programs," and a "less threatening conventional military posture."[18] In a pointed departure from Clinton's strategy, the new administration did not spell out what it was prepared to offer Pyongyang in return. And, most crucially, Washington did not reaffirm the commitment to "no hostile intent" laid out in the October 2000 communiqué that had been signed when Vice Marshal Jo Myong Rok visited Washington. According to Jack Pritchard, the thinking among the hard-liners who prevailed on this point was, "Anything that the North Koreans want we should view as a carrot, something that we possess that we can dole out. Certainly the North Koreans would like us to repeat the no-hostility pledge, so therefore, rather than taking that as a point of principle that it has already been declared, any repeating of that is a gift to North Korea, so that is going to be withheld."

The message to Pyongyang was clear. Despite Colin Powell's earlier assurances, the administration was not going to pick up where the Clinton administration left off. Instead, the administration had, in effect, imposed new conditions that Pyongyang was unlikely to accept. Already concerned about a more antagonistic U.S. policy, the North Koreans were now being asked for concessions not only on their nuclear and missile programs, including acceptance of intrusive verification measures, but Washington was demanding cuts in Pyongyang's conventional forces as well—in effect to scale back what North Korea saw as the key elements of its defense strategy with no promise of corresponding reductions in U.S. or South Korean forces.

While on the surface, demanding reductions in conventional forces appeared reasonable, to the North Koreans it appeared as if Washington's goal was to neutralize the central elements of their own national security. As Frank Jannuzi of the Senate Foreign Relations Committee, a frequent visitor to Pyongyang, noted looking back some years later, "The problem is these two goals are incompatible in fact, reducing their nuclear and reducing conventional. What are they left with? If you take away the nuclear security card and you also take away the conventional security card, all they're left with is what: The strength of their vibrant market economy? Their bankrupt ideology? By adding that to the mix, I think we complicated things."[19]

Moreover, it was clear the administration wanted North Korea to move first before Washington would reciprocate. In the absence of such movement, the administration appeared content to wait.

The policy review left few of the participants satisfied. To Michael Green, now handling Korea at the National Security Council, "It had this dyslexic, dysfunctional, schizophrenic conclusion. It was very hard to patch it together."

The review was "sufficiently muddled and vague that each side, each camp, could interpret it however fitted them best, or however they so chose," noted one senior official. "And it reflected, frankly, a failure in leadership at the highest levels to resolve the gridlock."

Under the circumstances, though, Jim Kelly felt things could have been much worse. "We got what we needed out of it . . . an ability to deal with the North Koreans on a broad array of items, and even though the Agreed Framework was hated, particularly by the administration's nonproliferators, it was going to continue. We weren't going to junk it."

Those who wanted to kill the framework had a different take on the policy review. John Bolton criticized it for authorizing "lower-level bilateral talks with the DPRK without condition."[20] One of his political allies said, "If I may be blunt . . . we ignored it."

Compounding the sense of confusion, moreover, the contents of the review were leaked to the media before the administration was able to brief its South Korean allies. As Jack Pritchard noted in his memoir, "The symbolism of taking a coordinated position on North Korea was important, especially following the disastrous—and from South Korea's point of view, humiliating—summit meeting between President Bush and President Kim Dae-jung in March."[21] Instead, to the irritation of the government in Seoul, the administration was forced to scramble to inform Kim Dae-jung's officials, even as they read accounts of the review in the press.

As for the North Koreans, no one bothered to contact their UN mission—the normal channel of communication—until after the review was made public. And even here, the administration's internal factionalism was painfully evident. Pritchard, as the special envoy for negotiations with North Korea, drafted a letter for Pyongyang's UN representative to transmit to Vice Foreign Minister Kim Gye Gwan. Hoping to avoid another fight, Pritchard waited until the last minute to invite someone from the National Security Council to accompany him, and he did not show her the letter he had written until they were in a taxi from Kennedy airport to Manhattan for the meeting. "I did not want predictable objections and word-smithing to delay a simple letter," he wrote.[22] The letter proposed renewed bilateral talks and left the time and date for the North Koreans to decide. It would be well over a year before high-level talks resumed. By then, the world had dramatically changed.

# 4

# "AXIS OF EVIL"

Twenty-four hours after the terrorist attacks of September 11, 2001, North Korea's Foreign Ministry released a brief statement. Carried by the official Korean Central News Agency (KCNA) the statement described the attacks as a "very regretful and tragic incident" that highlighted the "gravity of terrorism." North Korea, it stressed, "is opposed to all forms of terrorism and whatever support to it and this stance will remain unchanged."[1]

The statement, issued so soon after the event, reflected a desire in Pyongyang to reach out to Washington and head off a further deterioration in relations. Unsettled by the Bush administration's much harsher approach toward North Korea, Kim Jong Il's regime was deeply concerned that it might become a target of what undoubtedly would be an angry and powerful American response to the carnage of 9/11. Seeking to head off such a move, Pyongyang soon announced that it would also sign two important UN antiterrorism conventions it had not yet ratified, the International Convention for the Suppression of the Financing of Terrorism and the International Convention Against the Taking of Hostages. Explaining the move, KCNA declared, "We have made every possible effort to combat worldwide terrorism. We will make consistent efforts to fight terrorism in the future, too."[2]

To members of Dick Cheney's staff, a certain phrase became virtually a mantra. Almost from the moment of the September 11 attacks, every conversation Cheney had about North Korea began with the same line: "Here's what worries me most." Over and over, Cheney raised the specter that the next attack would be a nuclear one, with North Korea the source of the nuclear material. "The world's most dangerous technology in the hands of the world's worst people," said Stephen Yates, the Asia specialist on Cheney's staff. "Post-9/11, that was the big imperative—how do we keep that from happening?"

In the frightening weeks after 9/11, Cheney was hardly alone in imagining nightmare scenarios. David Frum, who had been hired as a Bush speechwriter, recalled that there "suddenly was a huge market for people who could give you vivid descriptions of potential disasters. There is a group of people in the national security field whose genius is imagining worst-case scenarios and scaring people to death. And normally they don't get that much of a hearing. But after 9/11 they did. They were talking to all kinds of important people and [saying] 'Well, if I were planning a terrorist attack, here's what I would do . . .' And then they would have some horrifying scenario. In a lot of these scenarios, a North Korean nuke featured and suddenly I think that jolted people."

Even the sober-minded analysts at the CIA shared the concern. According to John McLaughlin, who was then the Agency's deputy director, North Korea was a country in such desperate economic shape that "the temptation to sell some of this material would inevitably be there, and the market is there in the form of terrorists and also countries that are developing weapon systems but haven't got the long pole in the tent, which is the fissile material. So to me, the proliferation danger is the one we have to think about as earnestly as the one where we worry about the fact that they could actually mount a weapon on a missile and move it a long distance."

In Washington, a town suddenly in the grip of almost hysterical fear of another attack, Jack Pritchard noted Pyongyang's condemnation of the 9/11 attacks, disavowal of terrorism, and desire to avoid further inflaming tensions with the United States. He suggested that it might be useful to initiate a discussion with the North Koreans on terrorism. Although North Korea had been linked to terrorism in the 1980s, when a North Korean bomb killed many members of the South Korean cabinet in Rangoon, Burma, and North Korean agents had blown up a South Korean passenger airliner, Pritchard emphasized there was no evidence of any recent activity.

"Isn't it worth our while to enter into this kind of terrorism type of discussion with the North Koreans and see where it may lead?" he asked. "Do they have any contacts? Do they have knowledge? Is there something there that we can benefit with? And certainly we can go back to the September 2000 Jo Myong Ryok statement that they would cooperate on terrorism-types of information. So let's pull that string."

North Korean diplomats were certainly sending every signal they could that Washington should not consider Pyongyang in the same camp with the other "rogue states" being condemned for links to terrorism. Within days of September 11, Frank Jannuzi, the Democratic Party's Asia expert on the Senate Foreign Relations Committee, was contacted by the North Korean deputy permanent representative to the UN, Han Song Ryol. Han reiterated Pyongyang's expression of sympathy and determination to ratify the two UN terrorism conventions. Jannuzi was convinced the North Koreans were eager for Congress to be aware of their attitude. "The point was they understood 9/11 was drawing a stark division between the good guys and the bad guys and they wanted not to be in the bad camp, so they expressed sympathy and they signed on to counterterrorism conventions of the UN that they had before not ratified. And they thought to themselves, 'Hey, this inoculates us. We are part of the forces of order against the forces of chaos. Surely, they'll get it. This is a signal from us.' "

However, while Jannuzi's boss, Democratic Senator Joseph Biden, did make a public reference to Pyongyang's position, when Jack Pritchard raised the idea of talking to the North with government counterterrorism experts, he was told that no one thought Pyongyang would have any useful information. Pritchard was surprised by the lack of curiosity. Just after 9/11, he felt all avenues that might prevent another attack were worth exploring. Officials from the vice president's office and the NSC were even blunter, telling him he was just trying to find an excuse to engage North Korea and that was not administration policy.

"It was just not considered a serious proposal and it was a joke, and it really hurt his [Pritchard's] credibility and hurt State's credibility, that they tried to do counterterrorism cooperation with the North Koreans," said NSC Asia expert Michael Green. "It's just so flagrantly ridiculous that the North Koreans could be helpful on counterterrorism, and that we would somehow exchange things for that. It just wasn't credible."

Pritchard found himself a voice crying in the wilderness. The idea of trying to talk to the North Koreans after 9/11 went nowhere. A line was being drawn, with us or against us, and hard-liners in Washington made sure North Korea was put on the wrong side of that line.

Throughout the fall of 2001, President Bush kept up the rhetorical pressure on Pyongyang. On October 16, preparing to fly to Shanghai for a meeting of the Asia Pacific Economic Cooperation forum (APEC), he told South Korean, Japanese, and Chinese journalists that "Kim Jong Il needs to earn the trust of the world. I think he needs to take pressure off of South Korea and off of the DMZ. I know he needs to stop spreading weapons of mass destruction around the world."[3]

Three days later, in Shanghai, Bush described Kim as "suspicious and secretive." And in November, he appeared to expand his definition of terrorism. Speaking to reporters in the White House Rose Garden, the President said, "If they fund a terrorist, they're a terrorist. If they house terrorists, they're terrorists. I mean, I can't make it any more clear to other nations around the world. If they develop weapons of mass destruction that will be used to terrorize nations, they will be held accountable." Asked specifically about North Korea, he said, "I made it very clear to North Korea that, in order for us to have relations with them, that we want to know, are they developing weapons of mass destruction, and they ought to stop proliferating."[4]

Meanwhile, the Pentagon was at work on a secret review of U.S. nuclear strategy. On December 31, Defense Secretary Donald Rumsfeld submitted the classified report to Congress. The report provided a clear sense of the dramatic shift in U.S. thinking in the post-9/11 era and added to the sense of alarm in Pyongyang.

Reflecting the "new security environment," the document raised the possibility the United States might use nuclear weapons in a preemptive attack on rogue states or terrorist groups with weapons of mass destruction. "U.S. military forces themselves, including nuclear forces," the report stated, "will now be used to dissuade adversaries from undertaking military programs or operations that could threaten U.S. interests."[5]

The report explicitly listed North Korea—as well as Iran, Iraq, Syria, and Libya—as potential targets, and called for the development of nuclear weapons that "could be employed against targets able to withstand non-nuclear attack, for example deep underground bunkers or bio-weapons facilities."[6]

Most of the autumn of 2001, however, the primary focus of the White House was not North Korea. The U.S. assault on Afghanistan and the notion of a broader war on terrorism dominated the administration. By December, the Taliban regime that had been ruling Afghanistan since 1996 had been toppled, Osama bin Laden was on the run, and a pro-Western government had been installed in Kabul.

The fear of another attack on the United States was now tempered by a growing sense of confidence in the merits of the muscular use of American power. With what appeared to be victory in Afghanistan, President Bush authorized Defense Secretary Rumsfeld to begin looking at the possibility of invading Iraq. The idea itself was not new; going after Saddam Hussein had been proposed in the days immediately after September 11. Now, as the end of the year approached, with preparations for the president's State of the Union address underway, Bush's chief speechwriter, Michael Gerson, asked one of his junior colleagues, David Frum, to work up some language that would broaden the definition of the war on terror beyond the Taliban and al Qaeda. The speech would set the stage for the coming assault on Iraq.

Frum was a Canadian Jew with a degree from Yale, who during the '90s had emerged as a leading voice for neoconservative causes. Based at the neocons' leading think-tank, the American Enterprise Institute, Frum had authored a series of influential books and articles. By his own admission, domestic policy was his specialty, but in the aftermath of 9/11, like everyone else in his movement, he had been drawn into the issue of terrorism. Frum came to the White House sharing the general conservative contempt toward Clinton's North Korea policy.

"In 2000, I think for most conservatives it would have been exhibit A in what was wrong with American policy," he said. "More than al Qaeda, in that there was this deal and the U.S. had provided all these benefits for North Korea with no visible return. The U.S. had performed a legitimizing function for the North Korean regime."

As he drafted a memo for Gerson, Frum compared the Axis powers of World War II with the rogue states and terrorist groups now confronting the United States. "Together," he wrote, "these terrorist states and terrorist groups form an axis of hatred against the United States."

As drafts of the State of the Union speech circulated among the president's top advisers, Michael Gerson changed Frum's term to "Axis of Evil." Frum liked the phrase, as well as the notion of rogue regimes bound together by a common hatred of the West. He felt it was reminiscent of Ronald Reagan's famous characterization of the Soviet Union as the "Evil Empire."

Frum's initial draft of the speech did not include the reference to North Korea. According to an account by Gerson, National Security Adviser Condoleezza Rice instructed him to add Iran and North Korea "in order to avoid focusing solely on Iraq."[7]

The subsequent justification for adding North Korea, according to Frum, hinged on Pyongyang's nuclear program and history of aggression, which to administration hawks meant Kim Jong Il "needed to feel a stronger hand." When he saw the mention of North Korea, Frum also concluded the administration had a clear strategy for getting tough with North Korea. "I assumed there had to be the tip of the spear of a plan," he said. "You don't talk like that unless you have a carefully worked-out idea of what you are going to do."

In fact, with so much of the administration's attention on Iraq, it appears that North Korea was added almost as a casual afterthought to make the president appear less anti-Islamic. "There was a huge market for a way of presenting the post-9/11 security problem in a way that did not involve Islam and Arabs," Frum said. "You could raise this to a more abstract level—talk about terrorism, talk about WMDs, that was very very welcome in those days. North Korea fit into that."

The text of the speech was closely held—only a few senior officials were privy to the final version. Among them were Colin Powell and Richard Armitage. Neither voiced any concerns. "The Axis of Evil didn't leap out at us at the time as being a blueprint for military action," Armitage recalled. "It seemed to me to be fairly consistent with how we felt about things."

In the run-up to the speech, South Korea's enterprising ambassador in Washington, Yang Sung-chul, had picked up rumors that Bush might say something tough about North Korea. The night before it was to be delivered, Yang sought an urgent meeting at the State Department with Assistant Secretary of State Kelly.

"What's going on?" Yang asked. "Can the language be modified?" Kelly, who had not seen the final draft, told Yang the issue was out of his hands.

The next day—January 29, 2002—Bush spoke before Congress and an American public still traumatized by the attacks of four months earlier. He was defiant and confrontational: "Our . . . goal is to prevent regimes that sponsor terror from threatening America or our friends and allies with weapons of mass destruction . . . North Korea is a regime arming with missiles and weapons of mass destruction, while starving its citizens . . . Iran aggressively pursues these weapons and exports terror . . . Iraq continues to flaunt its hostility toward America and to support terror. . . . States like these, and their terrorist allies, constitute an axis of evil, arming to threaten the peace of the world. By seeking weapons of mass destruction, these regimes pose a grave and growing danger. . . . The United States of America will not permit the world's most dangerous regimes to threaten us with the world's most destructive weapons."[8]

Stephen Yates, the vice president's chief Asia specialist, applauded the president's bluntness. "Those were the heady days of strategic clarity," he recalled. "Call a spade a spade, and Kim Jong Il is nothing if not evil."

But many foreign policy experts who heard the speech were stunned by the Axis of Evil formulation. Among them was Brent Scowcroft, national security adviser to the current president's father. Scowcroft called Andrew Card, Bush's chief of staff and asked, "How did that ever get in there? These are regimes that have nothing to do with each other except that they are nasty regimes and hostile to the U.S. But Axis of Evil? I know how these State of the Union speeches get reviewed. Was it not reviewed?"

Yes, it was reviewed, Card replied, and he had even circled the term because it "seemed funny." When all the responses came back, however, no one had objected to it, so Card let it go. Card left Scowcroft with the impression that, because Axis of Evil was such a catchy phrase, no one in the administration had raised questions about how it would play in the press, or what in fact it meant.

The next morning, Colin Powell arrived at the State Department for his daily staff meeting. When aides asked about the speech, Richard Boucher recalled that Powell replied bluntly, "I saw it. I didn't object to it. The President said it. That's how he sees the world and that's how we are going to deal with it." In his memoir, John Bolton recalls Powell saying at the meeting, "No one should try to take the edge off what the president said, or try to spin it."[9] To other associates, Powell simply shrugged off the controversy. "It's just the speechwriters," he told one. "We can deal with it."

Elsewhere in the State Department, the reaction was much less sanguine. "How stupid," said one official then working for Assistant Secretary James Kelly. "This is totally gratuitous, and it's typical of the administration. Expressions of indignation have become the ultimate substitute for policy in this administration."

In Seoul, the speech created new headaches for Tom Hubbard, who had taken up his post as the American ambassador, to South Korea on September 11, and his deputy, Evans Revere. A week earlier, in his own state of the union speech, South Korean president Kim Dae-jung had publicly urged Bush to make a conciliatory gesture to get talks with Pyongyang going again.

Watching the American president's speech on CNN in the heavily guarded embassy compound, Revere was aghast. "When I heard that line, I said, 'Oh, my God!' Not only because of what it would do in terms of relationship or nonrelationship with the North—this would only confirm them in their growing paranoia about this administration—but what it would do in the South. This was going to send the South Korean population and the South Korean government through the ceiling because it would essentially be a declaration that North Korea was in the same camp as those who had attacked the United States on September 11. And you couldn't, from an American perspective, sit down and have a civilized negotiation or conversation with a power you had just characterized in those terms."

For Ambassador Hubbard, "All hell broke loose. I had been scheduled to meet with the entire Seoul press corps the next morning at eight A.M. for breakfast. I had to go before the press without any instructions. One of the first questions I got was: 'Kim Dae-jung had asked for a face-saving gesture. Is this your answer to his appeal?'"

Called in to meet Kim Dae-jung, the U.S. envoy found the South Korean president "obviously unhappy."

For an already frustrated Bob Carlin, the State of the Union address was the last straw. In Seoul that week, the longtime North Korea intelligence analyst was at the airport preparing to fly back to Washington when he called the speech up on the Internet at the United Airlines lounge. Appalled, he exclaimed in a loud voice, "Holy shit!" Startled passengers gaped at him.

For Carlin, the speech was another example of the handiwork of a group of people he called the "intellectual fascists" in the administration—people unwilling to tolerate opinions that differed from their own rigid worldview.

He then checked his e-mail, where a found a note from Chuck Kartman, who had resigned from the State Department the previous spring to become director of KEDO, the U.S.-South Korean-Japanese-EU consortium handling construction of the light-water reactors in North Korea as part of the Agreed Framework. Kartman had a job opening. Was Carlin interested?

Despite thirty-one years of government service, it took Carlin only "a millisecond" to accept.

The Bush administration no longer had the services of the intelligence community's most experienced North Korea watcher, and he would not be the last North Korea expert to quit or be sidelined in the early years of the Bush administration. The exodus significantly eroded Washington's already limited ability to understand the opaque and difficult North Koreans. "I think this was a serious problem," acknowledged one senior State Department official. "These were the strangest people in the world, with a strange style of negotiating. Yet, they have made deals. To not have people with the expertise, it's just stupid."

Predictably, North Korea reacted with anger. A commentary in the state-run Korean Central News Agency denounced the speech as "little short of declaring a war" on the North. KCNA quoted the first comment by Kim Jong Il, who said North Korea's military was "weathering out the raging wind raised by imperialists. No force on earth can overpower these great forces firmly determined not to allow any aggressors to dare invade the inviolable territory of our country but wipe them out to the last one at the risk of their lives."

For all the fiery rhetoric, Pyongyang remained cautious, with KCNA noting simply that "we are sharply watching the moves of the United States that have pushed the situation to the brink of war after throwing away even the mask of dialogue and negotiation."

The Axis of Evil speech came just two weeks before Bush was due to visit South Korea. The visit had been planned as a fence-mending exercise after Kim Dae-jung's traumatic trip to Washington the previous March. Now, the officials involved in making the final arrangements confronted a new crisis. Jack Pritchard was worried about South Korean perceptions. "You had for the first time in a long time concerns by people on the street in Seoul about potential war on the peninsula," he said. "They were worried about where the U.S. was taking them."

The reaction in South Korea, from President Kim on down, had been one of anger and alarm. "I was very concerned about the possibility of military action from the United States toward North Korea," Kim Dae-jung recalled. "A war against North Korea would mean the sacrifice of millions of people's lives. It could even lead to the miserable result of Korea being ashes, complete ashes. So it was a great shock to me, so I thought, 'I need to prevent that kind of military action against North Korea.'"

With the president's confidence boosted by the success of the U.S. intervention in Afghanistan, and facing large anti-American demonstrations on the streets of Seoul, Colin Powell felt the time was right to press Bush to focus again on Korean diplomacy. "We couldn't just sit there," he recalled. "We've got to do something." In meetings with Bush, Powell urged the president to placate Seoul and reengage with Pyongyang. The forthcoming Korea trip offered an ideal opportunity to do both.

In addition to his bilateral meetings, Bush was to make a major speech at Dorasan train station, the last stop on the South Korean side of what was called the "Unification Railway." Work on the station had just been completed as part of an agreement between the North and South to create a peninsula-wide rail link, although construction on the northern side had barely begun. With Kim Dae-jung at his side, Bush would have a chance to make a fresh start in his dealings with both the North and the South.

Arriving in Seoul on a bitterly cold day, Bush rode from the airport to the U.S. Embassy accompanied by his wife, Laura, Colin Powell, and Ambassador Hubbard. On the way, the president asked Hubbard how the South Koreans had reacted to the Axis of Evil speech.

"I don't think you'll get much argument from the South Koreans about the 'evil' part of it,'" Hubbard replied. "But the South Koreans don't know why you said it. They see the U.S. buildup for Iraq. The last thing the South Koreans want is a war on the Korean peninsula . . . and the speech, to them, raised that prospect."

Bush simply listened; his limousine arrived at the embassy before he was able to reply. Afterward, though, Hubbard was convinced that the conversation was a key factor in prompting Bush to say publicly during the visit that the United States had no intention of invading or attacking North Korea.

After arriving at the embassy, however, Condoleezza Rice showed the draft of the speech Bush planned to deliver at the Dorasan train station to Hubbard and his deputy, Evans Revere. To the consternation of both men, it contained a new reference to the Axis of Evil. Hubbard and Revere objected, warning Rice that to use the phrase again risked serious damage to the alliance between the United States and South Korea.

Before Bush's meeting with Kim Dae-jung, one of the officials traveling with the president provided to South Korean officials a summary of what Bush planned to say at Dorasan. At the Blue House (the South Korean White House), Hubbard and others waited outside the conference room as the Bush-Kim meeting stretched to twice its scheduled length. As he waited, Hubbard was approached by South Korea's ambassador to the United States, Yang Sung-chol. "We understand the president is going to mention the 'Axis of Evil' in his speech," Yang said. "We think this is terrible. It's anathema to everything Kim Dae-jung stands for."

The summit meeting ran long because the two leaders engaged in a forceful debate over their sharply differing views of how to deal with North Korea. In Kim's recollection, Bush began by making a blistering denunciation of Kim Jong Il to justify including North Korea in the Axis of Evil. The North Korean leader was violating human rights, Bush declared. His people were suffering from food shortages and many had starved to death. Yet Kim Jong Il continually expanded North Korea's military strength at the expense of people's lives. That was why Bush called Kim Jong Il a very bad dictator, why North Korea was part of the Axis of Evil, and why the United States would not engage in dialogue with Pyongyang. Unless North Korea abandoned its weapons of mass destruction, and unless it changed its attitude, Bush told the South Korean president, the United States can offer nothing to North Korea but retaliation.

Kim Dae-jung vigorously challenged Bush. "I answered that you can have dialogue even with evil if it is necessary," he recounted. "It's not for making friends; it's for pursuing your national interests."

Kim recalled that three Republican presidents—Eisenhower, Nixon, and Reagan—had conducted dialogue with hated Communist adversaries.

"Even as President Reagan called the Soviet Union an evil empire, he also had dialogue," Kim said. "So then, why not North Korea? Why can't you have dialogue with North Korea? If you do not pursue the option of dialogue, the only viable option here can be war. However, according to the UN Command [in Korea], about 1.5 million people in Seoul could die from that war, and that includes tens of thousands of Americans living in Seoul as well. So even if we have to wage another war on the Korean peninsula, that should be the last resort, the last option, after taking all the other options including dialogue. At the time, North Korea was consistently asking for dialogue with the United States. So why can you not have that option of dialogue?"

In addition to these broader issues, according to former American officials, either President Kim or his national security adviser Lim Dong-won (memories differ as to who) told Bush that it wouldn't be helpful to use the phrase Axis of Evil again in his speech at the Dorasan train station, noting diplomatically that the term was "misunderstood" by the South Korean public.

On February 20, in biting cold, Bush and Kim stood next to each other at Dorasan as the president delivered his speech. Heeding South Korean advice, there was no mention of the Axis of Evil, and some of his remarks were unquestionably conciliatory. "We're prepared to talk with the North about steps that would lead to a better future," Bush declared, praising Kim Dae-jung for putting forward a vision "that can illuminate the whole peninsula."

But the president could not resist lashing out at North Korea, labeling the country a "prison" and reiterating that the United States would not "permit the world's most dangerous regimes to threaten us with the world's most dangerous weapons."[10] Later, however, in a joint news conference with Kim Dae-jung at his side, he sought to reassure anxious South Koreans by telling reporters that the United States had no intention of attacking North Korea, and the two leaders went out of their way to stress their joint commitment to the U.S.–South Korea alliance.

Although Bush's underlying hostility toward Pyongyang remained clear, after all the ill-will produced during Kim's U.S. visit and by the Axis of Evil speech, the trip to Seoul helped ease tensions between the two allies and reduced fears of an all-out confrontation between Washington and Pyongyang. As for Bush himself, before leaving Seoul he told Ambassador Hubbard the trip had given him a better understanding of Korea and of Kim Dae-jung, even hinting at some regret over how he had treated the South Korean president on his trip to Washington the previous year.

In mid-March, Jack Pritchard was authorized to meet with North Korea's UN envoy Park Gil Yon in New York in the hope of getting talks restarted. This time, he brought with him Michael Green, the NSC's Northeast Asia expert. Green's presence was crucial.

"I was able to get a representative from the National Security Council to come with me to assure the North Koreans that what the president said was what he meant," Pritchard said, "that he really did want to get a dialogue going and that what the secretary of state was saying in terms of we are prepared to have talks any time any place was true. And it was for the first time we were getting some interest from the North Koreans and it had to do with that symbolic connection of having a White House person with me."

Green's presentation was blunt. "The president is not going to apologize or take back the Axis of Evil phrase," he said. "He meant what he said; but he's also prepared to have a very new and broad approach with the DPRK, comprehensive and therefore more difficult, but with bigger reward and gain at the end of it if we work together, and he's sincere about that."

The challenge facing Pritchard and Green was to convince the North Koreans that the Bush administration was indeed sincere after fifteen months of

sharply contradictory signals from Washington. During that time, the administration had discarded a series of diplomatic strategies for dealing with
Pyongyang that had been tested over the course of the previous decade. The
most important tool in that kit was regular contact to help North Korean diplomats make sense of developments in Washington.

"Since they have no diplomatic mission in Washington and no great reser-
voir of experience with the United States," Chuck Kartman recalled years later,
"they don't really know how to read all these public statements that emanate
from Washington, so you need to constantly hand-hold and explain these things
to them and keep them comfortable. You can't simply say, 'The president said
this but what he really meant to say was that.' You've got to do something a little more subtle. In the Clinton administration, we were trying to beat into the
North Korean system that there were only certain voices that could speak
authoritatively. What we felt we were doing was helping them to deal with the
white noise, but secondly, we were building up our interlocutor. So the Foreign
Ministry became stronger because of the way we were handling them. The Bush
administration did the opposite."

Underscoring this point, as Pritchard and Green were meeting with the
North Koreans in New York, another internal battle over North Korean policy
was reaching a climax. This time, the issue was whether the administration
would certify that Pyongyang was in compliance with the terms of the Agreed
Framework—a requirement imposed by Congress for the authorization of
funds to provide fuel oil shipments and other U.S. aid to the North. Hard-liners
in the administration were pushing for President Bush not to do so. In November 2001, Under Secretary of State for Arms Control John Bolton had argued
against certification on the grounds that North Korea had not fulfilled its obligations to allow the International Atomic Energy Agency to conduct inspections to determine the early history of its nuclear program—and specifically
whether it had deceived the IAEA about the amount of plutonium it had reprocessed in the late 1980s and early '90s.

"My argument was that the North Koreans were not in compliance with the
Agreed Framework because they had never made a complete baseline declaration of Yongbyon to the IAEA," Bolton said. "And because they had not com-
plied with their obligations to disclose fully to the IAEA what they were doing
in Yongbyon, that put them in violation of their safeguards agreement with the
IAEA and with the nuclear nonproliferation treaty. And my argument was they
could not be in compliance with the Agreed Framework if they were not in
compliance with the nonproliferation treaty."

The issue was a murky one. Pyongyang had consistently refused to reveal its
early nuclear history, feeding suspicions that it had indeed secretly reprocessed

more plutonium than it had admitted. This prospect led U.S. intelligence to conclude that the North, by the early 1990s, had enough weapons-grade plutonium for one or two nuclear bombs.

Under the terms of the Agreed Framework, the North would allow "special inspections" by the IAEA when a "significant portion of the LWR project is completed, but before delivery of key nuclear components," but no date for inspections had been specified. Although the framework had listed 2003 as the target date for completing the reactors, in early 2002 construction had yet to begin, and Pyongyang was under no formal obligation to permit inspections.

In the interest of keeping the broader rapprochement alive, and given the fact that there had been delays on the U.S. side with both building the LWRs and the regular provision of heavy fuel oil, the Clinton administration, in one of its final acts, had in January 2001 certified that the North remained in compliance.

Bolton's effort to block certification in 2002, a move in line with the administration's broader skepticism about all international arms-control agreements, was backed by the NSC, the Pentagon, and Vice President Cheney's office. Stephen Yates, Cheney's chief Asian adviser, noted, "I was of the view, why? What are we getting? Is this working or not? At what point do we look like fools for throwing American tax dollars at a process that's not really on the up and up?"

But the apparent effort to scuttle the Agreed Framework set off what one of Bolton's aides described as a "firestorm" in the State Department, with the Bureau of East Asian and Pacific Affairs, headed by Jim Kelly, "going ballistic." After a series of sharp debates between Bolton and his staff and Kelly and Jack Pritchard, an uneasy "gentlemen's agreement" was reached under which the administration would reluctantly certify North Korean compliance for 2002 but express concerns, thus laying the groundwork for potentially tougher steps the following year.

The Axis of Evil speech, however, had altered the power dynamics. Just after it was delivered, John Bolton triumphantly walked into the office of his key aide Mark Groombridge—a Sinologist who, like Bolton, had worked at the conservative American Enterprise Institute before joining the administration. "Remember that agreement we just had with the East Asia bureau?" Bolton said. "Gone."

Emboldened by the president's tough rhetoric, the hard-liners prevailed, those favoring engagement fell into line and the administration, for the first time since the Agreed Framework was signed in 1994, decided to declare North Korea not in compliance. In midwinter, Deputy Secretary of State Richard Armitage gave a classified briefing to members of the Senate Foreign Relations Committee. Armitage told the senators the administration no longer felt able to certify that North Korea was fulfilling its obligations. The committee chairman, Republican Richard Lugar, and the ranking Democrat senator Joseph Biden, pressed Armitage. Did the administration have evidence the North Koreans were cheating? No, Armitage replied, the administration did not have evidence of cheating but it also did not have confidence Pyongyang was going to comply. So, Biden asked sarcastically, is this a doctrine of preemptive breach of the contract? You expect they're going to violate it and therefore we're going to stop certifying now?

Armitage had little to say in response.

An irritated Biden subsequently sent his chief Asia staffer, Frank Jannuzi, to meet with Jim Kelly at the State Department. "Don't you understand how the North Koreans will interpret this?" Jannuzi asked. "They will interpret this as a sign that we are preparing to back out of this agreement."

But Kelly pushed back. "No, Frank," he said. "We've got to send a shot across their bow. They've got to get with it, in terms of their compliance. It's not adequate that they just have the freeze [of their nuclear program]. We need to get at the special inspections about what they did in the past."

In announcing the decision not to certify compliance, which he described as a "strong message" to North Korea, Bush's press secretary Ari Fleischer said that, to keep the Agreed Framework from collapsing, the president would use his power to waive the certification requirements in order to release $95 million so that fuel oil shipments could continue. Pressed by reporters as to whether any new information had prompted the reversal of long-standing U.S. policy, Fleischer said "no."[11]

Donald Gregg, the former CIA station chief in Seoul and U.S. ambassador to South Korea during the first Bush administration, watched the growing gulf between Washington and Pyongyang with alarm. As the head of the Korea Society, he had developed a relationship with the North Korean mission to the United States, whose diplomats were key figures in the so-called New York channel, which for years had been a key means of contact between the two countries. In the fall of 2001, following September 11, Li Gun, the second-ranking North Korean official in New York, had asked Gregg for advice.

"We're getting nowhere with the Bush administration," Li told Gregg. "What can we do to get things started?"

Gregg convinced the North Koreans to allow him to organize a group of four former U.S. ambassadors to South Korea to visit Pyongyang as a way of establishing contact with American figures able to speak on Korean affairs at home with some credibility. Following the Axis of Evil speech, however, the North Koreans canceled the invitation.

Soon after, Gregg decided to write a letter directly to Kim Jong Il. His message to the Dear Leader was blunt. "It was imperative that our countries talk," Gregg said. "Kim's interest in nuclear weapons, the fact that President Bush had included him in the Axis of Evil, were very bad harbingers of a future relationship, which we should try to deal with through conversation. A lack of conversation would cause us to drift farther apart."

Gregg showed the letter to Li Gun. The North Korean's first reaction, Gregg recalled, was to say, "How dare you write to our leader in such a way!"

"I'm writing it because I understand how your chairman's mind works," Gregg replied.

"How can you understand how my chairman's mind works?" retorted Li.

Gregg said he had spoken with Chinese officials who met Kim Jong Il on his visit to Shanghai in January 2001; to Russians who spoke with him during his summer trip to Moscow; to South Koreans who participated in the June 2000 North-South summit; and to Madeleine Albright. All of them came away with the impression that Kim realized that to survive, North Korea had to become a more modern, normal country. That's why he had written the letter.

"That's a good answer," said Li. "I'll send your letter in."

Gregg had informed the South Korean embassy in Washington and the State Department about his letter. The South Koreans were very enthusiastic, but there was no response from the State Department. Two weeks later, an invitation arrived for Gregg to visit Pyongyang, at which point State offered to send a Korean-speaking foreign service officer with him. In early April, the two flew to Pyongyang.

Gregg spent several hours in conversations with Vice Foreign Minister Kim Gye Gwan and a senior general of the Korean People's Army, Ri Chan Bok. The general was openly hostile. "We're ready to fight and die against you Americans if you drive us into a corner," he declared.

"I have no doubt," Gregg answered. "That's why I'm here, because that's the last thing that ought to happen."

Gregg's meeting with Vice Foreign Minister Kim was less bellicose, but the North Korean diplomat was full of questions. "Why is George Bush so different from his father? Why does George Bush hate Bill Clinton so much? Why does George Bush use such rhetoric in describing us? Why are you so suspicious of everything we do? Why do you threaten us?"

Gregg returned to Washington convinced the North Koreans remained open to talks and wrote a letter to President Bush, saying, "The North Koreans feel very threatened by us, they have no stake in their relationship with your Administration, but the things that almost happened at the end of the Clinton Administration are still on the table. A high-level letter from the White House, carried by someone whom you, the President, trust would get things started."

Gregg got no reply from Bush. But the same week of Gregg's visit, Lim Dong-won, the chief adviser on North Korean affairs to President Kim Dae-jung, also spent three days in Pyongyang, holding several hours of discussions with Kim Jong Il. Upon his return to Seoul, Lim had a dramatic announcement. The North Korean leader, he said, "has expressed a willingness to accept a U.S. envoy's visit to North Korea."

After ten months of delays, and despite its anger and confusion toward the United States Pyongyang was ready to accept the Bush administration's call for negotiations "anywhere, any time." The move was accompanied by new concil-iatory gestures toward South Korea, as the two sides announced plans to restart long-stalled talks on family reunions and the North-South rail link.

In Washington, Colin Powell continued to press President Bush for authoriza-tion to engage the North Koreans. The result was what became known as the "Bold Approach," a term Colin Powell attributed to the president. "So we talked about it and he started talking in terms of, 'I really want to help the North's peo-ple,'" Powell recalled. "I hate to see this starving, this terrible lousy regime, they're awful people, but I really want to help the people and so I want to have a bold approach to this.' I said, 'Got it.'"

Despite the misgivings of administration hard-liners who were opposed to any talks with Pyongyang, in the State Department, officials began a struggle to infuse some substance into the "Bold Approach," which remained little more than a catchphrase. The hope was for what one official described as "a sweeping series of developments in which we would, in exchange for step-by-step moves, change their entire relationship with us in the global economy."

"We were in fact for comprehensive negotiations with the North Koreans on a variety of issues," said Jim Kelly. "Weapons of mass destruction, the Agreed Framework itself, and how we were going to meet with the problem of finishing it up, a number of things being unresolved, the problem of terrorism, problem of conventional forces, and of course human rights."

Still, it took two months of internal debate before the United States told the North Koreans that Assistant Secretary of State Kelly would lead a delegation to Pyongyang on July 10. But before Kelly could depart, an explosive intelli-gence finding would shatter the shaky foundations for U.S. diplomatic dealings with North Korea and set the stage for the most dangerous crisis on the Korean peninsula since 1994.

# 5

# THE "SCRUB"

THE CLASS OF 2002 WAS THE FIRST TO GRADUATE FROM THE U.S. Military Academy at West Point after the attacks of September 11, 2001. On June 2, more than one thousand graduating seniors gathered at the Academy's historic plain overlooking the Hudson River to listen to their commander in chief deliver his most belligerent speech since the State of the Union address that had introduced the world to the term "Axis of Evil" less than six months earlier.

President George W. Bush declared that deterrence and containment—the two concepts that underpinned American strategy during the long decades of the Cold War—were no longer a sufficient response to the threats facing the nation. Instead, he spelled out a new post–September 11 doctrine of preemption—asserting the right to strike at potential threats before the United States itself was attacked.

"When the spread of chemical and biological and nuclear weapons, along with ballistic missile technology—when that occurs, even weak states and small groups could attain a catastrophic power to strike great nations," Bush asserted. "Our enemies have declared this very intention, and have been caught seeking these terrible weapons. They want the capability to blackmail us, or to harm us, or to harm our friends—and we will oppose them with all our power. We cannot defend America and our friends by hoping for the best. We cannot put our faith in the word of tyrants, who solemnly sign nonproliferation treaties, and then systemically break them. If we wait for threats to fully materialize, we will have waited too long. We must take the battle to the enemy, disrupt his plans, and confront the worst threats before they emerge. In the world we have entered, the only path to safety is the path of action. And this nation will act."

Iraq was clearly uppermost in the president's mind. But there's no question the message registered in Pyongyang as well.

Three weeks later, on the afternoon of June 23, 2002, the phone rang in the office of Under Secretary of State for Arms Control John Bolton. Alan Foley, the director of WINPAC, the CIA's Weapons, Intelligence, Nonproliferation, and Arms Control Center, was on the line. "John," he said, "I have something you have to see."

A veteran of more than two decades at the Agency, Foley was now the CIA's leading expert on weapons of mass destruction. He would subsequently become the focus of a public controversy with reports that he sought—unsuccessfully—to prevent the inclusion of the false allegation that Saddam Hussein had tried to buy uranium for nuclear weapons from Niger in President Bush's 2003 State of the Union speech.

On this humid June afternoon, uranium was also the focus of Foley's attention, but it was not Iraq that had prompted him to call Bolton. New intelligence had come in, Foley told Bolton, indicating that North Korea was procuring material for a program to enrich uranium for nuclear weapons, even as its plutonium-based program remained frozen under the terms of the Agreed Framework.

"It hit us all like a ton of bricks," recalled one former intelligence analyst who dealt with the material. U.S. intelligence had picked up traces of enrichment activities in the past, but nothing very conclusive. "This was a traumatic moment of realization that we had an entirely new and different problem to deal with here, and that dealing with this was going to be terribly difficult because it was very clear from this information that the North was violating the Agreed Framework by what it was trying to do here."

The first person Bolton told was his Asia specialist Mark Groombridge. Without knowing all the details, both men immediately felt this was a "gotcha" moment—a revelation that would be the stake through the heart of the Agreed Framework, a deal Bolton and those who shared his hard-line views had long wanted to discard.

"I thought clearly this should end the debate over the Agreed Framework," Bolton recalled. "This, to me, eliminated the article of faith about North Korean compliance."

On most days, Colin Powell liked to get to work by 6:30 A.M. The early hour gave him what he called his "quiet time," before the pressures of the day intruded. In late June, though, an early visitor disturbed Powell's calm. John Bolton burst into the secretary's seventh-floor office at the State Department. "See,"

Bolton exclaimed, brandishing the latest raw CIA intelligence. "Cheating! We've got to blow it open."

Despite their often sharp differences, Powell maintains he always had a good personal relationship with Bolton. Now, with the air of a parent calming down an overexcited teenager, he told Bolton, "Sit down, John. We're not blowing anything open until I've had a chance to read this, study this, and I want to hear from the intelligence community."

Knowing Bolton's predilection for leaking information to buttress his hard-line positions in Washington's bureaucratic power games—as well as his virulent opposition to the Agreed Framework—Powell put Bolton on notice. "We're not going to race off to the *Washington Times* or anybody else until I'm satisfied these guys know what they are talking about."

Producing weapons-grade uranium is not easy. The key challenge is to develop the fissionable material that produces the explosive chain reaction of a nuclear blast. Natural uranium contains two isotopes, U235 and U238. The more fissile of the two is U235, which can be split to release energy. But only 0.7 percent of natural uranium consists of U235. To build a bomb, uranium needs to be enriched, separating out the U238 to leave more than 90 percent U235. One way to do this is by introducing uranium hexafluoride gas into thousands of centrifuges linked together in what are known as cascades. A rotor within each of the centrifuges repeatedly spins the gas at extremely high speeds to separate out the slightly lighter U235 isotope. The technology for this process is extremely complex and costly, requiring a multitude of components and extraordinarily sophisticated engineering to build the centrifuges.

As Christopher Clary noted in a paper for the U.S. Naval Postgraduate School, "A country pursuing gas centrifuge technology would need to acquire nearly a hundred components each for thousands of centrifuges. Since a majority of these components cannot be easily manufactured, and because a majority of these components are proscribed by export control regimes, this necessitates a massive illicit procurement effort. States that successfully develop gas centrifuge enrichment must develop a network to funnel cash, often through middlemen, to shady businessmen. They then must transport the components from their point of origin, often relying on false end-user certificates and other techniques to deceive law enforcement and intelligence agencies. These goods are often transported through multiple third-party countries to further confuse watchful eyes before finally arriving in their destination."[1]

The hints about a North Korean uranium program had been around since the late 1990s. But the reports had always been sporadic, the information sketchy, and with Pyongyang's much more advanced plutonium program frozen by the Agreed Framework, the subject had not been high on the priority list of American intelligence.

"We had suspected for a long time, had tantalizing hints that they were working on a covert uranium enrichment program," said John McLaughlin, who was the CIA's deputy director until 2005, "but we didn't have confidence enough to say that we had a critical mass of data."

It remains difficult to ascertain with absolute certainty just what specific information came in that prompted Alan Foley's call to John Bolton and generated new high-level American attention to the possibility North Korea might be seeking a uranium enrichment capability. Throughout the spring, according to officials familiar with the effort, Bolton's office of Arms Control at the State Department, along with Robert Joseph and his deputy John Rood, a former CIA analyst who had handled nonproliferation issues at the National Security Council, had been looking for evidence to buttress their deeply held conviction that North Korea was cheating.

On May 6, 2002, in a speech delivered to the conservative Heritage Foundation, Bolton singled out "North Korea and Iraq for their covert nuclear weapons programs in violation of the Nuclear Nonproliferation Treaty," a claim he had first made public in comments in late January.[2]

Tantalizingly, it appears that one crucial source for what one U.S. official described as the key "alert" about the uranium effort may have been that rarest of assets—an agent inside North Korea. The existence and role of this person has been closely held, and even now no present or former official will provide any specifics. But four former senior officials who dealt with the North Korea issue all separately said that there was such an agent, and that the inside information from the agent was a crucial factor in refocusing attention on the North's uranium effort in June 2002.

It appears the agent was communicating not directly with the United States, but with South Korean intelligence, which passed the information to Washington. "It was credible single-source reporting," said one senior U.S. intelligence official. "It was very credible." The agent subsequently fled North Korea, and is now believed to be in South Korea.

The specifics of what the agent reported, as well as the time frame in which this person was actually operating in North Korea and the date of his/her defection to South Korea, remain secret. But in an interview for this book, a former senior intelligence official said, "In 2002, we had some reporting from one source that was credible but not complete, that caused us to go back and look again at the material that had been hard to interpret." The official wouldn't reveal any further details, but in the context of other sources appeared to be referring to the same agent.


In the intelligence business, it's called a "scrub"—a thorough review of material previously collected in the hope of finding a pattern of behavior or new nuggets of information that may have been missed when the information initially came in. With the U.S. intelligence community preoccupied and overworked by the "war on terror" and the aftermath of 9/11, North Korea had, until this moment, remained a relatively low intelligence priority, despite the Axis of Evil speech and other efforts by the administration to demonize the regime in Pyongyang.

"The intelligence community's capability of vacuum-cleaning data and retaining it is completely different from its ability to prioritize and sort through and see if there are any jewels in there," noted one former senior official with access to the intelligence. "And so, let me just say that it was a resource issue and it was a prioritization issue, and it didn't rise to the level where people took the possibility seriously. I would say that what happened then was a decision that it had now risen to the level that we need to take a really hard look at this. The information about a possible North Korean uranium enrichment program compelled us to a) no longer ignore the possibility and b) to do a scrub and go back and look at what we may have missed. Once we took it seriously and started looking, and turning over rocks . . . lo and behold . . . it was there unambiguously when we went back and looked at what we may have missed . . . a very aggressive procurement program."

The intelligence scrub brought a gold mine of raw data about North Korea's efforts to procure components that could be used to develop a uranium-enrichment capability. The CIA had intercepted faxes, monitored phone calls, acquired copies of bills of lading, and traced the movements of known or suspected North Korean purchasing agents in various parts of the world. Notwithstanding their penchant for secrecy, the "tradecraft" of these North Koreans was elementary enough that the United States had little difficulty keeping track. As one U.S. military intelligence officer noted, "James Bonds they ain't."

"When we began looking, when we went back," said one former intelligence official, "their commercial procurement activities were not exactly clandestine in nature, because they didn't have to be. They were out buying things and so it was reasonably straightforward once you devote the number of resources to go back and look . . . that if you know how to devote resources that you find what's there."

Even years later, U.S. officials remain tight-lipped about precisely which North Korean entities and individuals were being monitored at that time, but among the North Korean companies they acknowledge the United States was watching were Changgwang Sinyong Corporation, also known as the Korea Mining Development Corporation. It had offices in Macau, the former Portuguese colony that reverted to Chinese sovereignty in 1999, which had long been a base of operations for North Korean commercial and intelligence activities. The company had also been identified by the United States as active in North Korea's sale of missiles to countries such as Pakistan and Iran.

As U.S. intelligence officials examined the data, it became clear one key focus of the North Korean procurement effort was high-strength aluminum tubing to be used in the construction of centrifuges. One official who saw the information described it as "tons" of very high-quality tubing whose specifications, size, type [and] metallic characteristics" meant "there was absolutely no conceivable use for the material except for the rotors of a centrifuge."

The North Koreans were also seeking other critical components, including valves and electronic devices that would be needed to fine-tune the performance of a state-of-the-art centrifuge system. In addition, the North Koreans were looking for a high-strength alloy called maraging steel, rheostats, and specially refined petroleum to lubricate the system, as well as very expensive machining equipment called "four-access computer numeric control."

Taken together, U.S. intelligence calculated that all the equipment, when assembled, would allow the North Koreans to have as many as 3,000 functioning centrifuges. "This was not a laboratory effort," said James Kelly. "This was a production effort. We're not talking of tens of centrifuges but thousands, and some of that information clearly went back a number of years."

In their search for components, the North Koreans had scoured the world. U.S. intelligence identified numerous companies approached by Pyongyang's purchasing agents in China, Japan, Switzerland, and Russia. But as the scrub continued, new information came in that also suggested an ambitious North Korean attempt in Germany to acquire additional aluminum tubing with potential applications for a uranium program. Details of the case only became public in 2003, with the arrest, trial, and conviction of Hans Werner Truppel, a German businessman, on charges of illegally transporting equipment that could be used to make nuclear weapons.

In the spring of 2002, Truppel, who ran a tiny export firm called Optronic, was approached by a North Korean businessman claiming to represent an import-export company called Nam Chong Gang with an order for 214 tubes made of a special aluminum alloy known to be light, corrosion-resistant, and exceptionally strong. The North Korean said he was acting on behalf of Shenyang Aircraft, a leading Chinese aircraft manufacturer, based in the capital of Liaoning province next to China's border with North Korea. The tubes were supposedly intended to make gas tanks for Chinese airplanes. The businessman indicated the initial order was part of a broader plan to eventually acquire 2,000 tubes.

American officials familiar with this episode would not confirm whether the United States had tracked the 2002 order. But they referred me to a series of investigative reports published in 2003 by the German news magazine *Der Spiegel,* which remains the most detailed account of the case and from which I have drawn many of these details.[3] A *Washington Post* report on August 15, 2003, also noted that "throughout the second half of 2002, intelligence agencies in the United States and Western Europe picked up multiple signals that North Korea was attempting to acquire such tubes, along with other specialized metals used in centrifuges."[4]

The North Korean who placed the order was Yun Ho Jin, and he was no ordinary businessman. For fourteen years, he had been Pyongyang's envoy to the International Atomic Energy Agency, a highly visible figure, attending meetings, giving press interviews, and vocally defending North Korean policies.

Gary Samore, who had handled nonproliferation issues at the National Security Council during the Clinton administration, had dealt with Yun regularly. Samore remembered him as "a nice little guy." Now, in a curious move for a diplomat supposedly working on nonproliferation issues, Yun appeared to be taking the lead in an ambitious effort to acquire the components for a uranium-based bomb. And whatever Yun's explanation in his initial communications with Optronic, the fact was that the dimensions of the tubes he had ordered corresponded almost exactly to those used in a centrifuge designed by the European consortium Urenco—a design whose blueprints, back in the 1970s, had been stolen by the rogue Pakistani metallurgist A. Q. Khan, and which became the basis for Pakistan's own nuclear bomb.

American intelligence had been keeping a watchful eye on A. Q. Khan for years. As the head of Khan Research Laboratories, Khan presided over his own nuclear fiefdom, which in the late 1980s and early '90s, spearheaded Pakistan's successful development of highly enriched uranium. In 1998, Pakistan carried out a successful test of a nuclear bomb. Yet, confronted with the nuclear prowess of its neighbor and rival India, Pakistan still urgently needed a missile to deliver its bomb and was looking for a shortcut to avoid having to develop one on its own. Significantly, it was during the same time period that North

Korea had begun exporting ballistic missiles to countries such as Iran, Iraq, and Syria.

His triumph in developing the technology that had made Pakistan a nuclear power turned Khan into a national hero. It also emboldened him to embark on a new path—secretly selling nuclear technology, know-how, and equipment to other countries for his own personal profit. In any event, Khan began his enterprise in the late 1980s by selling centrifuges, blueprints, and other components to Iran. He would also eventually approach Iraq and Syria, and by the new millennium his client list had expanded to include Libya and North Korea.

It is widely believed that a visit to Pyongyang by Prime Minister Benazir Bhutto in December 1993 was the critical first step in an accelerating pattern of cooperation between Islamabad and Pyongyang.[5] Bhutto reportedly returned home with design details for a North Korean Rodong missile. Bhutto had consistently maintained it was purely a cash transaction—Pakistani money for North Korean missile technology.[6]

Following her visit, defense contacts between the two countries multiplied, leading, in either 1996 or 1997, to the delivery by North Korea's Changgwang Sinyong Corporation (North Korea Mining Development Trading Corporation) of key missile components—or possibly an entire missile. The Pakistanis eventually rechristened the 1,500-kilometer intermediate-range missile the Ghauri—the name of an ancient Muslim warrior who battled the Hindus—and successfully tested it in 1998.[7] Western analysts noted that the Ghauri was a close replica of the Rodong, although with some modifications.

By the mid-1990s, however, Pakistan was facing a financial crisis as its foreign exchange reserves plunged. It was at this point that the first real evidence emerged that Khan had offered nuclear know-how to the North Koreans. Whether the North Koreans accepted Khan's initial offer is unclear. Khan reportedly visited North Korea thirteen times. The precise arrangements are also unclear. It could have been a barter deal, under which Pakistan would compensate North Korea for ballistic missiles with uranium-enrichment technology. It remains equally possible that Khan was selling technology to Pyongyang for his own profit. The extent to which Pakistan's government and powerful armed forces knew of Khan's clandestine trade remains a matter of controversy, though some of the equipment was transported on Pakistani military aircraft and the flights were cleared by Pakistani air controllers. Whatever the case, flights of Pakistani military C-130 aircraft to North Korea increased sharply in the late 1990s.

At the time, U.S. intelligence was monitoring the flights and at least some of Khan's visits. Aware of the expanding contacts, Washington did not yet have sufficient details to put all the pieces of the puzzle together.

According to Robert Einhorn, who served as assistant secretary of state for nonproliferation from 1999 to 2001, "What we saw, and it was very very spotty at the beginning, we saw procurement attempts, attempts to acquire some dual-use items that had application in an enrichment program. And we were aware of the North Koreans shopping around."

But with the more immediate threat of Pyongyang's plutonium program frozen under the Agreed Framework, a possible North Korean uranium effort—which at this stage appeared to be more at the level of research and development rather than full-scale production—was not a top priority. The Clinton administration, according to officials who handled nonproliferation matters at the time, did decide, in the context of a broader thaw, to address the uranium issue with the North Koreans, but time ran out before it could do so.

In the final year of the Clinton administration, however, enough alarm bells had begun to sound about A. Q. Khan's proliferation activities that it triggered an ambitious joint U.S.-British intelligence operation to target the Pakistani nuclear scientist. The effort involved not just access to an incriminating paper trail, but actually placing agents inside the Khan proliferation network. After George W. Bush took office, the intelligence operation intensified. The initial target was Libya, which had become the focus for Khan's most elaborate effort thus far, involving an order from Col. Muammar Qaddafi for large numbers of centrifuges and 1.87 tons of uranium hexafluoride. Penetration of the network would lead Qaddafi to abandon his nuclear ambitions in return for better ties with the United States and Britain in 2003. Qaddafi's turnabout also yielded an intelligence bonanza, giving the United States enough incriminating details to force Pakistan's president Pervez Musharraf to place Khan under house arrest in early 2004 and assist in the dismantling of what was known of Khan's network.

In 2002, the investigation was still at an early stage. But it was already giving the CIA a better understanding not just of Khan's dealings with Libya, but of the alarming fact that his network had other clients—including Pyongyang and Damascus.

"Once we got inside that network it gave us windows into all of these countries, including North Korea," former CIA deputy director John McLaughlin confirmed in an interview.

In his book *At the Center of the Storm*, former CIA Director George Tenet wrote:

> Patiently, we put ourselves in a position to come into contact with individuals and organizations that we believed were part of the overall proliferation effort . . . we discovered the extent of Khan's hidden network, which stretched from Pakistan, to Europe, to the Middle East, to Asia. We pieced together a

picture of the organization, revealing its subsidiaries, scientists, front companies, agents, finances, and manufacturing plants. Our spies gained access through a series of daring operations over several years.[8]

One sinister episode from 1998 provides a revealing glimpse of the murky netherworld in which North Korea's nuclear acquisitions operatives—and their adversaries in Western intelligence services—operated. On June 7, 1998, ten days after Pakistan's first underground nuclear test, a North Korean woman named Kim Sa Nae was shot to death a few yards from A. Q. Khan's official residence in an upscale neighborhood of Islamabad. Officially, Kim was identified as the wife of Kang Thae Yun, a mid-level diplomat at the North Korean embassy. In 2004, Pakistani officials leaked word to Paul Watson and Mubashir Zaidi of the *Los Angeles Times* that Kim had actually been a member of a twenty-person delegation of North Korean experts invited by Khan to witness the nuclear test and learn more about the construction of uranium-based nuclear bombs. Her "husband," Kang, officially the North Korean embassy's "economic counselor," worked for North Korea's state-run Changgwang Sinyong Corporation, a company that continually featured in U.S. assessments of Pyongyang's missile export business. His presence in Pakistan appears to have been linked to the trade of North Korea missiles for Pakistani uranium-enrichment technology.

Publicly, the Pakistani authorities said almost nothing about Kim's death. When pressed, they offered vague and unconvincing accounts. One suggested she'd been accidentally killed when a gun belonging to a neighbor's cook went off. Another said that a different neighbor had accidentally discharged a firearm while cleaning it. Privately, Pakistani intelligence sources told the journalists from the *Los Angeles Times* that Kim had been suspected of spying for the United States. Her contact with unnamed Western diplomats caught the attention of Pakistan's military intelligence service, the ISI, which shared its suspicion with the North Korean embassy. Her murder soon followed.

Pakistani officials told the reporters that three days after Kim's death, her body was flown back to Pyongyang on a U.S.-built C-130 military cargo plane—the same kind of aircraft whose repeated flights into and out of North Korea from 1997 to 2002 had set off alarm bells among U.S. intelligence officials. The reporters were told that along with Kim's body, the plane carried both P-1 and the more sophisticated P-2 centrifuges, drawings, sketches, and technical data for centrifuges and warhead designs, as well as depleted uranium hexafluoride gas, which can be converted into weapons-grade material in centrifuges.

Reportedly, the plane was a charter flight operated by Shaheen Air International, a company set up in 1993 and run by retired officers from the Pakistani air force.[9] It may not have been a coincidence that one of Pakistan's ballistic missiles was also called the Shaheen. Named after a white eagle native to the country's rugged northern mountains, the medium-range missile was capable of carrying conventional or nuclear payloads of up to 1,000 kilograms.

By June of 2002, it became clear that the Khan network had provided North Korea with the "designs for Pakistan's older centrifuges, and for newer, more efficient models."[10] In 2005, President Musharraf confirmed that Khan had given the North Koreans "nearly two dozen" centrifuges, both the P1 and the more advanced P2. The designations P1 and P2 refer to two Pakistani types of centrifuges, one more sophisticated than the other. The designs for both had been stolen by A. Q. Khan when he was working at the Dutch company Urenco in the 1970s. While such a small number of centrifuges was far short of the thousands required for the cascades necessary for nuclear weapons, with Khan's detailed list of the remaining components, North Korea was now in a position to procure the necessary equipment to produce a uranium bomb.

"What was happening was, we had massive amounts of raw intelligence—signals intelligence, human intelligence . . . on North Korea's massive procurement efforts to buy everything they needed to develop nuclear weapons through uranium enrichment, based on the A. Q. Khan P2 centrifuge model," said one former senior official with access to the information. "And so the A. Q. Khan piece tipped us off that the North Koreans had gotten the blueprints to make one of these things, including a shopping list of what you need to make it."

"He gave them designs," said one senior U.S. military intelligence official. "He gave them actual functioning centrifuges, both type one and type two. I think that the deal was not just to give them the technology but also the drawings and all the components of the program as well as the know-how."

Taken together, the scrub of the earlier information and the evidence of more recent activities led U.S. intelligence agencies to a new understanding of North Korean activities.

The procurement effort, which began in the late 1990s, had been initially small scale—a research and development project involving just tens of centrifuges. By June of 2002, the intelligence suggested an effort on an entirely different scale. A senior NSC staffer recalled one briefing from the intelligence community. "The assessment was they'd gone from just small-scale dabbling in this to . . . I think they called it 'production scale.' "

Almost literally at the same time that the CIA's Alan Foley called John Bolton with new intelligence about North Korea's uranium procurement efforts, the factions within the Bush administration finally agreed to move ahead with re-engaging Pyongyang. Jack Pritchard contacted Pyongyang's UN envoy Pak Gil Yon to propose that Assistant Secretary of State James Kelly visit the North Korean capital on July 10. Kelly would bring with him the so-called Bold Approach aimed at getting negotiations under way again. Pritchard pressed Pak for an early and positive response.

After weeks of internal debate, the Bold Approach was still, in the words of Chuck Kartman, "a concept rather than an actual road map." It offered the possibility of dialogue and an eventual improvement in U.S. relations with North Korea. Yet, as would be true of the Bush administration's overall approach to the North in the following years, it was still heavily weighted toward demands that Pyongyang act first to satisfy American concerns on a host of issues before Washington would even begin to address any of North Korea's concerns. In a speech at the Asia Society on June 10, 2002, Colin Powell spelled out Washington's demands:

"The United States is prepared to take important steps to help North Korea move its relations with the U.S. toward normalcy," he declared. "However, progress between us will depend on Pyongyang's behavior on a number of key issues." North Korea, Powell insisted, "must get out of the proliferation business and eliminate long-range missiles that threaten other countries, come into full compliance with the International Atomic Energy Agency safeguards, and move toward a less threatening conventional military posture." Only then would the U.S. consider reciprocal steps.[11] In short, the North had to go first, which was antithetical to the simultaneous steps approach that had worked in earlier negotiations with the North.

On June 29, before the North Koreans could reply, the worst clash between North and South Korean forces in three years erupted in the seas off the peninsula's western coast. Two North Korean patrol boats challenged South Korean boats that had been fishing for crab north of the line dividing the waters claimed by each of the two Koreas. When challenged by eight South Korean naval vessels, the North Koreans opened fire, sinking one speedboat and leaving five dead. An unknown number of North Koreans also died when the South Korean vessels returned fire. The incident appeared to be a blow to Kim Dae-jung's hopes of rapprochement with Pyongyang. The North, however, appeared eager to play down the incident. The next day, acting as if nothing unusual had happened, Pyongyang congratulated the South on the performance of its World Cup soccer team. A month later, Pyongyang officially expressed "regret" for the incident.

John Bolton and other administration hard-liners had not been happy with the decision to send Kelly to Pyongyang. Bolton was in London when he got word of the North-South naval clash. He immediately called his senior aide Mark Groombridge. "I can't imagine this will take any effort," Bolton said, "but it probably will . . . so do whatever you legally can to stop the Kelly trip."

Groombridge then wrote an e-mail, intentionally copying everyone in the bureaucracy he could think of, arguing that in view of the clash, the trip should not take place. Within moments, he received a phone call from Jim Kelly's secretary asking him to come to Kelly's office. Kelly was furious at the blatant effort to sabotage his trip. Walking into Kelly's office, Groombridge found the assistant secretary standing at the door, his face beet red. "If you or John Bolton has a problem with what I'm doing, tell me directly as opposed to cc-ing your thousand friends," Kelly fumed. "Now leave."

Ironically, the South Korean government, despite the loss of its sailors, was desperate to see the resumption of diplomacy between Washington and Pyongyang and strongly urged the Bush administration not to let the incident lead to the cancellation of Kelly's visit. Indeed, Seoul was so eager to downplay the episode that President Kim did not attend the funerals of those who died. Yet the confrontation made it virtually impossible for proponents of engagement to argue in favor of going ahead. As one senior official exclaimed in a meeting to discuss the issue, "No, we shouldn't do the trip, because they sunk a goddamn patrol boat and killed five of our allies. That's why we shouldn't have the meeting—period."

When Ambassador Thomas Hubbard conveyed South Korean concerns to Washington, he got a similar response. Hubbard described the prevailing view in the administration as, "These South Koreans . . . care more about North Korea than their own sailors." In fact, though, given the new raw intelligence about North Korean uranium procurement—which U.S. intelligence agencies were now racing to analyze—the incident provided a useful fig leaf to cover the delay of any meeting while Washington assessed the new information and decided on a course of action.

On July 1, the North Koreans were told the meeting was off. "We can't go to Pyongyang to talk a bold approach, and now we have this new intelligence to say that they have a secret path toward another nuclear weapon—what are we going to do?" recalled Jack Pritchard. "So we used the 29 June incident between the North and South. I went back to the North Koreans—that we had been waiting for a response and in the meantime we had had this incident at sea, the atmosphere is no longer conducive for these talks. We are withdrawing our request for the meeting. But the basis for this withdrawal was the new information on highly enriched uranium."

"I didn't think there was any reason for [Kelly] to go," said John Bolton. "This was just the persistence of the East Asia Bureau bureaucracy [in the State Department]. They'd been trying to get him there since the administration started."

At a meeting on July 19 in Colin Powell's conference room with Kelly and Under Secretary of State for Political Affairs Marc Grossman, Bolton made the case that the United States should conclude the Agreed Framework was dead. Before the meeting, he asked his aide Mark Groombridge to put together a detailed presentation of all the available intelligence. Groombridge spent nearly twelve hours at a top-secret computer doing so, and Bolton brought the material to Powell's conference room.

Kelly began the session by saying he wanted to discuss the way forward. Bolton interrupted and said the intelligence proved the framework was finished, along with the policy approaches that had produced it. He then passed out the summary of the intelligence that Groombridge had prepared. The administration, he continued, now had to "address the range of policy issues that would immediately emerge [from the conclusion that the framework was dead, including] what military and other contingency plans to make in the event of an irrational North Korean reaction."[12]

Kelly responded by saying the intelligence was not clear about when North Korea might have enough highly enriched uranium to make a warhead, and warning that Pyongyang might start reprocessing plutonium if the United States publicly declared that the framework was dead. Bolton retorted that this was not a reason to save the 1994 deal. For his part, Grossman said the intelligence was indisputable, and Kelly too agreed that the United States now faced a very serious problem.[13]

Colin Powell and his colleagues at the State Department were convinced, however, that diplomatic engagement remained the only way to move the situation forward. Fearing that the newly scrubbed uranium information and the naval clash gave opponents of engagement fresh ammunition, Powell decided to act on his own. At the end of July, he was scheduled to attend a gathering of Southeast Asian leaders at the annual meeting of the ASEAN Regional Forum in Brunei. North Korean foreign minister Paek Nam Sun would be among those participating. Powell decided to have a "chance" meeting with Paek. Nothing about it was left to chance. The goal of holding what would be the highest-level encounter between the two sides since the Bush administration took office would be to revive the idea of dialogue and also to lay the groundwork for what Powell knew would be difficult future discussions about the uranium issue. He told National Security Adviser Condoleezza Rice of his plan, but deliberately avoided any interagency discussion of the idea because he knew that his critics would try to block the meeting. He never learned whether Rice told President Bush, and, if she did, what the president thought of the idea.

"I didn't ask for an interagency discussion of it because that would have gotten us nowhere," Powell recalled.

Acting on Powell's instructions, Jack Pritchard tipped off the North Korean UN mission to Powell's intentions. "So I get to the conference center [in

Brunei] about a half hour early," Powell said, "and we call the North Koreans and say hey, we've got half an hour, want to have coffee? And they came running down the steps—it's a wonder they didn't kill each other, racing to have coffee. And my colleague comes in with a whole bunch of translators and staff people to take notes. And it wasn't long, it was about fifteen minutes. I told them the president wants to take a new look at this, a bold approach. Please convey to your leadership how the president feels in a compassionate way about your people. We're not looking to attack you or invade you or anything like that. We want to get to talking again. And I said to get this started, I'd like to send Mr. Kelly to Pyongyang. And Paek immediately said, 'As soon as you ask, permission will be granted.'" Without mentioning the uranium issue, Powell sought to signal the North Koreans that the fact of a future meeting did not guarantee smooth sailing. "I said, now, when Mr. Kelly comes there are going to be some tough issues that we have to get on top of."

Powell's brief meeting with Paek infuriated hard-liners in Washington, including Vice President Dick Cheney's office, where suspicions of Powell ran deep. Cheney's staffers recalled the episode of March 2001, when Powell "leaned too far forward" on his skis by making positive comments about engaging North Korea as the Clinton administration had done.

"Powell is the person who at the beginning of this process declared a policy that wasn't the administration's policy," said one former Cheney aide.

On August 20, 2002, President Bush granted an interview to Bob Woodward of the *Washington Post*. The interview was for a book Woodward was writing on Bush's leadership in the aftermath of 9/11 and the war in Afghanistan, and would not be published until several months later. Yet it provided a unique glimpse of the president's thinking about North Korea at that moment. When asked about North Korea's leader, Bush declared, "I loathe Kim Jong Il. I've got a visceral reaction to this guy because he's starving his people . . . They tell me, we don't need to move too fast [against Kim] because the financial burden on his people will be so immense if we try to—if this guy were to topple. Who would take care—I don't buy that. Either you believe in freedom . . . and worry about the human condition, or you don't."[14]

For George Bush, North Korea was not just a foreign policy problem. It was personal.

At the end of the summer of 2002, in the conference room of the Director of Central Intelligence at CIA headquarters in Langley, Virginia, the agency's top leadership met to thrash out a consensus on the meaning of the uranium intelligence. Among those in attendance were CIA Deputy Director John

McLaughlin and Deputy Director for Intelligence Jami Miscik, who oversaw the agency's analytical staff and supervised the preparation of the president's daily intelligence briefing. Director George Tenet would pop in and out, listening to a series of analysts who had spent weeks poring over the raw data.

Unlike briefings in the U.S. military, which are usually characterized by elaborate PowerPoint presentations, these meetings were decidedly low tech. As one person who was present remembered, "It's literally passing pieces of paper across the table, different analysts with different specialties giving their piece of it . . . if you piece this together with that together with this, we would assess then that this is what's going on. . . . So it was much more pieces of a puzzle being put together than it was any smoking gun."

The agency analysts used the phrase "peeling of the onion . . . because you're looking through layers and layers."

Such meetings, said one former intelligence analyst, were "of course very technical . . . people who talk in a language that you can barely keep up with unless you're a physicist yourself." Still, the evidence of a procurement effort appeared compelling. "There were enough detailed dates and specifications that I don't remember anybody in the room sort of saying 'Well gee, I'm not persuaded.' I mean, we walked out of that room convinced that this was happening."

The judgment that emerged was that the North Korean uranium effort started over late 1997 and 1998, a period that followed North Korean warnings to U.S. officials that Washington was not living up to the Agreed Framework and coincided with the increase in contacts between the North and A. Q. Khan, who began to provide blueprints, uranium hexafluoride, and a small number of centrifuges. Once the North had the "shopping list," it began seeking to acquire the ingredients for a uranium weapons program. Until 2001, the effort remained small scale—"R&D" rather than a full production capability. By the end of the summer of 2002, though, the picture had changed.

"The picture was, with a high degree of confidence, that they were putting together materials and expertise and data that would allow them to produce a centrifuge enrichment program for uranium," said John McLaughlin. "The data on North Korea was of a quality that gave us high confidence."

McLaughlin and Tenet realized this was "blockbuster" news and ordered the CIA to pull together material so that President Bush and his key aides could be briefed. The meeting was scheduled for mid-September.

Junichiro Koizumi had a bombshell for Richard Armitage. The American deputy secretary of state was making a regular visit to Tokyo, with soliciting support for the forthcoming American invasion of Iraq high on the agenda. But he was also going to give the Japanese prime minister a hint, without revealing details, of the growing concern in Washington about the North Korean uranium effort. Armitage was the leading Japan hand in the Bush administration. Shortly before the 2000 election, he had spearheaded a report calling for closer cooperation on security, intelligence, and economics with Japan. The goal was to transform the U.S.-Japan alliance into an Asian version of the "special relationship" Washington had long maintained with Britain.

Koizumi, however, had his own surprise. Asking to meet privately, with no staff from the U.S. Embassy present, the prime minister on August 27 told a surprised Armitage that in three days he would be announcing plans to visit Pyongyang in September for a summit meeting with Kim Jong Il—plans that until now, the Japanese government had kept secret from its closest ally, the United States.

For a leader who had rapidly emerged as one of George W. Bush's closest friends abroad, it was a startling display of independence, a blunt repudiation of the administration's approach to North Korea and an indication of the extent to which Bush's policies were alienating Washington's key allies in the region. Koizumi believed Bush's confrontational approach was wrong and counterproductive. His advisers saw U.S. policy as harsh rhetoric combined with inconsistent, divisive, and poorly coordinated actions.

The gap between the two leaders had been publicly apparent for some time. In February 2002, en route to Seoul, the U.S. president had stopped in Tokyo. At a joint press conference with Bush, Koizumi told reporters, "Japan would like to work on normalization of relations with North Korea."

For Koizumi, normalization of relations with Pyongyang was the last unresolved issue from the Cold War. South Korea and Japan established relations in 1965, and China and Japan had done so in 1978. "North Korea was the last holdover," noted a close Koizumi adviser. And there was a second goal, the adviser said: "To get rid of the historical legacy. Japan had colonized Korea." Putting the painful past to rest, the adviser, said, was Koizumi's "hidden agenda." A more immediate objective, of course, was to resolve the case of more than a dozen Japanese citizens abducted by North Korean agents in the 1970s and '80s. The Japanese had apparently been used to train North Korean agents both to speak Japanese and to learn how to operate in the world beyond North Korea. The fate of the abductees, one of whom had been only thirteen at the time of her kidnapping, was a deeply emotional issue in Japan.

Bush's comment on North Korea at the same news conference revealed a sharply different view. "On the one side of a parallel we've got people starving to death, because a nation chooses to build weapons of mass destruction," he declared. "They should make no mistake about it, that we will defend our interests, and I will defend the American people."[15]

However disconcerting it may have been, Armitage responded to Koizumi's news in a low-key manner, diplomatically expressing appreciation that the prime minister had told him of his plan before making news of the trip public.

"We were gratified that our key ally in Asia—Japan—sought to inform us ahead of time," Armitage recalled. "And I told the prime minister that I'm sure the president would be very pleased with that. The prime minister assured me . . . he would do nothing to hurt our equities [interests]."

At this time, with the U.S. intelligence community still putting together its final assessment on the uranium question, Armitage was not in a position to provide Koizumi much detail. But he did give Koizumi a warning that there might be trouble ahead.

"I was able to tell the prime minister, please be a little careful, there are some new developments in North Korea that will soon come to light . . . that would be negative regarding North Korea, and I hoped that the prime minister would keep that in mind and be very careful."

Racing back to the U.S. Embassy, Armitage called Colin Powell at home to break the news. Powell in turn informed Bush, and then called Armitage back. Bush clearly had a lot of confidence in his friend Koizumi. "The president is comfortable with the prime minister's trip to Pyongyang," Powell told Armitage.

At least that was the official reaction. Privately, Jack Pritchard recalled a much less positive response. The news "caused alarm bells."

Hitoshi Tanaka, head of the Japanese Foreign Ministry's Asia Bureau, spoke with Armitage and asked him directly, "Are you opposed to the prime minister's trip to North Korea? Are you opposed to Japanese negotiations with North Korea? We have very significant problems . . . the abductions and all sorts of things. Are you willing to resolve this for us? You make use of all type of international relations for the sake of the national interest."

Tanaka was convinced the visit would enhance, not undermine, American interests because at that time Washington and Pyongyang were not talking at all about the huge issues they faced.

Clearly, the key concern in Washington was the new information on uranium. "We didn't want him to be going to North Korea without a fundamental understanding of what it might entail," noted Pritchard.

Just over two weeks after Koizumi's dramatic announcement, Koizumi and Bush met at the annual session of the United Nations General Assembly in New York. Koizumi was provided with further information about the North Korean uranium effort. At the same time, the Japanese leader, in a pattern that would be repeated regularly in the coming years, urged Bush to consider direct talks with North Korea. "You may not like Kim Jong Il," Koizumi said. "Kim

Jong Il is not a likable person. He can't be trusted. But you should have direct talks."

Under Secretary of State for Arms Control John Bolton and his Asia aide Mark Groombridge were about to board a plane for Seoul when they got a call from Robert Joseph, the fellow hard-liner who handled nonproliferation issues at the National Security Council, informing them of Koizumi's plan to visit Pyongyang. The prospect of a diplomatic breakthrough between Koizumi and Kim Jong Il did not dim Bolton's enthusiasm for the bellicose speech he intended to deliver in the South Korean capital—despite objections from Ambassador Thomas Hubbard and others in the Bush administration who were seeking to get Washington's own diplomacy with North Korea back on track.

The draft of the speech contained a harsh denunciation of Pyongyang. In South Korea, a country where the term had caused an angry backlash, Bolton planned again to label North Korea part of the Axis of Evil. Hubbard, alarmed by the potential for diplomatic damage, had urged Bolton to delete the phrase. The ambassador argued that it "had been misunderstood by the South Koreans when it was first delivered, and to my mind was not conducive to our working together with the South Koreans. I pointed out also that the president had not used the phrase when he visited South Korea in February of 2002, and that my guess was that he hadn't used it because he had drawn the same conclusion, that it had been misunderstood by the South Koreans. And Mr. Bolton's response, at the time was, 'The President said it. I'm going to say it too. It's the truth.' "[16] Bolton had little respect for Hubbard. He felt the ambassador "was a clear example of clientitis, wholly reflecting Kim Dae-jung's views on almost every issue."[17]

On August 29, two days after Koizumi had told Armitage of his plan to visit Pyongyang, Bolton, ignoring the appeals of the American ambassador, declared before an audience in Seoul, "President Bush's use of the term 'Axis of Evil' to describe Iran, Iraq, and North Korea was more than a rhetorical flourish. It was factually correct." It would not be the last time Bolton and Hubbard would clash over a speech in South Korea.

And Bolton's provocative remarks were hardly the only problem Hubbard faced in trying to manage an increasingly difficult American relationship with South Korea. Some of the tensions were inevitable, as a prosperous, modernizing South Korea sought to emerge from the shadow of its longtime superpower "big brother." But a series of incidents—from Bush's humiliating rebuff of Kim Dae-jung in March 2001 to the Axis of Evil speech to his thinly disguised personal animosity toward a regime in Pyongyang that many South Koreans saw not as an enemy but an errant relative—fueled hostility toward the United States.

This was followed on June 13 with a tragic accident that occurred just as the new information on North Korea's uranium procurement was emerging. An American armored vehicle on a routine journey along a narrow country road near the Demilitarized Zone ran over two fourteen-year-old girls who were walking to a friend's birthday party. Shin Hyo-soon and Shim Mi-sun were both killed.

Their deaths were initially overshadowed by other news; South Korea was in the grip of World Cup fever. The unheralded national soccer team had defied the odds to become the fairy-tale story of the 2002 World Cup tournament, which South Korea was cohosting, along with Japan. Reaching the quarter-finals, the team and its successes sparked an unprecedented wave of national pride. Huge crowds, dressed in red T-shirts and waving red banners representing the colors of the "Red Devils," packed the streets and city squares to watch the games on giant TV screens. Police reported a nearly 25 percent drop in crime of when the matches were broadcast. It was yet another sign of a confident, modern South Korea coming of age and taking its rightful place on the international stage.

But the focus of this intense outpouring of nationalistic sentiment quickly shifted to the case of the two girls. Their deaths became a national cause, sparking a wave of angry anti-American demonstrations and protests. "The combination of this sort of whipped-up nationalism, growing coolness between Washington and Seoul, and dissatisfaction with respect to U.S. policy toward the North, and then in the middle of that you had this incident. And it just became the perfect storm," noted Evans Revere, then Hubbard's deputy at the U.S. Embassy.

Further complicating the situation, the issue was swept up in South Korea's developing presidential campaign. Set for December, the election pitted a conservative, Lee Hoi-chang, who was clearly favored by Washington because of his tougher position on North Korea, against Roh Moo-hyun, a liberal human rights activist and longtime dissident, who campaigned with a promise not to "kow-tow" to the Americans.

The CIA was overwhelmed. As the first anniversary of the 9/11 attacks approached, the agency was working frantically to identify—and, if possible, to stop—any future attacks. It was a period of great anxiety and fear. At the same time, preparations were accelerating for the upcoming U.S. invasion of Iraq. The maneuvering, analytical debates and political pressure that contributed to the Iraq fiasco were steadily intensifying.

Against this backdrop, the agency's analysts finally completed their assessment of the available information on North Korea's uranium activities, and Deputy Director John McLaughlin prepared to make a presentation to a principals' meeting that would include President Bush, Vice President Cheney, Secretary of Defense Rumsfeld, Secretary of State Powell, National Security Adviser Rice, and Richard Myers, the chairman of the Joint Chiefs of Staff. To get ready, McLaughlin had been holding a series of two- and three-hour sessions with agency analysts to make sure he understood the issue in all its complexity. A team of six analysts and one technical expert had drafted a highly technical thirty-page paper and attached it to a new National Intelligence Estimate summarizing the agency's conclusions. So rushed was the process that the final draft came off the printer the night before the principals' meeting. The bottom line, according to one of those involved, was "that North Korea has a production-scale enrichment program."

Yet McLaughlin found assembling the material in a coherent form to present to Bush and others to be a daunting task. "I recall having a difficult time trying to put it together," he told me, "because these are busy people. They don't have time for all the technical details so I had to boil it down to about five or six points that took them through the history, up to the point of why we would be convinced that such programs existed."

The problem, McLaughlin acknowledged, was that there was no obvious smoking gun. "There were some unknowns here. There were questions which couldn't be answered with confidence."

Putting his notes together, he was struck that this was a more complicated intelligence story than most. In other situations, you often have a clear picture. In this case, there was no image of a centrifuge facility; instead it was a complicated detective story. *If I just hand the principals a pile of papers,* he thought to himself, *they won't able to make sense of it.* McLaughlin knew how much was riding on how he presented the material. If he hyped it or overplayed it, Bush might overreact and do something rash. The challenge was to get the right balance between what was known and what was not known.

After Bush and the other principals took their seats at the White House Situation Room, McLaughlin began his presentation, working from handwritten notes. "I came in and said, 'We have a complicated issue here. It's complicated because I'm not going to put one single piece of intelligence on the table that will show with crystal clarity where we are. I've got to take you back a number of years, I've got to walk you through some complicated old data and then I've got to show you some new pieces that throw a new and different illumination on those old pieces.'"

In a summary lasting about ten minutes, he took the principals through what was known in 1997, 1998, 1999—and what had only come together in a more coherent picture in recent months. McLaughlin felt Bush and the others realized the seriousness of what they had heard. "It was immediately apparent to them, you could see the lightbulbs going on all around the room—the frame-work agreement was in deep trouble. They had to devise a response to that."

Colin Powell spoke up first. This had major ramifications for the Agreed Framework, he said. How confident were we? Was there any reason for doubt?

Others in the room followed suit. How far along were the North Koreans? When would Pyongyang actually have a uranium bomb? Did the CIA know where the material was located or whether an actual facility existed? McLaughlin had to walk a careful line. He made clear the intelligence community did not have specific answers to such questions. He reiterated that there was high confidence the North was acquiring materials consistent with a centrifuge program, but the CIA did not know where such a program was based or how far along it was.

The discussion lasted an hour. The consensus was clear. Business as usual was no longer possible with North Korea. "People understood that this was an important development that radiated across a number of areas and concerned a country that everyone regarded as unpredictable and dangerous," McLaughlin recalled. "It was one of the soberest meetings I'd ever been to."

# 6

# HIGH-LEVEL
# MEETINGS

WITHIN THE AMERICAN INTELLIGENCE COMMUNITY, THERE was virtual unanimity about the reliability of the information on North Korea's uranium procurement activities.

"There was very high confidence," said one former senior National Security Council official, "with no dissent from INR [the State Department's Bureau of Intelligence and Research, which would later challenge flawed assessments that Iraq had weapons of mass destruction] or anyone else that the North Koreans were embarked on a clandestine HEU [highly enriched uranium] program, that they had ramped up significantly, that they were spending lots of money around the world getting all the pieces."

But many questions remained unanswered. How advanced was the program? Had a production facility actually been constructed? How many years would it take before bombs could be produced? Above all, what were Pyongyang's motivation and ultimate intentions in starting the acquisition effort? And here, the consensus that had been achieved on the procurement intelligence broke down. In interpreting the information, and considering a policy response, the same ideological biases and political turf battles that had marked earlier debates over what to do about North Korea reemerged.

"Nobody has ever been able to say with confidence that the components have been anything more than components," conceded one former high-ranking official who had access to the intelligence. "No one has ever reported, like A. Q. Khan or anyone else, that they have visited a functioning centrifuge facility. I think that's a fair statement."

"We didn't nail this thing," said former deputy secretary of state Richard Armitage. "If you look at how certain the agency [CIA] was about Iraq, they were nowhere near that certain about an HEU facility." This distinction—between credible hard intelligence that the North Koreans were trying to procure components for a uranium program and the absence of any solid data to show that an actual uranium enrichment facility existed—is crucial. Given the enormous technical challenges involved in assembling a working system of centrifuges that could enrich uranium in sufficient quantities to produce nuclear weapons, the best judgment of the intelligence community was that, as a November 2002 CIA report noted, it would be "mid-decade" at the earliest before such a plant would be fully operational. It was equally possible the process could take longer. "Based on what we had discovered in terms of what they were trying to purchase," noted one former senior State Department official, "they were years away—five, seven, ten years or more away—from this capability." While still a source of serious concern, the longer time frame meant it might be possible to negotiate a resolution to the issue, without sparking a major new crisis on the Korean peninsula.

For Colin Powell, the intelligence made clear that North Korea was cheating, but, as one senior State Department official recalled, "he was always skeptical as to the urgency of it. He was always objective about the fact that these were reports of procurement of material, of equipment, rather than saying they had it up and running and operating it. . . . It wasn't an imminent danger. It was just another thing to deal with."

The debate between moderates and hard-liners over the urgency of the uranium information—and how the Bush administration should respond to it—depended on how one assessed the motivations of Kim Jong Il. This too was a subject where opinions were sharply divided.

The North Koreans don't talk about their internal decision making, so any judgments on Pyongyang's motives are necessarily speculative. But it is possible the North's pursuit of a uranium capability came not from a long-standing determination to cheat on the Agreed Framework, but from a combination of domestic crises and mounting frustration at what Pyongyang saw as Washington's failure to fully implement the 1994 accord.

Virtually all the accounts of the uranium effort agree that it began in 1997 or 1998, a period when the famine of the mid-1990s was at its peak. With hundreds of thousands dying of starvation and the economy in a freefall, North Korean society was subjected to unprecedented internal strains, just a few years after the collapse of the Soviet Union and other longtime allies. Adding to the regime's sense of vulnerability was the fact that few of the benefits Pyongyang expected from the Agreed Framework actually materialized. While the United States achieved its key goal up front—freezing the North's plutonium program—Pyongyang had more ambitious goals. For Pyongyang, the framework was above all a political document, holding out the possibility of a fundamental trans-formation of North Korea's long-hostile relationship with the United States, which had been the country's key objective since the early 1990s. The supply of heavy fuel oil and the construction of two light-water reactors were, in addition to the obvious economic benefits, seen as political symbols of a new rapproche-ment with Washington. LWRs are not the sort of thing a country gives to its enemy.

By 1997, however, incremental movement toward a diplomatic thaw had stalled, and it was in February of that year that North Korea had issued the first of several public warnings that the United States wasn't living up to its commit-ments under the framework deal. "If the U.S. does not intend to keep its com-mitment," the official Korean Central News Agency declared, "we have no idea of keeping up our nuclear freeze."[1] Private warnings to U.S. officials were just as explicit. The effort to acquire components for a pilot uranium enrichment pro-gram appears to have started not long afterward, and could well have been a hedge against the possibility that the anticipated benefits from the Agreed Framework would not materialize.

The initial sketchy intelligence had described Pyongyang's uranium pro-curement activities in the late 1990s as modest in scale, aimed at acquiring research and development know-how rather than a full-fledged production ca-pability. That appeared to change in 2001 and 2002, when, as John Bolton noted, "We had substantial evidence that the North Koreans were trying to create a production-scale uranium enrichment capacity that would allow them to get weapons-grade uranium to fashion into nuclear warheads."

As in the earlier stages of the development of the North's uranium effort, the timing is intriguing. In a one-page statement issued on November 19, 2002, the CIA stated, "We assess that North Korea embarked on the effort to develop a centrifuge-based uranium enrichment program about two years ago." Some in-telligence experts contend that Pyongyang had begun ramping up its procure-ment effort in 2000, at the very time that the Clinton administration was seeking a breakthrough for better relations. But it may be equally possible that the change of administration in Washington in 2001, and the hostile signals coming from President Bush and other officials, prompted Kim Jong Il to accelerate his covert uranium program.

Equally uncertain is the broader question of whether the North was prepared to trade its nuclear arms program in return for a deal that led to a fundamentally different relationship with the United States. For all its flaws, the Agreed Framework had shown that Kim Jong Il was willing to shut down his reactors at Yongbyon and put his stocks of plutonium under international inspection in return for political and economic benefits from the United States.

Throughout the ups and downs of the 1990s and the first two years of the Bush administration, the North's plutonium capabilities had remained frozen. Moreover, during the summer of 2002, both in public and in private, Pyongyang had tried to send conciliatory signals indicating that all outstanding issues with the United States were negotiable. On August 31, 2002, two days after John Bolton issued a blistering denunciation of the North's nuclear and missile programs during his controversial speech in Seoul, a North Korean Foreign Ministry spokesman responded by noting Bolton's concerns and declaring, "The DPRK clarified more than once that if the U.S. has a will to drop its hostile policy toward the DPRK it will have dialogue with the U.S. to clear the U.S. of its worries over its security."[2]

North Korean diplomats had also used back-channel lines of communication in the hope of conveying a similar message to Washington. In mid-August, scholar Leon Sigal had lunch in New York with Li Gun, the deputy permanent representative to North Korea's UN mission and his newly arrived successor, Han Song Ryol. Fluent English-speakers, they were two of Pyongyang's most experienced "America hands." Li had served for the past several years in New York and was returning to Pyongyang to head the Division of North American Affairs. Han had served at the UN in 1993, been involved in the 1994 nuclear negotiations, and stayed on in New York for three years working on the implementation of the Agreed Framework before being promoted to deputy director of the North Korean Foreign Ministry's Division of North American Affairs. Now, he had returned to New York as number two in Pyongyang's UN mission.[3]

During the lunch, Sigal raised John Bolton's public allegation that Pyongyang had a "covert nuclear weapons program in violation of the nonproliferation treaty." Sigal urged Han to persuade his government to "reiterate more explicitly its willingness to address the nuclear issues." In early September, Han sent Sigal an e-mail stating that the North was ready to negotiate. "DPRK is in a position to make a deal with the U.S.," Han wrote. "Those in Pyongyang [are] ready to solve U.S. security concerns in return [for] normalization of diplomatic relations with U.S. after ending its hostile policy. They believe that the U.S. asks them to disarm first, then get normalization and aid. What they want is [to] exchange them simultaneously or hopefully first the normalization then disarm because they are much weaker with less military than the U.S. and its allies. Therefore, they need to start negotiation with the U.S."

The fact that such a senior North Korean official had put in writing a willingness to discuss the issues of greatest concern to the Bush administration marked a potentially significant step. Sigal immediately drafted a memo to Assistant Secretary of State James Kelly, summarizing his exchanges with Han. "A potentially useful development in North Korea's nuclear stance has emerged from recent contacts with North Korean diplomats in New York," he wrote. "In a series of exchanges, Ambassador Han Song Ryol has underscored North Korea's willingness to address nuclear issues of concern to the United States."[4] The letter was hand-delivered to Kelly; Sigal never received a reply.

The overtures from Pyongyang came amid signs the North Korean regime was cautiously exploring the possibility of economic reforms. In 2001, Kim Jong Il had spent a week in China. Accompanied much of the time by Chinese premier Zhu Rongji, a leading architect of China's experiment with capitalist economics, the Dear Leader visited China's most advanced semiconductor plant, a joint venture with the Japanese company NEC, an auto factory built with investment from General Motors, and the gleaming new Shanghai stock exchange.

As one Chinese official noted, "Kim Jong Il knows the dramatic gap between China and North Korea in terms of economic development, and also between China and South Korea. That's why he pays special attention to economic reform."

Shortly after Kim's return from China, North Korean TV broadcast forty minutes of footage from his Shanghai tour. Kim was shown visiting the home of a Chinese worker, whose apartment contained a TV, refrigerator, and stereo set—all unimaginable luxuries for most North Koreans.[5] While North Korea's system was so opaque that drawing definitive conclusions about the Dear Leader's intentions was always a guessing game, these developments suggested that Kim was at least contemplating reform.

Then, in mid-2002, Pyongyang announced a major change in economic policy. Overnight, the government abolished food rations and announced that supply and demand would henceforth determine prices. To soften the blow of rising prices, wages were immediately increased. At the same time, farmers were given permission to grow crops on small private plots and sell them for a profit. Small free markets were legitimized, and economic decision making was decentralized, giving local industrial and agricultural managers more authority. The North Korean currency, the won, which had been pegged at the artificial rate of 2.2 to the dollar, was devalued. The new rate—150 to the dollar—came close to the prevailing black market rate and was intended to encourage foreign investment and make it easier for North Korean companies to export.

In addition, the government gave further sanction to the idea of special economic zones intended to lure foreign companies. A fledgling zone had already been established at Kaesong, close to the DMZ, and had begun to attract South Korean companies. Now plans were under way for a second zone, at Sinuiju on the border with China.

These steps, all still experimental, nonetheless represented the biggest change to the North's economy in decades. In part, they were a recognition by the government of facts on the ground—such as the collapse of the state food distribution system and the emergence of farmers' markets—that had followed the dislocations of the famine years. But they also suggested that Kim Jong Il, aware of the weakness of the economy, was seriously interested in exploring at least the possibility of reform.

Introducing any changes into a system as rigid and inefficient as North Korea's was never going to be easy. And Kim Jong Il ran the risk that if he did decide to truly open up his economy he could well set in motion forces that could undermine his long-term control. Yet to some analysts, the Dear Leader appeared willing to take the risk, since he was also moving to reinforce changes at home with improvements in North Korea's security environment. The effort to start talks with the Bush administration in the hope of neutralizing what Kim likely saw as Washington's desire for regime change appears to have been one key part of his strategy. Another was to forge a thaw with Japan, which offered the prospect of billions of dollars of economic assistance from Tokyo.

While internal pressures mounted in Washington to get tough with North Korea, Junichiro Koizumi, the leader of the most important U.S. ally in Asia, embarked on an entirely different diplomatic path. On September 17, 2002, the Japanese prime minister arrived in Pyongyang for a historic summit with Kim Jong Il.

For Koizumi, the pressing immediate issue was the fate of a number of Japanese citizens abducted in the 1970s and '80s. In secret negotiations that led up to the summit, the Japanese had been given clear indications that Kim Jong Il would acknowledge the abductions and perhaps even apologize. One public signal had come on September 14, just three days before the summit. In written responses to questions submitted by Japan's Kyodo News Agency, Kim Jong Il said it was time "to clean up the past unpleasant events that have taken place between the two countries."[6] Kim was clearly referring to Japan's brutal colonization of Korea, but also appears to have been obliquely hinting at his intention to put the abduction issue behind him.

Koizumi's broader goal, however, was the normalization of Japan's relations with North Korea as part of an effort to ease tensions in Northeast Asia. "Koizumi's view on North Korea was very simple," noted Columbia University Japan scholar and longtime Koizumi confidante Gerald Curtis. "If we can resolve the nuclear issue with the North Koreans, the abductee issue will not stand in the way of a rapid normalization between North Korea and Japan."

In New York to attend the UN General Assembly just before traveling to Pyongyang, Koizumi had been briefed on the uranium intelligence by President Bush. The United States, however, did not want Koizumi to raise the issue directly with Kim Jong Il. Rather, the Japanese leader was asked to be mindful of the potential seriousness of the situation, and not to underplay the importance of the nuclear issue during his meetings with Kim.

Arriving in Pyongyang on September 17, Koizumi began the first of two long sessions with Kim. The two men covered a range of security issues, with Koizumi telling Kim Japan was seriously concerned about North Korea's nuclear program. Listening, Japanese Foreign Ministry official Hitoshi Tanaka found Kim to be surprisingly talkative, referring in positive terms to Pyongyang's diplomatic dealings with the Clinton administration, and complaining that "something was very wrong" with the Bush administration. Despite his criticism, Kim told Koizumi he remained committed to resolving the nuclear and missile issues through dialogue and reaffirmed that North Korea would continue to abide by "all relevant agreements" on nuclear matters—a reference to the Agreed Framework.

The morning session ended, however, without Kim's making any reference to the abductees. Given the depth of Japanese concern over the issue, Koizumi had rejected a North Korean invitation to a formal meal. Instead, his delegation had brought their own *bento* Japanese-style lunch boxes from Tokyo. Sitting in a room at a Pyongyang guesthouse they were certain the North Koreans had bugged, Deputy Chief Cabinet Secretary Shinzo Abe, a longtime hawk on North Korean issues, complained bitterly, telling Koizumi that if Kim was not going to be forthcoming on the abduction issue the delegation should simply return home.

Reconvening after lunch, Kim Jong Il delivered a bombshell. Reversing years of denials, he admitted that North Korean agents had kidnapped Japanese citizens in order to learn the Japanese language and utilize them for operations in South Korea. He said six of the Japanese had died, but confirmed that five were alive, and that he was prepared to let them return home temporarily. Kim was quoted as telling Koizumi, "This happened over decades of hostile relations and I want to talk about it frankly." He described the kidnappers as "misguided people," apologized for the incidents, and promised it would never happen again. That commitment was formalized in a "Pyongyang declaration" that the two leaders signed at the end of their talks.[7]

For the proud and usually secretive North Korean leader, taking public responsibility for such an unsavory episode was an unprecedented step. Kim had clearly calculated that openly admitting past transgressions would put the issue to rest and pave the way for a major improvement in Pyongyang's relations with Tokyo. The North had much riding on such an outcome. Tokyo had made clear it was prepared to offer a huge aid package—between $5 and $10 billion—to compensate for Japan's decades of harsh colonial rule in Korea. In Japan, opinion polls showed the initial public reaction to the summit was overwhelmingly positive. For his part, Koizumi was convinced that normalization could happen in a matter of months. Neither he nor any other senior Japanese officials, however, reckoned on the emotional public response in Japan to Kim's acknowledgment, and the news that so many of the abductees were dead. Within weeks, euphoria had turned to fury, fed by the conservative Japanese media and the bitterness of relatives of the abductees who had died. Support for a rapid improvement in relations evaporated.

In the immediate aftermath of the summit, however, Koizumi was more convinced than ever that it was possible to do business with Kim Jong Il. And he quickly conveyed that message by phoning his good friend George W. Bush.

As the news of the uranium finding reverberated through the Bush administration, hard-liners spoke out against the idea of any meeting with the North Koreans. Although there had been agreement earlier in the summer to send Assistant Secretary of State James Kelly to Pyongyang—a trip put off both by the North-South naval clash in June and the initial reports about uranium— now some leading figures, including Vice President Cheney and Defense Secretary Rumsfeld, objected to the idea of having the visit at all. Recalling the thinking at the time, a former aide to Cheney said, "What's the point of going and talking with the North Koreans about this? Say we confront them, all they're going to do is deny it, and then where are we? I thought what kind of a position are we in if we go and we confront them and then they say, 'No we don't, what are you talking about? Show me where the facility is?'"

Both John Bolton and Robert Joseph also opposed initiating diplomatic contact, as did Rumsfeld, who sent a memo making this argument to the White House. As a fall-back position, however, Rumsfeld said that if there were to be a meeting, then Bolton or Joseph, both trusted members of the hard-line camp, should lead the U.S. team.[8] At this point, according to a former senior intelligence official, "There was no guarantee there was even going to be a trip. There was no sense that we have to go and talk to these guys and solve the problem."

According to Randy Schriver, who was then chief of staff for Deputy Secretary of State Armitage, "The normal debate with Bolton, Joseph, the Office of the Vice President was, do you take whatever evidence you have, present it, and give them an opportunity to get out of the cul-de-sac or do you start punishing them right away? And I think that the Bolton notion was, why in the world would you take this to the North Koreans and potentially compromise [intelligence] sources but also express any confidence at all that they would do the right thing because they're not? So the approach should be to punish, talk to allies, friends, and others to punish rather than pursue this diplomatically. Powell and Armitage, despite their low level of confidence in Pyongyang, and Kim Jong Il doing the right thing, always came down on the side of talking to him."

Amid continuing debate, Japan's foreign minister Yuriko Kawaguchi arrived in Washington to brief the United States on Koizumi's visit. When National Security Adviser Condoleezza Rice was briefly called out of a meeting with Kawaguchi at the White House, the foreign minister turned to NSC Asia expert and longtime Japan hand Michael Green and asked if she should urge Rice to send someone to Pyongyang?

Green, weary of battling his NSC colleague Bob Joseph and other hardliners, encouraged her to do so. It was not the first time that the Asia analysts at the NSC would use the Japanese, who were widely respected throughout the administration, to buttress their own position in policy fights with nonproliferation hard-liners like Joseph and Bolton.

When Rice rejoined the meeting, Kawaguchi made her pitch. "I think it's an interesting question and a good time to think about it," the national security adviser replied. Soon after, Prime Minister Koizumi telephoned President Bush to make the same argument, telling Bush that based on his discussions with Kim Jong Il, it was a good time for an American envoy to go to Pyongyang.

The South Koreans had been urging the administration to hold talks ever since the United States canceled the scheduled trip to Pyongyang by Jim Kelly in July, but the intervention by the Japanese tipped the balance. A decision was made to resurrect the Kelly mission. But the debate now shifted to how he should conduct himself and what he should say. In many ways, this debate crystallized the Bush adminsitration's divisions over Korea.

In August, 2002 David Straub, a soft-spoken, bespectacled twenty-six-year State Department veteran, had become director of the department's Office of Korean Affairs. A fluent Korean speaker, Straub had just completed his third tour in Seoul. With the decision to send Kelly to Pyongyang, Straub, who would be part of the delegation, was given the task of drafting the assistant secretary's talking points, with the help of the Korea Desk's deputy director Ferial Saeed. On such a diplomatic mission, it was standard procedure for the State Department to take the lead, although the interagency process would require clearance by a host of other players at the State's Bureau of Nonproliferation under John Bolton, the National Security Council, the Pentagon, the Office of the Vice President, and elsewhere in the bureaucracy.

Straub had been around a long time and was not naïve; he had witnessed earlier power struggles over Korea policy from his vantage point in Seoul. Like his bosses—Jim Kelly, Richard Armitage, and Colin Powell—he favored tough-minded negotiations with North Korea to resolve the uranium issue, and he tried to keep the political environment in Washington in mind as he crafted Kelly's talking points. The strength of the hard-liners in that environment had been brought home to him by an episode that had occurred shortly after he had taken over the Korea Desk. One evening after he had prepared a memo on North Korea for Kelly, the assistant secretary looked at it, sighed, and said to Straub, "This is a 'kick-me' memo."

"What do you mean?" a puzzled Straub asked.

"If I send this out for interagency clearance," Kelly replied, "they're going to kick me in the rear."

S traub's initial draft of Kelly's talking points stressed the administration's commitment to the so-called Bold Approach. It noted the uranium issue as a matter of serious concern that had to be addressed, but folded that into a broader discussion of the many other questions on the U.S.–North Korea agenda as part of an overall process of rapprochement. It was only in that context, Straub believed, that it might be possible to make headway with the North.

The preliminary draft was sent to working-level officials elsewhere in the bureaucracy, where it ran into immediate opposition for failing to make uranium the central—or only—issue on the agenda. Mark Groombridge, John Bolton's chief Asia aide, led the criticism. "Our argument was that the nuclear issue should be front and center," he recalled. "They are in direct violation of the Agreed Framework. End of sentence. Stop."

Groombridge had developed key allies elsewhere in the bureaucracy who now worked with him to force a radical revision in the proposed talking points. Jodi Green at the Pentagon, Samatha Ravich at Vice President Cheney's office, and John Rood, who worked on nonproliferation issues with Bob Joseph at the NSC, all shared Groombridge's view that the diplomats at the State's Bureau of East Asian and Pacific Affairs (EAP) were little more than "EAPeasers." With their backing, Groombridge demanded that most of Straub's draft be deleted and replaced with a tougher approach.

At the NSC, Bob Joseph joined the chorus of criticism. In an interview for this book, he was scathing in describing Kelly's proposed approach. "What are you going to do, ignore that they're pursuing nuclear weapons through enriched uranium? Which is in violation of the Agreed Framework and the NPT and the safeguards? All of those commitments, the North-South Agreement, they violated everything. So what were the options? You could ignore it and go through with the Agreed Framework, which had now been demonstrated to be exactly what any of us had thought it was at first. Or you could call them on it, and be serious. You've got to be seen as serious if you have any prospect of them giving up their nuclear weapons and their program. If they don't think you're serious, they're not going to give it up."

Those who favored negotiations to resolve the uranium issue were convinced the hard-liners wanted to use the situation not to find a solution but rather to achieve their long-standing goal of getting rid of the Agreed Framework altogether.

Said Colin Powell, "They wanted to use this as a flaming red star cluster into the sky that the North Koreans have cheated, abrogated the Agreed Framework, we always told you this was a bad idea."

But the thinking behind the approach that Straub sought to articulate for Kelly was hardly woolly-headed. "We so-called EAPeasers, as we were known, okay, we're still trying to reach out to them [the North Koreans]," acknowledged one former State Department official. "But we were never trying to appease them. We understood their system was bankrupt, and if you didn't want a war, and you didn't want a collapse, there was going to have to be a change in that system. They could do it voluntarily, or it could happen involuntarily. So the HEU program, we wanted them to agree to stop it. 'Okay, you've been caught. And, okay, admit it, and here's what you've got to admit, sign on the bottom line, and let's start talking about real serious economic cooperation for transforming your system and doing a soft landing.' But it wasn't sudden and dramatic, and emotionally satisfying."

But in the climate in Washington that autumn—with an apparent military victory over the Taliban in Afghanistan and the president having made the decision to invade Iraq—there was little support for such a nuanced diplomatic approach. "At this point in the lead-up to Iraq, and in that mental frame, there was . . . a sense that we had a lot of coercive diplomatic leverage," recalled one former NSC official, "so of course we should keep the pressure on, and of course we should take advantage of this enormous leverage and momentum we had."

Deputy Defense Secretary Paul Wolfowitz and Deputy National Security Adviser Stephen Hadley weighed in, insisting that Kelly's presentation be toughened by adding language to emphasize North Korea's conventional military threat and its violations of human rights. And Groombridge and his allies played what they called the "Cheney card." They decided that Samantha Ravich, who worked for the vice president, would outline the rival positions to him and seek his active intervention with the president. Ravich held such hard-line views that her many critics in the State Department had disparagingly nick-named her Samantha "Rabid."

Soon after came a decision from what Groombridge called "the highest level" that the uranium issue would be "front and center" in Kelly's presenta-tion to the North Koreans. "We kept him on the tightest leash possible," acknowledged one leading hard-liner, "and for good reason. We didn't trust Powell and Armitage."

This decision was hardly the only example of the extraordinarily influential role Cheney had come to play in Bush's foreign policy. To Powell and Ar-mitage, it was a central reason why their more moderate approach—on North Korea and other issues—was so frequently torpedoed. "We didn't have the sense the vice president was going to be this sort of temple guard dog, gate-keeper," Armitage acknowledged. "The vice president would be in with the president all the time, so a lot of these decisions were made without being served up as I'd come to normally expect decisions—and they were just made."

According to Lawrence Wilkerson, Powell's chief of staff, "The network Cheney put in place was ruthless, single-minded, focused, and had a strategy and a vision. The way they implemented it was to go to meetings, whether they were official meetings like the policy coordinating committee meetings that Jim [Kelly] would chair with regard to North Korea, or whether they were just in-formal meetings like Jim's East Asia informal every Monday at three [a weekly gathering Kelly held to discuss current policy issues]. They just sat there, and they soaked up the debate and took it back to the vice president's office. If they sensed that the debate was going rapidly 180 degrees away from what the vice president wanted, they intervened and stopped the debate."

"The hard-line approach stems directly from the attitudes taken from the president and the vice president," David Straub observed years later. "And therefore, it was Secretary Powell and Deputy Secretary Armitage and Jim Kelly and the people I worked for who were out of step with the president. And it's no wonder we had difficulties, because Secretary Powell was trying to engage in real negotiations, or would have liked to I think engage in real negotiations with the North Koreans, and the president and the vice president did not want that. It was that simple."

Jim Kelly was not a confrontational person. Moreover, his dislike for the North Koreans was as deep as most of the hard-liners. Although he may have been privately frustrated, he accepted his final instructions, like the career military man he was, without complaint. In an interview for this book, he acknowledged, "I wasn't heading to Pyongyang to negotiate."

It was not just on the substance of the negotiations that the hard-liners imposed their views. They sought to control the atmospherics as well. In keeping with normal diplomatic practice, Kelly's delegation planned to host a dinner for the North Koreans, since they would unquestionably invite him to a welcoming banquet after his arrival. When she heard of the plan, National Security Adviser Condoleezza Rice reportedly went "ballistic." Kelly was ordered to cancel plans for the dinner and was also instructed not to make any toast to Kim Jong Il.

"We're going there to confront them on their cheating of a bilateral agreement with us," one former State Department official recalls her saying. "That is not an occasion for which you raise champagne glasses."

On October 3, 2002, a U.S. Air Force C-21, the military equivalent of the Lear Jet 35A business jet, roared down the runway at the American air base in Osan, South Korea—its destination Pyongyang. Apart from the two-man crew, the plane carried Jim Kelly and five other members of his eight-person delegation. The remaining two, one an interpreter, the other, a Korean-speaking foreign service officer, had set out for the North Korean capital by road, crossing the Demilitarized Zone north of Seoul for the two-hour drive along a mostly deserted four-lane highway to Pyongyang.

The transportation arrangements were highly unusual and full of diplomatic symbolism. Once the Bush administration had made the decision to send Kelly, Jack Pritchard, who was still nominally the point man for contacts with the North Koreans, met in New York with Pyongyang's UN ambassador, Pak Gil Yon, to discuss the logistics of the visit. The normal route for foreigners visiting the North was to take a North Korean Air Koryo flight from Beijing—a journey requiring a long detour through the Chinese capital and limited to two flights a week on ancient and uncomfortable Soviet-built Ilyushin or Tupolev jets. The other time-consuming route, used by U.S. officials in the past, was to fly from Japan through international airspace and then into North Korean airspace. Pritchard, however, requested special permission to bring the group directly from South Korea, where Kelly planned to stop to brief officials in Seoul before his meetings in Pyongyang. Given the long-standing suspicions on the divided peninsula, this kind of arrangement was not something the North Koreans readily granted. Pritchard saw the gestures as confidence-building measures that would require coordination between American and North Korean military officials. Somewhat to his surprise, it took the North Koreans just seventeen hours to respond positively. All the requests were granted, which Pritchard interpreted as a sign of how eager the North Koreans were to resume serious diplomatic engagement with the United States.

B ut the atmosphere began to sour the moment Kelly's group arrived. Normally, the protocol-conscious North Koreans would greet such a senior U.S. diplomat with an official of similar rank, usually Vice Foreign Minister Kim Gye Gwan, a veteran of many encounters with the United States. Instead, an anxious low-level functionary, the head of the American Affairs Bureau at the North Korean Foreign Ministry, was waiting at Pyongyang's bleak and virtually deserted Sunam airport. He escorted the Americans to a lounge and began to complain bitterly about the dinner arrangements.

The problem was that while Kelly's delegation was en route, the State Department's Korea Desk had advised the North Korean UN mission of Washington's decision—rammed through by the hard-liners—that Kelly would not host a reciprocal banquet on the second day of his visit. Somehow, when the news was transmitted to Pyongyang, North Korean officials had misunderstood and believed that Kelly was not being allowed to attend the dinner of welcome they had planned for the first night. It took some time for Kelly's team to explain that, while he would not be hosting a reciprocal banquet on the next day, he would attend the meal that first evening.

David Straub was appalled. "Of course, this is gratuitous and stupid. Diplomats have meals with each other. Unless they're ready to go to war, that's what diplomats do. It's part of the process, and there are good reasons for it. But we had these narrow-minded ideologues in the White House staff who were insistent that Jim Kelly, a man who had served his country with distinction for forty or fifty years, would do what they said or else. Now I can imagine why the North Koreans would be pissed, because I was pissed about it."

As another member of Kelly's team noted, "Arguing over dinner plans was not a good start."

The schedule agreed by the two sides called for an initial meeting with Vice Foreign Minister Kim Gye Gwan, a welcoming banquet that evening, a longer second session with Kim the next morning, and a concluding session with First Vice Foreign Minister Kang Sok Ju, who was Kim Jong Il's most senior foreign policy adviser. On the afternoon of October 3, the two sides convened at the North Korean Foreign Ministry—a stolid, Stalinist-style building just off Kim Il Sung Square, the site of so many of the regime's mass parades and rallies. As the host, Kim offered Kelly, his guest, the opportunity to speak first. Kelly had brought with him both a short and a somewhat longer version of his talking points. Reading from his approved short script, Kelly began by saying he had intended to start a dialogue about the Bold Approach. However, he continued, it was not possible to do so because the United States had irrefutable information and intelligence that led it to believe North Korea was involved in a covert program to develop weapons through uranium enrichment. Until that was undone, he stressed, no dialogue was possible.

Kelly offered no evidence. The U.S. intelligence community would not have allowed him to do so, and there was general agreement on the American side that it was to Washington's advantage not to let the North Koreans know how much the United States actually knew. But, realizing how much rested on North Korea's reply, Kelly urged Kim not to respond immediately.

"I asked him not to give a particular answer," Kelly recalled. "I wanted it to be a considered answer."

The assistant secretary spent the rest of his presentation, which lasted just under an hour, covering the other items on the U.S. agenda, such as missiles, conventional weapons, terrorism, and human rights. He also noted that not dealing with the uranium enrichment program would have an adverse affect on North Korea's efforts to expand its relations with Japan and South Korea. As he spoke, Jack Pritchard, who had spent literally thousands of hours in meetings with Kim Gye Gwan, carefully studied the North Korean official's response.

Kim sat silently, his lips pursed, his face flushed and set in a deep frown. North Korean officials would not agree to be interviewed for this book, but barely a month after the Kelly meetings, Kim Gye Gwan shared his reactions to Kelly's presentation with Senate Foreign Relations Committee staff member Frank Jannuzi, who was visiting Pyongyang. Kim said he arrived at the meeting full of optimism. Despite all the ups and downs, the North Koreans believed this would be the moment when they would really begin to move things forward with the Bush administration.

In a paper prepared a few weeks later for the Woodrow Wilson Center for International Scholars, Jannuzi elaborated on his November discussions with Kim. Describing Kim's talking points for the Kelly meeting as "consistent with this view of an insecure North Korean regime seeking a way in from the cold," Jannuzi said that "the North reportedly laid out a position marked by flexibility on four key issues of concern to the United States," including the timing of IAEA special nuclear inspections, North Korea's exports of ballistic missiles, the Bush administration's preference for conventional power plants rather than the light-water reactors stipulated in the Agreed Framework, and the status of U.S. troops in South Korea.[9] Kim said he was completely unprepared for, and totally stunned by, Kelly's accusation.

At the conclusion of Kelly's presentation, Kim called for a brief break. As the diplomats made small talk in the hallway outside the meeting room, Kim

Gye Gwan suddenly raced off down the corridor. Although members of the U.S. delegation were sure the room was bugged, they assumed Kim, who appeared unaware of any uranium program and genuinely shocked by Kelly's dramatic accusation, wanted to provide his superiors—especially First Vice Foreign Minister Kang Sok Ju—a personal report on what had just transpired before they saw the transcript from the hidden North Korean translator listening through the bug.

When the session resumed, Kim delivered his response. "I had asked him not to give a particular answer," recalled Kelly. "He, of course, did offer an immediate denial."

Kim declared that the claim of a secret uranium program was false, and part of a plot by those in the United States opposed to better relations between Washington and Pyongyang. He said the allegation had no more credibility than the U.S. accusation in 1998 that North Korea had a clandestine underground nuclear facility in Kumchangri—a claim that, when Chuck Kartman and other U.S. officials were allowed to inspect the site, turned out to be false. He also accused Washington of using the uranium issue to block Pyongyang from making progress on its relations with Seoul and Tokyo. Having made his denial, Kim returned to the rest of his talking points.

The meeting soon concluded, and after a brief rest, Kim hosted the Americans for an elaborate welcoming banquet. In his memoir, Pritchard described the dinner as "lavish," including "fruit, raw salmon, vegetables, fried pigeon, roast pork, lobster and steamed fish, rice cakes, quail egg consommé, rainbow trout, pine nut porridge, *sinsollo* [a kind of Korean hot pot], mushroom and pheasant meatballs, cold noodles and tea. It is little wonder," he concluded, "given the effort and expense involved, that the North Koreans appeared offended that the United States had withdrawn its offer to host a reciprocal dinner."[10]

The banquet also presented Kelly's first protocol challenge, as he had been expressly forbidden by the hard-liners from offering a toast to the North Koreans. When Kim Kye Gwan raised his glass, Pritchard and the other members of the U.S. delegation wondered how Kelly would respond. In a low-key manner, the assistant secretary raised his own glass—barely—in response. Wrote Pritchard, "I could imagine the consternation in Washington as one of [Kelly's] 'political minders' reported his transgression on their return."[11]

The next morning, the Americans held a second session with Kim. Kelly repeated almost word-for-word his presentation of the previous day. Kim, too, offered little new, simply reiterating his accusation that the United States was seeking to pressure North Korea, and dismissing the uranium allegations as "not worthy of a response."[12]

After a brief and awkward courtesy call on the head of North Korea's

Supreme People's Assembly, Kim Yong Nam, during which no substantive issues were addressed, Kelly's group returned to the Foreign Ministry to meet Kang Sok Ju in what was to be one of the most crucial encounters in the history of American diplomacy with North Korea. A close confidant of both Kim Il Sung and Kim Jong Il, the blunt, tough-minded First Vice Foreign Minister Kang was the dominant figure in the North Korean foreign policy apparatus and had been a key player in many of Pyongyang's diplomatic dealings with the United States during the previous half-dozen years.

His remarks at this meeting were a bombshell—words that Kelly and his stunned delegation took to be an acknowledgment of the U.S. claims that North Korea did indeed have a clandestine uranium program. When Kang's remarks were reported back to Washington, they became the catalyst that transformed dealing with North Korea from an important but second-tier Bush administration foreign policy concern into a major crisis with global ramifications—one that led to the unraveling of the Agreed Framework, the restarting of Pyongyang's plutonium weapons program, North Korea's withdrawal from the nonproliferation treaty, and a dramatic weakening of the entire international system to control the spread of nuclear weapons. The meeting further strengthened the resolve of the hard-liners in Washington and ultimately led to North Korea's October 2006 nuclear test and the diplomatic fallout that followed.

Yet even years later, precisely what Kang said—and what he intended—remains a source of controversy and dispute. The issue is dogged by questions about North Korean rhetorical style and use of language, the accuracy of interpretation, the lack of thorough follow-up questioning by Kelly's team, Pyongyang's misunderstanding of the Bush administration, and the disdain for all suggestions of subtlety or compromise in the harsh American policy response. The U.S. government has never released its transcript of the meeting. Repeated efforts by groups such as the National Security Archive—which is based at George Washington University and has successfully acquired thousands of previously classified documents—to gain access to the transcript through the Freedom of Information Act have been rebuffed. For their part, North Korean officials and the North Korean media have produced their own incomplete and politically tailored accounts. Under these circumstances, and without a publicly available transcript, reconstructing the meeting remains a difficult task.

The account that follows is based primarily on extensive interviews with Kelly and several other members of his delegation, supplemented by an account in Jack Pritchard's book, *Failed Diplomacy*; by observations and insights from several people at high levels in the U.S. government who did see the transcript after Kelly returned to Washington; by accounts of several Americans who had the opportunity to discuss the encounter with the North Koreans during visits to Pyongyang in the following months; and by several official commentaries in the North Korean media.

As Kelly and his colleagues arrived at the Foreign Ministry late in the afternoon of October 4, they were greeted with handshakes by Kang Sok Ju, Kim Gye Gwan, and other North Korean officials. On Kelly's team were three Korean speakers. One, Tong Kim, a naturalized South Korean, was the official U S. government interpreter. He had been a senior translator for many years, although some members of Kelly's delegation privately felt his skills had declined with the passage of time. The second, foreign service officer Julie Kim, was a Korean-American. The third Korean speaker, David Straub, had learned Korean for his assignments at the U.S. Embassy in Seoul.

Kang politely asked Kelly if the Americans wanted to go first, but Kelly replied, "You're the host. Please go ahead."

Kang, speaking from notes, then began a thirty-minute monologue, which was translated by the North Koreans' regular interpreter, Chae Sun Hui. Rumored to be the daughter of a senior official, she was a full-fledged diplomat at the North Korean Foreign Ministry. Although her primary function was as an interpreter, some of the Americans suspected she may have played a more important role in the internal deliberations of the North Koreans who dealt with the United States.

"She is clearly not your run-of-the mill interpreter," said one U.S. diplomat who subsequently had dealings with her. "She clearly has policy influence." She also had a close relationship with Kim Gye Gwan—so close that some American officials believed, with no way to confirm their speculation, that Chae and Kim were romantically involved.

There were also concerns on the part of some of Kelly's team about the quality of her translating work. Jack Pritchard recalled an episode at a meeting in New York some years before when Tong Kim had reinterpreted something Miss Chae had said, and she had gotten so angry she had stalked off muttering, "You don't need me here anymore," leaving Kim Gye Gwan in the embarrassing position of not having an interpreter for a brief period.

Kang Sok Ju began his presentation by saying that after receiving a detailed report from Kim Gye Gwan on the earlier session with Kelly, he had met through the night with senior officials from the armed forces, the defense procurement sector, and other government ministries to consider how to respond. As he listened, David Straub thought Kim was describing the Pyongyang version of a night-long deputies' meeting or principals' meeting. Although Kang made no mention of Kim Jong Il, several of the Americans assumed that on a matter of such importance, the Dear Leader himself must have been briefed. Stressing that he spoke on behalf of both the government and the Korean Workers' Party, Kang then launched into a scathing denunciation of U.S. policy. Pointing to the inclusion of North Korea in the Axis of Evil and on a list of potential targets for nuclear attack under the president's doctrine of preemptive strikes against rogue states, Kang said the Bush administration's actions had effectively nullified the Agreed Framework.[13]

In an interview, Kelly recalled Kang's tone as "deadly serious" but laced with sarcasm. To Pritchard, Kang "was flushed. He appeared angry. His voice was rising on occasion. He was lecturing. He was sarcastic on one hand and very defiant on the other." In his memoir, Pritchard quotes Kang as saying sarcastically, "We are part of the Axis of Evil and you are a gentleman. This is our relationship. We cannot discuss matters like gentlemen. If we disarm ourselves because of U.S. pressure, then we will become like Yugoslavia or Afghanistan's Taliban, to be beaten to death."[14]

As he spoke, Kang made a series of references to Kelly's allegations of a uranium enrichment program. All the Americans, however, agree that at no point did the North Korean official explicitly confirm the allegations. "That's the most sensitive part of this stuff, to say exactly what he said," recalled David Straub. "But I will go so far as to say he did not flatly say, 'We have a uranium enrichment program to build nuclear weapons.'"

What Kang did say, according both to the Americans and those who have seen a North Korean version of the transcript, was that North Korea was "entitled" to possess such weapons and had even more powerful weapons as well. In the official Foreign Ministry statement of October 25, the Korean Central News Agency described Kang's statement as follows: "The DPRK made itself very clear to the special envoy of the U.S. President that the DPRK was entitled to possess not only nuclear weapon but any type of weapon more powerful than that so as to defend its sovereignty and right to existence from the ever-growing nuclear threat by the U.S."[15]

The reference to an "even more powerful weapon" alarmed the Americans almost as much as the declaration about being "entitled" to possess nukes. In his book, Jack Pritchard notes, "We understood him to mean that Pyongyang was prepared to manufacture weapons that were even more developed than uranium-based weapons, whether they turned out to be biological or chemical weapons, plutonium-based nuclear weapons (which we suspected the North Koreans already had the capability to produce), or something else."[16] After news of the meeting became public, other North Korea watchers were convinced it was a reference to their spirit as a nation or their ideology of *juche* or self-reliance.

To Kelly, Kang's message was clear. "He didn't say that in so many words, but he clearly inferred that they were pursuing a uranium enrichment program as part of their broader nuclear weapons program." Listening across the table, Kelly scribbled a note to Pritchard, who was sitting to his left. "Jack," it read, "are you hearing what I am hearing?" Pritchard quickly scrawled an affirmative reply.

It was a reaction all the Americans shared.

"He did not flatly say, 'We have a uranium enrichment program,'" said David Straub. "But he spent thirty minutes responding to the previous presentations . . . talking about it in such a way that he left every single member of the delegation independently saying, 'He's acknowledged the program.'"

When Kang paused, Kelly responded. According to National Security Council Asia specialist Michael Green, "Jim said, 'If you are saying that you have this HEU program because of the president's utterances in reference to Axis of Evil in the last few years, that contradicts what we know, which is that you have been working this program since well before Madeleine Albright came here as Secretary of State.'"

In his book, Pritchard describes Kang as replying by repeating that the United States had said that North Korea was making nuclear weapons, and adding "But what about the U.S.? The U.S. is also making nuclear weapons; we have to do the same."[17]

Green struggled to decipher the piece of paper containing Kang's talking points, which he could see upside down from across the table. The NSC staffer noted what appeared to be four bullet points. Kang now proceeded to spell out three of them. If the Bush administration would agree to respect North Korea's sovereignty, sign a nonaggression treaty, and not interfere with its economic development, including improving relations with other countries, Kang declared, Pyongyang was willing to address the concerns Kelly had raised. He also hinted that the North was interested in resurrecting the idea of a meeting between the U.S. president and Kim Jong Il, something it had sought without success in the waning days of the Clinton administration.[18]

It was a classic North Korean response. Caught off guard, and ultrasensitive to the notion of being pushed around by anyone, especially the United States, Kang reacted with bluster, accusations, harsh rhetoric, and seemingly improbable demands. At the same time, however, he was in effect putting the uranium issue on the table, sending a strong signal that if Washington were willing to engage in a broad negotiation aimed at resolving the full range of issues dividing the two countries—which was, after all, what Pyongyang had believed Kelly's purpose was in making his visit—then the North was ready to address U.S. worries about the uranium program.

Looking back years later, David Straub came to believe Kang's strategy was neither to confirm nor deny the U.S. allegation, but to use it as a mechanism to jump-start the negotiations with Washington that Pyongyang had long desired, and that Kang's forceful, often combative personality created less ambiguity than he had intended.

"My very, very strong impression is that he had gotten instructions from his leadership to leave every one of us with the impression that they were acknowledging the program but they were willing to negotiate about it," said Straub. "And in fact, he specifically proposed negotiations, and he even hinted at the desirability of a summit meeting between our two countries. What happened, though, is he may have been a little too good, and they may have intended to leave a little more ambiguity in our minds about what he was saying than he intended. So we all generally came out of that meeting understanding him to be acknowledging the HEU program."

Straub was also convinced that Kang Sok Ju's behavior was the result of the North Koreans' fundamental misreading of George W. Bush. Pyongyang's previous experience of dealing with Americans was primarily during the Clinton administration, when Washington was consistently willing to seek negotiated solutions to even the most contentious of issues. "As of October 2002," Straub observed, "the North Koreans still did not fully understand George W. Bush and his administration, and thought they could get him to react like the Clinton administration did." What the North didn't realize was that things were different in the Bush administration, where most officials weren't interested in negotiations, but in North Korea's capitulation to U.S. demands.

To Jim Kelly, Kang's monologue was "a characteristic performance in the sense that it was bad news, worse news, terrible news, nothing can be done, but perhaps something can be done. He set out some conditions—one had to do with contact at a very high level—that offered some prospects." But even though Kelly recognized that Kang was offering negotiations, "I wasn't there to negotiate."

In fact, Kelly's hands were tied by his own rigid instructions, which were to confront the North Koreans and demand they end the uranium program while ruling out any negotiations on the subject. The process of drafting Kelly's talking points had been so dominated by the hard-liners that, prior to the trip, no one had even gamed out what he should say in the event that Pyongyang did acknowledge his accusation, as the U.S. delegation was convinced that Kang Sok Ju had just done.

"Of course we had talked about what happens if they admit to the highly enriched uranium program," Pritchard said later, "but the conversation then was that it was highly unlikely. So there really wasn't a plan in place to take that thought-process to what do we do if they admit to that program."

Moreover, in keeping with a pattern of behavior established earlier in the

administration, Kelly did little to press Kang for further details. "I don't remember a 'Please repeat for the tape recorder . . . are you saying you have an
HEU program?' " recalled Michael Green. "It would have been odd. It's hard
to describe the dynamic and the atmosphere at the time, but I think it was more
important that Jim was right. There was nothing in our minds from the translation that would make us doubt it." In fact, as Kelly acknowledged with some
chagrin years later, no one on the U.S. delegation had even thought to slip a
small recording device in a pocket.

Instead, Kelly said bluntly that what Kang had told him was most unwel-
come news, which he had to report immediately back to Washington.

"And the fact that he let them know he was not going to negotiate under
duress or under pressure like that after they cheated was a very important message too," added Michael Green. "It was very obvious the North Koreans
didn't expect that, and they looked shocked when [Kelly] said, 'I'm leaving.'
He closed his notebook dramatically and left."

Kelly's team returned to the Koryo Hotel in central Pyongyang, surprised,
disturbed, and, in the words of one member of the delegation, in a state of
"shock." Convinced that what they'd heard from Kang represented a "smoking
gun," most felt an urgent need to get the word back to senior officials in Washington. Stuck in a hotel where every phone was bugged, there was some consideration, even though it was the end of the day, of trying to leave Pyongyang
immediately, rather than the following morning as originally planned. Logistical
difficulties with securing permission for their plane to make a night-time departure and for a vehicle to cross back over the DMZ made that impossible. Instead, David Straub got on the phone and called James Hoare, Chargé
d'Affaires at the recently opened British Embassy in Pyongyang.


Jim Hoare was a thirty-three-year veteran of the British Foreign Service, a
longtime Asia hand who had served in both Seoul and Beijing. In early 2001,
he had arrived in Pyongyang to set up an embassy and pave the way for the eventual presence of a British ambassador, following the establishment of formal
diplomatic relations between Britain and North Korea in December 2001. That
move had been one of many Kim Jong Il had undertaken in 2000—including the
North-South summit and hosting Madeleine Albright—as the North Korean
leader sought to break out of his country's long-standing international isolation.
Although the Swedish Embassy in Pyongyang had long looked after U.S. interests in the North Korean capital, when plans for Kelly's trip were finalized, the
British Foreign Office offered the U.S. delegation the use of a newly established
secure communications system at its embassy should the need arise.

Since Kelly's arrival the previous day, Hoare had heard nothing from the U.S. team. Now, late on a Friday afternoon, Straub was on the phone, saying something had come up and the Americans wanted to take the British up on their offer. With work to further improve the still-shabby embassy premises under way, Hoare had abandoned his normal suit that day for much less formal attire. Looking, in his words, "very scruffy indeed," he set out with two embassy cars flying the Union Jack to collect the American delegation.

To David Straub and the rest of the anxious Americans, "the Brits felt at that moment to most of us sort of like the cavalry coming in to the rescue, and they picked us up and they took us over there." The agitation of the U.S. group was visible in their expressions. "Their faces were grim and flushed," Hoare recalled.

The British communications system was located in the embassy's only "secure" room, a tiny space barely able to accommodate two people. It consisted of one classified machine, which encrypted a message as it was typed for transmission to the Foreign Office. In an adjacent room, interpreter Tong Kim and Julie Kim sat at a table, going over their notes to compose an agreed-upon version of what they had heard. Straub, meanwhile, began to write a two-page memo summarizing the events of the day.

"The first thing we did was get together an agreement on exactly what was said there," Jim Kelly remembered, "to make sure Washington would get the full nuance of that." The Korean speakers were told to rely on their own notes and ignore the translation provided at the meeting by Miss Chae. According to David Straub, "We put together not a true transcript . . . we didn't have a recording device . . . but a quasi-transcript that tried to get as close to word for word as we could."

The two reached agreement on what one member of the group described as "a consensus document that seemed consistent, but was not exactly what Ms. Chae had said." But there was no disagreement on the main point—that Kang Sok Ju had acknowledged having a uranium program. Said Jim Kelly, "I don't think any of us were in any doubt."

To the surprise of British diplomat James Hoare, the Americans had not brought their own computers with them to the embassy. Instead, they typed their draft on an unclassified embassy Toshiba laptop, which was then retyped in the secure room. Julie Kim sent off the quasi-transcript first. Straub then transmitted the memo, under the heading, "North Koreans defiantly admit HEU program." Looking back years later, Straub wished he had used "acknowledge" rather than "admit," because "it was not an explicit 'yes we have it.'"

Straub had given Jim Hoare a brief and very general summary of the American take on the meeting, but Hoare also managed to sneak a quick glimpse at the cable being typed on his secure machine. "It was very negative," he recalled. ". . . confirm . . . after a twenty-four-hour delay that yes, they did have a powerful program, and that it had been raised in the context of the alleged highly enriched uranium program. The assumption was that that was what they were admitting to."

Given the poisonous politics in Washington, the Americans were concerned that the cable, signed by Jim Kelly, be closely held, along with the transcript, and asked that it be sent to the British Embassy in Washington to be hand-delivered directly to Secretary of State Colin Powell. But mere hours after the cable was sent, the memo had been distributed widely throughout the British intelligence system. Without the knowledge of Kelly's team, who believed distribution was limited only to the highest echelons of the State Department, it made its way to the Pentagon and, as Jack Pritchard observed, to other "places that we had no expectation that it would show up."

When Kelly and the rest of his group got off their C-21 at Osan Air Force Base in South Korea on the morning of October 5, ready to inform Ambassador Thomas Hubbard and the South Korean government of their dramatic news, they were greeted by a U.S. Air Force major. By his comments, the major made clear that, while the ambassador still knew nothing, he—like presumably many others in the U.S. military—had already read the cable. Kelly's team was taken aback. Even before they had reached Washington, the task of managing the information about Kang's "admission" within the Bush administration, let alone crafting a diplomatic response, was suddenly going to be much more difficult. To American hard-liners, however, the bombshell in Kelly's cable was manna from heaven.

# 7

# THE FOUR-
# LETTER
# WORD

COLIN POWELL WAS PREPARING TO ATTEND A NATIONAL SE-curity Council meeting in the White House Situation Room when the phone rang. Jim Kelly, just out of Pyongyang, was calling to give the secretary of state a firsthand report on the news of his dramatic confrontation with North Korean First Vice Foreign Minister Kang Sok Ju. Powell was astounded.

"And I walked in [to the meeting] and I sat down with all my colleagues," Powell recalled, "and I say, 'You're not going to believe this, but Kelly just checked in and we deployed our talking points, and guess what? The North Koreans admitted it.' And everybody went, 'What?' Yeah, they admitted it. They confirmed. What did they confirm? They confirmed that they had a program of some kind."

Powell also called John Bolton to his office to share the news. Bolton sat on a chair opposite the secretary's desk and read the cable sent from Pyongyang. Bolton was jubilant: *I'm vindicated. The Agreed Framework has just gone out the window.*

Once Kelly returned from Asia, having briefly summarized his encounter in Pyongyang for the South Koreans and Japanese—while avoiding any mention of Kang Sok Ju's remarks in his brief appearances before the media in Tokyo and Seoul—U.S. officials plunged into a round of intensive consultations to decide how to respond. Kelly was asked to give a briefing at a principals' meeting attended by President Bush, Defense Secretary Donald Rumsfeld, Powell, and other senior officials.

By this time, all of the participants had seen the initial transcript prepared by Kelly's team, and the discussion was less about what happened than what it meant. For the hard-liners, Kang Sok Ju's "admission" was the moment they had been waiting for—proof that there was no possibility of talking the North Koreans out of the nuclear program, and an opportunity to dismantle the entire structure of engagement built up during the Clinton administration, which administration moderates were seeking—with modifications—to continue.

"The first question for me," recalled John Bolton, "was how to get rid of the Agreed Framework and the entire superstructure of power based on it. That was the immediate objective because I thought it was a snare and an illusion, giving us the impression of security when in fact the North Koreans were un-doubtedly screwing us, which we now know they were."

Bolton pushed for the administration to go to the United Nations Security Council and demand it impose sanctions on North Korea. Bolton's view was that not only would such a step increase pressure on Pyongyang, it would also push Russia and China to take a tougher stance. And, if worldwide sanctions were not imposed, he added ominously, "Then at least we've checked the box and we can go on and do something else." The hard-liners also advocated cutting off the shipments of heavy fuel oil that the United States had been providing to Pyongyang every year under the terms of the Agreed Framework.

Colin Powell was hardly disposed to be generous toward the North Koreans. But privately he continued to be skeptical about the intelligence. As soon as Kelly returned, Powell asked one of the top technical experts on nuclear weapons at the State Department's Bureau of Intelligence and Research to go back and look at "every single piece of intel that involved HEU," an assignment that would consume the young analyst seven days a week for months.

In all the deliberations, it appears that the administration was so focused on Kang Sok Ju's "admission" that nobody paid attention to the fact that the North Korean had also offered to negotiate a way out of the crisis.

For its part, North Korea, in the first public comment on Kelly's visit, took an angry tone. "The special envoy . . . took a high-handed and arrogant attitude by claiming that DPRK-Japan relations and inter-Korean relations as well as DPRK-U.S. relations would be smoothly settled only when the DPRK first meets U.S. unilateral demands [on issues] such as nuclear and missile and conventional armed forces and 'human rights.' The U.S.-raised 'issues of concern' are nothing but products of its hostile policy toward the DPRK."[1]

Somewhat plaintively, the number two diplomat at the North's mission to the UN, Han Song Ryol, told a reporter for the Reuters news agency four days later that the U.S. is "refusing dialogue with us," adding in a more menacing tone, "We are prepared not only for dialogue but also for war."

As the internal debates continued, the administration said nothing in public; President Bush had insisted there be no leaks. Apart from Jim Kelly's classified briefings to a few senior congressional Republicans such as Senators Richard Lugar and Chuck Hagel, the dramatic confrontation in Pyongyang and the fact that the North Koreans appeared to have admitted possession of a secret uranium nuclear weapons program remained a closely held secret.

One reason for the secrecy may have been that during the same period in early October, the administration's attention was focused heavily on another member of the Axis of Evil, Iraq. The President was pushing for congressional authorization to use force against Saddam Hussein, and he and his lieutenants repeatedly invoked the specter of an Iraqi nuclear weapons program—despite sharp debate within the intelligence community over whether the Iraqi dictator actually had such a capability—to justify their plans for war. Revelation of the North Korean enrichment effort would have undercut the nuclear rationale for war or else created concerns about a two-front war.

On October 7, 2002, for example, just days after Kelly's return from Pyongyang, Bush warned of Saddam's nuclear ambitions before an audience in Cincinnati. "Knowing these realities," he said, "America must not ignore the threat gathering against us. Facing clear evidence of peril, we cannot wait for the final proof—the smoking gun—that could come in the form of a mushroom cloud."[2]

In the previous few weeks, National Security Adviser Condoleezza Rice had used a similar image, while Vice President Dick Cheney had declared that the United States had "irrefutable evidence" of an Iraqi nuclear weapons program, in the form of Saddam's effort to acquire aluminum tubes to be used for uranium centrifuges.

Four days after Bush's speech—on October 11—the U.S. Senate, by an overwhelming margin of 77 to 23, voted to authorize the President to use force against the Saddam regime. The vote in the House of Representatives was equally lopsided—296 to 133. Many of those who supported Bush, especially Democrats, emphasized the nuclear threat. In justifying her vote for the resolution, for example, California Democrat Diane Feinstein told the Senate, "The great danger is a nuclear one."

As the senior diplomatic correspondent for USA Today, Barbara Slavin had followed the North Korea story for years and was one of the few American reporters who had visited Pyongyang. Puzzled by the silence following what was, after all, the first trip to North Korea by a Bush administration official, she began working the phones. Soon she was hearing rumors that Kelly's meetings had not gone well. After scores of calls, she reached a former administration official who told her that friends at the State Department were describing the encounter as a "disaster."

On October 15, Slavin approached State Department spokesman Richard Boucher, who told her she was "on to something," but would not give her any further confirmation. Without a more solid source, Slavin's editors held the story. The next day, she lost her scoop.

Slavin's inquiries alerted the administration that the story was about to leak. In order to control the "spin," the administration made the decision to release the news itself. Late on the afternoon of October 16, Richard Boucher issued a statement which said that Kelly "advised the North Koreans that we had recently acquired information that indicates that North Korea has a program to enrich uranium for nuclear weapons in violation of the Agreed Framework and other agreements. North Korean officials acknowledged they have such a program. . . . Over the summer, President Bush—in consultation with our allies and friends—had developed a bold approach to improve relations with North Korea. . . . In light of our concerns about the North's nuclear weapons program, however, we are unable to pursue this approach."[3]

The revelation was a bombshell, with page-one headlines in the *New York Times*, *Washington Post*, *USA Today*, and other major media. But the immediate strategy of an administration preoccupied with plans for war in Iraq was to downplay the sense of crisis. While Bush, Cheney, Rice, and other senior officials had been making the public case against Saddam Hussein, it was left to spokesman Boucher, a lower-ranking official, to deliver the news about North Korea. And while in the following days, leaks to selected reporters provided some of the details about the uranium intelligence and the Pakistan connection, there was a conscious effort to emphasize using diplomacy to resolve the issue, and to avoid describing the new development as a crisis.

In a background briefing to a group of Washington reporters, Deputy National Security Adviser Stephen Hadley—identified only as a "senior administration official"—said, "We call on North Korea . . . to end its nuclear weapons program in a way that is verifiable. We want to resolve this peacefully. We don't want a crisis." The next day, the White House spokesman said, "The President believes this is troubling, sobering news. We are seeking a peaceful resolution. This is best addressed through diplomatic channels at this point."[4]

The fact that the administration had kept the North Korea news secret while using allegations about Saddam Hussein's nuclear program to secure congressional authorization for war with Iraq did not go down well with some members of Congress. Jim Kelly was asked to provide a classified briefing to the Senate Foreign Relations Committee. It was a stormy session. "When Kelly briefed, he was met with stunned expressions by senators and staff who were bitter about the fact that [the administration] had withheld this vital national security information [about the uranium intelligence] from Congress for four months and that they had not even briefed us on the North Korean alleged confirmation for ten days after he got back," said one committee staffer who was in the room.

According to Frank Jannuzi, an Asia specialist working for Democratic senator Joseph Biden, the questions for Kelly from senators and staffers were sharp.

"When were you planning to tell us this? You've known since June-July of 2002, during the months of the Iraq lead-up debate in Congress. You knew they were cheating then. You tell the North Koreans before you tell us about this information. When did you think the Congress, which pays the bills for the Agreed Framework, maybe should have been briefed about North Korea being in violation?"

In response, Kelly said the information was sensitive, and the White House wanted to avoid leaks while it considered its options.

"This is bullshit," recalled an aide to one senator. "They didn't want to muck up the Iraq debate all summer. There was a steady drumbeat. That's when Condi Rice is going around on TV and everybody's getting us ready for war in Iraq. They didn't want to be off message with North Korea being in breach. Imagine if there had been four months of discussion of North Korea being in violation of their nuclear commitments and pursuing an independent nuclear capacity before the Iraq vote."

The anger cut across partisan lines. In a letter to the White House, two Republican members of the House of Representatives joined with one Democrat to urge the administration to get tough with Pyongyang. "We regard the North Korean weapons of mass destruction threat to be at least as serious as the threat posed by Iraq," wrote Congressmen Christopher Cox, Benjamin Gilman, and Ed Markey, all of whom had long been critical of North Korea's nuclear ambitions. "We urge you to make a strong and vigorous response to this threat before it is too late."


On a trip to consult with the South Koreans and the Japanese, Kelly publicly held to Washington's position that there would be no negotiations without a "visible dismantling" of Pyongyang's nuclear program, and to start talks without such a development, he said, "In my view, got it upside down."

But while Tokyo and Seoul were also publicly critical of the North's nuclear activities, both governments urged the United States not to abandon the path of negotiations. In Tokyo, Prime Minister Junichiro Koizumi announced plans to proceed with normalization talks with North Korea, because he "judged that taking the first major step of moving from an adversarial relationship to a cooperative one would be in the best interests of Japan."[5]

In Seoul, South Korea, Deputy Foreign Minister Lee Tae-shik told reporters, "All problems related to North Korea's nuclear development should be solved peacefully through dialogue."[6] Underscoring the divergence in views, the South, in a gesture full of defiant overtones toward Washington, held ministerial-level meetings with North Korean officials from October 19–23 to discuss ways of further improving relations with Pyongyang. And President Kim Dae-jung weighed in, saying, "What I firmly believe is that it should be settled through dialogue, not economic sanctions or war. Scrapping the Geneva Agreement [the Framework] through economic sanctions would only result in North Korea being freed from the restraints of the agreement concerning the nuclear issue."[7]

As President Bush flew to Mexico for the APEC summit, an annual meeting of Pacific Rim leaders, the battle within the administration over whether the Agreed Framework was indeed dead, and whether diplomacy or coercion should be the central feature of U.S. policy, was being openly fought in the press.

*New York Times* correspondent David Sanger—the recipient of many leaks, especially from hard-liners—cited "senior administration officials" as telling him, "The Bush administration has decided to scrap the 1994 arms-control accord. One of them was quoted as saying, 'We think the framework as we knew it is dead.' "[8]

Soon after, Colin Powell, in Mexico for the APEC meeting, told the *Washington Post*, "I have not yet used the four-letter word [dead]—and have no plans to do so, at least at this time. No decision has been made . . . I'm not ruling out direct contact with the North Koreans. If they call us, we'll listen, and I hope vice versa. But that's not negotiating."[9]

The next day, another "senior administration official" fired back, telling the same *Post* reporters that Powell's conciliatory tone showed "a State Department in revolt . . . There is a discipline problem here . . . what that person said . . . may represent his view, the State Department view, but it does not represent the administration view."[10]

For his part, Bush lobbied the leaders of China, Japan, and South Korea to pressure North Korea. Yet, in a reflection of his personal ambivalence over how to deal with a leader he openly loathed, the president agreed in a joint statement with Koizumi and Kim Dae-jung to reiterate his February 2002 pledge in South Korea that "the United States has no intention of invading North Korea."[11]

Pyongyang, meanwhile, was still signaling its desire to find a negotiated way out of the crisis—without, of course, appearing to back down first in the face of American pressure. In midafternoon on Saturday, November 2, the head of the Korea Society, Donald Gregg, a longtime CIA operative in Asia who had been the U.S. ambassador to Seoul under the administration of George H. W. Bush, and Don Oberdorfer, a highly respected former *Washington Post* diplomatic correspondent and author of an acclaimed history of modern Korea, arrived in Pyongyang. The two men were old friends, having known each other since Gregg was the CIA station chief in Seoul in the early 1970s and Oberdorfer was a *Post* reporter in Asia. Both men had developed good contacts with the North Koreans and each had made several visits to Pyongyang. Their invitation had come just before the Kelly mission, and even though Kelly's visit went badly, it had not been canceled.

Indeed, in a gesture of goodwill, the North Koreans had offered to let the two men cross into North Korea through the Demilitarized Zone, as most of Kelly's group had done. But this time, the Bush administration refused to cooperate. The American military in Seoul said the corridor would only be opened for "official" delegations. Oberdorfer appealed to Deputy Defense Secretary Paul Wolfowitz, but the message was clear: Washington wasn't interested in gestures that might be interpreted as "conciliatory."

The importance of symbolic gestures to the North Koreans became evident when Gregg and Oberdorfer were hosted for dinner by Deputy Foreign Minister Kim Gye Gwan at the Potonggang Hotel in Pyongyang on the night of their arrival. The first thing that the North Korean official wanted to talk about was not nuclear weapons, but the fact that the Bush administration had made an issue out of whether Jim Kelly could attend formal dinners during his recent visit. Kim was indignant, telling the two visitors that the episode was an affront to North Korean dignity.

Over the next two days, Oberdorfer and Gregg spent more than ten hours in conversations with Kim; a senior North Korean general, Ri Chan Bok; and First Vice Foreign Minister Kang Sok Ju. Their meeting in Pyongyang's Palace of Culture with General Ri, who wore seven rows of medals on his chest, offered a revealing glimpse of the sense of siege that characterized so much of North Korea's approach to the world.

"As long as there is no guarantee against aggression," he declared, "we must be prepared militarily. We think the U.S. will attack our country militarily sometime in the future. We won't be slaves by kneeling down, but we will fight."

"Why did you start the HEU program?" Oberdorfer asked in reply.

"I do not need to answer that question," Ri shot back. "We do not think we should give up our nuclear program before coming to the table."

At no point in any of the meetings did the North Koreans deny the U.S. allegations about a uranium program, despite being given many opportunities to do so.

Vice Foreign Minister Kim Gye Gwan instead repeated complaints about the "high-handed and dictatorial attitude" that the Bush administration and Kelly had adopted. When pressed about whether the North actually had a uranium program, Kim employed the same language Kang Sok Ju had used with Kelly.

"We are entitled to have nuclear weapons," Kim said. "Whether we actually do or not we are not obliged to clarify."

But Kim was clear about Pyongyang's desire to find a negotiated way out of the crisis.

"We are hoping to resolve this great issue through dialogue and diplomacy," he told the two Americans. "We are trying to do everything possible. We have done the best we can to the best of our ability in light of the seriousness of issues and level of mistrust. It's time for the U.S. to move. The U.S. wishes to have us dismantle our program first. They want us to surrender first. Relations are most hostile. They are threatening us with a nuclear attack. We have been driven to the position of building our weapons to fight back. This is why we are driven to different kinds of tactical weapons."

"We discussed the issue for a day and a half," Oberdorfer recalled in an interview several years later. "There was not one word of denial that they had an HEU program. Nobody said explicitly, 'we have it.' But they didn't deny it. The topic was how they could get out of the situation. They were angry about Kelly not staying to negotiate. They thought he was a negotiator."

From the initial meetings onward, Donald Gregg pushed the North Korean officials for some kind of gesture or statement directly from Kim Jong Il that he and Oberdorfer could take back to Washington in the hope of jump-starting a meaningful diplomatic dialogue. On Monday afternoon, November 4, the day before their scheduled departure, they met with First Vice Foreign Minister Kang Sok Ju. Although North Korean officials had previously declared that American actions had "nullified" the Agreed Framework, Kang now described the accord as still alive but "hanging by a thread." Then Kang unveiled a surprise.

Kang announced that he had just come from a meeting with Kim Jong Il. "The things you discussed with Kim Gye Gwan have been reported to Chairman Kim Jong Il, Chairman of the National Defense Committee," Kang said. "Chairman Kim Jong Il has decided to send a verbal message to his Excellency President Bush." Kang gave the two men a piece of paper with a statement written in Korean. Although it was unsigned, Kang stressed that it was the text of a message from the Dear Leader to the American president.

The North Korean interpreter translated it for them. "At a time when positive changes are taking place in the region of Northeast Asia," the letter read, "we hope a new chapter will also open, overcoming the current crisis in the bilateral relationship between the DPRK and the U.S. We believe the current nuclear issue was generated essentially from the U.S. hostile policy of disregarding our sovereignty and of imposing blatant military threat." The letter emphasized that "if the U.S. recognizes our sovereignty and assures non-aggression, it is our view that we should be able to find a way to resolve the nuclear issue in compliance with the demand of a new century. . . . If the United States makes a bold decision, we will respond accordingly."[12]

Kang asked Gregg and Oberdorfer not to make the message public until after it was delivered to President Bush.

Arriving back in Seoul, the two men called Deputy National Security Adviser Stephen Hadley's secretary to request a meeting, saying they had just been to North Korea and were bringing back something important. They also arranged a meeting with Deputy Secretary of State Richard Armitage.

Soon after returning to Washington, they went to the White House to see Hadley. In Hadley's cramped office, the two men summarized their meetings in Pyongyang and gave Hadley both the original Korean text and a translation provided by Pyongyang's main interpreter, Miss Chae. Stressing that this was a rare personal overture from North Korea's top leader, they described it as a "golden opportunity" for diplomatic progress and urged the administration to respond.

"Even if this was the timetable or railway schedule to Poughkeepsie," said Oberdorfer, because it came from Kim Jong Il, "you can respond to it."

"No, the president couldn't do that," Hadley replied. "That would be rewarding bad behavior."

Although Hadley said he would give the letter to Bush or National Security Adviser Condoleezza Rice, Gregg and Oberdorfer left the meeting discouraged. "That was a very negative response," observed Gregg, "just about closing the door."

The next day, the two men went to see Richard Armitage and got a completely different reaction. "He already knew about the letter," recalled Oberdorfer, "and said he and Powell were very interested, hoped something would come of it, and thanked us very profusely."

Gregg and Oberdorfer told Armitage they felt the North Koreans really wanted to talk. Pyongyang had not expected the United States to discover its uranium efforts and was looking for a way out.

The administration never responded to Kim Jong Il's letter.

In the prevailing climate, according to Colin Powell's then–chief of staff Lawrence Wilkerson, even using the term "negotiate" was a recipe for trouble from the hard-liners.

"We hardly ever used the term 'negotiate' with NK," he recalled in an interview. "It was death with the vice president's office. We used 'talks,' 'exchanges,' 'process.'"

Armitage was more blunt. "Diplomacy in the Bush administration," he said, "is, 'Alright you fuckers, do what we say.'"

There was widespread agreement within the administration to ratchet up the pressure on Pyongyang by halting shipments of fuel oil to North Korea. Under the terms of the Agreed Framework, the United States was purchasing the bulk of the 500,000 metric tons of heavy fuel oil that KEDO was supplying to North Korea every year for power and heating. A cutoff would cause real pain in a country desperately short of energy. Now, even relatively moderate figures like Deputy Secretary of State Richard Armitage felt cutting off the HFO shipments was the right step.

"It didn't make sense for us to be shipping heavy fuel, which is something that has been agreed upon previously," he recalled in an interview, "in the face of the breaking of the agreements by the North Koreans. It didn't make any sense to me."

In Tokyo, on November 8 and 9, 2002, U.S., South Korean, and Japanese government officials gathered for a meeting of the Trilateral Coordination and Oversight Group (TCOG)—a regular forum for the three governments to coordinate policies—with a fuel cutoff the main item of the agenda.

In the days immediately before the meeting, Jim Kelly and Under Secretary of Defense Douglas Feith visited Seoul and Tokyo seeking to press Washington's key Asian allies to support harsh action against Pyongyang. Feith was a controversial figure who was to become one of the prime architects of the U.S. invasion of Iraq and its bungled aftermath. In his meetings with South Korean and Japanese officials, he struck a particularly belligerent tone.

At a news conference in Tokyo, he insisted that North Korea "must pay a price" for its violations of the Agreed Framework. He also pushed the Japanese to build a missile defense system—a central feature of President Bush's security agenda—to counter what he described as "the serious danger of a ballistic missile attack by North Korea on Japan."[13]

"If you were going to alter North Korean behavior," Feith told me in an interview, "we were much more likely to succeed through pressure than through blandishments." To some of his interlocutors this sounded exactly wrong.

As the meeting got under way, a tanker carrying the November shipment of 42,500 tons of heavy fuel oil was already at sea en route to North Korea from Singapore. Jim Kelly, pushing Washington's hard line, urged that the ship be turned around, but both the Japanese and South Koreans were uneasy, both with this drastic step and the broader confrontational posture the United States was taking toward Pyongyang.

"We were not enthusiastic," recalled a South Korean diplomat who was involved in the discussions. "There was a general sense in Seoul that this would cause an aggravation of the situation."

On November 13, President Bush chaired a meeting of the National Security Council, which decided to halt further U.S. funding for shipments of fuel oil. Even Colin Powell, who had reservations about the confrontational approach, went along. "I kept the fuel flowing for a little while longer," he recalled, "but there was no obvious way to resolve this conflict . . . and so ultimately, I could not keep justifying the provision of fuel under the Agreed Framework when the Agreed Framework had been violated. But I knew that if we cut off the fuel, we were heading into more difficult waters."

The HFO was the last commitment in the Agreed Framework that the United States had been fulfilling, the last link to the North's freeze of its plutonium program.

Despite the disputes over policy, the way in which the news of Kelly's trip had come out in mid-October—ten days after his departure from Pyongyang, with the administration's hand forced by the leak to USA Today's Barbara Slavin—essentially foreclosed reasoned discussion about what Kang Sok Ju had actually said and meant. The nuances of his language and the role the peculiarities of the North Korean mind-set may have played in how Pyongyang responded to Kelly's allegations were blurred by an overriding conventional wisdom: Kang had been challenged by Kelly and had confessed; the North Koreans had been caught cheating. In a sound-bite culture, the hawkish public comments by administration officials determined the way the issue was depicted in the media, setting up a steady drumbeat of North Korean culpability, with no acknowledgment that the reality might be considerably more complex.

For example, at his November 8 news conference in Tokyo, leading hardliner, Douglas Feith declared "What Assistant Secretary Kelly learned in North Korea was not that they may be pursuing nuclear weapons, but that they are. He got the North Koreans' confirmation that North Korea is working to enrich uranium."[14]

"Once North Korea was attributed to saying 'Yeah, we've got it,'" observed a former senior State Department official, "that became the single most important fact that we have on their program. It's the most compelling piece of evidence that we have."

Yet many of those who saw the actual transcript of the Kelly-Kang meeting had doubts. After returning to Washington, the three Korean speakers on Kelly's delegation revisited their original notes and, with the luxury of time, prepared a more detailed version of what they had recorded. The more carefully constructed written record, according to several of those who have seen it, lacked the sense of "confession" that so struck those who had seen and heard Kang Sok Ju's exposition in the Foreign Ministry building in Pyongyang.

"I was always convinced that the people who heard something in the meeting heard something different than what I read in the written transcript," observed one former senior intelligence analyst who read the document at the time. "I think you can come up with a different interpretation based on hand-gestures and body language. The shorthand out of the meeting was that they were working on an HEU unit. I looked and looked at the transcript, and there are words there that if you read into it, you may get it, but I don't see it. The North Koreans were caught off guard, they have an attitude that they can't be pushed around, so they said it. The notion that they admitted to the HEU isn't as clear-cut in the transcript as in the oral tradition that the meeting seemed to foster."

Kang's reference to "even more powerful weapons" underscored the potential for misunderstanding. At the time, it did not occur to anyone on Kelly's team to ask asked what he meant. Later, Fu Ying, the director-general of the Chinese Foreign Ministry's Department of Asian Affairs, asked North Korean officials for clarification. They told her the "weapon" was in fact a simply reference to "the great strength of the Korean people."

Similarly, as the administration made its fateful decision to cut off fuel shipments, there was little real discussion about how the North Koreans might react. "We didn't give ourselves any time to try to figure out if there were problems with that, or if there might be some other strategy that we could undertake," recalled David Straub. "So this was done like a six-year-old playing checkers. They only look if they can take the next piece then they've won." To hard-liners, putting the squeeze on Pyongyang was not only just punishment for the alleged admission of a secret HEU program, it fit into their broader goal of forcing the collapse of Kim Jong Il's regime.

For several months in 2002, Bush administration hopes that regime change might come soon in the North were fueled by what the CIA was describing as significant signs of unrest in the country. The CIA station in Seoul reported growing dissatisfaction within both the military and the general public. The evidence was said to include leaflets being distributed on the streets of Pyongyang calling for the overthrow of Kim Jong Il, and even accounts of efforts to organize dissident groups to oppose the regime.

These tantalizing accounts coincided with a report from the U.S. Agency for International Development that also stressed the fragility of the North Korean system. The study, which was commissioned by Andrew Natsios, the head of USAID, was classified because the man who conducted it, development specialist Robert Gersony, had traveled undercover along the Chinese border with North Korea. Posing as an NGO aid worker, Gersony interviewed dozens of refugees. His conclusion was that North Korea could be close to collapse and that, at the time of the 1997 famine, would in fact have collapsed had not assistance from the United States and the rest of the international community propped it up.

The CIA assessment and the Gersony report had been circulating at the highest levels of the U.S. government at precisely the time the uranium issue was coming to a head. By some accounts, Vice President Cheney and President Bush himself were briefed, with the conclusions lending further weight to the hard-liners' argument that Kim Jong Il was in trouble and that the last thing the United States should do was deal with or legitimize the North Korean regime.

However, after circulating this intelligence for several months in 2002, the CIA abruptly withdrew the entire stream of reporting. According to an American official who was briefed on the subject, the CIA determined that the sourcing was unreliable and may have been fabricated or exaggerated to give the United States what it was thought Washington wanted to hear. "Some of it was pretty hard to believe," noted one former intelligence analyst, "like KPA generals would put on paper plans for a plot to oust Kim Jong Il. That anyone would put it on paper so it would get out and be reported was either crazy or it was a counterintelligence effort by the North Koreans."

One senior official who saw the intelligence subsequently said that what was portrayed to the CIA as a major wave of antiregime activity was in fact an isolated episode of discontent in one North Korean army corps group. "It was just insubordination and rioting and looting of warehouses," the official noted. The more dramatic elements of the reporting couldn't be substantiated. "People had miscast it or misanalyzed it as a political revolt," the official added.

Even after the intelligence supporting its opinions had been withdrawn, however, the view that North Korea was poised for collapse remained widespread in the administration. "People at the top absolutely bought into it," according to the former intelligence analyst. "Even when it was withdrawn, people didn't give up feeling that North Korea was on the edge. And they could just use it to shoot down dissenting views."

The headquarters of the Korean Peninsula Energy Development Organization (KEDO) was a suite in an office building on New York's Third Avenue. On November 14, 2002, the representatives from the United States, South Korea, Japan, and the European Union who made up the KEDO executive board began the most critical meeting in the organization's history.

Although Chuck Kartman was KEDO's executive director, his old friend and former colleague Jack Pritchard was the formal U.S. representative to the consortium. But as the daylong discussion got under way, Pritchard was not his own boss. Instead, he was operating under instructions from the administration, shaped largely by hard-liners in the National Security Council, to push for as toughly worded a statement as possible, announcing an end to fuel deliveries to North Korea.

The other delegates, especially the South Koreans and Japanese, were not happy about that.

"The basic political argument," according to one South Korean who was there, "was that we should take our time and not do this abruptly. We were concerned the situation might escalate into a worsening direction. That was the basic message we were trying to convey to the Americans."

"I was of the view that cutting off fuel deliveries and scrapping the KEDO agreement would certainly invite North Korea to take countermeasures," said a senior Japanese official. "I thought the decision to stop the fuel oil would trigger a chain reaction."

Chuck Kartman voiced similar concerns about what Pyongyang might do in response. "I thought that the North Koreans then would suspend their own compliance with their own agreed framework. I had predicted to everybody on the board that if we did not get things restored in the context of the Agreed Framework that the North Koreans would reopen Yongbyon."

As the discussions continued, Pritchard was repeatedly called away to the phone. On the other end was John Rood, a hard-line official who worked under Robert Joseph at the NSC's office of nonproliferation. Rood insisted on even further toughening the language in the proposed resolution.

The fact that Pritchard had no real say on the issue and was being kept on such a short leash that even the fine details of the wording were being dictated to him from Wahsington "became embarrassing to Jack and the other delegates," observed Bob Carlin, the former intelligence analyst who had worked at KEDO since the previous spring. "It demonstrated where the policy was coming from."

At the same time, NSC officials were also calling their counterparts at the Prime Minister's office in Tokyo and the South Korean Blue House in Seoul, exerting more pressure for the South Korean and Japanese governments to order their delegates to back the U.S. position.

Eventually, both governments reluctantly gave way.

"The decision to cut off the oil aid to North Korea was the wrong decision," said former South Korean president Kim Dae-jung. "I rejected that decision. However, the U.S. stance was very firm at the time, and it was the U.S. who had all the control at the time, so I could not object any further."

When the Japanese and South Koreans were informed by their capitals to vote in favor of the U.S. position, they were, in Bob Carlin's words, "ashen-faced."

After a meeting lasting eleven hours, the KEDO executive board issued a statement announcing a suspension of heavy fuel oil supplies to North Korea. Using language imposed by administration hard-liners, the statement said the board "agreed" (a diplomatic fiction disguising the fact the decision had been rammed down the throats of the allies by Washington) "to condemn North Korea's pursuit of a nuclear weapons program, which is a clear and serious violation of its obligations under the Agreed Framework, the Nonproliferation Treaty (NPT), its IAEA Safeguards Agreement, and the Joint South-North Declaration on the Denuclearization of the Korean Peninsula."

The statement described North Korea's nuclear weapons program as "a shared challenge to all responsible states . . . that threatens regional and international security," and demanded that "North Korea must promptly eliminate its nuclear weapons program in a visible and verifiable manner."

The KEDO announcement, like Kelly's remarks to Kang Sok Ju and many administration statements after that meeting, adopted precisely the kind of tone most likely to spark a negative reaction from the always-suspicious and ultrasensitive North Koreans. It set out a series of nonnegotiable demands which, in Pyongyang's eyes, would undoubtedly be seen as an American demand for surrender.

Observed one appalled State Department Korea hand, "We had the moral satisfaction of saying, 'fuck you.' "

Having thrown down the gauntlet, however, the administration had no plans for dealing with a North Korean response, other than hoping that additional pressure would lead to capitulation—or even better—to collapse.

As they left the KEDO's office that chilly November evening, Kartman and Pritchard were more than a little worried.

Recalled Pritchard, "We knew that we had just taken a major step off a major cliff."

# 8

# MELTDOWN

THE YONGBYON NUCLEAR SCIENCE RESEARCH CENTER SITS in a rugged valley 100 kilometers north of Pyongyang, lined on either side by the stark granite peaks that define so much of the North Korean landscape. At the top of one of them is a guesthouse with a spectacular view often used as a retreat by Kim Jong Il. The Nine Dragons River cuts through the valley. According to Korean mythology, every year nine children die in the river, one to appease each of the nine dragons.

A bumpy dirt road along the riverbank leads into the main square of the town of Yongbyon. Here, a handful of nondescript apartment buildings, most covered with soot from the coal cookers on every balcony, house the staff of North Korea's key nuclear facility. Propaganda posters line the road, in which ferocious soldiers repel imperialist enemies, and muscular young men defiantly wave the North Korean flag.

Past the square, the dirt road reaches a ten-foot-high, twenty-foot-long sheet metal gate guarded by soldiers, with a machine gun nest dug into the ground. Inside, a series of buildings resembling a cross between a college campus and a laboratory complex are linked by a huge above-ground steam pipe that provides power and heating. Every few hundred yards, however, are gaps in the pipes. In the bitter cold of winter, steam shoots from the pipes, and, as it condenses back into water, freezes into icicles.

Another heavily guarded metal gate opens into the heart of the complex, the site of the five-megawatt reactor that produced the plutonium at the center of the 1994 nuclear crisis. Next to it, a cavernous building holds the storage pond where the spent nuclear fuel was kept under international inspection following Pyongyang's decision to freeze the Yongbyon facility under the terms of the Agreed Framework.

The pond itself, 100 feet long and 30 feet wide, was designed to hold hundreds of stainless steel canisters. Provided by the United States, each canister contained 40 spent fuel rods. In December 2002, 8000 rods—enough, when reprocessed, to produce weapons-grade plutonium for five to six nuclear bombs—were sealed here. Since the mid-1990s, the entire complex had been closely monitored by the International Atomic Energy Agency (IAEA), often with the help of American technical experts. All the canisters were sealed, while fifteen closed-circuit cameras enabled the IAEA to keep an eye on Yongbyon twenty-four hours a day. Two IAEA inspectors were also stationed regularly at the facility. Every evening, they would advise the North Koreans which buildings in the complex they intended to inspect the following morning. Occasionally, they would give only an hour's notice for a "surprise" inspection. It was a grim assignment. The inspectors stayed in the complex's drab and chilly guesthouse for two weeks at a time before rotating out. In a year, an inspector would have three stints at Yongbyon.

On the weekend before Christmas, 2002, the two IAEA monitors at Yongbyon—one from Lebanon, one from China—stood by helplessly, watching as North Korean officials systematically began dismantling the equipment that had allowed international monitoring of its frozen nuclear program over the past eight years. On Friday, December 21, the seals on equipment at the five-megawatt reactor were removed. Surveillance cameras were shut down, covered, and turned to face the walls. The next day, the North Koreans did the same thing at the pond containing the 8,000 spent fuel rods. By the end of the weekend, the seals and cameras in every building at the Yongbyon complex had been removed. Once they completed their work, the North Koreans celebrated by bringing out bottles of beer.

Pyongyang's nuclear breakout was under way.

At first, there had been silence from Pyongyang. For a full week after the KEDO board announced a cutoff of fuel shipments on November 14, North Korea said nothing—even after the *Washington Post*'s publication on November 16 of the first account of Bob Woodward's August interview, in which President Bush railed against Kim Jong Il. The page-one report described Bush as shouting and waving his finger in the air as he declared, "I loathe Kim Jong Il. I have a visceral reaction to the guy because he is starving his people." The article summarized Bush's attitude toward North Korea by saying it was "clear he was not content with the status quo."[1]

Three days later, the tanker carrying the final load of fuel—42,500 tons—docked at the port of Nampo. Three days after that, the Foreign Ministry in Pyongyang responded with a harshly worded statement blaming the United States for the collapse of the Agreed Framework.

"The U.S. has drastically delayed the construction of LWRs," the statement declared, "worked out a plan for a preemptive nuclear attack on the DPRK and listed the latter as part of an 'axis of evil.' "[2] The statement again called for the United States to sign a nonaggression treaty with the North. But it also warned, "The DPRK has exercised its forbearance to the full."

On November 25, 2002, a leading North Korean newspaper carried an even more blunt warning. "The DPRK has kept its nuclear facility frozen for the last eight years since the adoption of the Agreed Framework despite a huge loss of electricity," the official *Rodong Sinmun* noted. "The present grave situation is pushing the DPRK to the phase where it cannot respect the Agreed Framework any longer. The U.S. should be held fully responsible for the serious consequences to be entailed by its decision to stop the supply of heavy oil to the DPRK."[3]

As if things were not bad enough, as dawn broke over the horizon in the Arabian Sea on December 10, two Spanish warships, the *Navarra* and the *Patino*, confronted a rusty freighter about 900 kilometers from Yemen. The Spanish vessels were part of Task Force 150, a U.S.-led multinational naval operation initially intended to stop al Qaeda fighters from fleeing Afghanistan by sea. The freighter's name had been painted over, but its identity was no secret to the United States. The ship was the *So San*, and it had been tracked by American spy satellites and navy vessels since leaving its home port of Nampo, North Korea, in late November.

The Spanish ships signaled the *So San* to stop. Instead, the vessel tried to evade capture, prompting the *Navarra* to fire three bursts of warning shots. A sniper then shot out the *So San*'s mast cables, enabling a helicopter to lower Spanish troops on board. They quickly subdued the thirteen-man crew, all North Koreans. The ship's manifest listed its cargo as cement, but a search quickly found fifteen hidden Scud missiles, along with fifteen conventional warheads, twenty-three tanks of nitric acid propellant, and eighty-five drums of unidentified chemicals. As the Spanish carried out the boarding, the USS *Nassau*, loaded with marines, helicopters, and Harrier jump jets, patrolled nearby. The Spanish called for help. As U.S. explosives experts came aboard, the ship was turned over to the U.S. Navy.

Such missile exports were one of the few sources of hard currency for the North Korean regime. The sale of the missiles on the *So San* would likely have earned Pyongyang about $50 million. Washington had known of the trade for years, but this was the first time the United States had intercepted a North Korean shipment on the high seas. The aggressive move underscored the Bush administration's new use of preemptive measures to halt the spread of weapons of mass destruction. American officials gleefully declared that this was the first time North Korea had been caught red-handed.

In this case, however, what appeared to be a daring raid with a successful outcome turned into an embarrassing fiasco. The missiles had in fact been ordered by the government of Yemen, which promptly claimed it had made the purchase legitimately and demanded the *So San* be released to continue its voyage. The Yemenis had a point. Even if the *So San*'s paperwork was dubious, there was no law banning the international sale of ballistic missiles. Neither Yemen nor North Korea were signatories to the Missile Technology Control Regime, a voluntary association of states working to curb missile exports. To Washington's consternation, the transaction appeared legal. Adding to the embarrassment, since the al Qaeda bombing of the USS *Cole* in the harbor of Yemen's capital Aden in October 2000, the Bush administration had tried to forge good relations in the hope of enlisting Yemen's help in the war on terror. After a series of angry phone conversations between Yemen's president and Vice President Dick Cheney, the *So San* was allowed to proceed on December 11—just a day after its capture.

It was an inauspicious start to what was emerging as the Bush administration's new strategy for dealing with Pyongyang—"tailored containment"—the use of economic and political pressure to force a change in North Korea's behavior and, some within the administration hoped, in the regime itself. The term emerged after a series of papers were drafted in December for consideration by President Bush and his top advisers.

One was written by NSC Asia expert Michael Green, who had been part of Kelly's delegation to Pyongyang in October. Green called his proposals "The International Approach."

"The argument was, we need to get the allies on board to contain the problem," Green explained in an interview. "We have to make some diplomatic effort to keep them on board, but we also need them once diplomacy fails. So we have to show some ankle, we have to be a little more forthcoming, because the allies were not willing to be tough and put pressure on unless we were willing to create a diplomatic process. But we need to be very tough."

The second paper was written by Samantha Ravich in Vice President Cheney's office. Her hard-line views reflected those of her boss. Her paper was entitled "Regime Change," and proposed making the downfall of Kim Jong Il the top and immediate American policy goal.

Robert Joseph, the head of the NSC's nonproliferation department, and his deputy John Rood authored the third paper, "Tailored Containment."

"The idea was that you would not continue to give assistance to prolong the life of the regime, and by doing so the nuclear threat," Joseph recalled in an interview for this book. Instead, the proposal called for sanctions, heightened economic pressure, and the interdiction of North Korean weapons exports to deprive the regime of its sources of income. "It was morally repugnant to be part of extending the life of that regime," Joseph said.

"The objective was to slowly undermine the regime," said one official who supported the tailored containment approach. "Let's use the metaphor of a tree. You can chip away at it and it may not fall for a long, long time, but it helps to keep going at it. My thought was that we try to deal with the dangerous elements of the regime's behavior and we slowly undermine it, and over time, you hope that it will lead to the fall of the regime."

As the papers were circulated within the bureaucracy, there were bitter arguments over the right approach. Green and his boss, NSC Asia Director Jim Moriarty, backed by the State Department's Jim Kelly, battled with Bob Joseph and his hard-line supporters. Joseph favored unilateral American action. His opponents argued that even if tailored containment became U.S. policy, it wouldn't work without involving Washington's Asian partners. As David Straub, then director of the State Department's Korea Desk, observed, "How are we going to do tailored containment? Who's going to help us contain them?" One eyewitness recalled "huge fights—screaming and yelling."

"Jim Kelly is a very skeptical and cautious person about North Korea," said Straub, "but he is also a pretty reasonable person, and he would see in these positions no consistency, coherence, connection to the real world. So he would push back. He would push a little bit and Bob Joseph and other people would push back. I don't believe Bob Joseph by himself was able to do that. I've always assumed that Joseph had the support based on instructions from the president, vice president and Deputy National Security Adviser Stephen Hadley."

Eventually, National Security Adviser Condoleezza Rice endorsed the tailored containment option, and took it to the president at an NSC meeting. Bush, however, insisted that China be involved, thereby diluting the hard-liners' desire for the United States to act on its own, but by no means repudiating the long-term hope of seeing an end of Kim Jong Il's regime.

In the meantime, however, Joseph gave a background interview to Michael Gordon of the *New York Times* at the end of December and told him that tailored containment was the new U.S. policy. Michael Green accompanied him, but couldn't contradict the more senior Joseph in front of the reporter. Despite the internal confusion over how the new strategy would work, tailored containment became the public face of Washington's confrontational approach to North Korea.

This muscular attitude was also reflected in the publication in mid-December 2002 of a declassified version of a National Security Presidential Directive (NSPD), which had been signed the previous May 17. The directive dealt with the administration's new doctrine of preemption. "The United States will continue to make clear that it reserves the right to respond with overwhelming force" the document read, "including the resort to all our options, to the use of WMD against the United States, our forces abroad, and friends and allies." The *Washington Post* reported that a classified appendix listed North Korea among the countries that were the central focus of the U.S. doctrine.[4]

At the same time, President Bush secretly approved another NSPD that outlined his administration's policy of missile defense and explicitly named North Korea as a potential target. This one was not intended for public release, and only came to light when it was leaked to Bill Gertz of the conservative *Washington Times* six months later. Dated December 16, 2002, NSPD 23 said, "Some states, such as North Korea, are aggressively pursuing the development of weapons of mass destruction and long-range missiles as a means of coercing the United States and our allies. To deter such threats, we must devalue missiles as tools of extortion and aggression, undermining the confidence of our adversaries that threatening a missile attack would succeed in blackmailing us . . . In recognition of these new threats, I have directed that the United States must make progress in fielding a new triad composed of long-range conventional and nuclear strike capabilities, missile defenses, and a robust industrial and research development infrastructure."[5]

North Korea was the most secretive society on earth. Decision making in Kim Jong Il's regime was notoriously opaque, cloaked in a veil of bombast and rhetoric that often made deciphering Pyongyang's real intentions and policy positions a maddeningly frustrating task. With the state propaganda machine churning out ritualized denunciations of the "brigandish" behavior and "base plots" of the "American imperialists," coupled with fevered warnings that "the army and people of the DPRK with burning hatred for the Yankees are in full readiness to fight a death-defying battle" if the situation got out of hand, the North Koreans all too easily lived up to the caricature of the world's most kooky political system run by its most erratic and menacing leader.

In fact, though, as the crisis with the United States developed, Pyongyang went out of its way to make its concerns and its warnings unmistakably clear. Starting with the Kelly visit, Pyongyang had repeatedly appealed for direct negotiations with the United States, dropping broad hints that the nuclear program was on the table and that it was ready to satisfy American concerns about the uranium issue—but that those goals had to be reached in the context of a mutual agreement. North Korea would not take the first step of bowing to American demands. In the wake of the decision by KEDO to cut off shipments of heavy fuel oil, the North, while again calling for talks, signaled that its patience was running out and hinted that it might end the freeze implemented as part of the Agreed Framework that had halted its plutonium program.

Two days after the seizure of the *So San*, the North acted on its warnings. The state-run Korean Central News Agency (KCNA) issued a statement on behalf of the North Korean Foreign Ministry announcing that it would "immediately resume the operation and construction of nuclear facilities to generate electricity." The freeze, the statement said, had been implemented "on the premise that 500,000 tons of heavy oil would be annually supplied to the DPRK under the DPRK-US Agreed Framework."[6]

In a letter sent to Jack Pritchard, nominally still the administration's point man for contacts with the North Koreans, Pyongyang's ambassador to the United Nations, Pak Gil Yon, wrote, "The USA has completely broken the Agreed Framework by giving up unilaterally its HFO [heavy fuel oil] supply obligation after systematically violating the DPRK-USA Agreed Framework. We have already made clear who is to blame for it."[7]

KCNA's public statement, however, was also significant for what it did not say. The emphasis was on the production of electricity. There was no threat to reprocess the spent fuel rods into weapons-grade plutonium or to manufacture nuclear bombs. And the statement also contained yet another signal that Pyongyang's preferred course was direct negotiations—if Washington was ready to talk. "Whether the DPRK refreezes its nuclear facilities or not entirely depends on the attitude of the U.S."[8]

Given the range of provocative steps available to Pyongyang, as former NSC nonproliferation expert Gary Samore noted in a study of the crisis, "The announcement was seen as a relatively cautious move—intended to increase political pressure on Washington, rather than precipitate a full-blown crisis. As a practical matter, restarting the reactor did not present an immediate threat because the facility could not produce a significant amount of additional plutonium for at least a year."[9]

But Washington remained unyielding. Colin Powell repeated the administration's position that "what we can't and won't do is reward North Korea for its misbehavior." And in an interview with the South Korean paper *Chosun Ilbo*, Richard Perle, a prominent neocon who had been appointed by Bush to head the Pentagon's Defense Policy Board, said the use of force against North Korea could not be ruled out "because the dangers involved are so substantial."[10]

The North Koreans were not impressed. Two days after Christmas, officials

arrived at the guesthouse used by IAEA inspectors at Yongbyon. The two inspectors listened as the North Koreans read a letter formally ordering them to
leave the country. In a public announcement of the decision, KCNA said,
"There is no justification for them to remain" because "our freeze on nuclear facilities had been lifted, the mission of IAEA inspectors has naturally drawn to
an end."[11]

On the last day of 2002, the inspectors boarded an Air Koryo jet in
Pyongyang and flew to Beijing. They were allowed to take with them tapes
from the fifteen cameras that had been shut off, and they also carried a bagful
of severed seals. Ten days later, defying an appeal from the IAEA's Board of
Governors to allow the return of the inspectors and monitoring equipment, as
well as a warning that Pyongyang's noncompliance could be reported to the
UN Security Council, North Korea announced it was withdrawing from the
Non-Proliferation Treaty, making it the first country that had signed the
agreement to do so.


The way was clear for Kim Jong Il's regime to restart its reactor and reprocess the 8,000 spent fuel rods into weapons-grade plutonium. A North Korea with nuclear bombs and missiles capable of delivering them to targets in
South Korea, Japan, and possibly the United States—not to mention the option
of exporting fissile material to the highest bidder—was now a distinct
possibility.

Among administration hard-liners, concern at the implications of
Pyongyang's nuclear breakout was tempered by a sense of grim satisfaction—a
conviction that their unyielding hostility to North Korea had been vindicated,
and that their position in the bureaucratic warfare with the State Department
had been significantly strengthened. "Our view was—thank god for Kim Jong
Il," observed an aide to John Bolton. "Only he can save us from EAP (the State
Department's Bureau of East Asian and Pacific Affairs, headed by Jim Kelly).
"Our constant reaction was: 'Won't they finally get it now?' I'm tired of people
saying we need to test North Korean intentions. How many times, how many
agreements do they have to violate before you're going to get it? And so our
view was, fine, at least now there's no pretense."


Others, however, were convinced that North Korea's brinkmanship was intended to push Washington into talks, not into heightened confrontation.

"I think they wanted to be treated as a player, and that they felt that they
hadn't been," observed a senior figure in the intelligence community. "I compare

it to the movie *Fatal Attraction* with Glenn Close and Michael Douglas, and she's holding this big knife and she says, 'I will not be ignored.' I see North Korea playing the role of Glenn Close here. 'I will not be ignored. You have to take us seriously, you have to engage with us.' And doing something to bring back the attention, whether it's breaking the seals or whatever it is. I think it really was in my mind of that nature—pay attention to us, give us our due."

Nonetheless, the administration was caught off guard by the speed and decisiveness with which North Korea—in defiance of American warnings and appeals from the IAEA, South Korea, Japan, and other governments—had reopened its nuclear facilities. Despite its tough rhetoric, Washington struggled to find an effective response.

For all of Washington's muscle flexing, there were no easy options. The use of force—against a million-man North Korean army with over 10,000 artillery tubes pointed at Seoul and an arsenal of long-range missiles—was fraught with danger.

"The military options were on the table at that time" noted Jim Kelly, "and they weren't attractive."

Part of the problem was that while the hard-liners had managed to discredit the whole idea of talking to North Korea, in the process they had sharply limited the scope of any discussions about how to respond.

"From my vantage point," recalled John Wolf, who served as undersecretary of state for arms control at the time, "we did not have . . . we had not gamed out . . . what would happen, what we would do if certain things happened. I'm not remembering anything that said, 'Here's what we will do. The fleet will sail. The diplomats will do X. The intelligence agencies will do Y.'"

Instead, Wolf remembered the administration going into what he described as a tizzy. "How do we spin it? Then how do we deal with it if they boot the IAEA out and they move the plutonium. What do we do?"

Ironically, even as the administration was limiting its own policy options by acceding to pressure from the hard-liners not to negotiate, the challenge of North Korea was overshadowed by the impending invasion of Iraq. Although North Korea's actions raised the prospect that a charter member of the "Axis of Evil" would soon actually have nuclear weapons, and U.S. intelligence was unable to prove that Saddam Hussein's own nuclear program was anywhere close to success, toppling the Iraqi dictator remained President Bush's top priority.

Despite a warning from Defense Secretary Donald Rumsfeld that the United States had sufficient military power to prevail in a war with North Korea even in the midst of an invasion of Iraq, the fact was that within the administration, all other concerns, including the North's nuclear breakout, were subordinated to the upcoming assault on Baghdad. As the North cut the seals, shut off the cameras, and evicted the inspectors at Yongbyon, an administration that had made Iraqi interference with UN weapons inspectors one of its justifications for war drew no "red lines" with the North Koreans. Whatever Pyongyang did—and despite the pressure for action from some hard-liners—Washington was determined not to treat the situation as a crisis.

According to Jack Pritchard, "The feedback that I got from what the president was saying was, 'Nothing that the North Koreans do will cause me to view this as a crisis. Not the reprocessing, not firing a missile, not testing a nuclear weapon, nothing they could do.' He was so focused on Iraq that North Korea wasn't going to come up."

Steven Yates, who was Vice President Cheney's chief adviser on Asia, and who regularly fought with Pritchard over North Korea policy, had a similar recollection. "Alarm bells were ringing, but there was a palpable sense that there was a heavy burden already being carried by the government that affected at least one of the elements of strategy in this, the military option," he conceded. "So the alarm bells were going off, but we've got this ramp-up where we're still busy with Afghanistan, and homeland security, and preparing for Iraq."

In a study for the *Naval War College Review*, Jonathan Pollack noted that "a profound contradiction persisted between the administration's ominous portrayal of North Korea . . . and the seeming composure with which the United States reacted to Pyongyang's flouting of its nonproliferation obligations, especially in comparison to the administration's single-minded focus on Iraq."[12]

Appearing on NBC's *Meet the Press* at the end of December, Colin Powell was blunt. "It is not a crisis," he said, "but it is a matter of grave concern."[13]

Privately, Powell and his deputy Richard Armitage were in fact profoundly worried. "The North Koreans reacted boldly," Armitage said. "Secretary Powell and I thought we were in a fairly deep hole."

Politics in Washington prevented the secretary of state from making any direct effort to engage the North Koreans. Suddenly, an unusual interlocutor entered the picture—Democrat Bill Richardson, who had just been reelected as governor of New Mexico. A rumpled, folksy politician, Richardson had served as Bill Clinton's energy secretary and ambassador to the United Nations, where he had developed good relations with the North Korean diplomats and had made several trips to Pyongyang. In forging his North Korea connection, Richardson had been helped by K. A. "Tony" Namkung, a Korean-American scholar who had carved out a role for himself during the 1990s as a "back-channel" conduit between various American political and academic figures and the North Koreans.

In late December 2002, Richardson received a call on his cell phone from Han Song Ryol, Pyongyang's number-two man at the UN.

"What do you want?" asked a surprised Richardson.

"I want you to help us with the Bush administration," replied Han.

Richardson thought to himself, *These guys just don't get it.*

To the North Korean, he answered, "Han, there was an election two years ago. I am a Democrat. My guys lost. What the hell can I do?"

Still, Richardson informed the administration of the North Korean overture. Jim Kelly and others in the State Department urged Powell to avoid involving Richardson, arguing that as a member of the despised Democratic Party and a possible future presidential candidate, the New Mexico governor would only bring trouble. Yet as the situation deteriorated in January, Powell instructed the State Department to give the North Korean diplomats permission to visit Richardson in New Mexico. It was a symbolically important step, since normally Pyongyang's UN envoys were limited to traveling within a twenty-five-mile radius of New York. It underscored Powell's eagerness to maintain communication with the North Koreans.

Han Song Ryol and his colleagues arrived in Santa Fe just as Pyongyang was announcing its withdrawal from the Non-Proliferation Treaty.

"Han, this is not good," Richardson told the North Korean envoy.

"No," Han responded. "These are just tactics. Tell Powell they are just tactics to improve our negotiating position."[14]

During two days of discussions, punctuated by a visit to a downtown Santa Fe restaurant to introduce the North Koreans to authentic New Mexican chili, Richardson covered the entire range of issues at the heart of the crisis. After various intervals, he would call Powell, brief him on the contents of the discussion, and ask for guidance. Powell pressed him to explore whether the North Koreans might rescind their decision to quit the NPT and encouraged the governor to explore what options existed to reach that goal.

Richardson came away from the meetings convinced Pyongyang was prepared to deal. "They did say to me that they're ready to negotiate verification of some of their nuclear-reprocessing facilities," he told the *New York Times.* "They did say they would talk to the administration about the uranium enrichment facilities. They did say they want to improve relations with the U.S."[15]

"They don't negotiate like we do," Richardson told the Associated Press. "They believe in order to get something they have to lay out additional cards, step up the rhetoric, be more belligerent . . . so what I think the administration needs to do, with all due respect, is just pick up the phone, start the preliminary talks at the UN in New York at a low level to set up broader talks that address the issues."[16]

Given the resistance of administration hard-liners to any hint of a compro-mise, the otherwise promising meetings in Santa Fe produced no movement.

The confusion, posturing, mixed signals, and frequent paralysis exhibited by Washington at this crucial moment became the hallmark of the Bush admin-istration's approach to North Korea in the years that followed. In part this dys-function was the product of the bitter infighting between hard-liners who believed that pressure leading to regime change was the only option in dealing with Pyongyang, and pragmatists who were convinced that negotiations should be given a chance to succeed.

The impasse was made worse by the failure of Condoleezza Rice, in her role as National Security Adviser, to manage the internal battles and to help the president fashion a coherent strategy.

"She did nothing," said one former senior administration official. "She never tried to resolve the issue."

With Powell, Cheney, Rumsfeld, and their staffs engaged in a protracted in-ternecine war, this was not an easy task. It remains unclear whether Rice's weak-ness was a reflection of the president's wishes not to have a powerful national security adviser, or whether she was simply unable to stand up to the giants bat-tling around her.

There was another factor as well—a curious ambiguity in the president's own view of North Korea, which unquestionably influenced the battles over policy. As he had stated publicly, there was no question of his "visceral loathing" for Kim Jong Il and Kim's indifference to the suffering of his people.

It was this emotional reaction—something typical of Bush—that sustained opposition to talking to the North Koreans. "He did not want to be in a posi-tion of negotiating with a regime that does something like that," Powell contin-ued, "and he didn't want to get caught in the kind of negotiating morass that Clinton was caught in. He didn't like that kind of negotiation."

But it was equally clear that Bush had a pragmatic side, too. He understood that an Iraq-style military operation to topple Kim Jong Il was out of the ques-tion, and that he had little choice in the end but to support a policy that fell short of regime change.

"His instincts toward North Korea were not very friendly," said one senior State Department official, "so his basic attitude is that we need to take a hard line with these people. Then at the edge of the cliff he would turn and say 'Colin, get me out of here.'"

So Powell pressed the president. "That's what diplomacy is about," Powell said. "And sometimes it's very unpleasant, it takes a long time, but very often it works."

The contradictory elements of the administration's approach were evident when the president, in a news conference on the last day of 2002, declared, "I view the North Korean situation as one that can be resolved peacefully, through diplomacy . . . and we will continue to work that way. All options, of course, are always on the table. . . ."[17]

Diplomacy clearly meant enlisting South Korea and Japan, Washington's key Asian allies, as well as China, North Korea's oldest friend and one of Kim Jong Il's few remaining benefactors. Yet the administration's definition of negotiation did not involve give-and-take—a strategy that administration officials repeatedly described as "rewarding bad behavior." Instead, the administration's diplomatic efforts aimed at mobilizing international pressure to compel Kim Jong Il's regime to dismantle its nuclear program. If there were to be contact between Washington and Pyongyang, the sole purpose would be for the North Koreans to explain how they intended to comply with the Washington's demands—in other words, to discuss the terms of North Korea's diplomatic surrender.

Anti-American sentiment in Seoul in December 2002 ran deep. A poll released that fall by the Pew Research Center noted that 73 percent of South Koreans, the highest number in any Asian nation polled, said they believed the United States ignored their country's concerns in carrying out its foreign policy.[18]

And now, adding to this combustible mix, South Korea was in the midst of a presidential election campaign. Kim Dae-jung was stepping down. Lee Hoi-chang, leader of the conservative Grand National Party (GNP), a forceful advocate of the U.S.–South Korea security alliance and a skeptic on dealing with North Korea, was facing Roh Moo-hyun, a liberal human rights activist and labor lawyer, who called for continued engagement with North Korea and more independence from the United States.

Throughout the campaign, the Bush administration had signaled its preference for Lee Hoi-chang, giving him a warm reception on a visit to Washington—a stark contrast to the chilly relationship that had developed between the administration and outgoing president Kim Dae-jung. But the upsurge of anti-American nationalism in South Korea forced even the conservative Lee to modify his positions. In early December he declared that he was ready to meet Kim Jong Il at any time, without preconditions.

Roh's final campaign rallies were marked by renewed pledges to maintain the Sunshine Policy and increasingly sharp anti-American rhetoric, including warnings that a Roh administration would not necessarily side with the United States in the event the crisis led to armed conflict.

On December 19, 2002, the people of South Korea made their choice. With

48.9 percent of the vote, Roh Moo-hyun was elected president. Reflecting South Korea's generation gap, he received a much higher percentages of votes from people under forty than from older people. The stage was set for an already strained alliance to face the greatest crisis of its existence.

After the election, outgoing President Kim voiced his own opposition to the tough talk emanating from Washington. "Pressure and isolation have never been successful with Communist countries," he told his cabinet. "We cannot go to war with North Korea, and we can't go back to the Cold War system and ex-treme confrontation."[19]

For his part, even before taking office Roh Moo-hyun made clear that his views were more than just campaign rhetoric. On January 24, 2003 he sat down with me for his first television interview since winning the election, and outlined a position sharply at odds with the Bush administration on almost every aspect of the crisis.

"I think the best means of peaceful solution is dialogue, rather than unilat-erally demanding North Korea to abandon its nuclear ambitions," he told me. "If the tactic to pressure North Korea leads to a triggering of war or collapse of North Korean regime, I don't think South Korea is able to withstand the situa-tion, so I don't think it is a proper policy tool for the U.S."

Roh described the North's nuclear program as less a threat than "a political card to secure their political regime and to secure economic assistance for im-plementing reforms and opening up. I don't think it is accurate description or accurate presumption to consider North Korea's nuclear ambitions as a possi-ble, usable tool. Common sense tells us that North Korea will not confront U.S. with its nuclear weapons. And I think it is just trying to deter the possible at-tacks from United States by having a nuclear weapon and by guaranteeing its security."

Junichiro Koizumi had invested enormous political capital in a diplomatic breakthrough with North Korea. Despite his personal friendship with President Bush, the Japanese prime minister, in stark contrast to the U.S. ap-proach, had flown to Pyongyang in September 2002 and met Kim Jong Il to sign a document dubbed the Pyongyang Declaration, setting the stage for fur-ther negotiations on normalizing a long-tortured relationship—a development Koizumi believed was critical to the stability of Northeast Asia.

In the wake of the revelations from the Kelly visit to Pyongyong, Koizumi had repeatedly signaled his desire for negotiations between the United States and North Korea to resolve the crisis. His own behavior reflected such an approach. In late October, as American officials were declaring that no negotiations were possible, he authorized Japanese officials to hold a new round of normalization talks with Pyongyang. And his first reaction to news that North Korea was ending its nuclear freeze was to tell reporters, "If you read the North Korean announcement carefully, their consistent stance is to seek a peaceful resolution."[20]

As the Bush administration began to talk about tailored containment and sanctions, the Japanese became increasingly uncomfortable. They wanted to negotiate with the North Koreans. But a series of events since the Koizumi-Kim summit had thrust just one issue to the top of their agenda. The Japanese government and public wanted answers to a story that had become a national obsession—the fate of more than a dozen Japanese kidnapped by North Korean agents.

The story of the abductees obsessed the Japanese. Shock that so many had died, unanswered questions about what had actually happened to them, suspicion that some might still be alive, and anger at Pyongyang's refusal to let the children of the five survivors accompany them when they returned to Japan in October 2002 sparked intense public pressure for a harder line toward North Korea. The families of the abductees became national figures. They were embraced by the Japanese media, which provided saturation coverage, and by hawkish politicians, such as Chief Cabinet Secretary Shinzo Abe, whose public standing skyrocketed with his calls to get tough with North Korea.

Although the pressure forced Koizumi to make increasingly tough comments about North Korea, the Japanese leader recognized that the country's location—within range of North Korean missiles—meant it had much more to fear in the event of a military confrontation on the Korean peninsula. Even as he moved to strengthen Japan's security alliance with the United States, Koizumi continued to believe that negotiations still represented the best hope for resolving the saga of the abductees and the nuclear issue, and he sought to use his friendship with George Bush to encourage a more moderate American approach. When he spoke with Bush by phone in the last week of January 2003, Koizumi's message was clear. He told the president, "There is a need for a peaceful resolution of the issue."[21]

But suddenly, events seemed to be spinning out of control. At the very time Koizumi was speaking with Bush, American spy satellites detected trucks being loaded with cargo at the storage facility where the spent fuel rods had been kept at Yongbyon. All the indications were that the North Koreans were moving the rods to a reprocessing plant where they could be turned into plutonium for nuclear bombs. A move to reprocess would be a dangerous step; to many observers, it would constitute a justification for military action.

Colin Powell told the World Economic Forum in Davos, Switzerland, that "the United States has no intention of attacking North Korea." However, on the same day that Kim Dae-jung spoke with Bush, Admiral Thomas Fargo, commander of U.S. forces in the Pacific, requested that more American troops and warplanes be sent to the region. The admiral asked Defense Secretary Donald Rumsfeld to approve the dispatch of 2,000 troops, mostly Air Force personnel, to supplement the 37,000 U.S. soldiers already in South Korea, and to move two dozen long-range bombers to the U.S. territory of Guam, within striking range of North Korea. In addition, he requested that F-15E fighter-bombers and U-2s and other reconnaissance aircraft be deployed to American bases in South Korea and Japan. A week later, the long-range B-52 and B-1 bombers were placed on alert for deployment to Guam.

In Washington, the President's spokesman Ari Fleischer warned North Korea against taking "another provocative step" by reprocessing the fuel rods.

The North Koreans remained defiant. The official media reported that Kim Jong Il was inspecting military units and was "greatly satisfied to see all the servicemen trained as indomitable fighters capable of wiping out the aggressors by resolute and merciless blows."[22]

Across northeast Asia, worried leaders began to discuss what they could do to halt what seemed an inexorable drift toward war.

# 9

# WAR GAMES

HE WAS FAR MORE AT HOME IN THE RUGGED HILLS WHERE U.S. and South Korean troops trained along the Demilitarized Zone, slogging through the midsummer heat or shivering in the bitter midwinter cold. Now, David Maxwell, a colonel in the U.S. Army's Special Forces, was sitting in the comfortable State Department office of Lawrence Wilkerson, Colin Powell's chief of staff. Maxwell was a colorful figure, fluent in Korean and a veteran of years in the Special Forces. He was one of the U.S. military's leading experts on the peninsula, having served in and out of Korea since the 1980s. Wilkerson, a former Army lieutenant colonel who had a tour of duty in Vietnam, had summoned Maxwell to Washington and was grilling him intently. Wilkerson wanted to know what capabilities the Special Forces had to take out North Korea's nuclear facilities.

In keeping with his personality, Maxwell was blunt. "These are good facilities," he told Wilkerson. "They're probably underground. It would take several hundred members of Delta Force for such an operation, *if* the U.S. knew where the facilities were. Otherwise, it would be like trying to find a needle in a haystack."

And Maxwell had other questions for Wilkerson. "Do you really imagine there is any way to go in and take out the target and get out? You'd need hundreds of men and dozens of aircraft. That means the U.S. would have to take out North Korea's air defense capabilities. So from a North Korean perspective, it will look like we're attacking them."

To Maxwell, the conclusion was obvious. If the United States goes ahead, he asked Powell's chief of staff, "Are we prepared for catastrophe in the region?"

"I know," Wilkerson replied. "But I had to ask, because there are people up there who think there is a Special Ops capability to go in and take out their nuclear capability."

Said Maxwell: "They've been watching too much TV."

U sing the Special Forces was only one of the options being studied at the Pentagon. As U.S. spy satellites picked up increasing signs of activity at Yongbyon—indications that the spent fuel rods were being moved to a reprocessing plant where they could be made into weapons-grade plutonium—Defense Secretary Donald Rumsfeld was pushing his key advisers to prepare contingency plans for destroying the facility.

"What we did," recalled Douglas Feith, under secretary of defense and number three in the Pentagon after Rumsfeld and his deputy Paul Wolfowitz, "was . . . you look at the problem and you try to inventory what are the sources and types of leverages that we have. What are the various things we can do from talking, acting, acting by ourselves, acting with others, diplomatic, economic, intelligence, military—what's the full range of things we can do to induce or coerce a country like that to modify its behavior?"

The emphasis was on coercion. In one of the largest displays of American muscle flexing in Northeast Asia since the 1994 nuclear crisis, the Pentagon moved ships, planes, and troops toward South Korea, Japan, and the western Pacific. Two dozen B-52 and B-1 bombers, placed on alert at their home bases at the end of January, were deployed to Guam a month later. With each B-1 capable of carrying up to twenty-four one-ton, satellite-guided bombs and the payload of each B-52 weighing in at 70,000 pounds of bombs and missiles, it was a potent addition to the U.S. arsenal in the region. The aircraft carrier *Carl Vinson* was ordered to Japan to replace the *Kitty Hawk*, which had been sent to the Persian Gulf as preparations for the invasion of Iraq neared a climax. Six F-117 Stealth fighters and four F-15E fighter jets were deployed to South Korea. Ostensibly their mission was to participate in a training exercise, but, with conspicuous publicity, they were ordered to remain in the South once the exercise was over. And the training itself, code-named Foal Eagle, including staging a massive amphibious landing at Pohong, 220 miles south of Seoul, with 3,000 troops, including a thousand U.S. Marines, backed by warships and planes—a not-too-subtle rehearsal for a possible assault on North Korea.

In addition, despite the fiasco of the *So San* incident, in which a vessel carrying Scud missiles from North Korea to Yemen had been intercepted in

December 2002, only to be allowed to proceed after protests from the Yemeni government, the administration began to develop detailed plans to use the U.S. military to interdict or seize ships and aircraft from North Korea that were suspected of transporting missiles or nuclear weapons-related material.

At the same time, the rhetoric from Washington became increasingly belligerent. In his second State of the Union address, President Bush declared, "The North Korean regime is using its nuclear program to incite fear and seek concessions. America and the world will not be blackmailed."[1]

Shortly after Bush's speech, CIA Director George Tenet said that North Korea might already be capable of hitting the mainland U.S., as well as Alaska and Hawaii, with an untested long-range nuclear missile.[2] Another ominous warning came from an unlikely source. Jim Kelly, an advocate of diplomacy, told the Senate Foreign Relations Committee that the time line for Pyongyang to develop a uranium nuclear capability was much shorter than earlier estimates. "The enriched uranium issue, some have assumed, is somewhere off in the fog of the distant future," Kelly said. "It is not. It is probably only a matter of months and not years behind the plutonium." This suggested a greater degree of urgency than the original estimates by the intelligence community.

And President Bush for the first time explicitly raised the possibility of military action against North Korea as a last resort. If efforts to resolve the crisis "don't work diplomatically," he told reporters, "they'll have to work militarily."[3]

The posturing took place against the backdrop of the U.S. invasion of Iraq. It was a moment of supreme confidence—some would say arrogance or hubris—for the neocons, the time when their vision of remaking the international order according to their doctrine of preemptive war seemed to be becoming reality. A short time later, when the statue of Saddam Hussein was toppled in central Baghdad, John Bolton said, "We are hopeful that a number of regimes will draw the appropriate lessons from Iraq."[4] In a background briefing with the *New York Times*, an unnamed administration official said, "This is just the beginning. I would not rule out the same sequence of events for Iran and North Korea as for Iraq."[5]

"It looked like [President Bush] was prescient when the statue of Saddam came down," Richard Armitage recalled. "Everybody's saying, 'Holy shit, maybe he's brilliant.' So that side was feeling totally lusty and bold. They wanted to be muscular. They were full of testosterone."

According to Michael Pillsbury, a China expert and longtime Pentagon adviser, a "hawk position" on North Korea took shape and was presented to top hard-liners. "They were excited. They were sympathetic. And they felt that North Korea deserved an invasion far more than Saddam Hussein. We used to joke about whether the neocons wanted to invade Iran next or North Korea next. We used to say, is it in alphabetical order?"

But it was evident even to the most extreme hard-liners that a military strike against the North carried enormous risks.

Pillsbury characterized the tone of some of the discussions in the Pentagon: "Could this be done? Was it feasible? And then they would get back the mainstream view, which this was an invitation to World War Three," he recalled. "The mainstream view was if any kind of military strike starts against North Korea, the North Koreans would invade South Korea, and they will cause enormous destruction of Seoul. And we are not prepared to handle all this."

The signals sent by the muscle flexing were therefore meant to operate on several levels. First, the Pentagon wanted to be sure Kim Jong Il did not try to take advantage of the American preoccupation with Iraq.

"We had to make our deterrence completely credible," asserted Douglas Feith.

Although not stated as explicitly at the time, at least some of the more hawkish figures in the Pentagon appear to have had another goal—intimidation—to deploy American military assets in such a way as to make North Korea sufficiently frightened of an attack that it would rethink its nuclear breakout.

"Things were done involving beaches, ships, and various military deployments," said Michael Pillsbury. "It gave the impression that the U.S. was preparing for a strike on North Korea. Beyond just intimidation—actual preparations for an attack on North Korea."

Said one senior U.S. military figure, "You would hope that they picked up the signals clearly and they recognized that we were dead serious about their nuclear capability."

The U.S. buildup came amid continuing anti-American ferment in South Korea and the inauguration of the new president, Roh Moo-hyun, on February 25, 2003. In his inaugural address, Roh promised to continue the engagement policy with North Korea pioneered by his predecessor, Kim Dae-jung, and insisted that the nuclear crisis could only be resolved through dialogue.

At the Pentagon, Defense Secretary Rumsfeld watched the continuing wave of anti-U.S. protests—which regularly featured demands for American troops to leave South Korea—with mounting agitation, but also with a sense that they might become a catalyst for something he already wanted to do: orchestrate a major redeployment of U.S. forces in South Korea. For decades, the U.S.

Army's Second Infantry Division had operated in the shadow of the heavily for-
tified Demilitarized Zone, its function to be a "trip wire" in the event of a North
Korean attack. But changing military technology, U.S. planners believed, made
that concept obsolete.

The goal was to reconfigure an American military presence created during
the Cold War so it could more effectively deal with the challenges of the
twenty-first century, a project that predated the Bush administration. For decades, Washington had relied on fixed bases to deter or repel enemies that military planners expected to cross a clear border line. Now, in an era when
threats came from less conventional foes, the concept shifted to the creation of
a more nimble posture that would enable U.S. forces to respond swiftly to new
and unexpected crises in a time of terrorism, nuclear proliferation, and rogue
states.

"It wasn't necessary to have the 2nd ID sitting on the DMZ," recalled
one former senior American military officer. "We had so much invested in
capabilities. It wasn't the number of forces but the capability." Air and naval
power and high-tech weapons meant that the United States no longer needed
troops literally face-to-face with the North Koreans in order to defend the
South or take the battle to the North. Moreover, the numerous U.S. bases near
the DMZ, wedged in a small, densely populated area, increased the chances of
incidents like the tragic accident in which the two girls were accidentally killed
by an American vehicle. "This was an opportunity to reduce the footprint and
give back two-thirds of the land," the former senior officer added.

In early March 2003, with virtually no consultation, Rumsfeld sent shock-
waves through Seoul by signaling that a significant pullback—and possible
pullout—of U.S. forces from South Korea was on the table. From its forward
positions near the 38th parallel along the border with North Korea, the bulk of
the Second Infantry Division would be withdrawn to beyond the Han River,
well south of Seoul. Eventually, a portion of the division would be withdrawn
from South Korea altogether and sent to Iraq. At the same time, the Americans
began working on plans to relocate Yongsan, the sprawling U.S. military headquarters in the heart of Seoul. To an increasingly nationalistic population,
Yongsan had become a symbol of an overbearing and intrusive military presence that many had come to resent. The Pentagon's calculation was that establishing a new headquarters well away from Seoul would eliminate a major
political problem.

But in South Korea, the initial reaction to Rumsfeld's announcement was
one of alarm. Many South Koreans feared that moving the Second Infantry Division away from the DMZ might be a prelude to a U.S. preemptive strike on
North Korea. Within hours of receiving word of the planned redeployment se-

nior South Korean officials appealed to the United States to defer the decision, but to no avail.


The North Koreans were watching, too. In an interview with the BBC, a senior North Korean official was blunt. "In the United States, they published the fact that after Iraq, North Korea will be their next target," said Ri Pyong Gap, a Foreign Ministry deputy director. "A preemptive attack is not something only the United States can do. We can also do that if it is a matter of life and death. We are fully ready to have a conversation with the United States," Ri added. "At the same time, we are fully ready to have a war with the United States."[6]

Early on the morning of Sunday, March 2, 2003, a U.S. Air Force RC-135 Cobra Ball reconnaissance aircraft was flying about 150 miles off the coast of North Korea over the Sea of Japan. The RC-135, a converted Boeing 707, was packed with sophisticated equipment for collecting data on North Korean military activities.

"I saw on the U.S. side a desire to reach out and touch the North Koreans in an interesting way by having our aircraft up there sniffing, so to speak," said an American official based in Seoul at the time. "And that this was part of the overall demonstration effect of our military capabilities. But it was also a protective measure of putting aircraft there that could possibly detect nuclear-related activities."

At 10:48 A.M. local time, the RC-135 was intercepted by four North Korean fighter jets. For twenty-two minutes, two MIG-29s and two MIG-23s, all armed with missiles, shadowed the American plane, at one point approaching within fifty feet. At least one of the MIGs "locked on" its fire support radar. U.S. communication intercepts revealed that the North Korean plane had requested permission to shoot down the RC-135, but was ordered not to open fire.[7] But the confrontation forced the U.S. plane to break off its mission and return to the American airbase at Kadena, Japan. The incident was the most serious aerial confrontation between the two countries since the North Koreans had shot down a U.S. reconnaissance plane in 1969, killing thirty-one American airmen.

As he monitored the situation from his headquarters in Honolulu, Admiral Thomas Fargo, the commander in chief of U.S. forces in the Pacific, was convinced the North Koreans had been planning such a provocation for some time. Intelligence showed that the North Koreans had moved the MIGs from a base in the interior to one on the country's eastern coast. Moreover, the range and capability of the aircraft had been reconfigured for longer missions. "This was something they probably had been thinking about and planning for a long time," Fargo observed.

Back at the State Department, however, Colin Powell's chief of staff, Lawrence Wilkerson, studied the flight plans provided by the Pentagon to put together his own assessment of the incident for his boss Wilkerson was puzzled. "We looked at the flight plans," he recalled. "We wondered why the U.S. flight plan had been toughened up. It was a little more provocative."

Normally, Wilkerson said, a reconnaissance mission would fly parallel to North Korea's Air Defense Zone (ADZ), an area a certain specified distance from the shore that both countries saw as a line that could not be crossed. However close, the parallel flight path would reassure the North Koreans the U.S. plane would stay over international waters. In this case, though, Wilkerson saw that the RC-135's flight path was not parallel. Instead, repeatedly, the U.S. reconnaissance plane flew directly at the North Korean ADZ, only to veer away at the last minute. It seemed to Wilkerson that the plane's movements were intended to deliberately provoke the North Koreans.

"We were concerned that we were doing things that might cause an incident that would lead to where we didn't want to go," Wilkerson recalled.

There was no question all that the U.S. muscle flexing alarmed Kim Jong Il. After a visit to the Russian embassy in Pyongyang on February 12, 2003, he dropped from sight and did not make another reported public appearance for almost two months, even missing the annual session of the North Korean parliament in late March for the first time in six years. The speculation was that he was holed up in a secure position somewhere in the mountains, fearing that he, like Saddam Hussein, could soon be the target of a U.S. attack.

The day after the RC-135 incident, KCNA quoted Kim Jong Il as saying, "Should a war break out on the Korean peninsula due to the U.S. imperialists, it will escalate into a nuclear war."[8]

The combination of the imminent U.S. invasion of Iraq and the heightened American military posture in the western Pacific, however, set off alarm bells in Beijing, too. The Chinese suddenly saw the Bush doctrine of preemption becoming reality. And Washington did little to disabuse Beijing of that possibility; indeed, American officials were fanning its fears in order to get it to take diplomatic action. Chinese analysts in Beijing predicted that the war in Iraq would end with a quick American victory and warned that the next target might be North Korea. The possibility that Pyongyang appeared to be on its way to becoming a nuclear power—raising the prospect of a "domino effect," in which Japan, South Korea, and perhaps even Taiwan might follow suit and develop nuclear weapons—added to Beijing's worries. The upshot was a dramatic shift in Chinese foreign policy. For the first time, China took the diplomatic initiative on a major international crisis.

"We like to do things behind the scenes in Washington and Pyongyang," said one Chinese official, "by encouraging them to have more dialogue and exchanges. But by early 2003, the situation was very dangerous. My impression was that the Bush administration was so emotional," the official continued. "Many of its policies were not rational. Bush said, 'All options are on the table.' China did not see this statement as an idle threat. Also, we hated to see North Koreans withdraw from the Non-Proliferation Treaty and restart the reactor. Only when China realized the dangers of confrontation, even military confrontation, did China change its low-key manner."

The decision to abandon a long-held posture did not come easily. But it was pushed forward by a group of foreign policy analysts at the Chinese Foreign Ministry and some Beijing think-tanks whose members argued that the danger of inaction was far greater than the risks involved in taking a more activist role. The sentiments were echoed by the country's new leader, Hu Jintao.[9] The upshot of the policy shift was that China took on the role of intermediary and advocate of restraint on both sides.

In mid-February, Vice Foreign Minister Wang Yi met North Korean Foreign Minister Paek Nam Sun in Beijing and urged that North Korea moderate its provocative behavior. A few days later, oil shipments from China to North Korea were cut for three days. Beijing has never made clear whether the move was deliberate or merely a technical problem, but nonetheless appeared content for Pyongyang and others to interpret it as a sign of Chinese pressure.

Appeals for moderation were also made to Washington, most notably when Colin Powell met Chinese leaders in Beijing in late February, and when President Hu Jintao telephoned President Bush shortly after taking office. Bush, however, remained adamant that he would not agree to bilateral talks with the North Koreans.

As Powell continued to search for a formula to get negotiations under way, he was becoming increasingly frustrated.

"We knew we had to do something." he said in an interview. "And I couldn't go back to bilateral, the uranium enrichment specter is out, Yongbyon was humming, no more fuel oil. The Agreed Framework . . ." here Powell paused and made a shooting noise. "No way I could get the president or the system to go one-on-one. So I had to broaden it. The president and I came to the conclusion that, look, if I can spread it out with that deal, would you let me do that? And he said, 'Yeah.' "

In late January, Powell had authorized Jack Pritchard to meet with North Korea's UN envoy Pak Gil Yon in New York to present what was dubbed the "P5 + 5" approach—an unwieldy proposal for a meeting on the nuclear issue involving the five permanent members of the UN Security Council plus North

Korea, South Korea, Japan, Australia, and the European Union. The North Koreans rejected it almost immediately.

On his Beijing trip in February, Powell offered another idea—that China host some form of multilateral talks involving both Koreas, the United States, China, and Japan. He told Chinese leaders it was in their interest to broker talks. "I said, 'Look . . . you really should want a discussion to take place,'" Powell told his biographer Karen DeYoung. "You really have to be the spark plug in making it all happen."[10]

Two weeks later, in what Powell described as a pivotal moment, he met with Chinese foreign minister Tang Jiaxuan in New York. The two men had been in close contact on UN activities as the U.S. prepared to invade Iraq. Now, Powell unburdened himself to the Chinese diplomat about the political problems he faced in Washington winning support for engaging the North Koreans, and he appealed to China to host a multilateral meeting.

Eventually, Powell succeeded in convincing Tang and the Chinese leadership that Bush would indeed never accept bilateral talks. And the dangerous escalation represented by the near clash between the North Korean MIGs and the U.S. reconnaissance plane further fueled Beijing's concern.

On March 8, China's most senior diplomat, Vice Premier Qian Qichen, made a secret visit to Pyongyang. Qian conveyed a blunt message to the North Koreans, urging them to abandon their pursuit of nuclear weapons and pressing them to accept multilateral talks. Qian initially offered the five-party talks Powell had previously proposed. In his memoir, Pritchard recounts that, "When the North Koreans rejected the Chinese offer of five-party talks, Qian revised the suggestion on the spot, offering instead three-party talks involving only China, the United States, and North Korea."[11]

Pyongyang's immediate reaction was to stick to its guns. The North Korean media continued to insist that only direct talks with Washington could resolve the crisis.

And, predictably, Pyongyang also upped the ante. On March 31, Jack Pritchard and David Straub were asked to a meeting by North Korea's diplomats at the UN. After receiving permission from Armitage and Powell, the two men made the short trip to New York, where the North Koreans delivered a bombshell. As Jack Pritchard recalled, the message was blunt. "We've watched what you're doing in Iraq," the North Koreans told Pritchard and Straub. "The lessons we're getting out of that is that Iraq does not have weapons of mass destruction and you invaded them. So, we're going to reprocess the spent fuel rods [at the Yongbyon reactor], we're going to take them and create a nuclear deterrent so you cannot invade us."

Author with Kim Il Sung April, 1992.

Kim Jong Il's defiant public appearance at the height of the famine, April, 1997. *Photo by Eason Jordan.*

Mass Rally hailing Kim Il Sung and Kim Jong Il, Pyongyang, April, 1997. *Photo by Chris Goacher.*

State Department envoy Charles "Chuck" Kartman (on right, in white shirt) heads to a meeting with Vice Foreign Minister Kim Gye Gwan in Beijing to discuss a moratorium on North Korean missile tests and other issues. June, 1999. The bearded man in the background is intelligence analyst Robert Carlin. *Courtesy AP.*

The North-South summit. South Korean president Kim Dae-jung with Kim Jong Il, Pyongyang, June, 2000. *Courtesy AP.*

"No Hostile Intent." President Bill Clinton welcomes Kim Jong Il's personal envoy, Vice Marshal Jo Myong Rok, to the White House. Oct. 10, 2000. *Courtesy AP.*

Secretary of State Madeleine Albright with Kim Jong Il in Pyongyang. Oct. 2000. *Courtesy AP.*

President George W. Bush hosts South Korean president Kim Dae-jung at their disastrous White House summit, March 7, 2001. *Courtesy AP.*

The cooling pond at Yongbyon nuclear facility. The containers in the middle hold plutonium encased in spent fuel that was subsequently reprocessed and presumably turned into nuclear bombs. *Courtesy Jon Wolfsthal.*

The Kelly Mission: Assistant Secretary of State James Kelly and his team pose during their controversial visit to Pyongyang, Oct. 25, 2002. Left to right: Mary Tighe, Col. Michael Dunn, Michael Green, James Kelly, Julie Cheng, Jack Pritchard, David Straub.

U.S. and Spanish forces interdict the North Korean freighter *So San,* which was carrying a cargo of Scud missiles for Yemen. Dec. 2002. *Courtesy Department of Defense.*

The first round of six-party talks in Beijing, Aug. 27, 2003. Left to Right: Mitoji Yabunaka, director-general for Asian Affairs, Japanese Foreign Ministry; James Kelly, U.S. assistant secretary; Kim Yong Il, North Korea's deputy foreign minister; Chinese vice-foreign minister Wang Yi; Alexander Losiukov, Russian deputy foreign minister; Lee Soo-Hyuck, South Korean deputy minister of foreign affairs and trade. *Courtesy AP.*

Secretary of State Colin Powell, Deputy Secretary of State Richard Armitage, and President Bush at the President's ranch, Crawford, Texas, August. 2004. *Courtesy Richard Armitage.*

U.S. Ambassador to South Korea Thomas Hubbard with South Korean president Roh Moo-hyun. *Courtesy Thomas Hubbard.*

David Asher, driving force of the "Illicit Activities Initiative," in the cabin of the *Pong Su,* a North Korean freighter seized by the Australian navy with a cargo of heroin on board. *Courtesy David Asher.*

The headquarters of the Banco Delta Asia, Macau. *Courtesy AP.*

The Sept. 19 agreement. Christopher Hill shakes hands with North Korean envoy Kim Gye Gwan as a beaming South Korean deputy foreign minister Song Min-soon looks on. *Courtesy AP.*

Robert Joseph, John Bolton's hard-line successor as Under Secretary of State for Arms Control. *Courtesy Department of State.*

U.N. envoy John Bolton casts his vote in favor of a Security Council resolution imposing sanctions on North Korea after the Oct. 9, 2006 nuclear test. Sitting behind Bolton is his chief Asia expert, Mark Groombridge. *Courtesy AP.*

"A tough visit." South Korean president Roh Moo-hyun rebuffs an appeal from Secretary of State Condoleezza Rice to join in tough sanctions against Pyongyang. Oct. 20, 2006. *Courtesy Department of State.*

Assistant Secretary of State Christopher Hill, Korea desk director Sung Kim and State Department North Korea analyst Yuri Kim (in rear) on board "Mojo 55," the U.S. Air Force Cessna jet taking them to Pyongyang to deliver a letter from George W. Bush to Kim Jong Il, Dec. 2007.

Assistant Secretary of State Christopher Hill, wearing protective clothing, inspects the Yongbyon nuclear complex, Dec. 2007.

It was the first time North Korea had formally and unequivocally acknowledged it was trying to make nuclear weapons. While Washington had never made the warning explicit, reprocessing the fuel rods into weapons-grade plutonium had long been seen as a crucial red line, the crossing of which could be the death knell for a diplomatic process that had not really even begun.

As soon as they returned to Washington, Straub drafted a verbatim account of the meeting for Kelly, which was immediately sent to Armitage and Powell. The secretary and his deputy, however, made the decision to keep the information to themselves. While Powell asked the intelligence community to step up efforts to determine if reprocessing was indeed under way at Yongbyon, other government agencies—even the president—were kept in the dark. Powell was concerned that if the news leaked, the effort to arrange talks, which was still ongoing, would have been jeopardized.

When the news finally did come out, Bush was reportedly furious at Powell and the already acrimonious relationship between the hard-liners and Powell's diplomatic team was further poisoned. The Pentagon was particularly bitter. "We were not holding meetings with the North Koreans and not telling the State Department," said Douglas Feith. "Now Powell and Armitage—they were pumping out stories absolutely every day. The Pentagon didn't do that. And because it's all coming from the State Department leadership, when there were quarrels, the explanation is, the DOD [Department of Defense] people are quarreling."

According to one senior official, the episode did serious damage to Powell's standing in the administration. "That was a turning point on the president and Rice's willingness to let Powell and Armitage and Kelly have a relatively free hand," the official said.

Meanwhile, the Chinese had been playing a quiet double game to get Washington and Pyongyang to agree to a three-way meaning. To the Americans, Chinese diplomats made clear Beijing intended to be a full participant in any talks, and that the gathering would not be a fig leaf for bilateral U.S.–North Korea negotiations. To the North Koreans, however, the Chinese hinted that if they agreed to attend—which would mark a major shift in Pyongyang's long-standing position—there would be a chance for face-to-face talks with U.S. diplomats.

"That was the Chinese playing both ends against the middle here," recalled Jack Pritchard, "telling the North Koreans, 'Yes, you're going to have a bilateral meeting with the U.S., and then turning around and telling the U.S., 'Don't worry, this is truly a three-party session.'"

As a further sign of Chinese evenhandedness, Beijing blocked the UN Security Council from passing a U.S.-sponsored motion condemning Pyongyang's nuclear program. On April 12, North Korea informed the Chinese that Li Gun, the Foreign Ministry's deputy director for American affairs, would lead a delegation to three-way talks in Beijing. The talks were scheduled to last three days.

Having pushed for a broader multilateral format, Powell was concerned about the consequences of holding talks without the participation of Washington's key Asian allies, Japan and South Korea. In late March, to lay the groundwork for a possible meeting, Powell met South Korea's new foreign minister, Yoon Young-kwan. Yoon, a liberal-minded college professor, shared the concern of President Roh Moo-hyun that the Bush administration's rigid approach to the North was making the crisis worse. At the meeting, Yoon presented Powell with a three-stage "road map" to resolve the issue. The South Korean plan called first for a "standstill" (the word "freeze," with its associations with Clinton's hated Agreed Framework, was anathema in the Bush administration), followed by a return to the previous status quo, and eventual negotiations for a comprehensive settlement of all outstanding issues. Powell was noncommittal, but did tell Yoon about the possibility of three-way talks, while stressing his long-term desire to have Japan and South Korea be involved in any future meetings. Although South Korea would be excluded, Yoon and President Roh were so relieved to see the Bush administration commit to any kind of diplomatic process involving the North Koreans that they immediately gave their blessing, while also urging Washington to hold direct talks with the North as well.

Following the American invasion of Iraq, and over the objections of some of his advisers who opposed the invason, President Roh also secured the approval of the National Assembly for sending South Korean noncombatant troops to Iraq. While on one level it was a gesture of support for an ally, Roh made clear that his primary motive was to retain some additional leverage to enable him to press the Bush administration to engage with North Korea. "Extending help to the U.S. is far more helpful to resolving the North Korean nuclear problem," he told legislators, "than increasing friction for the sake of some [antiwar] cause."

For its part, the Japanese government was uncomfortable with the idea of three-way talks. While Tokyo had pushed Washington to encourage China to play a greater role, "Japan wanted to avoid a situation where the nuclear issue would only be discussed by North Korea, the U.S., and China," said one senior Japanese Foreign Ministry official. Eventually, Prime Minister Junichiro Koizumi gave his blessing, but only after a twenty-minute phone call with George Bush in which the president promised to work to include Japan in any future talks.[12]

Jim Kelly, the head of the U.S. delegation to the talks, was given instructions that reflected the imprint of those who thought talking to the North Koreans was a waste of time. Kelly was given permission merely to recite the official U.S. position.

He was told to inform Li Gun that the United States would not accept a freeze of North Korea's nuclear activity, insisting instead on the "verifiable, and irreversible dismantlement" of Pyongyang's nuclear weapons programs. This was a precursor of CVID—"complete, verifiable, and irreversible dismantlement"—which became the administration's mantra in subsequent negotiations. Moreover, if the North Koreans announced that they were in fact reprocessing the spent fuel into weapons-grade plutonium, Kelly was to immediately terminate the meeting and report back to Washington. The only concession to Pyongyang was that Kelly was authorized to assure the North Koreans the United States was not seeking to topple Kim Jong Il's regime, though for the hard-liners, even this was too much. Powell only managed to secure President Bush's approval for that proviso at a meeting that Donald Rumsfeld, preoccupied with the war in Iraq, was too busy to attend.[13]

The secretary of defense, however, was making his own push on Korea policy. After trying and failing to have John Bolton tapped to head the U.S. delegation, Rumsfeld circulated a secret memo to senior administration officials just days before Bush gave Powell the go-ahead for Kelly to attend the Beijing meeting, proposing that the explicit goal of U.S. policy should be the ouster of Kim Jong Il. The memo was drafted by Under Secretary of Defense Richard Lawless, a former CIA agent with years of experience in Korea, who had become the Pentagon's point person on Korea issues.

The central argument of the memo was that Kim Jong Il would never agree to negotiate away his nuclear weapons program, and therefore the most practical way to get rid of the North's nuclear weapons was to get rid of Kim Jong Il. The memo proposed that the U.S. work with China to push for Kim's ouster and his replacement by a regime "acceptable" to the United States—"regime modification" rather than regime change. It did not propose the use of force or the wholesale destruction of the North Korean system, but an increase in pressure in collaboration with Beijing to force the Dear Leader from power.

The proposal directly contradicted Powell's position of reassuring Kim Jong Il that, as a senior official told the *New York Times*, "We're not trying to take him out."[14] Coming just days before the scheduled meeting in Beijing, it seemed timed to pressure the administration to back out of the talks. Indeed, almost immediately after Rumsfeld sent the memo, it was leaked to the *New York Times.*

Pentagon officials believed the leak came from the State Department, where Powell and Armitage had received copies, and was intended to discredit Rumsfeld's position before it could be seriously discussed within the administration. The *Times* article included observations from unnamed pro-engagement administration officials saying it was "ludicrous" to think that China—now acting as intermediary between North Korea and the United States—would join in any American-led effort to bring about the fall of the North Korean government.

"The last thing the Chinese want," the *Times* quoted one senior administration official involved in the diplomatic effort, "is a collapse of North Korea that will create a flood of refugees into China and put Western allies on the Chinese border."[15]

Meanwhile, just days before Kelly was due to travel to Beijing, the North Koreans further muddied the waters. On April 18, 2003, the Korean Central News Agency released a statement in English announcing that "we are successfully reprocessing more than 8,000 spent fuel rods."[16] The public announcement set off alarm bells in Washington, as any confirmation of reprocessing could have led Bush to cancel the talks.

One U.S. official told the *Washington Post,* "We will look like fools if we get on a plane and go to those talks" after the North's statement.[17] Analysts noted, however, that the Korean-language version of the report was less explicit, and three days later, the original version was pulled from KCNA's Web site and replaced with one that read, "We are successfully completing the final phase, to the point of the reprocessing operation, for some 8,000 fuel rods." The issue remained ambiguous enough—at least in public—that the talks were not canceled before they began.

The Diaoyutai State Guest House is a place of uncommon beauty. With nineteen traditional-style buildings, artificial lakes lined with weeping willow trees, and carefully manicured gardens, it is an oasis of green tranquility in the heart of Beijing. On April 23, 2003, Jim Kelly, Li Gun, and Chinese Vice Foreign Minister Wang Yi in sat down in a large room at Diaoyutai for the first meeting attended by senior American and North Korean officials since the nuclear crisis had erupted. Sitting with Kelly were the members of his delegation, including David Straub, head of the State Department's Korea Desk, and Michael Green of the NSC—both veterans of Kelly's confrontation with Kang Sok Ju in October 2002. Also present were a brigadier general representing the Joint Chiefs of Staff and the Pentagon's hard-line Senior Country Director for North Korea, Jodi Green.

The meeting began with a plenary session where the head of each delegation read a prepared statement. A dinner was planned for later in the day, with a follow-up session the next morning. Smooth and cosmopolitan, Wang Yi, one of China's leading experts on Japan, kicked off the proceedings by urging both sides to be reasonable. To Korea Desk chief David Straub, Wang seemed to be "playing the role of the teacher and the mediator in kind of a condescending manner. We and the North Koreans were the recalcitrant students, little boys fighting with each other."

North Korea's envoy Li Gun went next. Li was short, stocky, and often pugnacious. He spoke excellent English, reportedly honed by listening to Miami radio stations while he was stationed at the North Korean embassy in Havana. He had also been based at Pyongyang's UN mission and had logged many hours in negotiations with American diplomats in the previous decade.

Li laid out what North Korean media later described as Pyongyang's own "bold approach"—a proposal clearly intended to be an opening position in what Pyongyang hoped would become a serious negotiation with the United States. He said North Korea was prepared to dismantle its nuclear program, allow international inspectors into its nuclear facilities, and end missile sales. In exchange, he demanded major concessions from the United States, such as normalized relations, economic aid, security guarantees, and a nonaggression pact. He also wanted Washington to take the first step. In the course of his presentation, he also stated that the North had begun reprocessing the spent fuel rods at Yongbyon and noted that the American side [Straub and Pritchard] had been informed of this development at the end of March.

Apart from Kelly and Straub, none of the other members of the U.S. delegation knew of the admission by North Korea's diplomats at the United Nations the previous month. When Li Gun mentioned it, the Pentagon's Jodi Green put down her pen and glared at Kelly, who refused to look directly at her.

When Li Gun finished, Kelly carefully recited his scripted instructions, insisting on the "verifiable and irreversible" elimination of North Korea's nuclear weapons program before any concessions or benefits could even be considered.

Kelly also made clear there would be no bilateral meeting. Li, however, insisted that without the promise of such a meeting, the North Koreans would not attend the three-way session scheduled for the following day. According to Pritchard, "The frustrated Chinese said, 'Wait a minute, why don't you act like a responsible adult here and just have a discussion?' Kelly said, 'I can't. I don't have those instructions.'"

The first day ended with the two sides far apart and the Chinese stuck awkwardly in the middle.


That evening, the Chinese hosted a banquet at Diaoyutai. Kelly sat with China's Wang Yi on his left and Li Gun on his right. Kelly and Li had met when Kelly had visited Pyongyang as a private citizen in 1992, and the two men chatted in English about inconsequential matters throughout the meal. At the end, though, when all the guests stood up, Li Gun motioned to his interpreter, Miss Chae.

"And all of a sudden," Kelly recalled, "we had this little bilateral. Li Gun immediately launches into Korean, clearly signaling to me that he was about to give us an official statement."

Despite his instructions banning any bilateral meeting, Kelly, almost literally cornered by the North Koreans and privately eager to hear what they had to say, made no effort to leave. Li then conveyed a blunt warning. He said North Korea had nuclear weapons, and that U.S. behavior would determine what Pyongyang did with them—whether they might demonstrate them or, most ominously, transfer them to another interested party. Li Gun ended by telling Kelly, "It's up to you."

Li Gun's statement, clearly prepared in advance, was a bombshell—and a typical example of Pyongyang's aggressive diplomatic style, ratcheting up tension through bombast and threats in the hope of securing benefits at the negotiating table. Still, this was the first time Pyongyang had acknowledged having a bomb, even though U.S. intelligence had long believed the North had manufactured one or two nuclear weapons before the 1994 crisis. And while the words Li used—"demonstrate" and "transfer"—were less threatening than "test" or "export," but it also raised the possibility that Kim Jong Il's regime might take such steps.

When the Americans returned to their hotel, tension within the group was high. Several members of the delegation, including the Pentagon's Jodi Green, challenged Kelly about Li Gun's reference to having previously informed the State Department about the uranium reprocessing. Green demanded that this assertion be included in the cable summarizing the day's events that was being prepared for transmission to Washington. "I work for Don Rumsfeld," she warned. "I don't report to you, and if you don't put it in the cable, I'm going to independently report it back myself."

Green's threat highlighted a central feature of the bureaucratic war in Washington—one that would play an increasingly important and destructive role in the diplomacy of the coming months. The contending factions each had their own separate back-channel e-mail and telephone networks. Whenever anything transpired at a meeting like this, representatives of different agencies would communicate back to their own bosses, often putting their own "spin" on developments to further a particular agenda or leaking to the press a version that might discredit their rivals.

"We had people from the Joint Chiefs of Staff and the Office of the Secretary of Defense and others," observed David Straub. "My impression of what was going on in the U.S. government was that people like John Bolton and Bob Joseph and Vice President Cheney's people had e-mail distribution lists, and Powell and Armitage and the people who worked for them had theirs, so here were these competing factions having literally the latest speed of light communications, battling each other all the time."

While Kelly sent an e-mail to Powell pleading for permission to hold a formal bilateral, his adversaries were on the phone almost immediately with their

own characterization of the day's events, which were promptly leaked to reporters. One of the recipients of the leak was CNN's State Department correspondent Andrea Koppel. Her source described Li Gun as "blatantly and
boldly" telling Kelly that Pyongyang had nuclear weapons and threatening to
test them. "The interpretation by the U.S. side," Koppel said, "is that this is
clearly an implication of blackmail."

"If you are trying to engage in diplomacy," noted Straub, "you don't want it
on page one immediately. You need for senior people to consider it, talk about
it, reflect on it."

Yet well before anyone in the administration had time to think the issue
through, the public had already been fed the perception of yet another reckless
North Korean move that amply justified the skepticism of the hard-liners. In
Kelly's view, "John Bolton or one of his running dogs immediately put it out to
her [Koppel]." While not admitting that he was the source of the leak, Bolton
saw Li Gun's brinkmanship as "another piece of evidence that these guys were
not going to give up their nuclear capability through voluntary action."

Kelly's request to Powell to hold a bilateral was rejected. Powell's comment
was, "That's more than the traffic will bear."

Asked about the latest developments, on April 24 President Bush told
NBC's Tom Brokaw on Air Force One, "See, they're back to the old blackmailing game." Then Bush added, "It's another reason, by the way, for us to advance
the missile defense system."

The next morning, Jack Pritchard's prediction that the talks would founder
came true. The schedule for the second day called for each side to comment on
the presentations made in the initial session. Under direct orders from
Pyongyang, however, Li Gun refused to attend a meeting with all the participants unless he could have a formal bilateral with Kelly first, something Kelly
was under orders to avoid.

"We were going to do this three-way meeting or not at all," recalled Kelly.
"And they wouldn't come to a three-way meeting, and we wouldn't come to a
two-way meeting."

China too had sought to convince the Bush administration to agree to a bilateral, with Beijing's ambassador in Washington making a personal appeal
to Condoleezza Rice. With the gathering degenerating into a fiasco, the Chinese
were exasperated by both sides and increasingly anxious about the loss of face
they would suffer if the meeting they had brokered collapsed altogether. So Beijing resorted to a classic diplomatic trick.

Early the next morning, China's new Foreign Minister Li Zhaoxing, a wily

Communist Party apparatchik who had served as ambassador in Washington, invited Li Gun to what was described to the North Korean as a private meeting at Diaoyutai. While the meeting was underway, Li arranged for Kelly and the American delegation to arrive at the same building and wait in a room just off the entrance.

"And so sure enough," recalled Kelly, "at the end of the meeting, out comes an expansive Li Zhaoxing, arm in arm with Li Gun, who is then horrified to see the whole American delegation milling around the front hall. And he cannot get out the door without walking past us. And all of a sudden a microphone materializes."

Kelly realized, "This was all a setup by the Chinese to force the North Koreans into a meeting, which would allow the Chinese to say this thing was a success and that we've agreed to have other meetings."

To his credit, in Kelly's view, Li Gun did not try to escape. "Li Gun is a stand-up kind of a guy," Kelly observed. "We had three-way photographs and he was willing to shake hands. He didn't run to the other side of the room or anything like that."

Speaking to reporters at Diaoyutai, the Chinese foreign minister tried to put a brave face on developments. "While discussing such an important issue, it is not strange for differences to emerge," he said. "While paying attention to the words and statements of the other side, we must emphasize even more their deeds."[18]

But this first attempt at international diplomacy only embarrassed Beijing and accentuated the gulf between Washington and Pyongyang. Shortly after the talks ended, North Korea's news agency said the situation "compels the DPRK to opt for possessing a necessary deterrent force and put it into practice."[19]

At the same time, U.S. spy satellites detected vapor from the cooling tower of the Yongbyon reactor, a telltale sign that the reprocessing of the spent fuel rods was in progress. Within days, Defense Secretary Donald Rumsfeld told the Senate Appropriations Committee that the U.S. military did not have weapons capable of dealing with targets buried deep underground. At the administration's urging, the Senate lifted a ten-year ban on developing new "bunker busting" nuclear weapons, specifically for use against North Korea.

# 10

# "READ MY STATEMENT"

A s AMERICAN, CHINESE, AND NORTH KOREAN DIPLOMATS were preparing for their ill-fated meeting in Beijing, German and French intelligence agencies were keeping close watch on a French cargo ship called the *Ville de Virgo*. In early April, the ship took on cargo at the port of Hamburg for a routine trip to Asia. At the last moment, a container with 214 ultra-strong aluminum tubes was loaded, apparently ordered by the Shenyang Aircraft Corporation in Northeastern China.

But hours after the *Ville de Virgo* steamed out of Hamburg, German intelligence confirmed that the tubes were not intended for use in aircraft construction and that their final destination was not China. Instead, they were to be delivered to North Korea, apparently to be used to make centrifuges for reprocessing uranium into nuclear bombs.[1]

For most of the previous year, intelligence agencies, including the CIA, had been watching North Korea's efforts in Europe to procure the ingredients to make a uranium bomb. Now, the ship's French owner was contacted and persuaded to order the *Ville de Virgo* to make an unscheduled stop at the Egyptian port of Alexandria. There, French and German agents came on board and removed the tubes. In late 2003, three German men would be indicted for their role in the scheme.

The episode underscored North Korea's continuing determination to acquire the components for a uranium enrichment effort—although, as was true in the earlier U.S. assessment of other intelligence on this issue, it remained unclear how much equipment had actually reached the North or been assembled and put into operation.

But the case of the *Ville de Virgo* spurred John Bolton, Robert Joseph, and other nonproliferation hawks in the Bush administration to expedite a new scheme for ratcheting up the pressure on Pyongyang.

It was called the "Proliferation Security Initiative" (PSI) and aimed to enlist other countries in an effort to target the illicit global trade in missiles and nonconventional—chemical, biological, or nuclear—weapons. Speaking in Poland on May 31, 2002, President Bush declared, "The United States and a number of our close allies . . . have begun working on new agreements to search planes and ships carrying suspect cargo and to seize illegal weapons or missile technologies."[2]

"We felt that if we could get international cooperation, we could do a lot more interdiction of international trafficking in WMD technology and materials," recalled John Bolton. "And it would have a deterrent effect."

The PSI was not an actual organization; rather, it was a "coalition of the willing"—a collection of nations with common views on counterproliferation. From the outset, it faced questions about the legality of interdicting ships on the high seas, the rules of engagement for any forces involved, and the political challenges of sustaining the coalition. Initially, the PSI attracted ten countries, who each signed a declaration of principles. Apart from Japan and Australia, all the others were in Europe. Two nations conspicuous by their absence were China and South Korea—a setback to American officials who had designed the PSI with North Korea very much in mind.

"North Korea was certainly a prime suspect," Bolton acknowledged, "both as exporters of ballistic missile technology and also in terms of importing technology and material."

The prospect of an American-inspired interdiction force stopping and searching ships on the high seas strengthened North Korea's view that, after the invasion of Iraq, it was going to be the Bush administration's next target. At Yongbyon, the reprocessing of spent fuel rods into weapons-grade plutonium went into high gear. And while hard-liners looked to the PSI as a new diplomatic stick, Washington's key partners in Asia, as well as the pro-engagement forces at the State Department, stepped up their efforts to convince the President to put some carrots on the table.

In mid-May 2003, South Korea's new president Roh Moo-hyun arrived in Washington for his first summit with George W. Bush. Both sides retained strong memories of the disastrous first meeting between Bush and Roh's predecessor, Kim Dae-jung, just over two years earlier. The new South Korean leader, however, was confident he could talk to Bush as one pol to another. In a CNN interview with me in January, just before taking office, Roh had said, "I heard that President Bush is a very frank and candid person. I am also a very frank and forward person to the point of being called dangerous because I am too frank, but I think we can have a candid and frank discussion when we meet each other."

Before the meeting, Roh made clear how much he differed from Bush on North Korea. "The mere thought of a military conflict with North Korea is a calamity for us," he told journalists.[3] "I think coercive measures have to wait until we have exhausted all possible efforts at dialogue."[4]

Roh was accompanied by Foreign Minister Yoon Young-kwan. Before the two presidents met, Yoon called on Deputy Secretary of State Richard Armitage (Colin Powell was out of the country). Yoon repeatedly stressed how important South Korea believed it was for the United States to have bilateral contacts with the North Koreans, even within a multilateral framework. Armitage was blunt in his response, saying it was U.S. policy to reject bilateral contacts with the North.

"What's the point of having a multilateral conference if your side won't meet and talk to the North Korean side?" Yoon recalled telling Armitage. "Of course the multilateral format is important because this is an international issue, but under this format there should be free discussions among all the members." Yoon continued, "Bilaterally, trilaterally, multilaterally . . . between the South Koreans and the North Koreans, the Japanese and the North Koreans, the Americans and the North Koreans. It's unnatural for the U.S. side not to meet with the North Koreans in Beijing."

One of his staffers later told Yoon he had used the word "bilateral" nearly ten times in his conversation.

Armitage responded like a broken record. "No," he would reply, "that's not the policy of our government." The South Koreans came away convinced that Armitage was repeating a policy with which he did not agree. Indeed, in testimony before the Senate Foreign Relations Committee in early February, Armitage had said, "Of course we're going to have direct talks with the North Koreans. There's no question about it. We're absolutely going to talk to them bilaterally."[5]

A few days later, Democratic senator Joseph Biden went to a meeting at the White House and told President Bush, "I'm so glad you're going to have one-on-one dialogue."

"What are you talking about?" Bush replied. "That's not my policy. We're absolutely not going to do that." The President was reportedly "off-the-wall angry" with Armitage's testimony,[6] and the deputy secretary came under criticism from Condoleezza Rice for "going off message."[7]

When Roh Moo-hyun walked into the Oval Office, Bush began the conversation by saying that he had been told that the average height of North Korean people was six to eight inches shorter than South Korean people because their diet was so bad, and that he had wept as he absorbed the shocking information. The South Koreans were struck by the depth of Bush's emotional response.

Although the personal dynamics were less tense than with Kim Dae-jung, Roh emphasized to Bush the need to resolve the North Korea issue diplomatically and reiterated his commitment to what he called a "Peace and Prosperity Policy"—his version of Kim Dae-jung's Sunshine Policy. The South Korean view was that since North Korea had offered a proposal—however unacceptable—to Kelly in Beijing in April, it was important for the United States to respond with a counterproposal. The American President was not interested. Bush made it clear that without an end to Pyongyang's nuclear program, no other steps were possible.

"Our policy toward North Korea can really be summed up as follows," Condoleezza Rice later told reporters. "No one should be willing to give in to the kind of blackmail that North Koreans have been practicing for a number of years now, especially not the United States."[8]

Pyongyang's response to the escalating pressure was no surprise. KCNA warned of an "immediate physical retaliatory step"[9] if the United States and its allies imposed a blockade. And on July 8, Jack Pritchard and David Straub met with North Korea's UN ambassador Pak Gil Yon and his deputy Han Song Ryol. Reading from a prepared statement, the North Koreans announced that they had completed reprocessing the 8,000 spent fuel rods, and were moving ahead to turn the material into nuclear bombs.


Dai Bingguo—intelligent, smooth, polished, and a good listener—was China's deputy foreign minister. The position was normally reserved for the senior Communist Party official in the Foreign Ministry, and in key ways Dai was more influential than his nominal boss, Foreign Minister Li Zhaoxing. Close to President Hu Jintao, until assuming his post in the Foreign Ministry Dai had been the head of the party's International Liaison Department, in charge of relations with North Korea, which was treated more like a fraternal party than an allied state. He had met Kim Jong Il frequently and was considered to have the best personal relationship with the Dear Leader of any Chinese official.

On July 12, 2003, Dai arrived in Pyongyang as the special envoy of President Hu on a crucial mission. Dai held six hours of meetings with Kim Jong Il and delivered a letter from the Chinese president explaining the importance of resuming negotiations over the North's nuclear program. In the letter, according to an account published in the *Hong Kong Economic Journal*, Hu made three promises. He told Kim that China was willing to mediate negotiations, to offer North Korea greater economic aid than in previous years, and to work to persuade the United States to make a promise of nonaggression in return for the denuclearization of the Korean peninsula.[10]

During their conversation, Kim told Dai that he was ready to reopen talks with the United States, but stressed his insistence on bilateral dialogue with Washington. Kim also indicated that he did not care about the overall format of the talks as long as his envoy could engage in meaningful negotiations with the United States. After extensive meetings with other top officials, including Kang Sok Ju and Foreign Minister Paek Nam Sun, Dai returned to Beijing.

While the Chinese diplomat was in Pyongyang, President Bush was in Africa on a trip that remains best known as the moment when former U.S. ambassador Joseph Wilson published an op-ed piece in the *New York Times* claiming that the administration had manipulated intelligence to justify invading Iraq. As Rice, Powell, and other officials scrambled to cope with the fallout from Wilson's assertion that, contrary to administration claims, there was no evidence that Saddam Hussein had sought to buy uranium from Niger, Powell also pressed the president on North Korea. Taking advantage of unusual "face time" alone with Bush on Air Force One, Powell, according to his biographer Karen DeYoung, reminded the president that the administration "had invited [the Chinese] to play a lead role in the initiative, and the fact that they were now doing so—and actively recommending ways to proceed—was a success for the White House. Allowing an opportunity for American officials to talk briefly to the North Koreans—not, by any means, a 'separate' meeting or negotiation, Powell assured him—while providing a blueprint for peaceful relations would in no way constitute an abandonment of U.S. principles."[11] Bush, while hardly enthusiastic, appeared open to the idea.

The Chinese were asked by the State Department to send Dai Bingguo almost immediately to Washington. In his memoir, Jack Pritchard notes that Beijing believed "it was premature to move directly into five-party talks. The Chinese thought that taking a more flexible approach and meeting with the North Koreans in a trilateral setting was the best and perhaps only way to move forward.[12] Upon arrival, Dai met with Condoleezza Rice, Colin Powell, Jim Kelly, and Dick Cheney, to whom he gave a letter for President Bush from Hu Jintao.[13]

"The Chinese were arguing for another three-party [negotiation]," Kelly recalled, "but I think they too understood that that wasn't going to work very well. Remember, we had done the three-party after trying to get a five-party together. We really wanted the Japanese and the South Koreans."

As Pritchard recounts, "Powell acquiesced to the Chinese request for trilateral talks, but only on condition that Beijing persuade Pyongyang to expand the talks immediately to include Tokyo and Seoul"—in effect, making the three-way and five-way meetings one single set of talks. According to Pritchard, when Powell explained the plan on the phone to Russian foreign minister Igor Ivanov, the Russian complained that Moscow was being excluded.[14] Other U.S. officials say China raised the idea of including the Russians after North Korea signaled that it wanted Moscow involved.

In any case, the Chinese diplomat was asked to convey a message back to Pyongyang: the United States was ready for a meeting with North Korea and China, as long as it was followed immediately by a larger multi-party meeting.[15]

On August 1, 2003, quoting a Foreign Ministry spokesman, the state-run KCNA announced that North Korea was prepared to attend six-party talks. The talks were set to begin in Beijing on August 27 and to last three days.

John Bolton thought negotiations would be a waste of time. "I kept saying it doesn't matter if you talk bilaterally or six-party talks or twenty-five-party talks. That's not going to get the North Koreans to give up nuclear weapons. And what we need to do is go to the Security Council, see what we can get there, and then whatever we do there ratchet up the pressure politically, economically, and, if need be, militarily."

A s arrangements for the meeting in Beijing were in their final stages, Bolton issued a blistering denunciation of Kim Jong Il. In a speech in Seoul peppered with forty-three references to the "Dear Leader," all of them unflattering, Bolton described Kim as a "tyrannical rogue-state leader."

"While he lives like royalty in Pyongyang," Bolton declared, "he keeps hundreds of thousands of his people locked in prison camps with millions more mired in abject poverty. For many, life in North Korea is a hellish nightmare." Bolton said it was time for the UN Security Council to take "appropriate and timely action."[16]

That Bolton gave such a controversial speech at a critical moment in the diplomatic process infuriated Powell and others at the State Department. Bolton had submitted the draft of his speech for routine approval with his colleagues at State. Korea Desk Director David Straub had taken a yellow marker and highlighted numerous passages that he thought could cause problems and had shown the document to Jim Kelly. Kelly's response was that it wasn't in the interest of the Bureau of East Asian and Pacific Affairs to have another ugly fight with Bolton. Reluctantly, Kelly gave his assent to the speech.

But when Tom Hubbard, the U.S. ambassador in Seoul, saw a copy the day before it was due to be delivered, he strongly objected. In testimony before the Senate Foreign Relations Committee when Bolton was nominated to be the U.S.

ambassador to the United Nations in 2005, Hubbard said, "We thought the tone was too strong, that he used derogatory terms about Kim Jong Il in virtually every sentence, and I and my staff argued that that was counter-productive to our interest in getting the North Koreans back into the talks."[17]

Hubbard also warned Bolton that "the South Koreans had consistently asked us to tone down our language in dealing with North Korea in an effort to get them back to the negotiating table,"[18] and that the speech would both infuriate Pyongyang and upset a key U.S. ally. According to Hubbard, Bolton "left in all the invective."[19]

For his part, Bolton said his main goal was to put the issue of human rights on the agenda in South Korea. "I thought it was unconscionable that the South Korean government didn't care about repression in North Korea," he said. "I wanted to get a discussion on that going."

"Would I have preferred that that speech not been given?" recalled Jim Kelly. "Yeah, it probably would've been better. It obviously antagonized a lot of people in South Korea and some in Japan, who simply felt that this would make it impossible to get a deal."

Soon after his return from South Korea, an angry Colin Powell summoned Bolton to his office at the State Department.

"Powell was pissed," an aide to Bolton recalled, saying it was one of the rare times when the two men got into "a screaming match."

"John, you can't give speeches anymore unless I approve them,'" Powell said sternly. "Public Affairs doesn't count. Rich [Armitage] doesn't count. Nobody counts. You can't give any speeches unless I approve them. Because John, whether you mean to or not, and most often you do mean to, you outrage people."

Powell won that battle. "Generally it had a pretty good effect," observed Richard Armitage. "I never found John, once he was spoken to, to wander off the reservation."

It was one thing for Powell to impose his will on a titular subordinate and quite another to win an interagency battle. Powell and his allies were about to lose a bigger and much more important battle over what Jim Kelly would be allowed to say at the forthcoming six-party talks.

As with Kelly's trip to Pyongyang in October 2002, it fell to State Department Korea Desk director David Straub to put together a first draft of Kelly's proposed talking points.

"We all knew what the general constellation of forces in the Bush administration was and what the president's strong personal beliefs were," Straub recalled. "So it was just on the margins" that he tried to insert a little flexibility—a reference to the "bold approach" that had been the center of the 2002 discussions on engaging Pyongyang, and that might give Kelly some flexibility on whether he could meet bilaterally with the North Koreans.

"Jim wanted to meet with the North Koreans," Straub said. "He felt it was the correct thing. We're in a meeting with six parties and our aim is to win the sympathy of the other four so that we can increase the leverage on North Korea, both positive and negative leverage on North Korea, to do what we want them to do. You have to take into account the other parties' feelings and attitudes. We didn't want to look like a bunch of bullies or idiots. So Jim wanted to be able to sit down and show that he was having a meeting with the North Koreans."

"Generally the State Department would try to get as much flexibility as possible," noted Richard Armitage. "Then we'd go to an interagency process where that flexibility would be whittled down. For the proliferation people, it was 'no, no, no,' and Kelly was looking for a little flexibility."

One of Bolton's aides said Straub's initial draft wanted to "fold in all the other issues—in terms of sequencing, who moved first, whether or not North Korea had a right to a civil nuclear program. You know, the whole panoply of issues. And we just laughed."

For his part, like John Bolton, Joseph was skeptical of the entire process. "I don't think the North Koreans were serious," he recalled. "I don't think they've ever been serious. The key is putting the pressure on."

Bob Joseph was concerned that Kelly would somehow manage to hold a bilateral negotiation with the North Korean envoy, so he drafted his own set of instructions for Kelly. "I think that there were a number of people that really thought that they could conduct bilateral negotiations within the framework of the six-party talks," Joseph said, "and I thought that was a mistake. So it was my view that it was better that I wrote the talking points than the EAP [Bureau of East Asian and Pacific Affairs] staffers."

Pentagon hard-liners weighed in as well. Deputy Defense Secretary Paul Wolfowitz insisted that Kelly emphasize the threat from North Korea's conventional weapons and missiles, as well as human rights abuses. And Secretary of Defense Rumsfeld demanded that any specific reference to the "bold approach" be taken out.

At the NSC, John Rood—the hard-line deputy to Bob Joseph in the Office of Nonproliferation—and Asia expert Michael Green had the task of arbitrating the conflicting pressures.

The final guidance for Kelly was strict. "There was always in the instructions that he was to avoid any bilateral meetings," said Stephen Yates, then Cheney's Asian adviser. "He was to avoid negotiation."

"And there was honestly some interagency instruction," noted State Department spokesman Richard Boucher, "saying you are not allowed to be in a room [with the North Koreans] without the other delegations."

For a man of Kelly's knowledge and experience, the instructions were so strict as to be almost humiliating. As an aide to John Bolton noted, "You could have had a trained chimpanzee who spoke English do it."

S ix days before the six-party talks were due to begin, Jack Pritchard finally quit. His final weeks on the job had found him again targeted by the hard-liners. This time, the issue was John Bolton. The North Koreans had been outraged by Bolton's speech in Seoul, with its dozens of personal barbs directed at Kim Jong Il. The state-run Korean Central News Agency (KCNA) immediately responded by labeling Bolton "human scum" and asking for a meeting with U.S. officials in New York. At the meeting, Pritchard and David Straub were the recipients of a long tirade read aloud by the North Korean UN envoy, denouncing Bolton in the strongest terms. In response, Pritchard repeated the instructions that he had been formally given by Colin Powell, telling the envoys that there were only two voices they should listen to—the president and the secretary of state. Pritchard made no direct mention of Bolton.

After returning to Washington from New York, Straub wrote a memo on the meeting for Powell and other top officials. Given Bolton's frequent opposition to Powell's policy initiatives, the secretary of state often would not authorize the distribution of certain internal documents to his under secretary for arms control. In this case, it remains unclear whether Bolton was copied on Straub's memo or heard about it on his own. In any event, Bolton was furious at what he saw as Pritchard's failure to defend him. Soon after, Senator Jon Kyl, a conservative Republican from Arizona and a Bolton ally, wrote an angry letter to Powell, which he copied to Vice President Cheney, Richard Armitage, and Bolton himself. The letter accused the administration of sending mixed signals to the North Koreans and demanded that Powell take "corrective action" against Pritchard. It is equally unclear how Kyl learned of the classified memo. But the episode was the most blatant attempt thus far by the hard-liners to force a leading pro-engagement figure out of the administration.[20]

Pritchard had long ago made up his mind to leave. The attack by Bolton and Kyl, coupled with the fact that the six-party talks were at last about to get under way, simply reinforced his belief that it was time to go.

T he hexagonal table was enormous—big enough to accommodate all six delegations in a cavernous meeting room at the Diaoyutai State Guest House in Beijing. The Chinese hosts had deliberately placed Jim Kelly next to North Korea's envoy, Kim Yong Il. The U.S. team was surprised to see Kim. A deputy foreign minister, he was a China specialist with no experience dealing either with Americans or the nuclear issue, unlike Kim Gye Gwan, who had participated in so many negotiations with the United States over the years. It was not a promising sign.

Yet when he made his opening statement at the plenary session on August 28, 2003, Kim put a new North Korean proposal on the table.

"The denuclearization of the Korean peninsula is the ultimate goal of the DPRK," Kim declared. "It is not our goal to have nuclear weapons. We can dismantle our nuclear program if the U.S. makes a switchover in its hostile policy and doesn't pose any threat to us."

Kim's proposal contained a series of steps based on the principle of "simultaneous action."

In return for a resumption of heavy fuel oil shipments and an increase in food aid, he said North Korea would "express its will to scrap its nuclear program." In return for the conclusion of a nonaggression treaty with the U.S. and compensation for the loss of electricity, Kim said the North would "allow the refreeze of our nuclear facility and nuclear substance and monitoring and inspection of them." He said the missile issue would be settled "when diplomatic relations are opened between the DPRK and the U.S. and between the DPRK and Japan. And we will dismantle our nuclear facility from the time the LWRs (light-water reactors) are completed."[21] Kim also denied U.S. claims that Pyongyang had a uranium enrichment program.

Of course, in typical North Korean fashion, it was an extreme response to the U.S. demand that North Korea disarm first before getting anything in return and a position that Pyongyang had to know would be unacceptable to the United States. But it was also clearly only an opening gambit. The key question was what might happen if a real negotiating process got under way.

In his presentation—which reflected the views of Washington hard-liners—Kelly made clear Washington's opposition to the kind of give-and-take process the North Koreans were looking for. Instead, he repeated the administration's demand that North Korea must "completely, verifiably, and irreversibly dismantle" its nuclear program before there could be any discussion of diplomatic, political, or economic incentives. In his one conciliatory statement, Kelly referred to President Bush's remarks that the United States had no intention of attacking or invading North Korea. But the statement Kelly read explicitly rejected Pyongyang's call for a nonaggression treaty. As one observer noted, Kelly "went to the table but put nothing on it."[22]

Before the opening session, David Straub had huddled privately with Chinese officials. He had a strange request—would they put some sofas in a corner of the room where the plenary session was being held? When Straub explained the reason, the Chinese were, to put it mildly, bemused. In the Washington battle over whether Kelly could talk bilaterally with the North Koreans, the final decision was that such an encounter could only take place within sight of the other delegations and could not in any way be seen as a negotiation. Recalled Straub, "I was so embarrassed for my country and my department."

The American rigidity frustrated the Chinese. "The U.S. position was pretty tough," noted one Chinese official. "No flexibility. We tried very hard to persuade the U.S. to have bilateral discussions with the North Koreans. The U.S. delegation rejected very strongly."

But the Chinese duly obliged Straub's request, and on the afternoon of August 28, during a break in the plenary session, Straub approached the North Koreans and asked whether they'd be willing to chat. Kelly was accompanied by a Pentagon official, Under Secretary of Defense Richard Lawless, and the NSC's Asia specialist Mike Green, as well as an interpreter. Their presence was a reflection less of interagency coordination than of the deep suspicion in which Kelly and the State Department were held by the more hard-line elements in Washington, who felt the envoy had to be monitored at all times to ensure he didn't try to exceed his instructions.

As Richard Armitage observed, "We were looking, at least to my mind, like something out of the old Soviet days, where there were watchers watching the watchers who were watching the prisoners."

As they sat on the Chinese-supplied sofas in a corner of the huge room, Kelly began the encounter by saying bluntly to Kim Yong Il, "This is not a negotiating session. This is not an official meeting."[23]

Recalled Kelly, "I was very careful to make clear we weren't in negotiation with them."

The awkwardness was palpable, Kelly felt. "Frankly, I think Minister Kim Yong Il would've rather been just about anywhere," he recalled, "other than interacting with Americans."

The Americans found Kim to be dour and "unimpressive," but the North Korean envoy said he had a list of questions. As the North Koreans so often do—out of built-up frustration but also for tactical reasons—Kim adopted a hostile tone, asking his questions, in the words of David Straub, "like a prosecutor."

"Question one," Kim began. "Is it your intention to end your hostile policy? Question two: Is it your intention to fulfill your obligations under the Agreed Framework?"

Altogether, Kim asked around ten questions.

Kelly was offended by being interrogated like a criminal suspect. In response, he said bluntly, "Read my statement carefully. Have Kim Jong Il read my statement."

In line with his rigid instructions, the entire testy exchange took place in full view, although not within earshot, of all the other delegations. As David Straub recalled, "All the other parties are there milling around in this huge hall. And of course they want to know what's going on, so pretty soon it's like . . . if you've ever lived on a farm you known how curious cows are . . . you had all of these people sort of coming like this, they were sort of all getting closer and closer. It was ridiculous."

One of those trying to edge closer was a South Korean diplomat. He shared Straub's assessment of the arrangement. "Frankly speaking," he said, "I think it was silly."

Sitting on a sofa in the corner, Kim Yong Il declared, "Clearly you have not ended your hostile policy. Therefore, we have no choice but to declare our possession of nuclear weapons and demonstrate our nuclear deterrent."

"This is a very serious matter," Kelly answered. "I'm going to share this with the other parties."

"So am I," retorted Kim.

The meeting ended after less than half an hour.

Kelly dryly recalled, "The conversations we had were in no way satisfactory."

Added a Chinese official, "All the words were confrontational. All the exchanges were just exchanges of policy statements."


That night, at Beijing's luxurious St. Regis Hotel, where Kelly's delegation was staying, there was a rush to the telephones. In what would become a regular pattern, various members of Kelly's delegation were conveying their own version of the day's events to their respective offices—the Pentagon, the NSC, and the Joint Chiefs of Staff.

Kelly, trying to draft a detailed cable for Powell and Armitage, was not happy.

"I had people who were reporting back to individual fiefdoms in Washington," he recalled, "fiefdoms that were not necessarily in support of the policy. And so this was aggravating. I wasn't very happy to have them reporting back, presumably over open lines, while we were writing cables. These guys were burning up the phone lines by criticizing us to others."

Kelly was deeply skeptical of the proposal Kim Yong Il had put on the table at the plenary session. Even the offer of a freeze, in Kelly's view, did not represent a step forward.

"The problem with pocketing the freeze is that that would simply return us to the Agreed Framework," he recalled. "I think that would be a big mistake. We have to have a commitment . . . to a complete end to the nuclear weapons program. A freeze might be a step along the way, but if it is a step that has a danger of becoming a goal in itself, which is what it ended up being in the Agreed Framework, then we fall badly short because we have failed to deal with the major part of their nuclear weapons program."

But given North Korea's history of brinksmanship, neither Kelly nor Straub were particularly alarmed by Kim Yong Il's threat of a nuclear test.

In Washington, though, media leaks from the hard-liners camp made sure the threat, rather than the new proposal for a diplomatic solution, dominated the headlines. "North Korea Threatens Nuclear Arms Test," read the page-one headline in the *Washington Post*. "North Korea Says it May Test an A-Bomb," fretted the *New York Times*.

On the second day of the talks, Kim Yong Il made good on his promise to repeat the threat to the entire group. Kim's warning, and his manner, did not go down well with the other delegations. "When Kim Yong Il spoke, sort of blustering, both in language and presentation," recalled David Straub, "that made a very bad impression, I think, on everyone, including the Chinese."

In a background briefing to reporters in which he was identified only as an "administration official," Kelly noted that the other parties also made it clear they would respond strongly if Pyongyang "moved from threat to action."

As had been true in the tripartite meeting in April, the sharp exchanges left the Chinese hosts scrambling to put a positive spin on a meeting that had produced no results and left Washington and Pyongyang in seemingly irreconcilable positions. Vice Foreign Minister Wang Yi pushed hard for a joint statement, even a bland one.

The possibility of a statement was under discussion at a working-level meeting with Li Gun, the North Korean official who had confronted Kelly in April, when one of his colleagues came into the room with instructions from Pyongyang. According to a Japanese diplomat who was in the room, "Li Gun shook his head and said, 'We can't agree to anything.'"

In the end, the only official statement came from Chinese Vice Foreign Minister Wang Yi, who announced that all six parties had agreed to meet again and urged both the U.S. and North Korea to "refrain from words or deeds that will further escalate the situation."[24]

Despite the lack of progress, American officials stressed that the mere fact that a multilateral meeting had been held was a vindication of the Bush administration's policy. As Douglas Feith, the hard-line under secretary of defense, recalled, "It wasn't that we thought necessarily that out of the six-party framework you would get an agreement that would solve the problem, but if that was what was useful to get the Chinese to work more effectively bilaterally with the North Koreans, then the six-party talks made sense."

Beijing, however, remained more frustrated with Washington than Pyongyang. Visiting the Philippines the week after the meeting, Wang Yi, who had been the official host at the meeting, was asked what he thought was the biggest obstacle to progress at the talks. His reply was blunt. "The American policy [toward North Korea]—this is the main problem we are facing."[25]

Wang's views were echoed by China's Foreign Ministry spokesman, Kong Quan. "How the U.S. is threatening the DPRK—this needs to be further discussed in the next round of talks," Kong said, adding that the next round of talks should address what he described as Washington's "negative policy" toward North Korea.[26]

Chinese officials also revealed that Beijing had appealed to Washington to postpone or scale back a large-scale naval exercise—part of the Proliferation Security Initiative—scheduled to be held off the coast of Australia in late September.[27] The exercise went ahead as planned.

On Saturday, August 30, Kim Yong Il and the rest of the North Korean delegation boarded a creaky, Soviet-made Air Koryo TU-154 in Beijing for the two-hour flight to Pyongyang. Also on board were two Americans— Frank Jannuzi and Keith Luse, the senior Democratic and Republican staff members on the Senate Foreign Relations Committee. Over the next three days, they would spend nearly twelve hours in conversation with the prominent North Korean official who had been absent from the six-party talks, the man who normally handled such diplomatic encounters—Vice Foreign Minister Kim Gye Gwan.

Jannuzi and Luce found Kim in a sour mood, depressed by the outcome at the just-concluded talks.

"The U.S. wants the DPRK to drop its pants and be naked and humiliated before the U.S. is prepared to improve relations," Kim told them. "We can't do that."

Kim equated the conditions Kelly had put forward to a call for unconditional surrender. Noting that the Korean War armistice had never been transformed into a peace treaty, he said, "We are technically at war with the U.S. You want us to surrender unconditionally. We are not Iraq."

Then Kim told the two men, "You two need to stop worrying so much about how to prevent North Korea from becoming a nuclear power and start thinking about how you're going to live with a nuclear North Korea."

Taken aback, Jannuzi and Luce concluded that Pyongyang was going to go nuclear as quickly as it could. With most of the 8,000 spent fuel rods now reprocessed into weapons-grade plutonium, it would not be long before the North Koreans could add new bombs to their arsenal. The two men also agreed that underlying North Korea's position was a desperate desire for respect and security.

The only hopeful note came when Kim Gye Gwan said, "This could all be resolved with high-level dialogue." It was yet another appeal for a summit, something they thought George W. Bush would never consider.

I t wasn't only the North Koreans who were unhappy with Washington's rigid position. While Luce and Jannuzi were in Pyongyang, South Korean foreign minister Yoon Young-kwan was in Washington, where he urged Colin Powell to come up with a detailed U.S. proposal in response to the one laid out by Kim Yong Il. Yoon also suggested that Powell consider proposing the establishment of a small U.S. diplomatic office in Pyongyang—something well short of an embassy, which would represent full diplomatic relations between the two countries—as an incentive for the North Koreans. The liaison office idea had been mentioned in the Agreed Framework but had never been implemented.

"That kind of gesture," Yoon recalled, "might have motivated North Korea to cooperate further. Even if the North Korean side did not respond to that kind of U.S. initiative, it would give a good impression of the U.S. attitude— that the U.S. had a sincere attitude in dealing with this issue through diplomacy."

Not surprisingly, the South Korean proposal got a frosty response. But the disagreement paled in comparison to the sharp exchange Powell and Yoon had later in the month, when they met again on the sidelines of the annual meeting of the UN General Assembly in New York.

The meeting got off to a bad start when Yoon gave Powell a copy of a new book by two American scholars called *Crisis on the Korean Peninsula: How to Deal with a Nuclear-Armed North Korea.* The book called for a "Grand Bargain," in which the United States, China, Russia, Japan, and South Korea would offer economic aid and security guarantees to North Korea, including a peace treaty and nonaggression pact, in return for significant reductions in both conventional and nuclear weapons. The idea was totally at odds with the approach of the Bush administration.

"You ought to do something like this," Yoon said to Powell. The secretary of state was visibly offended. And the meeting then got worse.

South Korean president Roh Moo-hyun had taken a major domestic political risk by supporting the dispatch of South Korean troops to Iraq—a critical step, Roh felt, that would give Seoul further leverage with Washington on North Korea policy. But Roh was coming under increasing fire from his left-wing political base, and after a meeting of his national security team in Seoul, Foreign Minister Yoon was told to deliver a blunt message to Powell.

"I was instructed to talk tough," Yoon recalled. Unless the United States demonstrated a more flexible attitude on North Korea, Yoon warned Powell, the dispatch of South Korean troops to Iraq would be in doubt.

Powell was angry. "That is not how allies deal with each other," he responded curtly.

"Colin recognized that the South Korean side was linking those two issues," Yoon recalled. "He was not happy. But I asked him to think about the difficult political situation President Roh Moo-hyun was facing at that time. The core group of his own supporters was against the idea [of sending troops]. I basically tried to explain the domestic political situation."

Indeed, while Roh's nationalistic suspicion of Washington ran deep, that sentiment was even stronger among his closest aides. Roh had surrounded himself with members of the "386" generation—people who were born in the 1960s, attended college in the 1980s, and were then in their 30s—who had come to political maturity demonstrating against military rule and perceived U.S. backing for it, who were deeply committed to the idea of a rapprochement with their northern cousins, and who saw the Bush administration's tough line as the greatest danger to peace on the peninsula. Chief among this cohort was Lee Jong-seok, who was initially named deputy national security adviser and later served as unification minister. A political scientist who had attended the 2000 North-South summit as a special assistant to President Kim Dae-jung, Lee was a longtime critic of U.S. policy and an advocate of engagement with Pyongyang at almost any price.

With Lee managing policy and Roh—who had seen his popularity drop sharply—lending his support, the tone in the Blue House became increasingly strident and anti-American. One result of the polarization was an internal turf war as South Korean policy makers split into two factions: the *jajupa* ("independence" or "self-reliance faction") associated with Lee Jong-seok and the National Security Council and the *dongmaengpa* ("alliance faction"), centered in the Foreign Ministry and which stressed the importance of the relationship with Washington.

The divisions had been exacerbated by a stunning revelation: the South Korean government had paid hundreds of millions of dollars to North Korea in order to secure Kim Dae-jung's June 2000 summit meeting with Kim Jong Il. The money transfers had been handled by a subsidiary of the South Korean conglomerate Hyundai and paid into North Korean bank accounts in the former Portuguese colony of Macau. Kim had acknowledged he was aware of the payments but defended them on the grounds that they helped lubricate the way for a dialogue with the North that was in the South's national interest. By the autumn of 2003, more than a half-dozen South Koreans had been convicted in court cases for their roles in the scheme. And just before the six-party talks began, the son of the founder of Hyundai leapt to his death from the company's headquarters in Seoul.

In the coming months, the infighting would intensify, further souring relations with Washington, undermining the U.S.–South Korea security alliance and putting Seoul increasingly at odds with the Bush administration on how to deal with Kim Jong Il.

Mitchell Reiss was vice provost for International Affairs at the College of William and Mary in Virginia. In the 1990s, he had negotiated many key protocols with North Korea while working for KEDO, the consortium responsible for construction of the light-water reactors under the Agreed Framework. In August 2003, Reiss joined the State Department as director of Policy Planning. Colin Powell told him to make North Korea a top priority.

Soon Reiss began a series of private meetings with what he dubbed the "circle of trust," a group of officials who favored a negotiated solution to the North Korean nuclear crisis. The most extreme hard-liners were excluded. Apart from Reiss, the "circle of trust" included Jim Kelly, Korea Desk director David Straub, the NSC's Mike Green, Joseph DeTrani—a longtime CIA operative who would replace Jack Pritchard as special envoy for talks with the North Koreans, Evan Feigenbaum, who was on Reiss's staff, and Kelly aide David Asher. The group gathered regularly to talk through different ideas about how to deal with North Korea, which Reiss and Feigenbaum then tried to incorporate into a new U.S. position.

The concept they came up with was dubbed "two plus two and a kicker." In the short term, Reiss proposed, the United States should demand an immediate cessation of North Korea's nuclear program, including a shutdown of Yongbyon (the word "freeze" could not be used because it was considered too "Clintonian"), and a public pledge by the North to halt its nuclear activities. In return, Reiss suggested that the United States offer a formal pledge that it would not attack North Korea. The goal of the new approach was a nonnuclear North Korea—its status verified by international inspections—with which the United States would have normal diplomatic relations. In the interim, it was suggested that Washington should offer to open a liaison office in Pyongyang. This was seen explicitly as a Trojan Horse—an opportunity to learn more about and explore ways to undermine from within, the North Korean regime. The strategy was enthusiastically endorsed by former CIA agent DeTrani. "Give me six guys who could go today," he would say. "We know how to do this."

While Powell did not accept all of Reiss's recommendations, he did push the president to offer a pledge not to attack North Korea. During a meeting with key advisers at Camp David the weekend of October 11, 2003, Bush agreed to test the idea with Chinese president Hu Jintao at a meeting scheduled to be held on the sidelines of the annual APEC summit in Bangkok the following week. "Powell knew you had to test the proposition," noted one member of the "circle of trust." "First, see if you could get a deal. Second, we had to manage the allies. Third, the U.S. had a certain position in Asia. If it was seen as not dealing with a security threat, that would diminish the U.S. standing."

For a president who had adamantly opposed the idea of offering any concessions to North Korea—let alone a security guarantee—until Pyongyang agreed to abandon its nuclear ambitions, it was a significant shift in emphasis. In his meeting with Hu, Bush signaled he was open to providing a written pledge not to attack North Korea as part of a multilateral security agreement involving all the participants in the six-party talks, although, as one senior official noted, "Any moves on our part would be conditioned on verifiable progress on their part."[28]

Bush bluntly rejected North Korea's long-standing demand for a formal nonaggression treaty, saying, "That's off the table."[29] But it marked the first time the American president had accepted that North Korea's security concerns had to be taken seriously if a diplomatic solution was to be found. And while Bush got a lukewarm public response from Hu, who said simply that China "will strive for a peaceful resolution" of the nuclear crisis, the Chinese president immediately dispatched Wu Bangguo, a senior Communist Party official and head of the Chinese parliament, to Pyongyang.

Following the first round of six-party talks, the North Koreans frequently repeated their desire for a negotiated solution, but their efforts to increase their nuclear arsenal continued. In early October, the Foreign Ministry in Pyongyang publicly declared that all 8,000 fuel rods had been reprocessed and that North Korea "will consistently maintain and increase its nuclear deterrent force" if the U.S. did not give up its "hostile policy."[30] As Bush set out for Asia, the KCNA said, "When an appropriate time comes, the DPRK will take a measure to open its nuclear deterrent to the public as a physical force."[31] And to drive home that point, while Bush was in Bangkok, the North Koreans test-fired a new cruise missile with a range of about 100 miles.[32]

In its first response to Bush's offer, KCNA described the proposal as "shameful."[33] Shortly before Wu's arrival, however, the North Korean Foreign Ministry, in an abrupt shift, announced it was "ready to consider" Bush's offer.[34] On October 30, 2003, China Central Television's national evening newscast showed Wu and a beaming Kim Jong Il shaking hands as the Chinese announcer declared that North Korea had agreed "in principle" that the six-party talks should be reconvened. But after the announcement, Pyongyang repeated its long-standing line that it would take part in the talks only "if they provide a process of putting into practice the proposal for a package solution based on the principle of simultaneous actions."[35] Still, Beijing's decision to play up Wu Bangguo's apparent achievement suggested China remained confident the North Koreans would indeed return to the table.

Beijing's hope was to convene a second round before the end of the year. Then Vice President Cheney intervened.

# 11

# "WE DON'T NEGOTIATE WITH EVIL. WE DEFEAT IT."

DICK CHENEY WAS, IN COLIN POWELL'S WORDS, "VERY hard" on North Korea.

"Cheney's view of the problem," observed Princeton University Sinologist Aaron Friedberg, who served as Cheney's deputy national security adviser from 2003 to 2005, "was that the regime was the root cause of the problem. Unless and until that is different, the proliferation problem will never be solved. The only lasting solution to the problem, therefore, is a change in the character of the regime."

But with problems mounting in Iraq, key U.S. partners in Asia all favoring negotiations, deep divisions in the administration, and the president himself stressing the need for a diplomatic solution, the desire of Cheney and others for an undiluted strategy of regime change remained frustrated. Instead, amid efforts by China to broker a second round of six-party talks, the hard-liners shifted their focus. Their goal: ensuring the U.S. position was so unyielding that the result would either be North Korean capitulation or a breakdown of the entire process.

For much of the fall of 2003, Paula DeSutter was leading this new movement within the administration. DeSutter was an extremely conservative staffer on the Senate Intelligence Committee working for Arizona Republican John Kyl, who had tried in August of 2003 to get Jack Pritchard fired for allegedly failing to defend John Bolton to the North Koreans. She was appointed Assistant Secretary of State for Verification and Compliance in the summer of 2002. The Bureau of Verification and Compliance was a relatively new addition to the State Department bureaucracy. It was established in 1999 under pressure from ultra-conservative North Carolina senator Jesse Helms, then chairman of the Senate Foreign Relations Committee, who wanted a separate unit to oversee verifying any arms-control accords, since he didn't trust the State Department's normal arms-control experts to be sufficiently vigilant.

DeSutter's bureau was under John Bolton's overall direction, and DeSutter and Bolton clicked immediately. Upon taking the job, DeSutter said a colleague had told her Bolton was "a great guy, very conservative." In Senate testimony during hearings on Bolton's nomination to be ambassador to the UN in 2005, DeSutter said she could not "ever remember a time" when she and Bolton disagreed.[1]

In the fall of 2003, following the first round of six-party talks—with the United States still demanding the "complete, verifiable, and irreversible dismantlement" of North Korea's nuclear program—DeSutter and her staff began work on a verification plan. Quietly meeting with likeminded officials in the intelligence community, Vice President Cheney's office, and Bob Joseph's nonproliferation office at the NSC, DeSutter eventually produced a thick, color-coded document laying out an exceptionally intrusive verification regime. The basic approach ignored the International Atomic Energy Agency, and instead proposed that the United States would be in charge, "with the right to investigate anywhere, anytime, on demand, no notice," as Bolton's deputy, John Wolf, the assistant secretary of state for Nonproliferation described it. To Wolf, the proposal was completely impractical because "there was no way you could have had the kind of intrusive, no-notice verification in North, Korea. The only way you could do it was through regime change."

"They had this concept of 10,000 inspectors linking hands along the DMZ and walking North," said one official involved in the process. "It was completely unrealistic."

DeSutter argued that intrusive measures were the only way to ensure that North Korea would in fact denuclearize, a view that Cheney's office shared. "Given the North Korean's skill at tunneling and concealment," noted Cheney's deputy national security adviser Aaron Friedberg, "we have to verify, and we can't verify through national technical means like we could in the Cold War." But John Wolf was not alone in viewing the DeSutter proposal as an effort to derail the still shaky diplomatic process by setting the bar so high that North Korea would never agree.

"No sovereign government in the world has ever accepted this kind of intrusiveness," observed the State Department's Korea Desk director David Straub. "The hard-liners were using this as a way to completely destroy any chance at negotiation."

In one paper for Powell, Mitchell Reiss, the State Department's director of Policy Planning, who had been asked by Powell to deal with the verification issue, described DeSutter's approach as a "nationwide proctology examination." Powell's secretary called Reiss and said, "This is the first time the word 'proctology' has ever been used at the State Department. Are you sure you want to?" Reiss said, "Yes."

Reiss subsequently went to Powell and said DeSutter's plan was a "nonstarter." Powell said, "Come up with an alternative."

In late fall, DeSutter, Bolton, Bolton's Asia specialist Mark Groombridge, Jim Kelly, Reiss, Powell's chief of staff Lawrence Wilkerson, and a small number of other officials met to try to resolve their differences. It was, in the words of one participant, "a knock-down, drag-out fight, a screaming match." Reiss asserted his right, under Powell's instructions, to take a leading role on verification issues. He urged that the burden be placed initially on the North Koreans to detail their nuclear facilities, with an overlay of verification measures to be applied at a later date. In this, he reflected Powell's view that it was better to bargain in the hope of capturing some of Pyongyang's programs than to insist on verification measures that would make an agreement impossible.

One person who was there said that "Paula lost it," and shouted at Reiss, "How dare you ever think of doing this?" Other participants remember Bolton raising his voice, being very difficult and acting as an "intellectual bully."

"You could call them the 'red team,'" joked one of DeSutter's critics, "because they tended to get pretty flustered and red in the face."

The upshot was what was known in the government as a "split memo." With no consensus, two conflicting positions were sent to Secretary Powell. Not surprisingly, the secretary rejected the hard-line view and accepted Reiss's ideas.

But even this more moderate approach remained caught in the ongoing fight within the administration. Having come up with a plan, the administration needed to brief the allies. The hard-liners, suspicious of the South Koreans, insisted on briefing the Japanese first. When it was pointed out that such a move, if it leaked, would infuriate Seoul, a briefing for South Korean diplomats was arranged just after the one to Japanese ended. But an interagency decision barred State Department briefers from giving the South Koreans or the Japanese a copy of the document. Instead, the allies were only provided a verbal summary.

"We were doing a briefing on a technical subject to people whose native language was not English," recalled David Straub. "Afterwards, a South Korean diplomat came to me and said, 'We didn't understand half of what you said, yet we have to inform our government. What should we do?'"

Straub was so irritated that, without getting permission, he arranged for one of his staff to meet privately with a South Korean embassy official. The Korea Desk official read the entire memo slowly enough that the Korean could write down every word. "We didn't give them a copy," said Straub. "But at least they got it."

But Powell was not the only powerful figure weighing in on North Korea policy.

On December 12, the President's key foreign policy advisers met to discuss the issue. In the preceding weeks, China had worked hard to arrange a second meeting of the six parties, with the hope the round could take place before the end of the year. On December 9, North Korea had sent a conciliatory signal. KCNA quoted a North Korean Foreign Ministry spokesman as saying Pyongyang was ready to freeze its nuclear program if the United States would remove North Korea from the list of terror-sponsoring nations, lift economic sanctions, and provide energy assistance. President Bush quickly rejected the offer, but Chinese officials nonetheless drafted a proposed statement to be released at the end of the forthcoming meeting. The Chinese told the United States that Washington's quick endorsement would be pivotal in getting North Korea to attend the session.

Vice President Cheney did not often attend such meetings, but on this day he unexpectedly showed up. As Aaron Friedberg observed, "He came in at the last minute on a number of occasions to prevent other people from giving away the farm by softening our position." The Chinese draft had not used the term CVID—"complete, verifiable, and irreversible dismantling" of Pyongyang's nuclear program. The term was central to the U.S. position; Cheney said the statement was unacceptable unless it was included—something Pyongyang would almost certainly reject.

As Karen DeYoung observed in her biography of Powell, "In the vice president's view, the six-party talks were a venue for the United States to set out its nonnegotiable demands with the support of the other four partners; anything less would be a return to the weak-kneed Clinton policies that had allowed North Korea to expand its nuclear program in the first place. Pyongyang would have to comply or risk facing the consequences."[2]

According to two participants who subsequently spoke to the *Washington Post*, Cheney declared, "We don't negotiate with evil. We defeat it." As the *Post*'s account noted, "that effectively ended the discussion: The Chinese draft was rejected."[3] The effort to hold a six-party meeting in December collapsed.

The headline in *USA Today* on January 2, 2004, was: "North Korea OKs U.S. Visit to Complex."[4] The story, by reporter Barbara Slavin, said Pyongyang had agreed to let a group of Americans see the Yongbyon nuclear facility, and that the trip had been approved by the Bush administration. At the White House, President Bush saw the paper and went ballistic. "I didn't authorize this," he fumed to Condoleezza Rice. "Shut it down."

The group had been organized by John W. Lewis, a distinguished Asian scholar at Stanford University and veteran of the Korean War. Lewis had been making regular visits to North Korea since 1987 and had maintained an ongoing dialogue with senior North Korean officials. For this trip, Lewis had invited two Senate Foreign Relations Committee staffers, Frank Jannuzi, who worked for Democrat Joseph Biden, and Keith Luse, whose boss was Republican Richard Lugar, and who, by coincidence, had been planning their own North Korea journey. Both had visited North Korea on previous occasions and were considered among the most knowledgeable Asia specialists on Capitol Hill. Lewis had also asked Jack Pritchard, now a visiting fellow at the Brookings Institution, a Washington think-tank. And, most important, with Pyongyang signaling that a visit to Yongbyon was on the itinerary, Lewis had invited Siegfried ("Sig") Hecker, one of the United States' leading experts on nuclear weapons, who had, from 1985 to 1997, been the director of the Los Alamos National Laboratory, where the first American nuclear bomb had been made.

Acting on Bush's instruction, Rice called Colin Powell, who then called Senator Biden, who in turn called Jannuzi.

"Frank," Biden said, "I just got off the phone with Secretary Powell. We had an interesting conversation. Powell says, 'The White House doesn't want me to send you.' He's spoken to Lugar. He's spoken to me. They don't want you going to North Korea. Powell says he was under instructions to shut it down."

But Powell disagreed with Bush's decision. In a subsequent conversation with Biden, Powell told the Senator he had informed the White House that he did not have the authority to block the trip. He could order the U.S. Embassy in Beijing not to extend any courtesies to the group, but he could not stop them from going to Pyongyang. The response at the White House, Powell said, was, "We don't care. Just shut it down."

Biden then asked Powell, "Are you, sir, saying it would be unhelpful for them to go."

"No," Powell replied. "I can't say that. I'm just telling you what I'm told to communicate."

"Fine," said Biden. "They'll go."


Pyongyang in mid-January 2004 was bitterly cold. But during the delegation's initial meeting with Vice Foreign Minister Kim Gye Gwan, the North

Korean stressed his government's continuing desire for a thaw with the United States. He repeated the offer to freeze all nuclear activities and provided an explanation for the decision to take the Americans to Yongbyon.

"We view the delegation's visit to Yongbyon as a way to help contribute to breaking the stalemate and opening up a bright future," Kim said. "We will not play games with you. We have invited you to go to Yongbyon. The primary reason for this is to ensure transparency. This will reduce the assumptions and errors. The visit can have great significance."[5]

The group also pressed Kim on the uranium issue.

"We wanted to give Kim a reasonable way out," recalled Sig Hecker, "to say, 'Yes, we have a uranium program but we aren't pursuing an enrichment program.' Kim didn't bite."

Instead, Kim denied the existence of any uranium effort.

"The answer then was, 'We never had a program,'" said Jack Pritchard. "'We do not now have a program; we do not have the scientists; we do not have the facilities; we have nothing to do with an HEU program.'"

The Americans drove from Pyongyang to Yongbyon in a van. The roads for part of the way were unpaved. The group was accompanied by Kim Gye Gwan's deputy, Li Gun, who was making his first visit to the facility. Li appeared excited, but when they arrived, he also seemed embarrassed. The Americans were convinced "he was expecting something out of James Bond, a modern, gleaming facility." Instead, they found a shabby, run-down complex with dials and other equipment that harkened back to the 1950s. But the scientists at Yongbyon were very proud and fawned over Hecker, a legendary figure in the nuclear field whose work they all knew.

"In a way that you do when you're really proud of something," recalled Jannuzi, "they became very talkative with him, probably letting their guard down. 'Just among us scientists, let's tell you about our toys. Let us show off to you, the world's expert, how much we know about plutonium.' So they gave us the tour of the facility."

Guided by Chief Engineer Liu Song Hwan, the group was taken to the spent fuel holding tank. The building was not heated, and a thin sheet of ice covered the storage pond. It was evident that many of the storage canisters in the murky water were empty, but others simply appeared closed. Afterward, the North Koreans said, "Now we've shown you that the fuel tank is empty"—meaning that all the fuel rods had been taken away for reprocessing into weapons-grade plutonium.

"No," replied Hecker. "You haven't. You've shown us there are many empty canisters but there could be many that are full."

The North Koreans asked what it would take to convince him. Hecker

asked for permission to choose a canister at random to open. In an extraordinary gesture for the normally secretive North Koreans, they agreed at once and
led him back to the tank. Hecker pointed to one at random. The North Koreans
pulled the lid off. It was empty.

"I'm satisfied," Hecker told them.

The Americans were then taken to the reprocessing plant. It was clear it had
not been used recently. The North Koreans insisted they had completed reprocessing all 8,000 spent fuel rods in 2003.

In a conference room following the tour, the North Koreans proudly declared, "Now you have seen our nuclear deterrent."

Again, it was Hecker who voiced skepticism. "You've shown us a facility,"
he said, "but you haven't shown us any product."

"Would you like to see some product?" the North Koreans asked. "Wait
here."

After an hour in the unheated room, bundled up in coats and scarves against
the bitter cold, two lab technicians came in carrying a metal container, which
they placed on a table and opened. Inside was a wooden box. The technicians
removed it and lifted the lid to reveal two glass jars. Their scene reminded
Jannuzi of the Russian stacking dolls that open to reveal another smaller container inside. The technicians said one jar contained 150 grams of plutonium
oxidate and the other had 200 grams of plutonium metal.

"The glass jars were fitted with a screw-on metal lid and were tightly taped
with transparent tape," Hecker told a Senate Foreign Relations Committee
hearing after returning to the United States.[6]

The North Koreans brought in a Geiger counter and waved it over the jars.
"It was hot," one of the Americans noted.

"Can I hold it?" Hecker asked.

"Yes you may," they answered, offering him the jars with their bare hands.

Hecker quickly requested a pair of rubber gloves, which the North Koreans
gave him.

Then, for a moment, it appeared the technicians were going to open the jar.
"No, no, no," Hecker told them. "That's not necessary. Just let me hold it in the
glass."

"I tried to get a feel for the density and heat content of the alleged plutonium metal by holding the glass jar in a gloved hand," Hecker said in his
testimony. "The glass jar (very thick-walled) was reasonably heavy and slightly
warm (importantly however it was not as cold as was everything else in the
building). The bottom line is with the rather primitive tools at hand I was not
able to definitively identify the purported metal and the powder as plutonium.
It was radioactive, however."[7]

As Hecker handled the jars, others in the group were watching the North Koreans. "They were like the cat that had swallowed the canary," said one American. "The scientists were cock-sure, confident, even a little showing off."

That night, back in Pyongyang, the group had dinner with Kim Gye Gwan, who repeated the assertion of the Yongbyon engineers. "Now we have shown you our nuclear deterrent."

It was evident to the Americans that the sole purpose of their remarkable day in Yongbyon had been to convince them of North Korea's nuclear prowess, so that they would take that message back to Washington and, Pyongyang clearly hoped, pressure the Bush administration into beginning serious negotiations.

Yet again, though, Hecker voiced a scientist's skepticism.

"No, you haven't shown us a deterrent," he said. "A nuclear deterrent has three components: plutonium, a bomb, and a delivery system. You might have shown us plutonium, but we don't really know for sure. It looks probable. I'm reasonably convinced. But you haven't shown us a bomb."

"Well," said Kim, "would you like to see it?'

"Yes," answered Hecker, "I would like to see the bomb."

"We don't have the authorization to show you," said Kim. "That's the military."

The other Americans chimed in, again repeating that they hadn't been shown the real "deterrent."

Still playing devil's advocate, one of the group asked Kim, "How would you feel if the U.S. doesn't conclude from our visit what you had hoped they would conclude?"

At that point, an obviously frustrated Kim turned to his interpreter, Miss Chae, and said, "What's that movie?"

Somehow, Frank Jannuzi immediately realized what Kim was referring to.

"It's *Gone with the Wind*, isn't it?" he said to Miss Chae.

"Yes," she answered. And then, speaking on behalf of Kim Gye Gwan, she said, "Our answer is: Frankly, I don't give a damn."

Returning from their visit to Yongbyon, Frank Jannuzi and other members of the delegation were puzzled at the reaction as they spelled out what they had seen and heard. In briefings at the NSC, the State Department, the Pentagon, and the intelligence community, their conclusion was the same: the North Koreans had reprocessed the fuel rods, were capable of producing weapons-grade plutonium and a viable nuclear device, and were not bluffing. When Senator Joseph Biden, raised the issue privately with Powell, the secretary told him, "It doesn't matter so much whether they have one or two or seven or eight. The threshold has been crossed when they went from zero to one or two, so I'm not going to get all worried about a little bit more plutonium."

Jannuzi was astonished. "Every bomb does matter with these guys," he recalled, "because of the risk of proliferation."

The Bush administration's hard line fueled tensions between the United States and South Korea. In January 2004, it also brought the turf war between leftists in the office of President Roh and pragmatists in the South Korean Foreign Ministry to the boiling point.

The split was bitter and personal. Word reached the Blue House that one member of the Foreign Ministry's Bureau of North American Affairs had compared the left-leaning coterie around Roh to the Taliban. In what became known in South Korea as the "night of the long knives," several leading Foreign Ministry officials were brought to the Blue House and interrogated about their behavior and loyalties, as Deputy National Security Adviser Lee Jong-seok, the most prominent of the leftists, watched.

"Those people were ferreted out, singled out," said one American defense official. "An inquisition was held in the Blue House where they were literally stood in front of a committee."

"Anybody who favorably viewed and negotiated positively for the alliance would be identified and charged with American ass-kissing and would therefore be penalized, excluded, exiled," noted another observer familiar with the event.

The resulting purge claimed the head of the North American Affairs Bureau and the junior official who had uttered the "Taliban" remark. Both officials were reassigned to other jobs, and their superior, Foreign Minister Yoon Young-kwan, was forced to resign. In announcing Yoon's resignation, a Blue House adviser emphasized that "some foreign ministry officials neither swerved from the 'dependent' foreign-policy paradigm of the past nor properly understood the basic concepts and direction of the [Roh] government's new 'independent' foreign policy."[8] However, in a sign of pragmatism, Roh appointed Ban Ki-moon, a career diplomat and future UN secretary-general who also had pro-American sympathies as the new minister of Foreign Affairs.

Acknowledging the Roh administration's accommodating posture toward Pyongyang, North Korea sent the government in Seoul a proposal in early 2004 and asked that it be passed along to Washington. Using a former South Korean official as an intermediary, the North said it was ready at the next round of six-party talks to offer what it called a "freeze for compensation." In return for freezing activity at Yongbyon, the North wanted heavy fuel oil, electricity, and a lifting of sanctions.

Despite the internal upheaval, South Korean Foreign Ministry officials felt the idea had some promising elements. They suggested accepting the freeze, reducing the compensation just to fuel oil, and changing the name to "freeze for corresponding measures." In meetings with Jim Kelly and other State Department officials, the South Koreans urged the United States to respond positively. But the proposal went nowhere.

On February 16, Bush's senior advisers met to finalize the U.S. position for the next round of six-party talks. A freeze was rejected. Instead, Jim Kelly was instructed to insist on CVID, with special emphasis on the North's uranium program. He was authorized to mention the possibility of security assurances, but not to offer a timetable for when the United States would agree to take such a step or to list any other inducements. As one official told the *Washington Post,* "We're not going to paint them a Western landscape with every detail that is some kind of road map."[9]

As round two of the six-party talks began on a chilly, smoggy February day in Beijing, Joseph DeTrani joined the American team. Asked by Colin Powell and Richard Armitage to join the State Department and fill Jack Pritchard's job of special envoy for talks with the North Koreans, he had been a CIA operative for years. He was well versed in dealing with wily Communist adversaries; fluent in Mandarin, DeTrani had served two stints in Beijing as CIA station chief before becoming the Agency's chief of operations for East Asia. In the early 1980s, during his first assignment in Beijing, DeTrani had played a critical role in convincing China to manufacture Soviet-designed weapons to provide to Mujahideen rebels fighting Soviet forces in Afghanistan. His admiring colleagues at the CIA nicknamed him "Broadway Joe."[10]

For the Americans, the head of the North Korean delegation was a familiar face. Kim Gye Gwan, who had handled so many negotiations with Americans over the years and was known as someone to make deals with, had replaced the stolid and uncommunicative Kim Yong Il. As the North had signaled prior to the meeting, Kim said Pyongyang was ready to freeze activity at Yongbyon for "corresponding measures." For his part, Kelly repeated the U.S. demand for CVID, covering both the plutonium program at Yongbyon and the uranium program the North Koreans insisted they did not have.

Unlike the first round, this time Kelly was able to hold two bilateral meetings with the North Koreans in a private room on the second floor of the Diaoyutai compound. Kelly took pains to tell reporters afterward that he "didn't negotiate, but it was a great way to communicate." He admitted the "differences and questions were sharp."

Both men went over the ground covered in their opening statements, but Kelly rebuffed Kim's offer of a freeze. "We kept saying we don't want to hear the word 'freeze,'" said one American participant. "We had our instructions. We weren't going back to the Agreed Framework. What we needed was a commitment to comprehensive dismantlement, and we told the North Koreans, 'You've got to give us something on that.'"

The central focus of Kelly's argument was uranium. "It was the core," said one U.S. official. "When we talked about CVID, we told them, 'We know you were making those procurements.'" Any North Korean commitment, the Americans insisted, "had to be inclusive of uranium enrichment."

"You've got it wrong," Kim Gye Gwan shot back, denying the existence of a uranium program. "You were wrong in Iraq, and you are wrong here."

Kim then asked Kelly for evidence to back up the U.S. claim of a uranium program. Kelly answered, "If I were to give you all that information it might make it easier for you to conceal it."

But Kelly also mentioned the case of Libya and expressed the hope that "they understand its significance. Once North Korea's nuclear issue is resolved, discussions would be possible on a wide range of issues that could lead to an improvement in relations."[11] Pyongyang still had to move first. Only then would Washington reciprocate.

Kim pushed back, asking whether the United States would put in writing the statements of President Bush that he had no hostile intent and no intention of invading North Korea, and pressing for specific details as to what the United States would do if the North dismantled its nuclear program. Kelly repeated Bush's promise of multilateral security assurances but said nothing about a written commitment or a willingness to provide electricity.

In an effort to bridge the gap, the South Koreans offered a three-stage proposal: first, an agreement in principle in which North Korea would state its willingness to eliminate all nuclear activities and the United States would declare its willingness to provide security assurances; second, a freeze that, if cast as "a step to dismantlement" and verified, would be accompanied by a "coordinated" response such as heavy fuel oil and other compensation; third, verified elimination. Kelly thought the proposal was "creative," but Washington remained opposed to a freeze and refused to join in providing heavy fuel oil. The South Korean ideas gained little traction.

As in the first round, the Chinese, having invested considerable diplomatic capital to arrange the meeting, were pushing for a joint statement. Joseph DeTrani did the drafting work for the Americans, with Li Gun representing the North Koreans. It was clear, however, that the North Koreans would not accept the CVID language. The drafting sessions were stormy. One witness recalls the pugnacious Li Gun as being "red in the face" and clearly under instructions to avoid reaching any kind of accord.

Kelly informed Powell of the deadlock. In the hope of maintaining some diplomatic momentum, Powell authorized him to explore modified language that would reduce the prospects of the North Koreans walking away from the negotiations altogether.[12]

One of those on Kelly's delegation was Mark Groombridge, John Bolton's chief Asian expert. Groombridge was alarmed by signs of a more flexible attitude on Kelly's part that meant CVID might not be included in any final statement. He felt the lack of clarity was dangerous and underscored the basic problem the hardliners had with the State Department. There was no point in having a piece of paper, he felt, unless there was agreement on the terms. "To the extent that the North Koreans were not even willing to admit that they had a uranium enrichment program," Groombridge recalled, "why were we even there?"

On the evening of February 26, Dick Cheney intervened.

"It became clear that we weren't getting a very decisive outcome," recalled Stephen Yates, who was Cheney's chief adviser for Asian Affairs. "And there were negotiations about a joint statement, and there was niggling about what was in the joint statement and not. And it looked like the joint statement was something that could be held up to appear strikingly similar to a return to the Agreed Framework."

Yates informed Cheney about what was happening in the talks. "And he did have a strong opinion," Yates said, "that this is no time to show weakness. Giving the appearance of walking back what standards we would require on counterproliferation was the wrong signal to send. And if that is where these negotiations are going, that's a mistake."

Colin Powell and Richard Armitage were at a black-tie dinner honoring veteran diplomat John Whitehead when they received a phone call from Deputy National Security Adviser Stephen Hadley.

"We got called out, sat in Powell's limousine, and talked [on the] secure [phone line]," Armitage recalled. Hadley said the White House wanted to modify Kelly's instructions. Powell had to return to the dinner, so he asked Armitage to handle the matter. "Steve and I finally agreed on something," Armitage recalled.

But that was not the end of the matter.

"I thought that we did have an agreement," said Armitage. "But it was contradicted by the vice president."

Meeting privately with Bush, Cheney persuaded the president to toughen Kelly's instructions to insist that any statement from the talks include a reference to CVID.

Without informing Powell or Armitage, Bush ordered the NSC to convey the new instruction to Kelly. Hadley told NSC Asia specialist Mike Green to call his NSC colleague Chuck Jones, who was with Kelly's delegation in Beijing, and order him to tell Kelly that any statement coming out of the talks had to include the following language, which came directly from the president and vice president: "The United States further declares that its continued support of the six-party process . . . rests on the complete, verifiable, and irreversible dismantlement by the DPRK of all nuclear weapons and all its nuclear programs."[13]

Kelly got the news in the middle of a meeting with his team. He was, in Mike Green's words, "pissed—really, really unhappy." Kelly turned to Joseph DeTrani and said, "I see the Bolton crowd got to the president." He then turned to Bolton's aide Mark Groombridge and, as one witness recalled, "shot him a look of death."

Groombridge was elated. "I loved it so much," he recalled. "It was exactly how I would have written it."

Powell first learned what had happened when he received a call from Chinese Foreign Minister Li Zhaoxing—at midnight Beijing time—telling him the North Koreans appeared willing to sign a more general statement agreeing to another round of talks and that the new American conditions put the statement in jeopardy. Powell was furious. Confronting Bush, he complained bitterly about Cheney's end-run when both Powell and Armitage were just a few blocks from the White House. After a sharp exchange, the secretary convinced Bush to accept a statement that did not include the U.S. demand for CVID.[14]

At 2:00 A.M. Beijing time, Kelly was informed that the CVID reference could be dropped. Instead, the language agreed on was "comprehensive dismantlement." In the wee hours of the morning, all six parties, including North Korea, reached a consensus. The document was sent back to the various capitals for final approval, with the understanding that, after so much effort, in the words of one delegate, "not a comma could be changed."

The next morning, as the exhausted diplomats were preparing for the final plenary session where the statement would be announced, the North Koreans suddenly demanded a change. Kim Gye Gwan insisted on adding the sentence: "All parties acknowledge differences remain and agree to narrow those differences in further discussion."[15]

When the Americans noted the previous night's agreement not to demand further changes, the North Koreans were adamant. One member of Kelly's team described the North Korean attitude as, "This is what we want. It's our way or nothing." As other delegations arrived for the final event at Diaoyutai, the North Koreans stayed stubbornly in their rooms. In the end, as was true after round one, Beijing was forced to issue a "chairman's statement" that papered over the differences by stressing the commitment of all parties to a nuclear-free Korean peninsula, their determination to seek a resolution "peacefully through dialogue," and to hold a third round of talks by June.

To Kelly, Pyongyang's last-minute obstinacy had allowed him to dodge a bullet by making the Cheney-inspired hard-line instructions irrelevant.

"There was some potential embarrassment [for the U.S.]," he recalled, "but the North Koreans, as usual, saved us from that situation."

Powell, though, continued to press his case with Bush.

In a background briefing to reporters before he left Beijing, Kelly made no mention of the Cheney episode. His spin was that the round had been important because "to a remarkable extent, the non-DPRK participants were on the same sheet." He portrayed the North Koreans as isolated and having antagonized the other delegates.

But Cheney's own deputy national security adviser, Aaron Friedberg, saw things differently.

"The only people who were really on board were the Japanese," he said. "The South Koreans, Chinese, and Russians all were trying to persuade the United States to be more accommodating, and were also providing the North Koreans with help that cushioned them from our pressure."

Washington's two key Asian allies now both took steps to go their own ways in dealing with North Korea.

Just days after the second round of six-party talks ended, South Korean president Roh Moo-hyun declared in a nationally televised speech, "Whether we are pro-U.S. or anti-U.S. cannot be the yardstick to assess ourselves. Step by step, we should strengthen our independence and build our strength as an independent nation."[16] On the same day, Seoul announced it was setting aside $40 million to develop the infrastructure for a new Kaesong joint economic zone on the northern side of the DMZ.

Roh's moves appear to have alarmed the White House. Two days later, the new South Korean foreign minister Ban Ki-moon set out for his first official trip to Washington. While driving to Seoul's Inchon Airport, Ban received a call from the South Korean embassy in Washington saying President Bush wanted to see him as soon as he arrived.

Ban was ushered into the Oval Office less than an hour after his plane touched down. The meeting was awkward. With a half-smile, Bush began by saying how precise and accurate U.S. weapons systems had become in recent years. "Our weapons systems are more lethal and more effective now," he told

Ban. "Unlike what we did in Yugoslavia, whatever target we want to destroy now we can."

The president's comment unsettled the South Korean. But Bush sought to allay Ban's anxiety by putting his observation in the context of the broader effort to transform and upgrade the U.S. military being overseen by Defense Secretary Donald Rumsfeld and stressing that even though the United States was scaling down its military presence in South Korea, Washington would stand by its treaty obligations.

Bush also told Ban, "Everyone [in South Korea] thinks I want to invade North Korea. That's not correct. I am not going to invade North Korea. I want to resolve this in a diplomatic way."

Hearing the president speak about pressuring the North into a deal, albeit without resorting to armed attack, the South Koreans left the meeting still uneasy, but somewhat reassured.

The message from Vice President Cheney was starker. Visiting Beijing in April, Cheney expressed frustration with the slow pace of diplomacy and warned Chinese leaders that "time is not on our side" in the six-party negotiations.[17] Signaling that the United States was losing patience, he portrayed North Korea as a growing threat. "We worry that, given what they've done in the past, and given what we estimate to be their current capability, that North Korea could well, for example, provide [nuclear weapons] . . . to, say, a terrorist organization," he emphasized in a speech at Fudan University in Shanghai. "We know that there are terrorist organizations out there like al Qaeda that have sought to acquire these kinds of weapons in the past."[18]

As Chinese leaders pushed for the United States to show more flexibility, the vice president tried to stoke China's own fears by warning that "other nations in the region" might go nuclear if North Korea's program was not eliminated. It was a thinly veiled reference to China's worst nightmare—the prospect that its main regional rival, Japan, might seek to develop its own nuclear capability, possibly leading South Korea and perhaps even Taiwan to follow suit. Cheney's aim was to get China to put pressure on North Korea to come to terms with the United States.

"He basically kept pushing the idea that this is a very serious situation, we're very concerned, proliferation of this technology would be a grave security challenge to us all," recalled Stephen Yates, the Chinese-speaking Asia adviser who accompanied the vice president. "And the mission of the trip was to urge the Chinese to lean a bit more forward on things related to North Korea."

Cheney made similar points during stopovers in Seoul and Tokyo. His efforts to link al Qaeda and the Pyongyang regime infuriated the North Koreans. "It is quite understandable that the United States cannot sleep in peace, terror-stricken by al Qaeda," said a North Korean Foreign Ministry spokesman in a statement carried by the official Korean Central News Agency (KCNA) on April 18, "but its [Cheney's] unreasonably linking the DPRK to such organization is an expression of total ignorance." The statement went on to denounce Cheney as a "mentally deranged person steeped in the inveterate enmity toward the system in the DPRK."[19]

The rumors began circulating within days of Cheney's departure from Beijing. Over the weekend of April 19, South Korea media reported than an official train had crossed the border from North Korea to China—Kim Jong Il was making yet another trip to the Chinese capital. In the following days, however, China and North Korea maintained official silence. There was no coverage in the state-run media in either country, se spokesman denied all knowledge of Kim's presence.

The secrecy was typical of the North Korean leader. When the visit was finally confirmed after Kim's departure, it became clear that China had heeded vice president Cheney's warnings. The official Beijing media announced that North Korea had agreed to continue the six-party talks and would participate in the next session, due to be held by June. Kim reportedly told Chinese leaders that he was committed to a peaceful resolution of the nuclear crisis, although he remained doubtful of America's unwritten promises not to invade.

Those suspicions continued to drive North Korea's nuclear program forward, despite talk of a new round in Beijing.

"We don't think [Bush] is at all serious about resolving the nuclear issue with us in a fair way," Kim Yong Nam, chairman of the Supreme People's Assembly, told visiting American scholar Selig Harrison in early May, "since we obviously can't accept 'CVID first.' My feeling is he is delaying resolution of the nuclear issue due to Iraq and the presidential election."

Eerily, Kim found one point of agreement with Vice President Cheney. "Time is not on [Bush's] side," Kim said. "We are going to use this time 100 percent effectively to strengthen our nuclear deterrent both quantitatively and qualitatively."[20]

But Cheney's effort to link al Qaeda with Pyongyang continued to anger North Korean leaders. "We make a clear distinction between missiles and nuclear material," Kim Yong Nam told Harrison. "We're entitled to sell missiles to earn foreign exchange. But in regard to nuclear material, our policy past, present, and future is that we would never allow such transfers to al Qaeda or anyone else. Never."

Added Foreign Minister Paek Nam Sun, "Let me make clear that we denounce al Qaeda for the barbaric attack of 9/11, which was a terrible tragedy and inflicted a great shock to America. Bush is using that that shock to turn America against us, but the truth is that we want and need your friendship."[21]

There was no meal, no communiqué, and little of the drama that had accompanied their first meeting. But in mid-May of 2004, in a striking repudiation of Washington's objection to bilateral contacts or substantive negotiations, Japan's prime minister Junichiro Koizumi held his second summit with Kim Jong Il in Pyongyang. The atmosphere in Japan had soured markedly since the first summit in September 2002. Public anger over the fate of the abductees had constrained Koizumi from moving toward his goal of normalizing relations. And the nuclear crisis had left North Korea more tense than it had been in years.

In meetings on the sidelines of the six-party talks in February, as well as in subsequent discussions, North Korean officials had signaled to Japanese diplomats that progress on the abduction issue in part hinged on progress in improving Pyongyang's ties with Washington. During a ninety-minute meeting, Koizumi offered Kim $10 million in medical supplies and 250,000 tons of food. Kim agreed that eight family members of the five abductees who had been allowed to leave in 2002 would now be permitted to rejoin their relatives in Japan. Five left with Koizumi that day. Three, however, remained behind: Charles Jenkins, an American GI stationed in South Korea who had defected in 1965 and married one of the Japanese abductees, and their two children. Jenkins feared being imprisoned for desertion by U.S. military authorities if he went to Japan. It would take many more months of negotiations before he was able to depart, and, after serving a nominal thirty-day sentence at a U.S. base in Japan, the case was closed.

The nuclear issue was also high on Koizumi's agenda. "I told [Kim] face to face, 'If you compare what you gain from nuclear weapons and what you gain from dismantlement of your own nuclear program, there would be a difference of heaven and earth,'" Koizumi said. In response, Kim told the Japanese prime minister he was committed to eventual denuclearization. Stressing his eagerness for direct talks with Washington, Kim reportedly told Koizumi that he wanted the other participants in the six-party talks "to play music" so North Korea and the U.S. "can dance well." Kim said he wanted his negotiator to talk to the United States so much that the envoy's "voice will become hoarse."[22]

As the summit ended, Koizumi told reporters, "I felt personally that North Korea is interested in moving forward in a positive way with six-party talks. I believe North Korea wants this to happen. It is up to the U.S. to make a decision of what sort of approach it should take."[23]

Upon returning to Tokyo, Koizumi called his good friend President Bush, conveyed Kim Jong Il's request for direct talks and urged Bush to accept. The president was not interested. Two weeks later, the two men met at the G8 summit at Sea Island, Georgia, and Koizumi again pressed Bush, telling him Kim Jong Il might indeed be serious about a nuclear deal. Bush replied, "He [Kim Jong Il] is an untrustworthy liar. I cannot trust such a country. I will only talk to them if there are witnesses."[24]

# 12

# "SOME GOOD, SOME BAD, SOME UGLY"

ALMOST NO ONE WHO DEALT WITH DAVID ASHER IN WASH-
ington was neutral about him. To his supporters—like his boss,
Jim Kelly—he was "a brilliant guy" who did "exceptional work."
To his detractors, he was "decaf Dave," "a bomb-thrower," and a "loud-
mouth nutcase."

With a Ph.D. from Oxford University, Asher was a Japan specialist
with a background in finance. He had spent the 1990s working for
hedge funds doing business in Asia before ending up at the American
Enterprise Institute, the conservative think-tank that had sent so many
people to important jobs in the Bush administration. When Kelly became assistant secretary of state for East Asia, he brought Asher to the
State Department as one of his key advisers. Asher's original brief was
the Japanese economy, but in late 2003 and early 2004, he became the
driving force behind what was dubbed the Illicit Activities Initiative—
an ambitious effort to pressure and weaken North Korea by targeting its
dirty dealings.

Asher's hyperkinetic personality played a central role in this effort.
With his light brown hair and glasses, he looked and acted like a college
professor on speed—constantly moving, talking, pushing. Jim Kelly,
whose calm demeanor led one admirer to describe him as a "thoughtful
Buddha," once commented to a colleague, "You know Dave—he comes
up with fifteen ideas an hour. Most are crazy. But a few are very good."

By 2003, Asher was focusing his not inconsiderable energy on North
Korea's illicit activities. "It's important to understand that there'd been a

lot of evidence of North Korean counterfeiting of the dollar and illegal activities for many years," he recalled. "But no one had done anything about it."

Asher became convinced that North Korea was, in effect, a "*Sopranos* state"—one vast criminal enterprise. "The more we dug into the illicit activities arena," he said, "the more we found that they were engaged in. Most disturbingly: the increasing evidence of a large-scale distribution of U.S. currency, which was having a destabilizing impact on confidence in the dollar to some parts of the world—at least on a temporary basis. We felt that it was the right thing to do to start to enforce our laws against North Korea and to the extent that the North Korean government was involved."

A U.S. effort to target Pyongyang's illicit activities, he thought, could inflict real pain on Kim Jong Il and perhaps undermine his grip on power. Moreover, by counterfeiting U.S. dollars, Asher argued, North Korea was engaging in "economic warfare" against the United States, something that, under international law, could be regarded as a *casus belli*. Asher drew up a memo asking for the creation of an interagency task force to target these activities, and proposed that he be put in charge. The idea was thrashed out with Kelly and Deputy Secretary of State Richard Armitage.

"They've got the methamphetamine, they've got this, they've got the money in Macau and all," Armitage recalled. "We could do this and we can really hurt the elite on this without further hurting the people. And will you support this? Kelly was there in my office, and I said that basically, 'Yeah, let's write it up.' And we took it to Powell and told him, and he said, 'Yeah.' "

Not everyone was comfortable with Asher's plan. David Straub, director of the State Department's Korea Desk, thought it was a bad idea that would undermine the prospects for progress at the six-party talks. Moreover, he resented what he saw as Asher's naked grab for power on Korean issues within the bureaucracy.

Jim Foster, who succeeded Straub as head of the Korea Desk in mid-2004, was equally critical. Foster argued that the initiative was only giving ammunition to the hard-liners. It wasn't complementing U.S. diplomacy, Foster felt, but instead simply provided a rationale at every interagency meeting for those who believed the U.S. couldn't—and shouldn't—deal with North Korea.

Colin Powell, however, brushed the objections aside.

"You couldn't push this stuff under the table and say we can't do anything about this because it would affect the negotiations," he said. "These guys were counterfeiting our money, they were running drugs, they were doing a lot of illicit things. And so it seemed like we had them cold and we had to use it, and we did."

In an administration where the hard-liners had such an influential voice on Korea policy, part of the appeal for Powell and his key aides was that the Illicit

Activities Initiative would allow them to act in a muscular way toward Pyongyang—a fact that was recognized by their bureaucratic rivals. As Stephen Yates, Vice President Cheney's Asia specialist, noted, "Part of the psychology of what was going on was the State Department team—Powell, Armitage, and the people who worked for them—saying 'We know, we're tough, we can handle this, we're the policy makers and implementers, just get out of our hair, trust us, trust where we're going.' And they had their own sort of projects going."

The rivalries meant that, even with Powell's backing, Asher's idea for an Illicit Activities Initiative encountered skepticism elsewhere in the bureaucracy.

"We had a little trouble selling it in the NSC and others," Armitage recalled. "In fact, I went and sold it with [Deputy National Security Adviser Stephen] Hadley at a deputies meeting. And Hadley didn't like Asher, and others there, particularly the non-pro [nonproliferation] people didn't like him very much. And I told David, 'Sit in the back and don't say a fucking word on this. If anyone else asks anything, don't answer.' Because David is his own worst enemy sometimes."

Indeed, initially, Asher, with his bosses' support, sought to keep prominent hard-liners at arm's length, both to ensure the project remained a State Department initiative and out of concern that what David Straub and Jim Foster worried about—that skeptics of the six-party talks would use any opening to destroy the diplomatic process—might become a reality.

"State didn't want to let anyone in on what their project was," recalled Cheney aide Stephen Yates, "because they were afraid that the right-wing crazies in the White House might seize upon this as a pretext to kill the talks."

Among the other skeptics were John Bolton and Bob Joseph. "They felt it was a threat to PSI [the Proliferation Security Initiative, the Bolton-inspired but so far largely ineffectual plan to interdict North Korean shipping]," said Lawrence Wilkerson, who was Powell's chief of staff. "PSI was essentially . . . a bunch of people who said, 'We're committed to PSI and oh, by the way we'll throw a naval vessel in and we'll sail the high seas and we'll act like we're doing something.' So I think Bolton and some others thought this was a threat to PSI because it had every prospect of being effective."

For his part, though, Asher argued that pressing Pyongyang on illicit activities was simply another way to gain leverage in any negotiations: if Pyongyang was being recalcitrant, pressure on this front could be increased.

But for it to work, supporters agreed it had to be kept out of public view.

"The whole program was predicated on being quiet and not saying anything about it," observed Armitage. "If you say something about it, then it just forces the North Koreans to be more . . ." Armitage paused . . . "so just be quiet and don't say anything."

In Washington, getting government agencies to cooperate is often an impossible task. But Asher pushed and pushed, eventually bringing representatives from State, the Treasury Department, the Secret Service, law enforcement agencies, and the intelligence community together in the same room.

"Asher railroaded everyone," observed one official, "by sheer force of his crazy personality."

With the entire project designated top secret, many of the planning meetings were held in a secure room at the State Department. Some of the ideas under consideration seemed to come right out of a spy movie. As the North Koreans often used diplomatic pouches to move counterfeit cash, "taking down a North Korean diplomat" and seizing his pouch was one suggestion. Infiltrating North Korean embassies and using the electronic eavesdropping capabilities of the National Security Agency to get inside banks where the North Koreans did business were other options.

"It's safe to say the plan incorporated almost everywhere the North Koreans had money," said Lawrence Wilkerson, who attended many of the meetings, "whether that money was illicit or legitimate."

Eventually, it was agreed that one of the targets would be Banco Delta Asia, a small bank in Macau, the former Portuguese colony that had reverted to Chinese sovereignty in 1999.


By early summer of 2004, the Bush administration's policy toward North Korea was facing conflicting pressures on several fronts. The Christian right—a key part of the President's domestic political base—was pushing to put North Korea's appalling human rights record high on the U.S. agenda, a development that inevitably would fuel an even tougher position. Inside the supposedly "moderate" State Department, the Illicit Activities Initiative was taking shape, even as the internal bureaucratic warfare continued. And pressure of a different kind was coming from Washington's key Asian partners—treaty allies Japan and South Korea, and China, host of the six-party talks—for the United States to show some flexibility in the stalled negotiations, with another round scheduled in Beijing in late June.

Similar calls were coming from Senator John Kerry, who would become the Democratic Party's candidate for president in the November 2004 election. In a campaign speech on June 1, Kerry said the administration "essentially negotiated over the shape of the table while the North Koreans have allegedly made enough fuel to make six to nine nuclear bombs. . . . We must be prepared to talk directly to North Korea. This problem is too urgent to allow China, or others at the table, to speak for us."[1]

As in the earlier rounds, State Department Korea Desk director David Straub prepared the initial draft of Kelly's presentation for the forthcoming talks and tried to take advantage of the pressure from the South Koreans, Japanese, and Chinese to moderate the administration's previously unyielding position.

"For the third round, I drafted an initial presentation that tried to push the envelope a little," Straub recalled. "Bits and pieces, areas in which you can try to go a little farther. And I did that and showed it to my bosses, and we sent it out for circulation, and I was feeling, this was at least something that was presentable. It was a little more developed than what we had the previous session."

"There was this feeling that, even if we were not prepared to give them something before they did what we wanted them to do, we should at least be able to give them a little bit of detail, outline the type of things we would be willing to talk about and contemplate if they did dismantle," said one member of the U.S. delegation. "So there was a lot of effort and preparation for trying to lay out a score card of the things we would be prepared to talk to and to present them there."

Then, predictably, came the pushback from hard-liners at the NSC, the vice president's office, and the Pentagon.

"State was trying to push the envelope," recalled a Pentagon official involved in the process, "and people had to keep reining them back in. Frankly, we didn't support the concept of offering the North Koreans benefits to get them to dismantle."

"And at that point," said Straub, "just shortly before we left, all of a sudden we got a brand-new paper, from [NSC nonproliferation director] Bob Joseph [with backing] from the White House. And we were told, 'This is what you're going to do.'"

What Straub and his State Department colleagues did not know was that both Vice President Cheney and Defense Secretary Donald Rumsfeld had personally intervened to toughen Kelly's proposed talking points. Their intervention followed a South Korean government initiative to deal directly with the White House, sparked by Seoul's frustration at State's inability to prevail in the internal U.S. policy battles. After Straub circulated his initial paper, officials from the South Korean National Security Council met in mid-June with their U.S. counterparts and hammered out ideas for a joint position for the upcoming talks, which included U.S. acceptance of an interim period when North Korea would freeze its nuclear program before dismantling it. This represented a modification of the previous American position. When Cheney learned of the new proposal, he instructed his aides to insist that any reference to a freeze— even if it was called something else—be removed. At the same time, Rumsfeld objected to the idea of giving Pyongyang six months to dismantle its nuclear capability. He successfully lobbied for the time period to be cut to three months.[2]

In an effort to rebut the charges of inflexibility, the administration did decide to drop the term "CVID" and to offer, for the first time, a proposal that contained some specifics. But the proposal still required that North Korea act first, while holding back any concrete benefits from the United States until Pyongyang had dismantled its nuclear capability.

In his statement at the opening plenary session in Beijing on June 23, 2004, Jim Kelly insisted that the North first make a unilateral declaration agreeing to dismantle all its nuclear programs. Then, in the three-month period demanded by Donald Rumsfeld, Kelly said Pyongyang had to "provide a complete listing of its nuclear activities, and cease operations of its nuclear activities; permit securing of all fissile material and the monitoring of all fuel rods; permit the publicly disclosed and observable disablement of all nuclear weapons, weapons components and centrifuge parts."[3]

Once Pyongyang had made its declaration, China, South Korea, Russia, and Japan—but not the United States—would resume shipments of heavy fuel oil. A State Department proposal to offer security assurances to the North as the fuel shipments began had been rejected by President Bush after Rumsfeld protested.[4] While Kelly said a "discussion" on the lifting of U.S. sanctions might be possible as the process moved ahead, he stressed that any "lasting benefits" from the United States to the North would come only "after the dismantlement of its nuclear programs had been completed."[5] And he said that a "wholly transformed relationship with the United States" would not happen until North Korea agreed "to change its behavior on human rights, address the issues underlying its appearance on the U.S. list of states sponsoring terrorism, eliminate its illegal weapons of mass destruction programs, put an end to the proliferation of missiles and missile-related technology, and adopt a less provocative conventional force disposition."[6]

For his part, North Korean envoy Kim Gye Gwan also added some details to Pyongyang's offer to freeze its nuclear activities—for the right price. But what Kim called "reward for freeze," in which the North would receive benefits long before any final dismantlement, was an entirely different approach than Kelly's. Kim said Pyongyang was prepared to "freeze all the facilities related to nuclear weapons and products churned out by their operation, refrain from producing more nukes, transferring and testing them and the freeze would be the first start that would lead to the ultimate dismantlement of the nuclear weapons program."[7] In return, though, he demanded the lifting of U.S. sanctions and the provision of two million kilowatts of electricity—the amount that would have been generated by the two light-water reactors North Korea had been promised under the Agreed Framework. The size of the request translated into about 2.7 million tons of heavy fuel oil—a sign of the scale of North Korea's shortage of energy.

Hoping to improve the strained atmosphere at the talks, the Chinese scheduled a lavish outdoor reception and banquet on the grounds of the Diaoyutai State Guest House after the opening plenary session.

"It was meant to be a sort of icebreaker," said one member of Kelly's delegation, "where the Americans can sort of casually mix with the North Koreans." But the Chinese hadn't taken into account the unpredictable Beijing summer weather. "What happens is everyone gets on a shuttle bus and takes maybe 250 yards to go over to this beautiful outdoor garden area," said a member of Kelly's team. "Here the Chinese have set up this elaborate outdoor buffet with ice sculptures, beautiful girls in traditional Chinese outfits, tiger prawns, and other food. And we get over there and within ten minutes a huge torrential cloud front moves in and dumps water over everything. People barely get two shrimp in their mouths, before they're running inside to get shelter, and of course they immediately go home instead of staying around and talking."

It was not an auspicious end to the first day of the new round of talks.

On the second afternoon, however, Kelly, Kim Gye Gwan, and their aides held a private meeting that lasted around two hours. According to one witness, Kelly told Kim the United States didn't like the word "freeze," preferring to use the term "halt."

Kim immediately shot back, "It's still ABC [Anyone But Clinton]."

Kelly responded, "We're talking about a halt in preparation for ultimate dismantlement. Once you make that commitment, everything else starts flowing."

But the two men remained at loggerheads over the issue of Pyongyang's uranium program.

"You say you'll halt Yongbyon," Kelly told Kim. "We need some assurances that you're talking about more than you have at Yongbyon."

Kim repeated the North's long-standing denial of any uranium effort.

Then Kim startled the Americans by threatening a demonstration of Pyongyang's nuclear "deterrent."

"The North Koreans said there were some, not identified, in the DPRK who wanted to test a nuclear weapon," Kelly said afterward, "and might presumably do so if there was no progress in the talks."[8]

But when a surprised Kelly pressed for more details, Kim said nothing more.

"He got our attention," noted one participant in the meeting, "and then walked away."

Despite alarming headlines triggered by leaks of Kim's warning, Kelly and his colleagues downplayed the threat, insisting there was no evidence a nuclear test was in the offing. Officials from the South Korean delegation shared a similar assessment. But Kelly resisted appeals from China—which, as the host, was eager to show that progress was being made by having all six parties issue a joint statement at the end of the round. Even a call from China's foreign minister to Colin Powell could not convince the U.S. side. Instead, for the third successive time, the head of the Chinese delegation issued a "Chairman's statement," trying to put a positive spin on a meeting that had produced scant progress.

As the meeting ended, Kelly described it to reporters as "some good, some bad, some ugly." North Korea noted a "sincere atmosphere" and the fact that Washington had dropped the use of the objectionable term "CVID." The gulf between the two sides remained vast, but optimists could at least convince themselves that both had staked out opening positions—an essential first step in any negotiation. It remained far from clear, however, whether either side was prepared to compromise.

A week after the talks ended, Colin Powell, acting on his own, arranged another "chance meeting" with North Korean foreign minister Paek Nam Sun at the Regional Forum of the Association of Southeast Asian Nations in Brunei, two years after he had orchestrated a similar encounter.

"It's good to see you again," Paek said.

"Last time I spoke first," Powell answered, giving Paek the chance to do so this time.

Paek began by reading a prepared statement that repeated word for word the proposal Kim Gye Gwan had just put forward in Beijing. But he then offered some additional insights into North Korean thinking.

"The U.S. suspects we would evade dismantlement [of the North's nuclear program]," he told Powell, "while we suspect you will attack us if we freeze. If the U.S. takes positive steps to participate in offering rewards, such as supplying energy, lifting sanctions, or taking us off the terrorism list, we will move toward dismantlement. If the U.S. studies our proposal carefully and participates in the rewards, a breakthrough is possible."

"We are studying carefully," Powell replied. "My view and the president's view is that we have made progress but there is a long way to go. We have no intention to invade or attack and no hostile intent. The U.S. has relations with many countries with whom we have serious differences and with whose ideology we disagree. The U.S. wants to see action. We can enter into a provisional security agreement. A freeze must be linked to dismantlement as well as ultimate removal."

Powell stressed that for any final agreement, the uranium issue had to be resolved. "We are confused by your position," he told Paek. "We have to work out what programs you have as a way of building trust. As we prepare for the next round, we need to get into details, we need to get specific."

He also cautioned Paek about the North's repeated threats to stage a nuclear test. "Statements that you will test make it more difficult. We need to build trust and move forward."

In response, Paek said, "You have convinced me this can be resolved smoothly. If both sides have the attitude of resolving this issue, it can be resolved smoothly. We have never said officially that we would test. We don't have a uranium enrichment program and we are willing to prove it. If the U.S. renounces its hostile policy, we are willing to clear this issue up."

Around the same time, a North Korean ship left the port of Nampo bound for the South Korean port of Busan, watched closely by the United States. The vessel was packed with fake American cigarettes—a target of opportunity for David Asher's Illicit Activities Initiative. Asher was convinced the production of counterfeit cigarettes was big business for North Korea. "Indeed, counterfeit cigarettes may well be North Korea's largest containerized export sector," Asher asserted in a 2005 speech "with cargoes frequently coming from the ports of Najin and Nampo for shipment via major ports in China and the ROK [Republic of Korea] throughout the world. . . . A 40-foot container of counterfeit cigarettes might cost as little as $70,000 to produce and have a street value of $3–4 million."[9]

Going through normal channels, the United States alerted the authorities in Seoul. But with its top priority to reduce tensions with Pyongyang, especially given Washington's tough line in the six-party talks, the government of President Roh Moo-hyun chose not to act. Undeterred, the Americans found another way to intercept the shipment.

"There was a relationship between the U.S. Coast Guard and the South Korean Coast Guard," said one former official involved in the effort, "so some people said, 'Jeez, let's let them squabble in Seoul while we actually do it' because the [two] coast guards are friends and buddies who work together all the time—and by God, they won't ask permission from Seoul. We'll just tell them, and if it comes in we'll take it down."

When the North Korean ship arrived in Busan, the South Korean Coast

Guard alerted customs officials, and several containers of counterfeit cigarettes were seized.

At the end of July, North Korea pulled down the last propaganda billboard on its side of the Demilitarized Zone and ended the propaganda broadcasts that had been a feature of the DMZ for decades. The final broadcast said, "We, from one blood and using one language, can no longer live separated. We must put the earliest possible end to the tragedy of national division."[10]

In mid-August, North and South Korean athletes marched together in the opening ceremony of the 2004 Olympics in Athens.

These steps underscored not only the links developing between the North and South, but also the sharp differences between South Korea and the Bush administration. In September 2004, South Korea's foreign minister Ban Ki-moon met Colin Powell in New York on the sidelines of the annual session of the United Nations General Assembly. Reading from prepared notes, Ban, stressing the need for "creative ideas, wisdom and flexibility," pressed Powell to come up with a new and better offer for the North Koreans. Ban went on at some length, but got nowhere. "Powell was pretty rough on him," recalled one State Department official, "and completely rejected the request.

The June 2004 round of six-party talks would be the last for David Straub, as his two-year term as Korea Desk Director was ending in the summer. At the beginning of the year, he told Jim Kelly that he had decided to resign soon from the State Department. The problem was not just his disagreement with the president's confrontational approach to North Korea. As a young Foreign Service officer, Straub had handled human rights issues for the U.S. Embassy in Seoul during the years of military dictatorship in the early 1980s, where he documented the use of "waterboarding"—the simulated drowning of prisoners that had been authorized by the administration as a legitimate post–9/11 interrogation technique. Watching reports of the harsh treatment of prisoners captured in Iraq and in the broader war on terror, Straub concluded, "I didn't want to work for an administration that condoned the use of torture. Coupled with that was my direct experience with the Bush administration working on North Korea policy. It seemed to me that the president was personally responsible for much of the wrongheadedness."

Later that spring, however, the position of Japan Desk director suddenly opened up. Freed from the nightmare of Korea policy, Straub decided to do one last assignment, then leave government. His replacement was Jim Foster, a longtime Japan hand who had been involved in negotiations with the North Koreans during the 1990s. The first thing Foster did was to read into the intelligence on enrichment. He was unimpressed. It clearly showed North Korean operatives trying to procure components for a uranium program, but he could see little evidence that the effort had amounted to much. Whatever Pyongyang's intentions, there was nothing to show they actually had a production-level facility capable of producing sufficient uranium to create a weapon.

And Foster felt the focus on uranium—the way it had become a stumbling block to progress on a broader deal—was both wrong and dangerous. Almost immediately, he became embroiled in fierce disputes with John Bolton and other hard-liners. In meeting after meeting, Foster pointed out that even if the uranium intelligence was a smoking gun, the really critical issue was the plutonium program, which was churning out material for bombs every day. It only took a half-dozen kilograms for each weapon, he argued. To insist that the North had to first acknowledge the uranium program was preventing the United States from addressing the much more critical immediate issue.

Foster's doubts crystallized as he put together material for a trip to Beijing in September 2004. Along with Jim Kelly, Joseph DeTrani, and Robert Walpole, Foster had been asked to present evidence on the uranium program to the skeptical Chinese. Walpole, who wrote the final briefing paper for the China trip, was the CIA's top nuclear-weapons expert. He had played a crucial role in preparing material for Colin Powell's infamous February 2003 UN speech making the case for war in Iraq. In the days before the speech, Walpole had briefed Powell that aluminum tubes intercepted en route to Iraq provided convincing evidence that Saddam Hussein had a nuclear program—evidence that was subsequently discredited.

Before leaving for Beijing, Foster read the briefing paper Walpole had prepared. He found it less than compelling.

The Chinese were not impressed either. Originally, Vice Foreign Minister Wu Dawei had agreed to bring together officials from the Chinese armed forces and intelligence services to listen to the U.S presentation. The Americans hoped that by sharing the information, the military and security people would be convinced and make an argument to the political leadership in Beijing that the uranium issue was a serious one.

Upon arrival, however, Wu Dawei found an excuse to avoid seeing the group. Instead, a much more junior Foreign Ministry official chaired a meeting one participant described as "desultory," in which the Chinese participants voiced considerable skepticism about the American case, questioning whether the North

Koreans had the technology, were capable of making a uranium bomb, and the length of time required to achieve such a goal.

"We really questioned the American assessment," said one Chinese official. "It was hard to reach a conclusion North Korea had an HEU program."

"This was supposed to be our breakthrough moment to explain to the Chinese why we were so firm on this thing," recalled one U.S. official. "And we just got nowhere with it."

E ven by North Korean standards, the vituperation from Pyongyang was extreme. "Bush is a thrice-cursed fascist tyrant and man-killer," thundered the KCNA, "a political idiot and human trash."[11]

The angry outburst was sparked by a Bush campaign appearance in Wisconsin in which he said the other parties in the six-party talks had to work together to say "to the tyrant in North Korea, disarm, disarm."[12] It reflected not just Pyongyang's extreme sensitivity and propensity for bombast, but the fact that the North Koreans—along with the rest of the world—were paying close attention to the 2004 presidential campaign. Democratic candidate John Kerry repeatedly blamed Bush's refusal to talk to the North for Pyongyang's nuclear breakout. In a televised debate on September 30, Kerry said, "While they didn't talk at all, the fuel rods came out, the inspectors were kicked out, the television cameras were kicked out. And today, there are four to seven nuclear weapons in the hands of North Korea. That happened on this president's watch."

Bush, however, again ruled out bilateral negotiations. "It's not going to work if we open up a dialogue with Kim Jong Il. He wants to unravel the six-party talks, or the five-nation coalition that's sending him a message."[13]

In October, just weeks before the election, President Bush signed the North Korea Human Rights Act after it had been unanimously adopted by the U.S. Senate. The act authorized removing barriers to granting North Korean refugees asylum in the United States, stepping up American radio broadcasts to North Korea, funding the smuggling of Bibles into the country, and providing financial help to organizations promoting democracy and human rights. Pyongyang described the legislation as "one more declaration of the hostile Korea policy which fully disclosed the U.S. real intention to slander and insult the DPRK, a dignified sovereign state, and topple the socialist system chosen by its people. . . . This has deprived the DPRK of any justification to deal with the U.S., to say nothing of the reason for holding the six-party talks for settling the nuclear issue. The DPRK is now left with no option but to put spurs to increasing the deterrent force to counter the U.S. force to the last."[14]

On November 2, 2004, George W. Bush won a second term in office, defeating John Kerry. It was nearly two weeks before North Korea made any comment. Pyongyang's first reaction was cautiously conciliatory. On November 13, KCNA quoted a Foreign Ministry spokesman as saying the North "stands for settling the nuclear issue between the DPRK and the U.S. through dialogue and negotiations." If the U.S. was ready for "coexistence," KCNA said, "it will be quite possible to settle" the nuclear issue.[15] But the statement made no reference to whether—or when—Pyongyang would agree to return to the six-party talks.

The prospect of a prolonged boycott worried South Korean president Roh Moo-hyun. The following day, in a speech to the Los Angeles World Affairs Council, Roh rebuked Bush by rejecting the use of force and the idea of regime change, denouncing talk of economic pressure against North Korea and declaring, "There is no alternative left in dealing with this issue except dialogue."

Roh's speech got a chilly reception in Washington, but his aides contended it was aimed as much at Kim Jong Il as at Bush.

"Roh's real intention was not to provoke the Americans," said one senior South Korean official, "but to persuade Kim Jong Il to come back to six-party talks—to let him know that Roh was sympathetic. If they came back, they would get some help."

"South Korea was deeply concerned that if you pressured the North Koreans too much they might start to do wild and stupid things and destabilize the situation," observed one State Department official. "They were convinced pressure tactics weren't going to work. The big factor was—they didn't think we had a workable policy."

# 13

# "WE HAVE MANUFACTURED NUKES"

THE REELECTION OF GEORGE W. BUSH SPELLED THE END OF Colin Powell's tenure as Secretary of State. Battered by Cheney and Rumsfeld, unable to create a strong personal chemistry with the president, and finding his pragmatic approach to foreign policy out of sync with the ideologues who dominated the first Bush administration, Powell could not persuade the president to adopt a coherent or effective policy toward North Korea. Richard Armitage, Powell's deputy, and Jim Kelly, the assistant secretary of state for East Asia, also left— dispirited and worn out by the infighting within the administration and lack of progress toward greater global stability.

"We used to have a nasty saying in Vietnam," said Richard Armitage, using typically earthy language. " 'The dicks are in the wire,' And you know what it means? Well, our enemies were inside our wire! So you have to fight the enemies of our country out there, and then you're fighting your own battle here. So I realized that I was spending sixteen hours a day fighting outside, and then the other eight just writhing over." Here Armitage paused. "It was at great personal cost," he mused, both to himself and to Powell.

Chris Hill was fond of jokes. That quirk was part of his wry, acerbic personality, as well as his diplomatic style. In talking about the state of the Bush administration's North Korea policy as the president began his second term, the longtime Foreign Service officer liked to tell the perhaps apocryphal story of the New York Mets in their first, disastrous season in the major leagues in 1964, when they set a record for the most baseball games ever lost by a single team. The Mets' manager was the legendary Casey Stengel, then in his seventies. Stengel, the story went, was watching two third basemen miss ball after ball in practice. So he grabbed a glove and took the field himself. Of course, he botched all the grounders batted his way as well, prompting him to complain, "You guys have messed this up so bad that no one can play this game!"

Yet Hill was not one to avoid a challenge. In 1995 he had served as deputy to UN Ambassador Richard Holbrooke in the negotiations that ended the war between Serbs, Muslims, and Croats in the former Yugoslavia. In dealing with the Serbian leader Slobodan Milošević and other stubborn, embittered Balkan leaders with blood on their hands, Holbrooke described Hill as "brilliant, fearless, and argumentative" and "an extremely good negotiator." With the retirement in mid-2004 of Tom Hubbard, Hill lobbied successfully to become the U.S. ambassador to South Korea. True to form, once he arrived in Seoul in August 2004, he ignored diplomatic conventions by visiting universities known for anti-American sentiment, engaging in public debates with critics of American policy, and becoming the first senior U.S. official to pay his respects at a memorial for pro-democracy protestors killed by South Korean troops during a military crackdown in 1980—the same year that Kim Dae-jung had been sentenced to death.

In December 2004, Hill visited Washington for what he thought would be routine consultations with the Bush administration's revamped national security team. Bush had announced that Condoleezza Rice would replace Powell as secretary of state, and her longtime deputy, Stephen Hadley, would be promoted as the new national security adviser. Hill scheduled a meeting with Hadley, where he intended to press for a more flexible policy on North Korea, but was surprised to discover Rice joining them for a wide-ranging discussion of Asian issues.

"I had a meeting with Steve Hadley, and then Rice took over the meeting," Hill recalled. "So I realized that they were considering me for more than just an incoming ambassador giving his two cents' worth."

It became clear to Hill that he was under consideration for Jim Kelly's job as assistant secretary for East Asia, which would put him in charge of dealing with the North Koreans.

Hill made his pitch to Rice. "I told Rice 'I need to be able to talk to these people. It doesn't mean I like them, but I need to talk to them,'" Hill recalled. "'This is the only way we're going to make some progress.'"

Although his statement wasn't presented as a "take it or leave it" proposition, Hill made clear he wouldn't take the job unless he were given what he saw as the necessary tools to do it. He'd already had what he felt was a great career in the

Foreign Service—including three ambassadorships. If he didn't get what he needed, in his own mind, he was quite prepared to walk away.

Hill's selection as assistant secretary was a sign that Rice might be open to a strategy that involved real negotiations, and she had a critical advantage over her predecessor. Unlike Colin Powell, she was extremely close to George W. Bush, with a kind of personal bond and a level of access Powell never enjoyed. That fact offered possibilities that had been almost unimaginable during Bush's first term.

Other personnel changes also raised the possibility of a shift in U.S. policy. Rice convinced Bush to appoint Under Secretary of State for Arms Control John Bolton as ambassador to the United Nations. The job gave Bolton a high public profile, but it removed him—and his hawkish views and bureaucratic scheming—from a day-to-day role in policy making in Washington. Bolton was replaced by the equally hawkish Robert Joseph, who had handled nonproliferation issues at the NSC, where he was bureaucratically at least as skillful as Bolton, but Bolton's departure was still taken as a significant public sign of the gradually eroding fortunes of the hard-line camp.

One other factor was also of critical importance to the future of U.S. relations with North Korea. By 2005, the war in Iraq had become a disaster. U.S. forces were bogged down in a civil war with no end in sight. Public support for the war in the United States had begun to plummet, and the most vocal advocates of the invasion were put on the defensive. Throughout the administration, senior officials who were increasingly struggling to manage a rapidly deteriorating situation in Iraq were also too preoccupied to devote much time or energy to North Korea.

Throughout 2004, Victor Cha waited impatiently. Cha, a mild-mannered, highly respected professor of international relations at Georgetown University, had been asked by Condoleezza Rice to join the National Security Council as an Asian expert. But it took almost a year for the South Korea–born Cha to receive his security clearance.

Cha had attracted the attention of Rice and President Bush with an essay in *Foreign Affairs* on North Korea titled "Hawk Engagement." Deeply suspicious of Pyongyang, Cha nonetheless advocated the use of diplomacy to resolve the nuclear crisis, not least because if the United States wanted to adopt more coercive measures, it was important to show Washington's Asian partners that the Bush administration had exhausted every opportunity to find a nonconfrontational solution.

In December, Cha was finally able to start his new job. Accompanied by Joseph DeTrani, the former CIA operative now in charge of dealing with the

North Koreans, and other American officials, he went to New York for two informal meetings with Pyongyang's UN envoys. The message from DeTrani was
clear: with the election over, it was time for the North to return to the six-party
talks. U.S. officials who favored diplomacy had become increasingly frustrated
at their inability to convince Pyongyang that the Bush administration did not
have the "hostile policy" the North Koreans continually complained about.

"They were saying it was hostile policy," recalled one member of the U.S.
team. "And we said, 'All right, we'll go to New York and *tell* you we don't have
a hostile policy."

But the North Koreans remained unconvinced and made it clear that they
would be studying what Condoleezza Rice said in her forthcoming confirmation
hearings and how President Bush referred to North Korea in his second inaugural address and his State of the Union speech. "To them," one senior official
noted, "that was a clear sign of what direction the administration was going."

In the run-up to all three public events, NSC staffers Victor Cha and
Michael Green went through the drafts of Rice's and Bush's speeches word by
word. While they tried to ensure that no unexpected rhetorical flourishes like
Axis of Evil were included, the language, tone, and overall message of all three
speeches left the North Koreans with much to ponder.

In the president's inaugural address, North Korea received no explicit mention. But the speech's main foreign policy theme, against the background of the
toppling of Saddam Hussein, was democratization. And Bush's speechwriters
did include this ringing declaration of U.S. policy: "So it is the policy of the
United States to seek and support the growth of democratic movements and institutions in every nation and culture, with the ultimate goal of ending tyranny
in our world."[1]

In the State of the Union, there was only one mildly worded sentence about
North Korea: "We're working closely with the governments in Asia to convince
North Korea to abandon its nuclear ambitions."[2]

But three days before the inauguration, in her opening statement during confirmation hearings before the Senate Foreign Relations Committee, Rice called
North Korea, along with Cuba, Burma, Iran, Belarus, and Zimbabwe, "an outpost of tyranny."[3] To the always paranoid North Koreans, the almost throwaway
comment obscured Rice's repeated references to Washington's commitment to
the six-party talks. It underscored the ambiguity over whether, at its heart, the
Bush administration wanted confrontation or engagement with Kim Jong Il.

The first leak came in the *New York Times* on February 1, 2005.
Correspondent David Sanger—a longtime recipient of leaks from the

intelligence community—and his colleague William Broad reported a dramatic development.

"Scientific tests have led American intelligence agencies and government scientists to conclude with near certainty that North Korea sold processed uranium to Libya," they said in a page-one story, "bolstering earlier indications that the reclusive state exported sensitive fuel for atomic weapons."[4]

The article was literally a bombshell. When Libyan leader Colonel Muammar Qaddafi had abandoned his nuclear weapons program in early 2004, Libya had given the United States a huge cask containing nearly two tons of uranium hexafluoride—a gaseous form of uranium which, when fed into centrifuges, can be enriched into fuel for nuclear bombs. The *Times* reported that the United States had concluded the material had come from North Korea. The paper said the information had sparked a "hunt to determine if North Korea had also sold uranium to other countries, including Iran and Syria."[5]

Just hours later, the *Washington Post*, quoting an unnamed "U.S. official," repeated the claim and added new details—two senior officials from the National Security Council, Michael Green and William Tobey, had been sent to Tokyo, Seoul, and Beijing to brief Washington's key Asian partners and seek their support for a tougher approach to North Korea. If Pyongyang was indeed proliferating nuclear weapons material to rogue states, then it would have crossed a clear "red line," lending strength to the hard-liners' arguments in favor of confronting Kim Jong Il. The alarming headlines—"Tests Said to Tie Deal on Uranium to North Korea," "North Korea May have Sent Libya Nuclear Material, U.S Tells Allies"—certainly helped to create a renewed sense of urgency around the North Korean nuclear issue.

The problem was that U.S. intelligence agencies were sharply divided over whether the central allegation in the report was actually true. In the following days and weeks, conflicting assessments were provided to the *Times* and the *Post*, as bureaucratic rivals within the intelligence community fought a battle of leaks, as the administration's North Korea policy hung in the balance.

Just two days after the initial report in the *Times*, the *Post* quoted "analysts and officials familiar with the data" as saying the evidence of the alleged North Korean shipment of uranium hexafluoride to Libya was so uncertain that it "could just as easily point to Pakistan."[6] The first story in the *Times* said that U.S. government scientists had reached their conclusion by analyzing samples of the uranium hexafluoride supplied by Libya, and by comparing "its isotope fingerprint with those of uranium samples from other countries and, by process of elimination, concluded that the uranium had come from North Korea."[7] But the experts quoted in the latest *Post* report said the International Atomic Energy Agency, which also conducted tests on the material, did not

reach the same findings, and that U.S. experts had not shared their own results
with the IAEA.[8]

Moreover, the suspect cylinder had originated not in North Korea, but in
Pakistan—part of the nuclear proliferation network run by A.Q. Khan. Since
North Korea had considerable natural deposits of uranium, it was possible the
uranium hexafluoride had been produced there and shipped to Pakistan as part
of the two countries' long-standing trade in missile and nuclear material and
know-how. But it was equally possible that Khan had shipped a small amount of
uranium hexafluoride to Pyongyang to enable the North Koreans to test the
centrifuges he had supplied, and that the empty cask was then sent back to Pakistan, where Khan reloaded it for shipment to Libya.

Siegfried Hecker, perhaps the most knowledgeable American nuclear expert
to have visited North Korea's reactor and other facilities, observed, "Whether
Khan was packing cylinders that had been in North Korea or whether the uranium hexafluoride came from North Korea is not clear."

And there were other doubts. The shipment to Libya had occurred in 2001,
at a time when the Yongbyon facility was under close international observation
and when, according to U.S. intelligence, the North Koreans were still at a very
early stage in the development of an HEU capability. For the North to have actually manufactured such a large amount of the material for export at that time
suggested it had a functioning uranium hexafluoride plant, a capability well beyond what U.S. intelligence had detected.

In mid-March, the *Post*'s Dafna Linzer published a follow-up article with an
even more dramatic allegation. Linzer quoted "two officials with detailed
knowledge of the transaction" as saying that Pakistan—not North Korea—had
sold the uranium hexafluoride to Libya. Moreover, the officials told Linzer that
"Pakistan's role as both the buyer and the seller was concealed to cover up the
part played by Washington's partner in the hunt for al Qaeda leaders."[9]

Reports that intelligence on weapons of mass destruction may have been
manipulated in support of a hard-line agenda echoed the run-up to the invasion
of Iraq, when the Bush administration ignored or silenced those who voiced
skepticism about Saddam Hussein's weapons program. In this case, the goal appears to have been to convince all of Washington's Asian partners of North
Korean perfidy—and in particular to use the intelligence to convince China to
ratchet up the pressure on Pyongyang.

According to several people familiar with the episode, Condoleezza Rice and
others were intrigued by the notion that China held the key to a solution. Beijing
was becoming an increasingly responsible "stakeholder" in the international
system, they were convinced, and with larger interests than just propping up
Kim Jong Il's regime, the information might prompt China to act.

But most of the State Department's China and Korea experts disagreed. "They really believed that we could create an intelligence case that would get the Chinese to put pressure on the North Koreans to dismantle their program," recalled one former senior official, "when it was very, very clear that the Chinese had no intention of doing that. The Chinese had exactly the opposite philosophy. They weren't going to bring down the regime."

One official involved in preparations for the trip was scathing in his recollection. "This is the U.S. foreign policy establishment—they're a bunch of fucking idiots! Where do these guys come up with this stuff? Where it comes from is that they haven't been out to the region, they haven't lived there for a period of time. You have to go to these countries, spend some time there, and understand that the U.S. and our particular notions of human rights and nonproliferation, which were our two major concerns, are not the concerns of the region. The region is scared to death that this place is going to implode and that all of them are going to be drawn into a conflict with each other. Why? Because they haven't figured out what's going to happen to the Korean peninsula. And they don't know. And in the absence of that, removing Kim Jong Il is as dangerous as removing Saddam Hussein."

In his version of the episode, NSC Asia expert Michael Green argued that the media reporting on both sides of the issue had been exaggerated. The point of the presentation to Japanese, South Korean, and Chinese leaders was to emphasize the danger of North Korea's having any nuclear material at all, to put them on alert that Washington, in an age of terrorism, would not stand idly by if the North exported such material and to stress the urgency of leaning on Pyongyang to resume the six-party talks. But he acknowledged the United States could not prove that the North was deliberately exporting the uranium hexafluoride, even though the initial leaks to the *Times* and *Post* had presented that allegation as proven fact.

In any event, as the pragmatists in Washington had predicted, the Chinese remained skeptical, and the episode did not help Washington's already shaky credibility with other key Asian partners.

"Another Intelligence Fiasco," screamed the headline in the *Korea Times*. "Did Washington Lie to Seoul?" asked the conservative *Chosun Ilbo*.

"The South Korean government has never been fully persuaded that North Korea ever had an HEU program," said one official in Seoul. "We asked the U.S. side again and again, 'Please provide us with the evidence.' Green showed the 'evidence,'" the official scoffed. "It was just a description. No copies of transactions or any other hard evidence."

Another senior South Korean was blunter. "I was very angry," he recalled, "I showed some displeasure to Green. 'What are allies all about? Do we have to get the U.S. position through the *New York Times?* If you are going to come to Korea, you should come to us. Is that new info you showed the *New York Times,* or just another twist and turn?' "

This was hardly the only irritant in increasingly strained relations between the United States and South Korea. Throughout 2004, American and South Korean military planners, acting under orders from General Leon LaPorte, the commander of U.S. forces in South Korea, had been working to refine and update what was known as CONPLAN 5029 (for "Concept Plan"), which spelled out how the alliance would respond to the possible collapse of North Korea. The plan reportedly mapped out actions to be taken in the event of a coup or civil war, famine, mass disorder, a major nuclear accident, or waves of refugees pouring across the DMZ to the South. As part of this process, U.S. officials proposed that the guidelines be upgraded and expanded into an OPLAN ("Operations Plan"), which would elaborate in greater specificity the military steps to be taken in response in a given contingency.

In January 2005, South Korea's National Security Council, with the left-leaning Lee Jong-seok in the lead, rejected the proposal, saying the plan could limit "South Korea's exercise of its sovereignty." In April 2005 to the consternation of U.S. officials, the government in Seoul leaked details of the OPLAN and made its opposition public. "So a con-plan, or an op-plan, designed to make sure instability in North Korea doesn't spill into the South, is somehow going to limit South Korean sovereignty?" complained one exasperated senior U.S. military officer. "We didn't know what to say when they came to us and told us this. What it really was about was they were practicing something they got very good at . . . premature capitulation to the North."

In a background briefing to reporters, President Roh explained his position. "We have to rework the details of Contingency Plan 5029," he said. "The current plan fundamentally focuses on U.S. forces going into the North and taking control of the situation. The situation would be serious if this happens to be the case."

"It could have given the wrong signal to the North," noted one former Blue House official who defended Seoul's position. "We did not want to alarm the North unduly."

But the North was already alarmed—mostly about Condoleezza Rice's use of the term "outpost of tyranny." On February 10, 2005, Pyongyang upped the stakes dramatically. A Foreign Ministry statement conveyed by KCNA announced, "We have manufactured nukes for self-defense" and "we are compelled to suspend our participation in the [six-party] talks for an indefinite period."

It was a definitive policy pronouncement—not the vague references to a "nuclear deterrent" Pyongyang's envoys had previously used in meetings with U.S. officials, but the first time North Korea had officially declared itself a nuclear power. While, in the absence of a nuclear test, it was not possible to confirm the claim, the declaration was consistent with the evidence that the North had been reprocessing fuel rods into weapons-grade plutonium and with Pyongyang's repeated warnings of the consequences of the Bush administration's not altering its hard-line policy.

The announcement also made clear how closely the North Koreans were watching the official statements in Washington as Bush began his second term.

"The remarks made by senior officials of the administration clarifying the official political stance of the U.S. contained no word showing any willingness to co-exist with the DPRK or make a switchover in its policy toward it," KCNA said. "On the contrary, they have declared it as their final goal to terminate . . . the DPRK. . . . The U.S., turning down the DPRK's request to roll back its anti-DPRK hostile policy, a major stumbling block in the way of settling the nuclear issue, treated it as an enemy and, not content with this, totally rejected it, terming it 'tyranny.' This deprived the DPRK of any justification to negotiate with the U.S. and participate in the six-party talks."[10]


Predictably, there was debate in Washington over whether North Korea was simply employing a scare tactic as part of a negotiating strategy to win diplomatic concessions before returning to the table, or had actually crossed a line from which there was no turning back. Hard-liners urged a sanctions resolution at the United Nations. Christopher Hill was convinced that the U.S. and North Korea would eventually have to talk face to face.

Condoleezza Rice, the new secretary of state, was sending mixed signals. In March, on her first trip to Asia after her confirmation hearing, she arranged a highly publicized visit to a secret bunker in South Korea that would serve as the command post for U.S. forces in the event of war. In Tokyo, however, she delivered a major speech in which she acknowledged that "North Korea is a sovereign state" and repeated a formulation used by Bush and Powell that "we have no intentions of attacking or invading North Korea."[11]

But in Beijing, she publicly raised the idea of increased pressure, noting that "there are other options in the international system" if diplomacy failed. The option of seeking a UN Security Council resolution authorizing stepped-up political and economic sanctions against Pyongyang had long been advocated by hard-liners in the Pentagon and the office of Vice President Cheney. The Chinese quickly made clear, as had the South Koreans, that they would not support a tougher line, and even urged Rice to sweeten the offer Kelly had laid out in the June 2004 round of the six-party talks. Rice refused.

Soon after her China trip, Rice again raised the prospect of seeking UN action against Pyongyang. In an interview with Fox News, she said, "We reserve the right and the possibility of going to the Security Council should it be necessary, of putting other measures in place should it be necessary. I think the North Koreans are not confused about the fact that the United States maintains a significant deterrent against North Korean nuclear weapons."[12]

Later in the spring, President Bush himself raised the decibel level, issuing a blistering personal denunciation of Kim Jong Il at a televised news conference.

"Kim Jong Il is a dangerous person," Bush said. "He's a man who starves his people. He's got huge concentration camps. And there is concern about his capacity to deliver a nuclear weapon. We don't know if he can or not, but I think it's best when you're dealing with a tyrant like Kim Jong Il to assume that he can."[13]

Vice President Cheney also chimed in, telling CNN's Larry King that Kim Jong Il was "one of the world's most irresponsible leaders."

In response, North Korea's official media outlets denounced Bush as a "hooligan bereft of any personality as a human being . . . a half-baked man in terms of morality and a philistine whom we can never deal with."[14] And it described Cheney as a "cruel monster and blood-thirsty beast."[15]

The name calling was accompanied by belligerent gestures on both sides. In April, North Korean officials told visiting American scholar Selig Harrison that fuel rods would soon be unloaded from the Yongbyon reactor to be reprocessed into more weapons-grade plutonium. This would further augment a nuclear capability underpinned by the 8,000 fuel rods that had already been reprocessed in early 2003 after the North ended its freeze and expelled inspectors at the end of 2002. [16] Pyongyang also warned that any effort to bring North Korea before the UN Security Council would be regarded as "an act of war."[17]

Meanwhile, *New York Times* reporters David Sanger and William Broad— to whom had been leaked the questionable allegations about North Korea's transferring uranium hexafluoride to Libya in February—were the recipients of another alarmingly sensational leak. In a story headlined, "U.S. Cites Signs of Korean Preparations for Nuclear Test," the *Times* reported that American spy satellites had spotted "rapid, extensive preparations for a nuclear weapons test."[18] The story quoted officials "who had reviewed the imagery" and offered fascinating details about the mechanics of constructing the tunnel where the North Koreans apparently planned to conduct the test. But the source also noted that "satellites could not divine the intentions of Kim Jong Il," and speculated that the exercise could simply be a way to "put pressure on the Bush administration to offer an improved package of economic and diplomatic incentives" in return for curbing its nuclear program.[19]

At the same time, there was another round of American muscle flexing in the region. After B-2 and F-15E aircraft were sent to Guam, within easy range of North Korea, the United States deployed fifteen F-117 Stealth bombers from Holloman Air Force Base in New Mexico to various U.S. bases in South Korea. The Pentagon also sent B-2 and F-15E fighter jets to Guam for what was described as "routine training," but both squadrons extended their stay when the training exercise ended.[20]

The Chinese were growing increasingly frustrated with both the North Koreans and the Americans. Within days of the North Korean announcement that it had "manufactured nukes" and would boycott the six-party talks, Chinese president Hu Jintao sent Wang Jiarui, head of the Communist Party's International Liaison Department, to Pyongyang to deliver a personal message to Kim Jong Il appealing for a change of heart.

In early April, Kang Sok Ju, North Korea's first vice foreign minister, visited Beijing for three days of talks with top Chinese leaders. Kang spelled out Pyongyang's view of the Bush administration. The Bush Doctrine, he said, consisted of three elements: regime change, preemptive strikes, and the Axis of Evil. Although he said that North Korea's long-term goal was denuclearization, under the current circumstances, Pyongyang had no choice but to expand its "nuclear deterrent."

The meetings were intense, sometimes erupting into arguments. Chinese officials bluntly told Kang they were "opposed" to the North's nuclear efforts. In the carefully calibrated world of diplomacy, this was significantly stronger language than the previous Chinese formulation, which used the words "do not support."

In response to Kang's three-point description of the Bush doctrine, the Chinese had their own three-point formula. It was called the "three upholds"— uphold denuclearization, uphold peace and stability, and "uphold" using the six-party talks to resolve the issue. Kang was told Beijing understood North Korea's concerns, but that the talks were the best way to address those concerns.

At the same time, a senior Chinese diplomat, in a rare public comment, told the *New York Times* that the Bush administration bore much of the responsibility for the failure to resume talks. "A basic reason for the unsuccessful effort lies in the lack of cooperation from the U.S. side," said Foreign Ministry official Yang Xiyu. Yang told the *Times*'s Joseph Kahn that the personal attacks on Kim Jong Il by President Bush and other U.S. officials had created a "loss of face" for North Korea. "Mr. Yang said that when President Bush referred to the North Korea leader, Kim Jong Il, as a 'tyrant' in late April," the *Times* reported, "Mr.

Bush 'destroyed the atmosphere' for negotiations, undoing weeks of efforts to persuade North Korea that the United States would bargain in good faith."[21]

Yang urged the Bush administration to find some way to talk directly to the North Koreans. "I know the U.S. is reluctant to have even informal contacts with North Korea," the *Times* quoted him as saying. "But as the world's superpower, I would hope it can show more flexibility and sincerity to make a resumption of talks possible."

Christopher Hill spent much of the spring of 2005 trying to come up with a new way to approach the six-party talks and break the worrying deadlock. One reason the diplomatic process had produced so little progress, he believed, was that there was no overriding vision of how to proceed. Hill borrowed a concept he had used during the Dayton peace talks between the warring states that made up the former Yugoslavia.

"What we did in Dayton," he recalled, "was we had a set of agreed principles. Then, once we got everyone on the same page, we'd go to a more comprehensive thing which would show how the principles would work. So I just shamelessly imported these ideas. My feeling was, let's get them to the negotiations and see where we are. I felt we should get them to negotiations and test them with a set of principles. If they couldn't agree to the principles, screw it, we had no basis for working out an agreement. If we could agree to the principles, we could then work it through." It was the same approach the Clinton administration followed: agreement in principle followed by practical steps.

Hill's thinking was also strikingly similar to the approach China had tried to apply since the start of the six-party talks. Beijing saw the notion of starting with principles and moving to implementation as a way to push the United States and North Korea to each make concessions. This explained why the Chinese were always so eager for participants to issue a joint statement at the end of each round of talks, even though, so far, the rounds had ended with China issuing its own "Chairman's Statement" since Washington and Pyongyang remained so far apart on all the key issues.

An important new player on Rice's team shared Hill's desire to see some diplomatic movement. Philip Zelikow was a professor at the University of Virginia who had worked with Rice on the National Security Council during the administration of the first President Bush, had coauthored a book with her on U.S. policy toward German unification, and had been executive director of the 9/11 commission. Rice had made him the State Department counselor, and as such a key adviser to the new secretary.

"We concluded that the basic model for negotiations with the North Koreans was not likely to succeed and actually was conceptually flawed," Zelikow said. "We'd basically created a six-party framework but the substance of that framework was locked around a concept of bartered concession for denuclearization in which we had our stand and they had their stand and the situation was frozen. The kind of tit-for-tat model—we'll give you a barrel of oil, you'll give us a girder—was never going to be satisfactory to us and actually kind of reinforced the worst tendencies on the North Korean side."

The central premise, as Zelikow noted, was "to offer the North Koreans a much richer agenda for diplomatic action than they had been offered in the past."

But Zelikow's approach had another track as well—one which particularly appealed to Rice—the campaign against the North's illicit activities. "We needed to at once both escalate and move to make it clear that the costs of continuing to develop their nuclear program and being an outlaw state were going to be increasingly significant and painful for the North Korean government," Zelikow said, "and that the United States would adopt various measures to defend itself against North Korean criminal behavior."

The problem was whether the two parts of the approach were complementary or contradictory—whether continuing hard-line resistance in Washington would permit any space for genuine diplomatic efforts—and how, under the circumstances, could the North Koreans be coaxed back to the table.

On the fifth anniversary of the June 15, 2000, North-South summit, a delegation of South Korean officials traveled from Seoul to Pyongyang for a commemoration. The leader of the South Korean group was Chung Dong-yong, a British-educated former TV news anchor who had been named minister of unification by President Roh Moo-hyun in April 2004.

Chung had met Condoleezza Rice when she made her first swing through Asia as secretary of state in March 2005. He had tried to explain to her why Pyongyang took such offense at the term "outpost of tyranny" and other harsh remarks made by senior U.S. officials.

"The characteristic of this regime is that if you attack the leader," he told Rice, "those people who are under him start competing to express their loyalty to him," making any prospect of compromise out of the question. Chung repeated the standard South Korean appeal that the United States talk to North Korea. He recalled that Rice "just listened."

Now, in Pyongyang, Chung was invited to meet Kim Jong Il at a lavish building on the outskirts of Pyongyang that had been built in the 1970s for a state visit by Yugoslavian leader Marshal Tito. The meeting lasted five and a half hours, and ninety minutes were devoted to the nuclear issue.

Kim expressed frustration that the United States was ignoring his hopes of developing a normal relationship with Washington. He complained that the Bush administration had never reaffirmed the communiqué signed by Vice Marshal Jo Myong Rok on his historic October 2000 visit to Washington, where each government pledged they had "no hostile intent" toward the other. While that attitude continued, Kim told Chung, North Korea had no choice but to continue its nuclear program. Citing his father's legacy of supporting a denuclearized Korean peninsula, Kim said if the United States was willing to have a normal, friendly relationship, there would be no need for him to possess nuclear weapons. And Kim hinted that he was prepared to return to the six-party talks, as long as North Korea was "respected and recognized."

Like other visitors who had spent time with Kim Jong Il, Chung came away with the impression he was "well-informed, well-briefed on the nuclear and other international issues," and that his professed desire for a nuclear deal should be tested by a serious U.S.–North Korea dialogue.

In the hope of enticing the North Koreans back to the table, the South Korean government followed Chung's visit by offering Pyongyang two million kilowatts of electricity if Kim Jong Il would move toward ending the North's nuclear program.

In June, Donald Zagoria, a New York–based scholar with the National Committee on American Foreign Policy, organized a so-called Track II meeting— ostensibly an academic meeting that would enable Americans and North Koreans to hold informal discussions away from the public spotlight. North Korean diplomats at the UN had signaled that if a senior official from Pyongyang was invited to the gathering—and would be able to meet privately with U.S. officials—Pyongyang might be willing to return to the six-party talks. Hill convinced Rice to authorize a visa for Li Gun, director general of the North Korean Foreign Ministry's America department.

Two weeks after Kim Jong Il's conversation with South Korean unification minister Chung Dong-yong, Li was hosted for lunch in New York by Joseph DeTrani, the U.S. envoy in charge of talks with North Korea; Victor Cha, the Korean-American National Security Council Asia specialist; and a small number of other Americans.

By now, DeTrani had dealt with Li Gun for two years. The former CIA agent saw the North Korean as hardnosed but a basically decent guy. Before the meeting, DeTrani told Hill, "I think you'd like him."

"Maybe I should speak to him," Hill replied. DeTrani and Hill agreed to try to arrange an "informal" phone call.

When the meeting began, DeTrani was blunt.

"Let's get back to the table," he told Li Gun. "This is going down the tubes. The name calling back and forth isn't helping anybody."

Li Gun was equally blunt.

"The only way we're going to come back to the talks," Li declared, "is if your secretary of state retracts the statement about the 'outpost of tyranny.' "

"That's not going to happen," DeTrani shot back.

"Well," Li Gun said, "can we say that we met and indicated our indignation at your use of the term?

"You can say you're indignant about anything you want," replied DeTrani.

"But will you respond?" asked Li.

"No," said DeTrani. "You can say you're indignant. We're not going to respond to that. But don't ask us to retract anything."

After the meeting, DeTrani called Hill in Washington and told him there were some signs of movement. It was clear the North Koreans were looking for a face-saving way to return to the six-party talks, and it was time for the phone call they had discussed.

Later the same day, the Americans and North Koreans met again.

"So the phone rings in the meeting," recalled one person who was there. "We take it. We sort of say, 'Oh, hi Chris. We're just in a meeting with Li Gun. Oh? You'd like to speak to him?' And so we handed the phone to Li Gun, and you should have seen the look on his face."

After all the snubs the North Koreans had received at the hands of Jim Kelly, "they were like little children" receiving a gift, one of the Americans said.

Hill knew that the only way to develop the trust necessary for any negotiations to succeed was to develop personal relationships with his main interlocutors. This was an important first step. And unlike Jim Kelly, who had been hamstrung by rigid instructions from the hard-liners, Hill had the latitude from his bosses to do so—but only up to a point.

The North Koreans made clear that, while they were open to returning to the talks, they wanted a bilateral meeting with Hill before making any announcement. Hill's problem was that Rice and other senior officials, while willing to sanction a meeting, insisted that it be trilateral, with China participating as well.

On July 9, 2005, as Condoleezza Rice was in the air en route to the Chinese capital, Hill arrived at the lavish St. Regis Hotel in Beijing, where Chinese officials, in response to U.S. requests, had agreed to host a dinner with the Americans and the North Koreans. But neither the Chinese nor the North Koreans were there. It soon became clear to Hill that the Chinese were not going to show up at all. Hill had to make an instant decision as to whether to go ahead with only the North Koreans in attendance. He could have called Rice on her plane to ask for guidance. Instead, displaying the willingness to take risks and to stretch—if not ignore—his instructions that would characterize his modus operandi in the coming months, Hill decided to go ahead on his own and present her with a fait accompli. During the meal, North Korean vice foreign minister Kim Gye Gwan confirmed that Pyongyang would return to the talks, with the next session scheduled for the end of July.

When Rice arrived in Beijing later that night, Hill went to her hotel suite. "The bad news," he told her, "is that the Chinese didn't show up. But the good news is that the North Koreans announced they would come back to the talks." Rice was not amused, although Hill felt that, since getting the talks under way again was one of her goals, her anger would pass. The next morning, however, she complained to Chinese foreign minister Li Zhaoxing. In his biography of Rice, *Washington Post* reporter Glenn Kessler quotes her as sternly telling Li, "You were supposed to host the dinner, but then you don't show up." Li simply told her to concentrate on the outcome, not the process.[22]

The North Koreans kept their promise. After the dinner, KCNA made the official announcement. "The U.S. side at the contact made between the heads of both delegations in Beijing clarified that it would recognize the DPRK as a sovereign state, not to invade it and hold bilateral talks within the framework of the six-party talks, and the DPRK side interpreted it as a retraction of its remark designating the former as an 'outpost of tyranny' and decided to return the six-party talks."[23]

After a thirteen-month hiatus, serious diplomacy was about to begin.

# 14

# THE SEPTEMBER 19 DECLARATION

HE TALKS THAT GOT UNDER WAY AT THE DIAOYUTAI STATE
Guest House in Beijing in late July 2005 were very different from
any of the previous sessions. For the first time, the United States
had a negotiator who was allowed to use his own judgment about meeting bilaterally with the North Koreans—and to engage in serious give-
and-take. No longer was the United States simply listing demands and
awaiting North Korean capitulation.

Christopher Hill went out of his way to convince Kim Gye Gwan
that things really had changed. In the previous rounds, the talks had
been characterized by long plenary sessions, with delegation heads recit-
ing prepared statements and relatively little time or opportunity for side
meetings or informal bilaterals.

Now, the plenary sessions were shorter, and the delegations moved
quickly into more substantive discussions. Hill sought to assure the North
Koreans that face-to-face meetings were no longer a point of contention.
His first bilateral with Kim lasted an hour and a half—longer, one of Hill's
colleagues joked, with only slight exaggeration, than the sum of all the
face time Kim had been granted with Jim Kelly. He also stressed that the
United States was serious about reaching a deal and was prepared to stay
in Beijing for as long as it took to do so. He even signaled that he was
ready to visit Pyongyang if the parties agreed on a good final statement.

But not everything had changed. The hard-liners still had clout in
Washington and remained both skeptical of the whole process and
concerned that Hill might make inappropriate concessions.

"Chris Hill, I think, suffers from a problem that many State Department officers have, which is they want to see their name at the end of a deal, and they
think that talking solves all problems," said one prominent hard-liner, reflecting
a view widely held in his camp. "And I think communication is important, but
sometimes that means not talking. And he wants a deal, and he thinks he can get
a deal. I think he's out of his mind."

Like Jim Kelly before him, Hill's delegation had representatives from numerous different agencies in Washington, many of which did not share his goal of
reaching a deal, and each of whom was making regular calls to bosses or allies in
Washington. The NSC's William Tobey was in touch with the head of the NSC
Nonproliferation's Office, the conservative John Rood. Anthony Ruggiero, a
young intelligence analyst, was liaising with Robert Joseph, who had been appointed to take John Bolton's job as under secretary of state for arms control.
Scott Feeney was dealing with the Pentagon, and Victor Cha was in contact with
National Security Adviser Stephen Hadley. Hill, meanwhile, was dealing directly
with Condoleezza Rice. It was not a recipe for a smooth-running operation.

Moreover, the mere fact that Hill was able to hold bilateral meetings with
Kim Gye Gwan did not mean the two sides would agree. While all six parties
accepted the new concept of trying to reach a consensus on overall principles
and goals and leaving the specifics to be worked out later—the Chinese had independently reached the same conclusion as Hill about the need to move away
from particular items and take a broader approach—differences between the
United States and North Korea quickly became apparent.

The first issue was what to call any North Korean move to give up its nuclear
program. Hill was instructed to insist on the word "dismantlement." The
North Koreans objected, complaining that the term implied they were being co-
erced into acting. Kim Gye Gwan insisted on "abandon," which implied that the
North was acting on its own volition. Although "abandon" suggested something
less than full dismantlement to some observers, Hill was flexible. The Americans
eventually accepted the North Korean language.

Other issues proved much more contentious. Washington remained adamant
that the uranium issue be addressed in any statement. While Hill was ready not
to have a specific mention of HEU, the United States insisted that the language
refer to "all nuclear weapons and all existing nuclear programs." The word "programs" was clearly intended to refer to the North's uranium effort.

The North Koreans instead wanted to use the phrase "abandon all nuclear weapons." The result was a deadlock, prompting the Chinese to offer a
compromise. Cui Tiankai, the director-general of the Chinese Foreign Min-

istry's Department of Asian Affairs and his staff were handling the actual drafting of the proposed document. Cui was smooth, polished, careful, and detail oriented, but his cautious exterior disguised a streak of creativity. As the talks progressed, his team would take the various proposals and come up with new drafts to be circulated among the six delegations for debate and discussion. At the end of each day, the delegates would contact their capitals for fresh instructions, and the process would begin all over again.

Cui Tiankai suggested a different wording: that North Korea "abandon all nuclear weapons and nuclear programs prohibited by the 1992 Joint Declaration on the Denuclearization of the Korean Peninsula" that had been signed by the governments of North and South Korea. This accord had committed Seoul and Pyongyang not to "test, manufacture, produce, receive, possess, store, deploy or use nuclear weapons," and not to "possess nuclear reprocessing and uranium enrichment facilities."[1]

Chinese diplomats argued that the 1992 accord was even more sweeping than the Agreed Framework. The North Koreans didn't like it, but having signed it in 1992 they couldn't easily reject it. According to Chinese sources, the Americans objected because it did sanction the use of "nuclear energy solely for peaceful purposes." Opposition to that position was a reflection of the continuing clout of Washington hard-liners, who believed North Korea could not be trusted with—and was not entitled to—any kind of nuclear program, even a peaceful one.

As the process inched forward, Hill faced opposition within his own delegation, especially from NSC staffer Tobey (who had accompanied Michael Green to Tokyo, Seoul, and Beijing earlier in the year to present the questionable "evidence" that North Korea had sold uranium hexafluoride to Libya), the Pentagon's Feeney, and, to a lesser extent, from NSC Asia expert Cha. Hill also had to deal with conservative critics in Washington who were reviewing the proposed language for any final agreement. These included Robert Joseph, under secretary of state for arms control; John Rood, who had assumed Joseph's, nonproliferation duties at the NSC; Under Secretary of Defense Douglas Feith; and two members of Vice President Cheney's staff: the ultra-conservative Samantha Ravich and Lewis "Scooter" Libby, the vice president's chief of staff.

"I always interpreted a lot of these debates, which were fueled largely by Will Tobey and Victor Cha and some of the other wordsmiths on the team, [to mean] basically they didn't want an agreement," recalled one member of Hill's team, "and they were looking for excuses."

The U.S. position on this key negotiating point remained unyielding. Although the Chinese argued that North Korea, as a sovereign state, was entitled to the right of peaceful nuclear use, Hill was instructed to demand that

Pyongyang would have to agree to "abandon all nuclear weapons and all existing nuclear programs."

"What happened of course is that we sent it back, and the boys and girls
wordsmithed it to death," caustically noted an aide to Hill, "which then allowed
the North Koreans to come and start wordsmithing."

The Chinese included the American demand in a revised draft that was circulated to all six parties. But Chinese diplomats shared the concern about how
the North Koreans would respond. These concerns quickly became reality. Ten
days into the round, Kim Gye Gwan told Cui Tiankai, "If the documents say
'abandon all nuclear weapons and all nuclear programs,' it means we give up
the right to peaceful nuclear use. If the Americans insist on 'dismantling all
nuclear programs,' we demand light-water reactors."

In a meeting with Hill, Kim Gye Gwan—clearly acting on instructions from
Pyongyang—not only brought up the demand for the LWRs, but also appeared
to backtrack on the earlier pledge of denuclearization, saying the North's nuclear
program had to be dual use because it needed a "deterrent" against Washington's hostile policy. Hill was furious at what he regarded as outrageous behavior.

"Tell me how deterrence works," Hill challenged Kim. "We attack you. And
then what do you do?"

Kim was silent.

"Are you going to attack us with your weapons?" Hill went on. "Is that
what that means? Are you going to attack South Korea? Just explain. How does
it work?"

At that point, Hill refused to continue the bilateral meetings. When the
North Koreans expressed dismay, Hill asked them, "What's the point?"

To the hard-liners in Washington, meanwhile, the demand for the LWRs
raised the specter of Clinton's hated Agreed Framework, which they had spent so
much time and effort in recent years trying to tear up. "The North Koreans raised
that," Hill recalled, "and people just went ballistic. I had people in Washington
say, 'We will never give them a light-water reactor.'" Rice too heard the criticism.
"She was certainly encountering a lot of resistance," Hill acknowledged.

Although Joseph DeTrani and Li Gun—at the instruction of their bosses
Christopher Hill and Kim Gye Gwan—met in the hope of narrowing the areas
of disagreement and Hill resumed bilateral meetings with Kim, the talks remained at an impasse. The round was recessed for three weeks.


While the talks were suspended, I made my fourteenth trip to Pyongyang.
In opening its doors ever so slightly, North Korea appeared eager to use
the international media to make its case on the nuclear issue. But my week there

also provided some revealing glimpses of the small but significant changes that had occurred since I last visited the capital in October 2000. The immediate impression was still the same: streets devoid of cars, giant monuments to Kim Il Sung, people with the Kim buttons pinned to their chests. As on my previous visits, I was accompanied everywhere by two government minders whose job was to prevent any unauthorized contact with ordinary people. But in the center of Pyongyang I saw kiosks where private street vendors were selling snacks, drinks, and cigarettes. A handful of privately run restaurants were operating, and in the capital's Tong Il market, fruit, vegetables, meat, clothing, and other consumer goods were available to anyone with the cash to pay. The people appeared better and more stylishly dressed. I even noticed women wearing heels, something unheard of in years past.

All were consequences of the government's still tentative experimentation with market mechanisms that had been announced in mid-2002. Another sign was the recent arrival in Pyongyang of a small but determined group of resident Western businessmen. They were a colorful lot—an intrepid British banker, a former East German diplomat with ambitions to become the country's first expatriate Internet entrepreneur, and a Swiss who had just established the Pyongyang Business School, offering classes on management, finance, accounting, and marketing to eager North Korean officials. All were convinced that the changes, although still at an early stage, were real, and that over time, the regime would be ready to expand reforms and permit North Korea to become more connected to the international economy.

Even with the signs of progress in Pyongyang, aid workers told me that the reforms had had a sharply negative impact on the lives of many citizens. The market reforms had driven up the price of food and other goods, and the weakening of the state-run food distribution system meant that many North Koreans could not afford what was available. Outside of the capital, food shortages were becoming more serious, and for most people, chronic hunger remained a way of life. It was not hard to understand why the government continued to demand food aid, shipments of fuel, supplies of electricity, and the right to peaceful nuclear energy in the six-party talks.

During my weeklong stay, I had the opportunity for two extended discussions with Kim Gye Gwan. It was the first time I had met the North Korean negotiator. I found him friendly and charming—not the stereotypical hatchet-faced apparatchik—but he never strayed off message. The message he sought to convey through CNN as the resumption of the talks approached clearly contained hints of compromise. Kim insisted that Pyongyang could not give up its right to have a civilian nuclear program, symbolized by the light-water reactors. But he sought to soften the demand by saying that if the reactors were built, the North would accept "strict supervision" over their operation in which the United States could play a role. He also offered to return to the Non-Proliferation Treaty and to abide by IAEA safeguards. On the contentious uranium enrichment issue, while repeating the government's standard denial, he did offer what seemed to be an opening for further discussion. "In the future if there is any kind of evidence that needs to be clarified," he said, "we will be fully prepared to do so."

As an illustration of the government's desire to end the years of enmity with America, I was taken to see the USS *Pueblo,* the American spy ship whose seizure by the North Korean navy in 1968 as it intercepted communications off the North Korean coast almost triggered a new Korean War. The ship was moored in the Taedong River, which flows through the center of Pyongyang where it was open for visitors. The bullet holes from the 1968 confrontation were still visible, and an introductory video about the ship's history contained numerous references to the "American imperialists." The symbolism of the exhibit was that North Korea would fight the Americans if necessary. But the now-retired North Korean naval officer who had captured the *Pueblo* insisted that he, like the rest of the government, wanted to put the past behind him and begin a new relationship with the United States.

When the talks resumed at the end of August, the Chinese came up with more joint-statement drafts trying to find common language. So many versions were sent to the printers that one Chinese official joked, "The environmentalists would oppose us. It cost us a lot of trees!"

The fourth draft produced by the Chinese made no explicit reference to light-water reactors, instead only mentioning "peaceful nuclear use." The Japanese, South Koreans, and Russians wanted to accept it, as did Hill and his State Department colleagues. If the North Koreans refused, Hill argued, they would be isolated. But in Washington, the hard-liners objected to language that committed the United States to "bilateral dialogue" with Pyongyang. In *The Confidante*, his biography of Rice, Glenn Kessler published the sentence at the center of this dispute. The Chinese draft read, "The United States stated that it recognizes and respects the sovereignty of the DPRK, and that it undertakes to take steps to normalize its relations with the DPRK, subject to bilateral policies and dialogue." Hard-liners in Washington insisted on changing the language to, "The DPRK and the United States undertook to respect each other's sovereignty, exist peacefully together, and take steps to normalize their relations subject to their respective bilateral policies." The reference to "bilateral dialogue" was removed.[2]

When Washington rejected the language about "bilateral dialogue," the North Koreans insisted the statement contain an explicit reference to light-water reactors. The talks were again deadlocked.

In their frustration, the Chinese tried to pressure Hill, warning that Washington would take the blame if the talks broke down. Hill pushed back, and China's lead negotiator, Vice Foreign Minister Wu Dawei, threatened to go the press.

"You want to go to the press," retorted Hill, whose media savvy had become apparent as the talks progressed, "I can handle that. I'd love to go to the press. Let's go together, I can't wait."

The Chinese backed off.

Hill had gradually become convinced that a way had to be found to address the North Korean demand for LWRs, or else the talks might indeed fall apart. Although the demand appeared to have less to do with Pyongyang's real energy needs than the political symbolism of reacquiring what had been promised under the Agreed Framework that the Bush administration had discarded, Hill felt the hard-liners' argument was silly. If North Korea got out of the nuclear business, rejoined the Non-Proliferation Treaty, and allowed IAEA inspectors to monitor the process of denuclearization, there would be no harm in agreeing to discuss the LWR issue.

Over the weekend of September 17, Hill spoke by phone with Rice, who was in New York at the meeting of the UN General Assembly. He was frustrated. At one point, a colleague heard him muttering, "If she doesn't want me to negotiate, she shouldn't have sent me over here." Meanwhile, the Chinese came up with a fifth draft, whose careful wording acknowledged the North's desire for LWRs. The draft read, "The DPRK stated that it has the right to peaceful uses of nuclear energy. The other parties expressed their respect and agreed to discuss, at an appropriate time, the subject of the provision of a light-water reactor to the DPRK."

The Chinese made clear that this time, it was a "take it or leave it" proposition.

"The question was: Were we prepared to leave in 'discuss a light-water reactor at an appropriate time?'" Rice later said. "We did have concerns that if 'at an appropriate time' was vague, that the North might try and tie up the next round saying, 'Where's our light-water?'"[3]

At midnight Beijing time on September 18, Hill finally convinced Rice to take a chance and accept the joint statement. In return, though, Rice insisted that Hill, at the final plenary session, read a unilateral American statement dictated in Washington offering the U.S. "interpretation" of the joint declaration—to ensure no one mistook American acceptance of the accord to mean that LWRs would be on the agenda any time soon. Hill, convinced the declaration was the critical document, did not object.

In his dealings with Rice, Hill exhibited another trait that was to become a standard part of the way he operated. He effectively froze out the rest of his delegation and the agencies they represented, especially the critics at the NSC and the office of the vice president. When they found out, other members of the U.S. team in Beijing were furious.

"People in the U.S. delegation were literally screaming at each other in the hallways of the St. Regis Hotel," said one American official.

"There was the general impression that we have caved on issues we had said we were resolutely against talking about, like the light-water reactors," said one of Hill's critics on the U.S. delegation. "To cobble together something that looks like the Agreed Framework again was just silly."


As members of the U.S. team looked over the final Chinese draft, alarm bells over a different issue went off in Victor Cha's head. The statement mentioned "peaceful coexistence" between North Korea and the United States. While Cha admired Hill's negotiating skills, the Korean-American scholar believed Hill had a limited understanding of the divided peninsula's tortured history. In Cha's view, "peaceful coexistence"—an expression widely used by the Soviet Union during the height of the Cold War—had a specific meaning to the North Koreans. It meant a Korean peninsula with no American troops and ultimately reunified under North Korean terms. Although that may not have been the North Korean interpretation, Cha's concerns were shared by his NSC colleague Michael Green, as well as the more hard-line members of the U.S. delegation.

Without informing Hill, Cha called his boss, National Security Adviser Stephen Hadley, and raised his objections. "Hill doesn't seem to understand the meaning of the term," Cha told Hadley, "and its symbolism to the North Koreans." Hadley immediately informed Rice.

On the morning of Monday, September 19, Hill and the other delegates were waiting at the Diaoyutai State Guest House where the joint declaration would be announced at a news conference. As he chatted with Chinese Vice Foreign Minister Wu Dawei, Hill's cell phone rang. Condoleezza Rice was calling. She had a problem with the phrase "peaceful coexistence," she told Hill, and instructed him to have it removed from the document.

When Hill told the Chinese, they were astonished and alarmed by what seemed such a petty demand. Making any changes at such a late stage might create a chain reaction. If the Americans insisted on a change, the North Koreans would likely follow suit, and the entire deal could unravel. Wu Dawei's initial response was to say, "No."

"My boss instructed me to make the change," Hill said.

"And my boss says, 'No,'" Wu shot back.

Hill called Rice and told her the Chinese had rejected the change. Rice demanded to talk to Foreign Minister Li Zhaoxing. Wu Dawei told Hill that Li was out of Beijing. No matter where Li was, Rice insisted that she needed to talk to him. A conversation was quickly arranged, and a classically Chinese compromise was reached. The Americans were told the phrase could be changed to "exist peacefully together," which Rice accepted. Meanwhile, the Chinese informed the other delegations—including the North Koreans—of the U.S. demand. Kim Gye Gwan was angry; however, because the change in wording in English did not change the basic meaning, the Chinese diplomats told Kim that the language in both Korean and Chinese versions of the statement would remain unchanged. The North Koreans acquiesced.

The final document, dubbed the September 19 Declaration, marked an important breakthrough. It was the first time that North Korea, the United States, and the other four parties had put in writing an agreed set of principles to resolve the nuclear crisis.

In the declaration, Pyongyang committed to "abandoning all nuclear weapons and existing nuclear programs and returning, at an early date, to the Treaty on the Non-Proliferation of Nuclear Weapons and to IAEA safeguards."

The United States affirmed that "it has no nuclear weapons on the Korean Peninsula and has no intention to attack or invade the DPRK with nuclear or conventional weapons."

After all the arguments over its wording, the section on light-water reactors read, "The DPRK stated that it has the right to peaceful uses of nuclear energy. The other parties expressed their respect and agreed to discuss, at an appropriate time, the subject of the provision of a light-water reactor to the DPRK."

The United States and North Korea both agreed "to respect each other's sovereignty, exist peacefully together, and take steps to normalize their relations subject to their respective bilateral policies." Respecting the North's sovereignty was diplomatic language for not attempting to overthrow its government. And China, Russia, Japan, South Korea, and the United States agreed to provide energy assistance to the North, and Seoul reaffirmed its July offer of two million kilowatts of electric power.[4]

Preoccupied with the final details of the joint declaration, Hill had left the drafting of the unilateral American statement to Washington. That produced an opening for the hard-liners to reassert themselves. As President Bush was later to do when attaching "signing statements" to many bills the Democratic Congress passed after 2006, the unilateral declaration was drafted to largely undermine the agreement. Robert Joseph, Deputy National Security Adviser J. D. Crouch, and NSC nonproliferation chief John Rood collaborated in drafting a statement that, in both tone and substance, amounted to a hard-line manifesto. It appeared to be formulated to remove any diplomatic flexibility, and used language deliberately calculated to elicit a negative North Korean reaction that could jeopardize what progress had been achieved.

Resurrecting a term the United States had discarded the previous year because of objections not only from the North Koreans but also from the South Koreans, Chinese, and Russians, the statement demanded that North Korea "completely, verifiably and irreversibly" eliminate all nuclear programs. On the sensitive issue of light-water reactors, where the joint declaration had acknowledged that the issue could be discussed at "an appropriate time," the statement defined such a time as to make it virtually never.

"That 'appropriate time' will only come when the DPRK has:

- Promptly eliminated all nuclear weapons and all nuclear programs, and this has been verified to the satisfaction of all parties by credible international means, including the IAEA; and,
- When the DPRK has come into full compliance with the NPT and IAEA safeguards, *and* has demonstrated a sustained commitment to cooperation and transparency and has ceased proliferating nuclear technology."

Only at that point, the statement continued, would the U.S. "support" a discussion—but nothing more. And just to emphasize that the LWRs were, in Washington's view, a nonstarter, the statement also announced that the consortium set up under the Agreed Framework to construct the LWRs was being disbanded.

That was not all. The statement said North Korea had to address U.S. concerns about "human rights, biological and chemical weapons programs, ballistic missile programs and proliferation, terrorism and illicit activities" before normalization of relations would be possible.[5]

When the statement came in from Washington, Hill's reaction was, "Oh shit. I can't believe this." Hill felt it was bloodcurdling, impolite, and rude, deliberately designed to goad the North Koreans into being angry. But as he looked it over, Hill concluded it would only be a minor irritant because the document that mattered, the one that would endure, was the joint declaration endorsed by all six parties. So, reluctantly, he read the entire statement at the closing plenary session.

Afterward, he realized he had made a big mistake.

Victor Cha was sitting next to Hill, with a clear view of Kim Gye Gwan. In front of him, the North Korean envoy had a prepared statement to read. After hearing Hill, however, Kim discarded his prepared remarks. Instead, he said, "I see that we have climbed one mountain—only to find a taller one ahead." The next day, North Korea made clear just how tall the new mountain was. "The U.S. should not even dream of the issue of the DPRK's dismantlement of its nuclear deterrent," the Foreign Ministry in Pyongyang warned in a statement issued on KCNA, "before providing LWRs, a physical guarantee for confidence building."

To make matters worse, while Hill had been preoccupied with the final days of negotiations, the U.S. Treasury Department had announced it was targeting a small bank in Macau called Banco Delta Asia as a "primary money-laundering concern" and a "willing pawn for the North Korean government to engage in corrupt financial activities." This routine-sounding announcement would have enormous implications for Hill and the entire negotiating process.

To the always suspicious North Koreans, all the reassuring signals from Hill appeared to be little more than empty gestures. The September 19 agreement began to fall apart almost literally before the ink was dry on the declaration.

# 15

# ILLICIT
# ACTIVITIES

MACAU HAD LONG DESERVED ITS REPUTATION AS A "BACK-water." Founded in the sixteenth century as a base for Portuguese traders and missionaries seeking to penetrate China, the enclave was the oldest continuous European settlement in Asia. Eclipsed in the mid-1800s by its new neighbor across the Pearl River Delta, the British colony of Hong Kong, Macau entered a steady period of decline, known, from the early twentieth century on, largely as a center for gambling and its related pleasures, prostitution and drugs.

With its cobblestone streets, outdoor cafés, fading Mediterranean architecture, and tacky casinos and nightclubs, Macau retained a kind of decadent charm, although its reputation suffered in the late 1990s as rival gangs of Triads—Chinese gangsters—fought a bloody war for control of the territory's gambling industry. Even here, though, the gang war had a certain cinematic appeal. The leader of one of the gangs was nicknamed "Broken-Tooth Koi." A flamboyant character, he financed a Hong Kong production company to make a film about his life. In the end he was arrested by a bearded Portuguese policemen and hauled off in handcuffs directly from the casino at the gaudy Lisboa Hotel.

Then, in 1999, after five hundred years of colonial rule, Portugal returned Macau to Chinese sovereignty. A local tycoon handpicked by Beijing took over to lead the Special Administrative Region. Intimidated by the presence of a garrison of the People's Liberation Army, the Triad gangs called off their war. In the hope of reviving the economy, the local authorities ended the casino monopoly controlled by billionaire Stanley

Ho—who had ties to North Korea and had set up a casino in a Pyongyang—and invited American gambling tycoons from Las Vegas to set up shop. The first U.S.-owned casino, the Sands Macau, opened in 2004, followed by a Venetian hotel and casino complex, complete with fake canals and gondolas right out of Las Vegas. Thousands of China's new rich—unable to gamble in the mainland where the practice is still illegal—poured across the border. Macau suddenly became a boomtown.

In the mid-1970s, when it was still a sleepy colonial outpost, Macau became North Korea's most important economic outlet to the rest of the world. The relationship began after the 1974 revolution in Portugal, when a leftist government in Lisbon established diplomatic relations with Pyongyang. The North Koreans soon opened several trading companies, staffed by "businessmen" with diplomatic passports. The most important was the Zokwang Trading Company, which operated from a fifth-floor office in a shabby concrete building on the Avenida Sidonio Pais. Officially, the enterprise traded rubber, cloth, and ginseng. But it also acquired and shipped luxury goods to the elite in Pyongyang—TV sets, Hennessy cognac, fresh fruit. For years, it was suspected by local and Western law enforcement and intelligence agencies of involvement in money laundering, counterfeiting, and other illicit activities.

As the North Korean presence in Macau grew, the government in Pyongyang began to use the territory for other dubious activities. It became a training ground for North Korea spies—a place where they could learn to blend into modern, capitalist societies. In 1987, two North Korean agents placed a bomb on a South Korean jet, killing all on board. One of the agents, Kim Hyon Hui was arrested before she could take a suicide pill. Kim later told authorities that she and her partner had used Zokwang's office in Macau as a base to learn the necessary skills—such as how to shop in a supermarket and use a credit card—to enable them pose as innocent tourists from Hong Kong.

In the early 1990s, Zokwang and other North Korean companies began doing business with a small Macau bank. The Banco Delta Asia (BDA) was a family-run concern whose major shareholder was a colorful local businessman, Stanley Au. Au was also a member of the Macau legislature and would later campaign unsuccessfully to be the territory's chief executive after the 1999 return to Chinese sovereignty.

In 1994, several Zokwang executives were arrested for depositing counterfeit U.S. dollar notes at the bank; BDA itself alerted the Macau and Hong Kong police authorities. All the suspects carried North Korean diplomatic passports and were sent home without facing trial. Zokwang, however, remained in business.

It was hardly the only case of counterfeiting and money laundering linked to North Korea. The U.S. Secret Service, which is responsible for combating counterfeiting, had been watching North Korea for years and had grown increasingly concerned at the profusion of what were dubbed Supernotes—forgeries of such high quality as to be almost indistinguishable from the real thing.

"I certainly wouldn't be able to tell," said one senior Treasury Department official. "To the naked eye, to someone who is not trying to detect it, they are very difficult to detect. We have no doubt that the Supernote is manufactured and distributed by the government of North Korea."

In September 2004, Deputy Assistant Treasury Secretary Bruce Townsend noted, "For the past several years, the Secret Service has investigated a family of counterfeit notes which utilizes complex and expensive printing methods such as intaglio and typographic. This form of counterfeit notes is emanating from North Korea. The sophisticated techniques used in producing this family of counterfeit U.S. banknotes is evidence of a well-funded, ongoing criminal enterprise, with a significant scientific and technical component."[1]

In a 2005 study of Pyongyang's illicit activities, Stanford University researcher Sheena Chestnut compiled a list of at least ten incidents involving counterfeiting linked to North Korea. Apart from the 1994 Zokwang episode, these included: a former member of the Japanese Red Army detained with a North Korean diplomatic passport and tens of thousands of dollars in fake U.S. bills in Cambodia and Thailand; a trade attaché at the North Korean embassy in Moscow caught with $30,000 in counterfeit U.S. currency and another episode involving Zokwang employees in Macau in 1999.[2]

While North Korea consistently denied such allegations, a variety of reports linked counterfeiting and other illicit activities to a shadowy office in Pyongyang known as Bureau 39. Reportedly housed in a six-floor building in a heavily guarded compound near the Koryo Hotel in downtown Pyongyang, Bureau 39 was said to be the headquarters for all of North Korea's foreign-exchange-earning businesses—licit and illicit. For a regime hard-pressed for hard currency, the bureau played a crucial role in propping up a rickety economy.

Press accounts and information from defectors described Bureau 39's key responsibilities as procurement of luxury goods—from Mercedes-Benz automobiles to Rolex watches and TV sets that Kim Jong Il used himself or distributed to senior party, military, and government officials to ensure their loyalty—and the management of counterfeiting, money laundering, and the profits from drug trafficking.[3] Macau was a key base of operations for these activities. In the late 1990s, the North Korean airline Air Koryo began regular service to Macau from Pyongyang. (In late 1999, I spent a morning with my CNN camera crew at

Macau Airport shooting video of an Air Koryo Tupolev-154 being loaded with one enormous Sony TV set after another for the weekly return flight to the North Korean capital.) The Zokwang Trading Company was widely believed to be the Bureau 39 office in Macau.

In 2000, Bureau 39 was said to have managed accounts at the Bank of China branch in Macau, which received several hundred million dollars in secret deposits from South Korea. The payments, handled by the Hyundai conglomerate and only acknowledged by President Kim Dae-jung years later, helped smooth the way for Kim's June 15 summit that year with Kim Jong Il.

There were, in addition, intriguing reports that Kim Jong Il's own family had a Macau connection. Portuguese intelligence officials told me that Kim himself had maintained an apartment in the territory that was frequently used by his wife. His oldest son, Kim Jong Nam, also reportedly spent time in Macau, and photographs are said to exist showing him gambling at the Lisboa casino.


David Asher believed he'd found North Korea's Achilles' heel. As the adviser to assistant secretary of state Jim Kelly working on the Illicit Activities Initiative, Asher became convinced that Kim Jong Il's regime was so dependent on the funds it received from counterfeiting, drug dealing, and other dubious transactions that it would be vulnerable to pressures that cut the flow of such money.

"The money really goes right to the top," he said. "This distinguishes it from other sorts of kleptocracies that we've observed in the past—be it Noriega's Panama, which was in collaboration with some of the Cali [drug] Cartel members, or Milošević's Serbia, which was engaged in counterfeit cigarette trafficking. I think the difference is that with North Korea, the leadership has made it a core part of its economic survival strategy and it is using facilities—diplomatic facilities, trading companies, intelligence officers, diplomats around the world—to actually traffic these items."

In January 2005, as she prepared to take over as secretary of state from Colin Powell, Condoleezza Rice received a briefing from Asher. In his usual ebullient way, he outlined the concept behind the illicit activities effort. According to one official who attended the meeting, "Condi was fascinated by the idea of the potential to hurt the North Koreans"—so much so that one skeptical senior State Department official, in the hope of cooling Rice's ardor, asked Asher whether the IAI could bring regime change. Asher's answer was no. It just was leverage. But Rice loved the idea.

As the Bush administration began its second term, high-level approval—it remains unclear whether it came from Rice or Bush or both—was given to the

Treasury Department, the Secret Service, the CIA, and other intelligence and law enforcement agencies to target North Korea's illicit activities. But Asher would not be around to see the results. Christopher Hill, the incoming assistant secretary of state for East Asia and the Pacific, disliked Asher's over-the-top style and had little regard for the entire Illicit Activities Initiative. Asher, to his dismay, was fired.

Two senior officials at the Treasury Department now made going after Pyongyang's dirty dealings a top priority. Daniel Glaser had worked at a high-powered New York law firm. After 9/11, he joined Treasury and in 2004 was appointed Deputy Assistant Secretary for Terrorist Financing and Financial Crimes. He was widely respected within the Department as someone who could get things done. Glaser's boss was Stuart Levey. A Harvard Law School graduate, Levey was also a Republican Party activist who, like John Bolton, had worked for George W. Bush during the controversial Florida recount following the 2000 presidential election. He joined Treasury in mid-2004 as the first Under Secretary of the Treasury for Terrorism and Financial Intelligence, a new office to combat the financial dealings of terrorists and rogue states. At the NSC, they were supported by NSC hard-liner Will Tobey, and, to a lesser extent, Victor Cha, and by the State Department's hard-line nonproliferation chief, Robert Joseph.

In a series of interagency meetings in the spring of 2005, attention was increasingly focused on Banco Delta Asia (BDA). There was little doubt among American officials that the bank had a long-standing and unsavory relationship with North Korea.

"Banco Delta Asia provided a tolerant environment for North Korean illicit activities," recalled Daniel Glaser. "Many notorious North Korean–related companies were doing business with Banco Delta Asia, laundering money through Banco Delta Asia, attempting to pass currency through Banco Delta Asia."

A variety of means were used to collect information on BDA, including enlisting the National Security Agency (NSA) to monitor the bank's internal communications.

"We've had a very sophisticated operation in NSA for a long time for monitoring financial transactions around the world," noted one former senior State Department official. "And if it wants to focus like a laser on a particular national entity, or a particular bank or a particular consortium, it could really turn out more information than you can even analyze. It just flows in. They can get everything. It's that sophisticated."

In its pursuit of BDA, the Treasury Department had a new weapon—the USA Patriot Act, which had been adopted after 9/11. Section 311 of the act allowed Treasury to designate a suspect foreign financial institution as one of "primary money-laundering concern." Such a designation would effectively cut off the designated bank from the U.S. financial system, which would trouble depositors with business dealings in the United States. In today's interconnected financial world, such a designation would also likely make the country whose accounts were targeted a global pariah, with other financial institutions unwilling to jeopardize their own relationship to the U.S. financial system by maintaining contact with those on Washington's blacklist.

By midsummer of 2005, as the six-party talks were about to resume, Treasury and its allies were convinced they had enough information against BDA to designate the bank as a "primary money-laundering concern." The evidence was supplemented by two FBI sting operations—"Smoking Dragon" and "Royal Charm." In parallel undercover operations, agents posing as drug traffickers and arms merchants infiltrated Chinese criminal gangs on the U.S. East and West coasts that were involved in smuggling counterfeit cash, fake brand-name cigarettes, Viagra, and weapons into the United States.

The investigations would ultimately lead to the arrest of dozens of people and the seizure of about $4.5 million in fake $100 notes.[4] Indictments in Los Angeles against four Chinese men that were issued in June 2005 offer revealing insights into how the smugglers—and the sting operation—worked. Although details of the financial transactions and the names of the offending countries remain sealed, it is possible to make a tentative reconstruction of the arrangement.

The indictment said that defendant Chao Tung Wu "told the Undercover Agent (UCA) that he had met with an unindicted co-conspirator in a foreign country (hereinafter referred to as 'Country One') regarding exporting counterfeit U.S. currency to the United States."[5] The unidentified "Country One" appears to be China.

Wu "told the UCA that the government of a foreign country (hereinafter referred to as 'Country Two') was making counterfeit U.S. currency which Wu could sell to the UCA."[6] "Country Two" appears to be North Korea.

In March 2005, Wu met the undercover agent to discuss payment and asked that money be wired to another foreign country identified only as "Country Six." This appears to be Macau. According to the indictment, "the UCA wired $25,000 to an account in Country Six at the direction of Wu . . . as payment for Supernotes to be shipped from Country One to the United States."[7]

After the cases were made public, U.S. officials, in background briefings, made it clear that North Korea was the source of the fake dollars, and told the *New York Times* that the financial trail led to BDA in Macau.

The "investigations had significance for Macau banks, including Banco Delta Asia," the *New York Times* reported, "because they produced evidence of illicit financial transactions through the Chinese territory that was strong enough to be presented in court and to meet the test for designating banks as money-laundering concerns, according to American officials who reviewed the results of the investigations."[8]

Not everyone in the bureaucracy, however, was convinced that the evidence against BDA was strong enough to hold up, let alone prove the involvement of the North Korean government, as opposed to individual North Koreans. The skeptics included virtually all the State Department's leading Korea experts: Korea Desk Director Jim Foster and most of his staff, including the head of the Desk's North Korea unit; Sue Bremner; John Merrill, a veteran North Korea analyst at State's own intelligence arm; the Bureau of Intelligence and Research; Robert Manning, a longtime Asia hand in the Department of Policy Panning; and several others.

The skeptics repeatedly asked for details of the intelligence to substantiate the claims Treasury was making about BDA, but remained dissatisfied with what they were told.

"They never really produced anything, quite frankly," noted one of those who challenged Treasury's conclusions. "I kept on going back and all I got was sort of vague allegations . . . and 'by the way we know the North Koreans are involved in all these kinds of activities, and this will send a very very firm warning to them.'"

Apart from the fact that the North Koreans had accounts at BDA, the skeptics argued the evidence of money laundering and counterfeiting—particularly of taking counterfeit funds and introducing them into the financial system—didn't add up.

"It was just like the weapons in Iraq," said one critic. "They weren't there."

Christopher Hill shared some of the doubts. But the pressure from the NSC, the White House, and the Treasury Department was relentless. Eventually, Hill felt he had no choice but to give his assent or risk his own standing within the administration.

"After all," he said in a meeting with Jim Foster and his deputy negotiator Joseph DeTrani, "this is law enforcement."

"Chris," Foster shot back, "this is not law enforcement. This is pure and simple blackmail. It's going to backfire on us. These guys are going to walk away from the talks."

"Well," replied Hill, "we've got to do this. I've got to preserve my credibility. If we don't do this, I'm going to lose my negotiating leeway."

Although the official line was that any U.S. action was nothing more than law enforcement, the temptation for hard-liners to use the move to undermine the prospects for diplomacy while boosting the chances or internal collapse in North Korea was strong. On September 8, 2005, as a formal Treasury Department announcement designating BDA as a "primary money-laundering concern" was being readied but had not yet been announced—and just days before the six-party talks were due to resume—the story was leaked to The *Wall Street Journal*.

Christopher Hill was furious about the timing. His first reaction was not to look at the content, but to wonder who had leaked it, and why.

"The neocons seized on BDA," said one former official who had worked on the issue from the start.

Added a longtime intelligence officer, "Someone leaked it to discredit the other track of negotiations."

It remains unclear who was the source of the leak, but in any event on September 15, 2005, two days after the six-party talks resumed in Beijing—as Christopher Hill struggled to find a way out of the deadlock—the Treasury Department made it official. Banco Delta Asia was designated "as a 'primary money-laundering concern' under Section 311 of the USA Patriot Act because it represents an unacceptable risk of money-laundering and other financial crimes."[9]

In making the announcement, Under Secretary for Terrorism and Financial Intelligence Stuart Levey accused BDA of a host of misdeeds. These included:

- providing financial services for over twenty years to North Korean government agencies and front companies, including some involved in illicit activities
- helping North Korean agents conduct surreptitious, multimillion dollar cash deposits and withdrawals
- working with DPRK officials to accept large deposits of cash, including counterfeit U.S. currency, and agreeing to place that currency into circulation
- facilitating several multimillion-dollar wire transfers connected with alleged criminal activity on behalf of a North Korean front company
- servicing a multimillion-dollar account on behalf of a known international drug trafficker.[10]

The allegations were sweeping—and damning—but the statement contained no specific names, dates, or other concrete evidence.

When he heard the news in Beijing, Hill was unsure whether the timing of the announcement, like the leak, was politically motivated, but he was concerned it might complicate the negotiations. The North Koreans, however, said nothing. The fallout from Pyongyang would come later.

In Macau, though, the fallout was immediate. The announcement had been made Thursday night Macau time. On Friday morning, September 16, thousands of worried depositors rushed to all of BDA's eight branches to withdraw their funds. It was a classic bank run. About $133 million was withdrawn in a single day—a third of the bank's total assets. Within twenty-four hours, the Macau government intervened and appointed a three-man committee to run the bank. Soon after, the Macau authorities froze $25 million worth of North Korean accounts at BDA.


Christopher Hill boarded his plane in Beijing after the signing of the September 19 Declaration, cautiously hopeful that the groundwork had been laid for diplomatic progress. When he arrived at Dulles Airport in Washington, he discovered the situation had changed. While he was in the air, Pyongyang had issued its statement that denuclearization was not possible unless North Korea received light-water reactors.

Hill had two reactions. At one level, he felt the demand was typical North Korean bluster and should be ignored. But he was also concerned that this could undermine his position within the Bush administration and make it harder to convince the hard-liners that North Korea was—as he had begun to believe—serious about negotiations.

Hill had hoped to build on the progress in Beijing by traveling to Pyongyang in the fall of 2005. South Korean officials were strongly in favor, and the North Koreans were eager to welcome him. To protect himself politically, he had told the North Koreans he intended to bring Jay Lefkowitz. Lefkowitz had been chosen by President Bush in August to be the U.S. special envoy on human rights in North Korea—a position mandated by Congress in the North Korea Human Rights Act it passed in October 2004. The White House had waited ten months to fill the job, as the State Department had warned that the envoy could complicate the prospects for diplomatic movement with Pyongyang. Under pressure from conservative Christian groups, the administration finally acted.

Lefkowitz was a dyed-in-the-wool neocon. A lawyer and regular contributor to such neocon publications as *Commentary* and *The Public Interest,* he had worked in the White House Office of Management and Budget from 2001 to 2003 before returning to New York to resume work at Kirkland, the law firm run by Kenneth Starr, who had headed the Whitewater investigation of President Bill Clinton and his wife, Hillary, in the 1990s.[11] Lefkowitz was a devout Jew, whose brother-in-law, Michael Horowitz of the Hudson Institute, was a prominent figure in right-wing circles and a key player in leading the charge against North Korea on human rights. Lefkowitz had, interestingly, also been a liaison for Bush to Christian conservatives, who were also among the strongest backers of pushing North Korea on the issue.

His appointment was yet another mixed signal from the Bush administration. Pyongyang's human rights abuses were appalling, and the strength of the president's personal view on the issue was hardly in doubt. Bush had even held a highly publicized meeting at the White House earlier in the summer of 2005 with Kang Chol Hwan, a North Korean defector who had written an acclaimed memoir of his years as a child prisoner in a labor camp, *The Aquariums of Pyongyang: Ten Years in the North Korean Gulag.* But the conservative coalition that had pushed for creation of the position generally supported regime change in North Korea—at precisely the moment when finding a way for the United States to acknowledge the legitimacy of Kim Jong Il's regime was a key part of the negotiating process being spearheaded by Christopher Hill.

Somewhat to Hill's surprise, the North Koreans accepted his bringing Lefkowitz, even though the human rights envoy, in his first public comment after being confirmed in mid-September, had accused Pyongyang of holding "200,000 people in concentration camps," subject to "torture, starvation, disease and exposure."[12]

Still, the idea of any visit was strongly opposed by the Pentagon, the National Security Council, and the Office of the Vice President, who remained deeply suspicious about the prospects for a deal and highly suspicious of Hill himself. In a reflection of their antipathy, his critics within the administration came up with a nickname for the Assistant Secretary. They called him "Kim Jong Hill."

"We didn't want a PR fiasco," said one senior Pentagon official. "We didn't want another Madeleine Albright thing frankly. We had visions of him going over there and pulling a Madeleine Albright, taking him into a stadium with roaring crowds, mass gymnastics. We didn't want North Korea to make a spectacle out of him, and we didn't think it was appropriate, given that North Korea really still at that point had not shown any intention or sincerity that they wanted to dismantle."

In addition, Condoleezza Rice also remained skeptical about the value of such a trip at this stage in the process. "Don't sell yourself short," she told Hill.

Soon, a new precondition was given to the North Koreans. If Hill were to visit, Pyongyang would have to shut down the Yongbyon nuclear reactor while he was there. It remains unclear whether this idea came from Hill, in the hope of further protecting himself from the hard-liners, or was imposed by Vice President Cheney's office—interviewees offered both versions of the story. In any case, the demand meant asking North Korea to give up one of its key bargaining chips—stopping the reactor—in return for a short visit from a U.S. official. Not surprisingly, Pyongyang said no, and the trip never happened.

With diplomacy at a standstill, Hill was increasingly discouraged. After returning from Beijing, he had been granted a brief meeting with President Bush. Hill thought the president would at least offer some words of praise or encouragement. Instead, Bush was noncommittal about Hill's efforts. In mid-October, Rice called him in for a "pep talk."

"Don't worry about all the people against dealing with North Korea," she told him. "They're on the team."

"That's the problem," Hill replied. "They're on the team."

At various points that fall, Hill seriously considered quitting.

Meanwhile, long-simmering tensions between the United States and South Korea boiled over at the annual meeting of the two countries' defense ministers in the fall of 2005. For weeks, U.S. and South Korean officials had worked to draft an official communiqué—an annual exercise that spelled out the current and future goals of the alliance. The night before the formal meeting was to begin, South Korean negotiators advised their American counterparts that, under instructions from President Roh Moo-hyun's left-leaning Deputy National Security Adviser Lee Jong-seok, Seoul wanted to remove a long-standing reference to South Korea's remaining under the U.S. nuclear umbrella. According to one South Korean official, Lee's reasoning was that "since North Korea was insisting that the nuclear umbrella be removed from the peninsula, why should we provoke the North Koreans?"

The demand infuriated the American side. After hours of angry discussions, Richard Lawless, the deputy under secretary of defense for Asia and Pacific affairs, put down his foot. Either the nuclear umbrella reference remained, he insisted, or there would be no communiqué. The South Koreans backed down. But the episode added to the sour tone over the alliance, a sourness made worse as President Roh abruptly began a campaign to fundamentally alter the structure of the alliance's Combined Forces Command (CFC). For years, the CFC had been the backbone of the alliance. While Seoul maintained control over its own soldiers in peacetime, should war break out, the two governments had long agreed that the general in charge of U.S. forces in Korea would immediately become the commander of an integrated military command involving both forces. It was partly a matter of military efficiency and also a way of further guaranteeing that the United States would come to South Korea's aid in the event of a North Korean attack. Now, in late 2005, for what appeared to be a combination of personal conviction and political calculation—boosting his flagging popularity by appealing to national pride—Roh pushed very publicly for OPCON to be transferred to South Korea, portraying the regaining of wartime command as a matter of national pride and sovereignty.

In doing so, though, he was at odds with his own military establishment, which feared that such a step would jeopardize the effectiveness of the alliance. "The president and a lot of Blue House advisers were for it," recalled one former Blue House official. "The Ministry of National Defense was not comfortable with it, and they were concerned that it was being pushed too fast for essentially a political motivation rather than a military motivation." So strong was the opposition that more than a dozen former South Korean defense ministers and senior military officials publicly warned of the dangers of Roh's policy. "Under this president, in this atmosphere, if it's done, the consequences might be disastrous," noted Hyun Hong-choo, South Korean ambassador to Washington under general-turned-president Roh Tae-woo.

At the Pentagon, there were concerns about South Korea's ability to handle what it was demanding. "Since the South Koreans have never done it, they have a lot of learning to do," observed one American officer. "They aren't going to replicate U.S. capability. They need more attack helicopters, multiple rocket launcher systems, high performance aircraft; and especially C4I—command and control, communication, computers, and intelligence."

Still, given the broader reconfiguration of U.S. forces on the peninsula, and the nationalistic sentiment driving President Roh, the decision was made in Washington to accede to Seoul's request. When South Korea's defense minister formally raised the issue with Defense Secretary Rumsfeld, he was told, to his surprise, "You're pushing through an open door. We're comfortable with that."

"The ROKs [Republic of Korea] have to be in charge if we want this relationship to be politically viable," says one Pentagon official. "If we want to sustain the viability of the alliance for the long term we've got to change some fundamental ways that we're doing business."

Meanwhile, for the first time in a year, North Korean and Japanese officials met to discuss the increasingly contentious issue of the abductees. During the last encounter in November 2004, North Korea had turned over a box of bones and ashes that Pyongyang said were the remains of the most well known of the Japanese citizens kidnapped by North Korean agents decades before. Megumi Yokota was just thirteen when she disappeared while returning home from a badminton match in November 1977. Her distraught parents had become the public face of the movement to demand an accounting of the fate of the abductees. Soon after, however, the Japanese government claimed that DNA testing showed the remains were in fact not those of Megumi—who according to the North Koreans, had committed suicide in Pyongyang in 1993.

The impact on public opinion of what appeared to be a cynical act of North Korean duplicity was huge, fueling calls for sanctions or other retaliatory steps. Subsequently, the prestigious scientific journal *Nature* raised doubts about the way Japanese scientists had conducted the DNA tests and the veracity of their conclusion. But the doubts were lost amid the clamor to get tough on Pyongyang—a groundswell of anger that boosted the popularity of Chief Cabinet Secretary Shinzo Abe, who would succeed Junichiro Koizumi as prime minister in 2006.

In the new talks between Japan and North Korea there was no progress. Japanese officials said normalization of relations between the two countries would not be possible without a resolution of the abduction issue, but the North Koreans were not forthcoming. Officials in Tokyo promised to pursue the issue when the six-party talks reconvened.

But the new round in Beijing in November 2005 lasted barely three days and achieved nothing. All sides remained locked in their previous positions. The United States again rejected a North Korean offer to freeze production of nuclear fuel in return for aid. Instead, Christopher Hill called on Pyongyang to shut Yongbyon down altogether.

Then, just as some State Department officials had worried they might, the North Koreans raised the issue of the U.S. sanctions against Banco Delta Asia. North Korean envoy Kim Gye Gwan angrily warned that unless the sanctions were lifted, it would be "impossible to discuss the nuclear weapons issue." Kim said the U.S. move showed "an utter lack of basic trust."[13] From Pyongyang's perspective, it appeared that, despite the September 19 Declaration committing the two countries "to respect each other's sovereignty, exist peacefully together, and take steps to normalize their relations," the hard-liners had reasserted themselves, using the BDA issue and other sanctions to undermine the North Korean state.

The exchanges were difficult. One report said the meeting was "so tense that the other delegates could hardly continue dialogue."[14] The round ended with only a vague agreement to meet again; no date was set. Shortly afterward, a

North Korean Foreign Ministry statement declared, "Though the U.S. claims to stand for a negotiated solution to the nuclear issue, it is, in actuality, seeking to 'bring down the system' by isolating and pressuring it. It is quite unreasonable for the DPRK to sit at the negotiating table with the party keen to 'bring down its system' and discuss the issue of dismantling the nuclear deterrent built up to defend it."[15]

The atmosphere was further soured by a misunderstanding over the only accommodating gesture Christopher Hill had been able to make. As the measures against BDA were unquestionably a bilateral matter, Kim told Hill that bilateral negotiations were necessary to resolve it. In response, Hill said U.S. officials would be willing to provide a briefing to the North Koreans on the laws that had set the sanctions in motion. Believing this was an opening to hold a bilateral discussion on all the issues, including the BDA sanctions, Kim Gye Gwan returned to Pyongyang and made plans to visit Washington in early December. But administration hard-liners opposed to any bilateral talks with the North objected. In late November, the invitation to Kim was "withdrawn," although his deputy Li Gun was invited for a "technical" briefing from the Treasury Department. The North Koreans were convinced the United States had broken its word, and the entire trip fell through.[16]

The designation of Banco Delta Asia as a "primary money-laundering concern" had been followed by the Macau government's seizure of fifty-two North Korean accounts at BDA, among them North Korean banks and trading companies, North Korean citizens, Macau-based companies that conducted business with North Korean entities, and some Macau residents.

In response to the American claims, the Macau government hired the accounting firm Ernst & Young to conduct an audit of BDA. Ernst & Young collected 300,000 pages of materials—virtually every single transaction sheet in the bank's possession. In the hope of getting the U.S. designation lifted, Ernst & Young was authorized to turn all 300,000 pages over to the Treasury Department, which provided more leads to pursue as Washington sought to tighten the financial squeeze on Pyongyang.

The U.S. moves had a devastating effect. North Korea, as one analyst noted, had placed "so many of its foreign exchange eggs in the BDA basket" that it was particularly vulnerable to the cutoff. Moreover, other foreign businesses and banks became increasingly unwilling to conduct even legal business in North Korea and began severing their ties, fearful that any association, however legitimate, carried the risk of being tainted with U.S. accusations of complicity in illicit activities and being shut out of the American financial system. American officials

openly encouraged this trend. Representatives from the Treasury Department visited Macau, Hong Kong, Vietnam, Singapore, and China to urge banks there to
cut ties to North Korea as well. And the Treasury Department issued an advisory
warning all U.S. financial institutions to guard against any dealings that could
bring them in contact with North Korea. The Treasury Department's Stuart
Levey gloated that the U.S. effort was having a "snowballing . . . avalanche effect."[17] Shunned around the world, North Korea's ability to conduct international
business was under stress.

To leading hard-liners the financial pressure appeared to be proving far
more effective than anyone had dreamed, reigniting hopes that it could become
a weapon to produce a change of regime.

"This is a criminal enterprise," said Robert Joseph, under secretary of state
for arms control. "We need to see transformation. It's not just the nuclear issue.
It's a brittle regime. It's an argument for not throwing them a lifeline."

Many American officials believed Pyongyang's involvement in illicit activities was so extensive that there was no such thing as a "legitimate" North Korean transaction. As David Asher noted, "North Korea has become a 'Sopranos
state' . . . whose actions, attitudes and affiliations increasingly resemble those of
an organized crime family more than a normal nation."[18]

When I visited Pyongyang in August 2005, Nigel Cowie—one of the tiny
handful of foreign businessmen living in the North Korean capital—took me to
dinner in one of the growing number of newly opened private restaurants there.
Cowie was the general manager of Daedong Credit Bank, a joint venture that
was the only foreign-owned and managed bank operating in North Korea. Established in 1995 by the Hong Kong finance group Peregrine, which collapsed
during the Asian financial crisis of 1997, Daedong had become the only bank
available for Pyongyang's small foreign community. Its 200 customers included
foreign aid organizations, foreign-funded joint venture investment projects, and
some individual foreign residents. Of the fifty-two accounts totaling $25 million
that had been frozen at the Banco Delta Asia, $7 million belonged to Daedong,
including $2.6 million owned by the British American Tobacco Company,
which had set up a cigarette factory in North Korea.

Given long-standing suspicions about North Korean dirty dealings, Cowie
stressed to me that Daedong only engaged in legitimate transactions. After
Treasury's designation of BDA, he repeatedly insisted that Daedong's business,
like that of many other legitimate North Korean companies, had been severely
hurt by the U.S. effort. And he subsequently published an article recounting an
incident that showed the reach of the U.S. campaign.

In late 2005, Daedong had opened an account with the Golomt Bank in
Mongolia. In February 2006, Daedong sent couriers with $1 million in U.S

dollars and 20 million Japanese yen to deposit in the new accounts. The use of cash, Cowie said, was common in North Korea. The country's long-standing international isolation, its inability to obtain credit, and its primitive financial infrastructure meant that more modern banking methods were rarely employed. (This was certainly my own experience on all my visits to North Korea beginning in the late 1980s. My CNN team always brought large amounts of dollars to cover hotel bills, satellite transmission costs, and other fees; paying by credit card, check, or wire transfer was never an option.)

Upon arrival at Ulaanbaatar airport, the Daedong couriers were detained by Mongolian intelligence agents who accused them of smuggling counterfeit currency. Cowie raced to the Mongolian capital to try to resolve the situation. After conducting further inspections of the cash, the Mongolians returned the currency, which was deposited in the Golomt Bank. Cowie made clear that the Mongolians were acting with the encouragement of U.S. officials.[19]

The year 2006 began with the promise of the September 19 breakthrough a fading memory. In an effort to revive the diplomatic process, China offered to host a meeting between Christopher Hill and Kim Gye Gwan in Beijing on January 18. The offer came following a weeklong visit to China by Kim Jong Il. In a meeting with Chinese president Hu Jintao, Kim spoke of "difficulties" in the negotiations, but stressed, "There is no change in the DPRK's basic stand of maintaining the goal of denuclearizing the Korean Peninsula, implementing the joint statement issued at the fourth round of the six-party talks and pursuing a negotiated peaceful settlement."

When the Chinese invitation was received in Washington, it set off yet another round of internal battles between Hill and his supporters who wanted to accept the invitation, and hard-liners opposed to any meeting, even with the Chinese in attendance. Eventually, responsibility for the decision went all the way to the White House, and President Bush gave Hill approval to go. Hill felt the episode was one of the lowest points in his entire experience in dealing with the North Korea issue. But the fact that Bush ruled in his favor was a sign that, for all his rhetorical bluster and visceral dislike of North Korea, the president had not abandoned the idea of reaching a diplomatic solution to the nuclear crisis. Given the vast gap between the two sides, however, it was almost inevitable that the brief three-way meeting in Beijing would make no progress.

Leon Sigal was getting worried. With diplomacy going nowhere, the New York–based North Korea scholar felt the absence of dialogue was dangerous.

In early February, he worked with Donald Zagoria of the National Committee on American Foreign Policy to organize another Track II meeting in New York. North Korea's deputy permanent representative to the UN, Han Song Ryol, was invited to join about a half-dozen American experts and scholars, including two mid-level officials from the State Department for an informal, unofficial brainstorming session.

Han was quick to cite the BDA issue as the main impediment to resuming six-party talks. Sigal suggested setting up a "bilateral mechanism" for the two countries to discuss both the financial measures and the North's illicit activities. Han appeared interested.

"But it's our money!" he insisted, adding that if Washington had evidence that it was obtained illicitly it should present it and ask for Pyongyang's cooperation.

Sigal acknowledged that the United States had no business holding the proceeds of legitimate trade, but stressed that unless Pyongyang could identify the legitimate proceeds in its accounts, it wouldn't get any money back.

Perhaps one way out, Han said, would be for North Korea to open an account at an American financial institution like Citibank. That would be much easier for Washington to monitor and would help assure the United States that North Korea's funds were being used in a legitimate way.

Sigal and some other participants felt the proposal was worth exploring. Discussion then turned to what would happen if—or when—the six-party talks resumed. In response to questions, Han indicated that Pyongyang's offer to freeze its nuclear facilities was still on the table, and that some of the plutonium reprocessed in 2003—the start of the current crisis—and since might be put under international inspection.

Since the Bush administration continued to say a freeze was not enough, Han was pressed to consider other steps, such as providing a list of all nuclear facilities and material, or putting some fissile material under international inspection, or taking additional measures to make it difficult to resume operations at the Yongbyon complex. When asked what North Korea wanted in return, Han said that it wanted to get off the terrorism list and an end to all U.S. sanctions.

During breaks in the discussions, one of the State Department officers was on the phone to Washington, to either Hill or one of his aides, providing a running commentary on what the North Korean envoy was saying.

Following this meeting, North Korea decided to accept the U.S. offer of a briefing on the financial sanctions, and in March, Li Gun, the Foreign Ministry's director-general of American affairs was sent to New York.

Yet again, there were battles in Washington over who would meet with him. John Rood, the NSC's proliferation expert, and Deputy National Security Adviser J. D. Crouch—both among the most active members of the hard-line camp—were skeptical of the value of talking with the North Koreans and didn't want anyone from the State Department to attend the briefing. Hill fought back and eventually convinced Secretary of State Rice to send Kathleen Stephens, the principal deputy assistant secretary for East Asia, a Hill protégé but someone who had no experience dealing with the North Koreans. Hill, Korea Desk director Jim Foster, and anyone else who had actually been involved in the six-party talks were not allowed to attend.

The meeting on March 7, 2006, lasted three hours. Most of the talking on the American side was done by Deputy Assistant Treasury Secretary Daniel Glaser. When it was Li Gun's turn to speak, it was clear the North Koreans had embraced some of the key ideas that had emerged from the Track II meeting the month before. While Li predictably denied any wrongdoing and demanded the lifting of the sanctions, he also proposed the creation of a joint U.S.-North Korean task force to examine the issue, and asked for North Korea to be allowed to open an account at a U.S. bank.

The proposal came in the wake of other signs from Pyongyang that the North was looking for a face-saving way out of the deadlock. Shortly before Li Gun's departure for New York, a Foreign Ministry spokesman was quoted by KCNA as saying, "We have already told the U.S. side that we were ready to cooperate in the efforts to settle the issue of 'fake dollars,' a worldwide trouble, and urged it not to bar the DPRK from participating in the normal international financial activities but cooperate with it. If the U.S. is truly interested in the protection of its currency, it should stop such reckless act as linking the issue of 'fake dollars' with the DPRK in a far-fetched manner, lift financial embargo on the DPRK at an early date and opt for mutual cooperation in normal banking transaction."[20]

Not surprisingly, Li's suggestion did not get a positive response. The idea of a joint task force was widely viewed as yet another North Korean ploy to circumvent Washington's ban on bilateral negotiations outside the context of the six-party talks. As one senior U.S. official noted, Li was basically told, "Stuff it."

But Li's presence in New York nonetheless marked an important moment— the point when Henry Kissinger began to get seriously involved with the North Korea issue. The day before the briefing, Donald Zagoria had hosted yet another Track II meeting, this time, with Kissinger in attendance. The former secretary of state had quietly become a regular visitor to the White House, and his voice appeared to carry significant weight with George W. Bush. In discussions with Li Gun, Kissinger sought to put the North Korea issue in a broader regional context.

"You want a new relationship with the U.S.," he told the North Korean envoy. "We want you to get rid of your nuclear weapons." Kissinger urged both sides to stop fixating on side issues like the BDA sanctions and begin talks on how to resolve the nuclear issue as part of a wider set of new security arrangements in the region.

Kissinger noted that he thought there were some constructive elements in what Li Gun had said. The former secretary of state said the United States wanted all the nations in Northeast Asia to have constructive relations with it and others in the region. If the nuclear issue could be resolved it would be possible to develop a regional security framework. If not, North Korea's prospects for economic growth would be limited and pressures on it would grow.

Kissinger acknowledged that it was necessary to understand the North's concerns about regime change. The central issue to focus on was whether it would be possible to do away with North Korean nuclear weapons while providing assurances for its security and economic and social development. Since the United States thought the North wanted to keep its nuclear program and stall, and to the DPRK it looked as if the United States wanted it to disarm before deciding what to do in return, the problem had to be broken up into stages and tangible quid pro quos worked out for both sides at each stage

Just as it took a right-wing Republican, Richard Nixon, to open the door to China, Kissinger also told the North Koreans that their prospects of a deal would be better with the Bush administration than with whoever came into the White House next. He was "basically telling the North Koreans, 'You should make a deal with this administration,'" said one senior U.S. official, "because it's not going to get any better, either under a Democrat or a Republican administration."

To the North Koreans, the chance to interact with Kissinger was a significant development. Kissinger led Li Gun to believe he was in touch with the White House. The involvement of the man who, along with Richard Nixon, had been the architect of the U.S. opening to China, was not lost on the North Koreans. He appeared to represent the possibility of a change, although at this point it was far from clear that George Bush was listening to the advice the wily old diplomat may have been offering.

Kissinger subsequently spelled out his thinking in an op-ed piece in the *Washington Post*. Warning that continued stalemate risked the possibility of Japan and South Korea going nuclear and North Korea possibly proliferating nuclear material, Kissinger wrote that "diplomacy needs a new impetus." And

he was blunt about what would be involved. "Inevitably, a negotiation on nuclear disarmament will involve compensation in security and economic benefits
in return for abandonment of nuclear weapons capabilities and is, in that sense,
incompatible with regime change."[21]

C hun Yung-woo was pleased with himself. South Korea's new chief negotiator
for the six-party talks had just agreed to arrange what he jokingly called a
"blind date" between Christopher Hill and North Korea's Kim Gye Gwan—a
way, Chun hoped, to get around American restrictions on bilateral communication and get the two countries to begin talking again.

All three men, along with the six-party envoys of China, Russia, and Japan,
were in Tokyo in early April 2006 to attend another Track II conference; this
one was called the Northeast Asia Cooperation Dialogue. These sessions had
been held annually since the early 1990s. Now, Chun believed, the conference
provided an opportunity for diplomatic reengagement.

In Washington, Hill had encountered predictable opposition from hard-
liners who did not want him to attend any meeting where Kim Gye Gwan was
present. Eventually, though, he was given the green light to fly to Tokyo, but he
made it clear that unless Kim was ready to announce North Korea's return to
the six-party talks, Hill was not prepared to hold a bilateral meeting. The U.S.
envoy was uncomfortable with this restriction, but given the prevailing sentiment in Washington, felt unable to do anything more to challenge it.

When Hill arrived in Tokyo, Chun pushed him to reconsider and meet Kim
face to face. But Hill's instructions were clear.

Chun was deeply frustrated by Washington's intransigence. He felt the Bush
administration placed a higher priority on not holding bilateral negotiations
with North Korea than taking meaningful steps to stop the North's nuclear program. All of the Bush administration's "principles," he believed, were harming
South Korea's interests and making a negotiated settlement harder to achieve.

The delegates to the conference were housed in the luxurious Akasaka
Prince Hotel in the center of Tokyo. Chun Yung-woo found himself on the
same floor as Kim Gye Gwan. Out of public view, with access to the floor
guarded by police, the two Koreans spent hours together in Chun's room, talking while drinking copious amounts of a mixture of beer and whiskey that Koreans dubbed *poktan ju* or "bomb liquor."

Kim told Chun that getting the BDA money back remained the top priority
and the chief obstacle to Pyongyang returning to the six-party talks.

Chun pressed the North Korean. "We are ready to resume the supply of
heavy fuel oil," the South Korean said. "That's worth about $200 million. And

from the moment you have completely denuclearized, we're prepared to give you two million kilowatts of power. That's worth a billion dollars a year. So on an annual basis, you'll be getting well over a billion dollars. So you're wasting all that to get $25 million back from BDA. That is nonsense to me."

Kim acknowledged Chun's point. But he said that the owners of the BDA accounts were very powerful in Pyongyang, and the North Korean Foreign Ministry could not defy this power. And these powerful forces had decreed: Don't go back to the six-party talks until you get the money back. That was an order. Kim did not mention any names, but there had been much speculation that at least some of the BDA accounts were for the personal use of Kim Jong Il and his family. That would explain why Pyongyang was making such a fuss and why its diplomats had little choice but to press their demands even if, as Chun noted to Kim, it was costing the North hundreds of millions of dollars in potential benefits.

After this conversation, the South Korean envoy was more determined than ever to get Kim and Hill together. He came up with his idea of a "blind date." Chun told Hill he would invite him to his room for a drink. "You don't have to report to Secretary Rice that you are meeting with Kim Gye Gwan," Chun said. "Just accept my invitation to stop by. There will be a stranger . . . actually not a stranger but Kim Gye Gwan. You don't have to act like you're not following your instructions." If it worked, the two men would be able to speak frankly, without anyone else knowing of the encounter.

Hill, seeing a way to circumvent his rigid instructions, agreed to the plan, as did Kim. But before the appointed time, the North Korean received an invitation from China's envoy, Vice Foreign Minister Wu Dawei, for dinner at the Chinese embassy. Unaware of Chun's plan, and also intent of brokering a meeting themselves, the Chinese had asked both Kim and Hill to attend the meal. Given North Korea's dependence on China, Kim felt he had no choice but to accept. For his part, Hill refused to accept the Chinese invitation unless he received an assurance that Kim would inform him the North was returning to the talks. The dinner—without Hill—was a flop. Kim returned to the hotel having not eaten anything. Arriving at Chun Yung-woo's room, it was clearly too late to pull off the "blind date." The two Koreans spent the evening eating sashimi and getting drunk.

As the conference ended, Hill's refusal to meet Kim received scathing criticism in South Korea. "Hill has snubbed North Korea's second-ranking diplomat, who was willing to meet him without any conditions attached, humiliating the man and forcing him to return home empty-handed," noted the usually conservative *Chosun Ilbo*. "Kim is left with no good explanation when he reports to the North Korean leadership. The episode has also left a sour taste in the mouths of the other nations in the talks, all of whose delegation chiefs were in Tokyo, sending a message that their influence counts for little in Washington's eyes."[22]

Kim held a brief session with the press before returning to Pyongyang. To the surprise of some reporters, he did not describe the meeting as a failure. "We tried to meet Christopher Hill to confirm the U.S.'s final position," Kim said, "but in the end we could not meet with him. Now we know what the U.S. position is. And it has only cemented our resolution."[23] Then the North Korean envoy said provocatively, "If the U.S. tries to pressure us, we will only take stronger measures. We will employ our traditional tactic of direct confrontation. There is nothing wrong with delaying the resumption of the six-party talks. In the meantime we can make more deterrents."[24]

North Korea's rhetoric was so regularly full of bombast and threats that many American officials and others simply dismissed what Pyongyang and its representatives said as overheated posturing. But the North in fact had a consistent pattern of clearly signaling its next move; Kim Gye Gwan's statement was no exception. The stage was now set for the event the United States—and the region—had worried about since the moment the crisis erupted—a North Korean nuclear test.

# 16

# GOING BALLISTIC

U P AND DOWN THE EAST COAST, JULY 4, 2006, HELD THE
promise of a perfect Independence Day holiday—cloudless
skies, brilliant sunshine, warm temperatures. At the White House,
staffers and their families gathered on the lawn to enjoy the celebrations.
The president was at Fort Bragg in North Carolina, to give a speech before a friendly military audience, but was due back in Washington for
fireworks planned in the evening. Adding to the festivities, in the early afternoon the space shuttle *Discovery* was set to blast into orbit from Cape
Canaveral in Florida—the first U.S. space launch on America's national
day and only the second since a disastrous accident killed the crew of the
shuttle *Columbia* in 2003.

But almost literally as *Discovery* was lifting off, on the other side of
the world a new crisis was about to cast a shadow over the holiday festivities. Far above the earth, an American spy satellite detected the hot
plume of a missile being launched from a test facility in North Korea. It
was the first such launch since 1998. North Korea had ended a self-
imposed moratorium on missiles tests.

Immediately, land-and sea-based sensors—part of the fledgling antimissile shield that George W. Bush had made a centerpiece of his
defense strategy—began tracking the course of the missile. As the White
House situation room called senior aides away from the July 4 celebrations, a second missile was launched, then a third, and a fourth. The fourth
one sharply raised the level of American anxiety. It was a Taepodong-2—
an intercontinental ballistic missile with the potential, American experts

believed, to hit Alaska and possibly the continental United States. In California and Alaska, eleven long-range interceptor missiles were placed on alert. It was the first time the U.S. missile defense system—which was still in its early stages and has not yet proven to be effective—has been primed in reaction to a real event.

"It was a rehearsal of missile defense, the first one ever," noted a senior White House official. "With everybody trying to think about what systems should be activated, what collection platforms should be where, what were the orders that the president of the United States would give to his commanders as to what would happen and what authorities would the commanders have in this situation."

"I think we had a reasonable chance of shooting it down," Bush said afterward. "At least that's what military commanders told me."[1]

Before the president could make a decision as to whether the interceptors should try to bring the North Korean missile down in mid-flight, however, the Taepodong broke up and fell into the sea just forty-two seconds after launch. It did not appear to be carrying a warhead and the danger that it might pose a real threat to the United States had passed. But other launches kept coming. Altogether, over a four-hour period, the North Koreans fired six missiles, and, a few hours later, a seventh. In addition to the long-range Taepodong, three were medium-range Rodongs, capable of hitting targets in Japan, and two were short-range Scuds, easily able to reach all parts of South Korea. The design of one missile remained unclear, but it may have been a new medium-range missile capable of reaching Japan.

The message from the launches—and the end of a moratorium, which Pyongyang had once explicitly linked to the continuation of talks with the United States and later to talks with Japan—was clear enough. "The North Koreans tried diplomacy first," noted one U.S. intelligence analyst, only to have the United States go after their hard-currency accounts in the Banco Delta Asia and elsewhere. "Then they went back to in-your-face."


The test preparations had begun soon after the mid-April 2006 conference in Tokyo, where Christopher Hill had rejected Kim Gye Gwan's appeals for a bilateral meeting to discuss the freezing of North Korean accounts, leading Kim to warn of a strengthening of North Korea's "deterrent." Just days later came another development that Pyongyang appears to have interpreted as a "hostile" gesture. The Japanese government introduced a measure in the Diet on April 28 titled the "Bill on Response to Abduction and Other Human Rights Abuse Issues by North Korean Authorities." It called for implementing sanctions against North Korea on the long-festering abductee issue.[2] Although there is no way to determine just when Kim Jong Il made the decision, within a week, American intelligence picked up the first signs of preparations for a possible North Korean missile test. In early May, American spy satellites observed tractor trailers carrying the distinctive Taepodong to the test site. Knowing they were being watched, the North Koreans made no effort to hide their work. In the following weeks, they began to assemble rocket components, large fuel tanks, and other essential items.[3]

While the North Koreans were fixated on what they saw as Washington's "hostile" intent, as so often was the case with the Bush administration, Washington's messages toward Pyongyang were mixed. Even as administration hard-liners were preventing Hill from holding a bilateral with Kim, and Treasury Department officials were traveling the world to urge governments and banks to scale back or cut financial ties with North Korea, George W. Bush was hosting Chinese premier Hu Jintao in Washington, where the tone on North Korea was one of cooperation and conciliation.

E nlisting Chinese help to deal with North Korea had been a central theme of administration thinking for years. There was a widely held view that, as the North's main conduit for food, energy, oil, and aid—with China's long, if now frayed, history of "fraternal" relations with the neighboring socialist state— Beijing wielded special influence in Pyongyang. At various points, Washington hard-liners had sought—without success—to pressure Beijing to "punish" the North for its behavior, or to join the United States in pushing for the ouster of the Kim Jong Il regime. At other times, U.S. officials urged the Chinese to act as an intermediary in convincing the North to return to the six-party talks. While the Chinese always insisted they had less leverage with Pyongyang than Washington imagined, Beijing's higher profile on the nuclear issue was a reflection of its increasingly important role in dealing with its intractable neighbor.

On April 20, President Hu Jintao was due for a formal banquet at the White House. Usually at such occasions, the two presidents did not sit side by side. Protocol dictated each would sit next to the other's wife. The conversation tended to be polite and sometimes awkward small talk. But on this day, Bush told his senior advisers before the meal, "I'm calling an audible. I want to sit next to Hu."

As the two leaders made their way to the dining area, Bush looked at Hu and said, "You know, we have more to talk about, so we are going to sit next to each other at lunch." Hu, in mock horror but with a twinkle in his eyes, replied, "Oh. I had been looking forward to a relaxing social lunch."

Instead, recalled a senior administration official, the next two hours were "a remarkable lunch at which the two of them really discussed North Korea in a way that no American and Chinese leaders had ever discussed it."

As the two men ate, Bush asked Hu if North Korea would ever take the route China had followed in introducing economic reforms. Hu pointedly answered that China at that time faced a much more benign external environment than North Korea did now.

Bush said to Hu he would be ready to create that kind of international environment if Pyongyang would get rid of its nuclear weapons.

"Look, I am ready for peace on the Korean peninsula," Bush told Hu. "I am ready to end the Cold War in Northeast Asia, but I can't do this myself. I can deliver my side of this deal, but you have to deliver your side. You have to get the North Koreans to understand that a diplomatic solution is within reach, that I want a diplomatic solution, and that I want a permanent peace on the peninsula."

Bush's blunt words grew out of a sense the U.S. president had developed over a series of meetings with Hu that the Chinese leader was someone he could work with on North Korea.

"Hu is a very inward-faced Chinese president," focused on his country's enormous internal problems, observed one of Bush's advisers. "I think Hu just found North Korea completely annoying and distracting. So Hu was ready to hear the message the president gave to him."

Bush had reached one other conclusion about Hu.

"What you find with Hu is he really doesn't say very much, he'll use the standard line of the party," said a senior administration official. "But you talk to him and you find things happen. He's a real good listener, and he internalizes what the president says." And Bush was convinced that, whatever its denials, Beijing did have real clout with Pyongyang.

"He's always believed that the Chinese had the leverage, that the road to a solution lies through Beijing, not Pyongyang," said the same senior official. "The North isn't going to change, [but] the dynamic that could be changed is the Chinese position, and that through working on the Chinese and making them see that the North was doing them no favors, that there was a possibility of moving this to a better place."

Hu was reportedly so struck by Bush's conciliatory comments that he immediately dispatched a senior adviser—State Councilor Tang Jiaxuan, who had previously served as foreign minister—to Pyongyang to meet with Kim Jong Il. The importance with which Hu viewed Tang's mission was underscored by the fact that Tang had been scheduled to accompany Hu on the rest of his U.S. visit, but instead left at once for the North Korean capital.

Bush's statement marked a significant evolution in his thinking about how to deal with North Korea. But Pyongyang, looking at other American actions, and probably suspicious that Washington and Beijing might be "ganging up" on the North to push for concessions, did not respond directly.

Tang's visit to Pyongyang was not made public, and even now few details have emerged. But after briefing Kim on Bush's comments and urging North Korea to return to the six-party talks, the Dear Leader reportedly said the North would only come back to the table when the U.S. financial sanctions against BDA were lifted.

When the Chinese conveyed to the administration what Tang had heard from Kim, they emphasized another point as well. In addition to unfreezing the BDA funds, the United States needed to articulate a clear vision of the sort of economic and diplomatic cooperation Washington was prepared to pursue as part of a nuclear deal.

"The Chinese agenda was that unless the U.S. was ready to come forward with some guarantees with respect to economic assistance and other sorts of things," recalled one former senior State Department official, "they were a little bit skeptical about how serious we were."

E ven as they stepped up preparations for a possible missile test, the North Koreans made one last formal appeal for bilateral talks, which contained the hint of a response to the Bush position that had been relayed by Chinese envoy Tang Jiaxuan. On June 1, Pyongyang publicly invited Christopher Hill to visit Pyongyang. In a long statement carried by KCNA, a Foreign Ministry spokesman sent several conciliatory signals. "The DPRK has already made a strategic decision to abandon its nuclear program," the statement said. "We will not even need a single nuclear weapon once we get convinced that the U.S. does not antagonize us and confidence is built between the DPRK and the U.S. . . . We are fully ready to discuss the issues of bilateral relations, peaceful coexistence, the conclusion of a peace agreement, the provision of light-water reactors and other points mentioned in the [September 19] statement along with the issue of abandoning the nuclear program on the principle of 'simultaneous action.' . . . If the U.S has a true political intention to implement the joint statement, we kindly once again invite the head of the U.S. side's delegation to the talks to visit Pyongyang."[4]

The invitation was rejected almost immediately.

"The United States is not going to engage in bilateral negotiations with the government of North Korea," White House spokesman Tony Snow declared.

Instead, President Bush telephoned Hu Jintao in early June and pressed him to use China's influence to urge Pyongyang not to go ahead with a missile test.

By mid-June, North Korea had completed fueling the Taepodong missile at its test site in the eastern part of the country. Photos from U.S. spy satellites showed booster rockets loaded onto a launching pad and liquid fuel tanks fitted onto the missile. The preparation sparked another frantic round of diplomatic efforts to pressure the North not to test, with Condoleezza Rice telephoning the Chinese and Japanese foreign ministers, and UN secretary-general Kofi Annan calling on Pyongyang to show restraint.

In response, on June 21, a senior North Korean Foreign Ministry official declared that Pyongyang no longer felt bound by the missile moratorium. At the same time, however, Pyongyang's deputy permanent UN representative Han Song Ryol held out the prospect that the launch could be put off—if the United States agreed to direct talks.

"We know the U.S. is concerned about our missile test launch," Han told the South Korean news agency Yonhap. "The DPRK as a sovereign state has the right not only to develop, deploy, and test missiles, but also to export them. It is not right for others to tell us to do this or that about our sovereign right." Still, Han continued, "Our position is to solve this situation through discussions."[5]

As tension mounted, President Bush received sharply conflicting advice from three figures who played key roles in handling North Korea policy during the Clinton administration. Former secretary of defense William Perry and former assistant defense secretary Ashton Carter published an op-ed piece in the *Washington Post* calling for military action to destroy the North Korean Taepodong before it was launched.

"We believe diplomacy might have precluded the current situation," Perry and Carter wrote. "But diplomacy has failed, and we cannot sit by and let this deadly threat mature. A successful Taepodong launch, unopposed by the United States, its intended victim, would only embolden North Korea even further. The result would be more nuclear warheads atop more and more missiles."[6]

The following day saw a reply from Jack Pritchard, who had been a key figure in negotiations with Pyongyang that had climaxed in the visit of Clinton's secretary of state Madeleine Albright and had stayed on as special envoy for talks with the North until he quit the Bush administration in 2003. In his own *Post* op-ed, Pritchard wrote, "The missile test is not a violation of anything more than our pride, ripping a gaping hole in the false logic that talking with the North Koreans somehow rewards and empowers them. To the contrary, we should be opening avenues of dialogue with Pyongyang."[7]

President Bush, however, simply repeated warnings that a test would be "unacceptable" and warned that the United States and its Asian allies, especially Japan, "cannot be held hostage to rockets."[8] Meanwhile, the U.S. military told Japan it planned to station Patriot PAC-3 interceptors at the American Air Force base in Kadena, Japan, and was considering deploying the Aegis cruiser *Shiloh*, with its advanced missile defense system, to waters near Japan.

Beijing watched the mounting tension with anxiety. On June 28, Premier Wen Jiabao issued what was, for the cautious Chinese, an unprecedented public warning. "We are paying close attention to the information showing there might be a possible missile-testing launch by North Korea," Wen said. "We hope that the various parties will proceed for the greater interest of maintaining stability on the Korean Peninsula and refrain from taking measures that will worsen the situation." The reference to "restraint" appeared partly to be a reaction to the talk in Washington about a U.S. preemptive strike, but it was also aimed at Pyongyang. Coming from the Chinese, it represented a major public rebuke to the North Koreans.

In Pyongyang, where bowing to outside pressure was not only unthinkable but would likely be seen as the kind of capitulation to foreigners that could undermine Kim Jong Il's authority—especially with the armed forces—the appeal from Wen was ignored.

"What I hear is, Big Brother is telling Little Brother, 'Don't do that,'" Kim Gye Gwan was quoted as saying. "But we are not boys. We are a nuclear power."[9]

J ust before 4:00 A.M. Tokyo time on Wednesday, July 5 (the afternoon of July 4 in Washington), Ambassador Thomas Schieffer was awakened by a phone call from Japan-based U.S. military officials informing him of the missile tests. The embassy immediately put into operation a prearranged plan for liaising with the Japanese that had been worked out in a series of meetings during the preceding weeks between American and Japanese diplomats, military and intelligence officials. Their goal was to avoid a repetition of the fiasco of 1998, when North Korea had launched its first Taepodong missile and U.S.-Japan coordination was so bad that when an American official called to inform the Japan Defense Agency, no one picked up the phone.

This time, Schieffer—a longtime personal friend of President Bush who had been a co-owner with Bush of the Texas Rangers baseball team—drove through the predawn gloom for urgent meetings with Japanese chief cabinet secretary Shinzo Abe and the ministers of defense and foreign affairs. The Japanese prime minister had already spoken with his key security advisers. By 7:00 A.M., both men had made public statements condemning the launch, and Japan's TV networks had interrupted their regularly scheduled programs to broadcast the news.

"This is a very provocative act," Schieffer said. "This is a very dangerous thing that they've done this morning, and we are going to continue to work with our allies and friends around the world, and that's why we're considering taking it to the United Nations."[10]

The first North Korean missile—a short-range Scud—had been launched at 3:33 A.M. local time. It was the same hour in Seoul and Tokyo. The second, a medium-range Rodong, went up at 4:00 A.M. But for another hour—while Ambassador Schieffer was in touch with Washington and Prime Minister Koizumi consulted his closest aides—South Korean President Roh Moo-hyun was asleep. Only after the launch of the long-range Taepodong, at 5:00 A.M., did Roh's advisers decide to awaken him. Moreover, apart from a few brief news flashes, South Korea's TV networks continued with their coverage of World Cup soccer from Europe until nearly 7:00 A.M., and South Korea's National Security Council did not meet until 7:30, well after U.S. and Japanese officials had already spoken to the press. Lee Jong-seok, the former deputy national security adviser who had recently been made minister of unification, explained the response by saying, "Because these missiles were shot toward the East Sea, it was not thought that they posed a direct threat to national security."[11]

The difference in the immediate reactions of the South Korean and Japanese governments reflected a broader gulf between the two most important U.S. allies in Asia over how to respond to North Korea. The South Koreans, used to living with the North Korean threat, much more readily shrugged off a new round of saber rattling. As we have already seen, in the wake of the June 2000 North-South summit, growing numbers of South Koreans had come to view the North Koreans not as enemies but as wayward cousins to be coaxed out of their isolation and poverty with trade, economic assistance, and soothing words. Moreover, many in Seoul saw the current deadlock as less a consequence of Pyongyang's belligerence than the Bush administration's intransigence, and they worried that too harsh a response risked encouraging an even tougher American line.

South Korean officials did eventually condemn the tests and announced that they would withhold 500,000 tons of rice and 100,000 tons of fertilizer the North had sought in aid. Roh himself, however, said nothing publicly about the incident for a week, and the government in Seoul continued to hold high-level consultations with Pyongyang. Barely a week after the test, Unification Minister Lee Jong-seok met North Korea's chief cabinet councilor in the southern port city of Busan. After Lee called on Pyongyang to cease missile launches and dismantle its nuclear program, however, the North's delegate walked out. Still,

Roh's government continued to argue that engagement was the only way to reduce tension.

In Japan, however, the tests set off shock waves, producing widespread anxiety and strong public support for a tough response. Although the launch of the long-range Taepodong had failed, the Japanese government and people were well aware that the medium-range Rodongs, which performed well, could easily reach any target in Japan, including the U.S. bases in Okinawa far to the south. Indeed, with the South Koreans less and less inclined to view the North as a threat, the rattled Japanese—already furious over the abductee issue—were coming to see themselves as the likeliest target of any North Korean missile attack. The sense of vulnerability and anger shaped the Japanese response.

"The most direct threat to Japan is an attack by a Rodong missile with a nuclear warhead," said one Japanese official. "Japan's location is almost equal to Israel if Saddam had nuclear weapons near Tel Aviv."

Within hours of the launches, Japan announced it would ban North Korean officials from visiting Japan and suspend operation of the *Mangyongbong-92*, the only regular ferry service between Japan and North Korea, for six months. "We will consider every type of sanctions possible," Chief Cabinet Secretary Shinzo Abe said.[12] Abe, a prominent right-winger who had built his political career on a hard line toward North Korea, and who was considered the leading candidate to replace the retiring Koizumi in September, also raised the possibility that Japan might consider staging a preemptive attack on North Korea's missile test site. At the same time, the strong public reaction gave new momentum to the effort by Abe and other Japanese rightists to amend the country's pacifist constitution and allow Japan's armed forces to play a more active role.

"The missile tests were very ominous in Japanese eyes," noted a former senior Japanese diplomat. "They changed the Japanese security perception in favor of stronger defense and a stronger U.S.-Japan alliance."

In Seoul, the tough talk from Tokyo set off alarm bells.

"This created a lot of alarm in Korea," noted one senior South Korean official, "because Japan's rearmament and constitutional amendment is a far bigger issue than North Korea's missile test, from the standpoint of the geopolitical landscape of Northeast Asia. So when there was a perception that Japan was taking advantage of the missile crisis to achieve the long-standing political goal of the conservative agenda regarding the use of force, that put us in a very awkward situation."

With South Korea appearing more concerned about Japan's attitude than North Korea's behavior, the Japanese, with strong backing from the

Bush administration, took the lead in pressing for UN sanctions against North Korea. In Tokyo, the driving force was Shinzo Abe. The morning after the tests, Japan introduced the first version of a strongly worded draft resolution at the United Nations. The resolution condemned the tests and demanded an immediate halt to the North's development, deployment, testing, and proliferation of ballistic missiles. It also called for sanctions to prevent North Korea from receiving funds, material, or technology that could aid Pyongyang's missile or nuclear programs. The draft was in the form of a binding resolution under Chapter Seven of the UN Charter—a provision that would make sanctions mandatory and allow the use of force to enforce them.

Along with Japan's UN ambassador Kenzo Oshima, John Bolton—now Washington's envoy to the UN—became the most forceful advocate of the tough Japanese resolution.

The tests had given a strong boost to the hard-line camp. As he worked to drum up support for the strongest possible action, including invoking Chapter Seven, Bolton saw the crisis as an opportunity "to go after the DPRK the way I wished I had been able to do so from the start."[13]

For his part, President Bush made clear there was no chance of bilateral talks with Pyongyang, telling reporters he would not "get caught in the trap of sitting alone with North Korea at the table."[14]

Even among administration moderates, moreover, the test was seen as an outrageous provocation that required a tough response.

"The North Koreans didn't want to work the diplomatic side of this," observed State Department counselor Philip Zelikow, "so they were going to work the 'be scared of us' side of this. And we decided we needed to have a strong response."

Immediately after the tests, Bush dispatched Christopher Hill to Asia to consult with the Chinese, Japanese, and South Koreans. Before leaving, Bush gave Hill a message to deliver in Beijing. "You tell the Chinese I can't solve this," the president said to Hill. "They need to solve this."

In an effort to pressure Beijing, before his departure Hill publicly pointed out that Pyongyang had ignored Chinese calls for restraint.

"China said, 'Don't do it,' and the DPRK went ahead and did it," Hill said. "Now we need for China to be very firm about what's acceptable behavior and what's not acceptable behavior."[15]

Bush himself added to the pressure for Beijing to get tough, telling Chinese president Hu Jintao in a phone call that "the great Chinese people have been slapped in the face by North Korea."[16]

But at the United Nation, both the Chinese and the Russians quickly made clear they would not accept the Japanese-U.S. resolution—especially the reference to Chapter Seven. After the U.S. invasion of Iraq, both Beijing and Moscow had serious concerns about what they saw as the Bush administration's preference for using military means to resolve international disputes, and neither wanted to give Washington any excuse for military action against North Korea. South Korea shared similar concerns and also opposed the original draft.

In the days after the missile tests, Condoleezza Rice had several phone conversations with Chinese foreign minister Li Zhaoxing, which she described to colleagues as "disappointing" and "unpleasant." In one conversation, she said she had been "pretty raw" with Li, who had warned Beijing would veto the draft resolution in its current form.[17]

Publicly, a Chinese Foreign Ministry spokeswoman criticized the proposal as "an overreaction. If approved, it will aggravate contradictions and increase tension. It will harm peace and stability in the Korean peninsula and the Northeast Asia region, and hurt efforts to resume six-party talks as well as lead to the UN Security Council splitting."[18] Convinced that a sanctions resolution would be counterproductive, China's UN ambassador Wang Guangya urged instead that a much milder, nonbinding statement from the Security Council's president be adopted. Wang reiterated the threat Li Zhaoxing had made—that China would use its veto to block a tougher resolution.

For his part, Bolton was not too bothered by the Chinese threat. If China did exercise its veto, he wrote in his memoirs, "it would demonstrate that the Security Council was not up to the job, freeing us to do what we chose to do outside the UN."[19]

Despite their public concerns about American intentions, privately, the Chinese were furious at the North Koreans—as much, it appeared, for ignoring appeals for restraint from a country that had long viewed itself as North Korea's "older brother" as for the potentially worrying military implications of the tests. In a meeting with Dennis Wilder, the National Security Council's senior director for Asia, a high-ranking Chinese general vented his anger. "After all we've done for them," the general fumed, "they couldn't give us any warning they were going to do this. How dare they?"

Shortly after the test, President Hu Jintao, in a meeting in Beijing with the vice president of North Korea's parliament, said, "China opposes any actions that will worsen the situation and hopes that all relevant parties will do more things conducive to the peace and stability of the region."[20] For the Chinese leader, who rarely spoke publicly on the North Korea issue, the statement was a firm rebuke.

Hu followed this public comment by sending Deputy Foreign Minister Wu Dawei, who had led the Chinese delegation at the six-party talks, to Pyongyang along with Deputy Prime Minister Hui Liangyu. Hoping to bring the North Koreans around, the Chinese requested, and Washington and Tokyo agreed, to delay any Security Council vote on the resolution until the outcome of this Chinese diplomatic mission was clear. But although Wu and Hui spent several days in Pyongyang, Kim Jong Il, in what appeared to be a calculated snub, refused to see them. The Chinese envoys left the North Korean capital empty-handed.

The North Korean tests and subsequent behavior and the feverish press coverage it generated, especially in Japan and the United States, fueled the perception of Kim Jong Il as reckless and bellicose. Part of Pyongyang's motivation appeared to be to send a signal that North Korea would not bow to pressure from any quarter, whether it was the "hostile" Americans and Japanese or the "fraternal" Chinese. But in a long statement carried by KCNA and issued shortly after the tests, a spokesman for North Korea's Foreign Ministry linked the launches to the absence of direct dialogue with Washington and the lack of progress in normalizing Pyongyang's relations with Tokyo.

The statement noted that the moratorium on missile tests which the North agreed to in 1999 "was valid only when the DPRK-U.S. dialogue was under way. The Bush administration, however, scrapped all the agreements its preceding administration concluded with the DPRK and totally scuttled the bilateral dialogue."

The statement also justified the tests as a response to American financial pressure, saying, "The DPRK's missile development, test-fire, manufacture and deployment, therefore, serve as a key to keeping the balance of force and preserving peace and stability in Northeast Asia."

Significantly, however, the statement left open the possibility of a return to negotiations. "The DPRK remains unchanged in its will to denuclearize the Korean Peninsula in a negotiated peaceful manner just as it committed itself in the September 19 joint statement of the six-party talks." But, in typical blustering fashion, it made clear Pyongyang would consider even stronger measures if the United States did not meet its demand for bilateral negotiations. "The DPRK will have no option but to take stronger physical actions of other forms, should any other country dare take issue with the exercises and put pressure upon it."[21]

Meanwhile, negotiations at the UN became increasingly contentious. In a compromise gesture, China and Russia abandoned their opposition to a formal resolution and introduced their own draft, which did not include the sweeping sanctions in the Japanese version or the reference to Chapter Seven. The United States and Japan rejected it.

"We have felt from the time we learned of the launch of North Korean missiles that a Chapter Seven binding resolution is necessary because we want to bind North Korea," said U.S. ambassador John Bolton.

"A quick glance at the text [of the Chinese and Russian resolution] shows that there are very serious gaps on very important issues," noted Japan's envoy Kenzo Oshima. "I believe that it will be very difficult for us to accept that as it is."[22]

Intense negotiations followed. In the wake of the failed Chinese diplomatic mission to Pyongyang, China and Russia finally agreed to accept tougher language on the specific sanctions. In return, though, they insisted that all mention of Chapter Seven be dropped. The result was that instead of using the milder language initially put forward by Beijing and Moscow, which said the council "calls upon" North Korea to halt its missile activities and "urges" member states to prevent the transfer of technology or material that would help the North's WMD programs, the final version used the much stronger terms "demands" and "requires." But in deference to Chinese and Russian concerns, the resolution also dropped the original U.S.- and Japanese-backed reference to the "development, testing, deployment and proliferation of ballistic missiles," using instead the milder language of "all activities related to its ballistic missile program."[23] John Bolton strongly objected to the concessions but was overruled by Condoleezza Rice and the White House, who believed that it was more important to win China's support for the resolution, even with somewhat watered-down language.

On July 15, the Security Council, in a unanimous vote, passed Resolution 1695. The administration characterized even the watered-down document as an important achievement that would add significantly to the pressure on Pyongyang. Afterward, John Bolton said the resolution "sends an unequivocal, unambiguous and unanimous message to the government in Pyongyang: Suspend your ballistic missile program, stop your procurement of materials related to weapons of mass destruction, and implement your September 2005 commitment to verifiably dismantle your nuclear weapons and existing nuclear programs."[24]

Unquestionably, the fact that even the Chinese and the Russians signed onto a resolution criticizing North Korea was a major diplomatic step. Still, the Chinese, South Koreans, and Russians showed no meaningful inclination to curb their economic links with North Korea, ensuring that Pyongyang would in all likelihood be able to ride out increased international pressure. In his memoirs, Bolton acknowledged, "We were in fact caving in to the threat of a Chinese veto."[25]

For his part, North Korea's UN envoy Pak Gil Yon said his country "totally rejects the resolution." Pak then got up from the council's horseshoe-shaped table and stalked out of the room. The next day, a North Korean Foreign Ministry spokesman said, "Our republic will bolster its war deterrent for self-defense in every way by all means and methods now that the situation has reached the worst phase due to the extremely hostile act of the U.S."[26]

The next bombshell from Pyongyang came in a North Korean Foreign Ministry announcement on October 3, 2006.

"The U.S.'s extreme threat of a nuclear war and sanctions and pressure," it said, "compel the DPRK to conduct a nuclear test." No date was given, but consistent with its past behavior, North Korea was telegraphing its intentions in advance.

Lost in the alarmist headlines, however, was the statement's final line. "There is no change in the principled stand of the DPRK to materialize the denuclearization of the peninsula through dialogue and negotiation."[27]

Concern about a possible nuclear test had arisen almost immediately after the missile tests. By early August, U.S. intelligence had begun to pick up the first signs of telltale activity, including "suspicious" vehicle movements and the unloading of long rolls of cables at what Washington believed was an underground test facility in the northeastern part of North Korea. Along with the initial press leaks, the language some U.S. officials used in discussing the issue was tough. If there was a test, one unidentified senior official told ABC News, "We would try to hermetically seal the hermit kingdom." The same official said that much more stringent sanctions—even a naval blockade—would be considered.[28]

The announcement of the planned test underscored the fact that, for all its bluster, Pyongyang's behavior was becoming increasingly predictable. Throughout the spring, the North had sought bilateral talks and a willingness by the Bush administration to end the sanctions against Banco Delta Asia. With little sign of movement, Pyongyang very openly prepared for and then staged the missile tests. The move fit the "tit for tat" pattern of engaging when Washington was prepared to talk and ratcheting up the pressure when the United States tried to get tough. And in ignoring appeals for restraint from the United States, South Korea, China, and others, the North was also signaling that it would not bow to external pressure from any source.

"If the North Koreans feel they are not getting interaction with the U.S.," observed Chuck Kartman, the Clinton administration's lead negotiator with the North, "they tend to do things to get our attention. The tools that they have are all bad ones. They really don't have anything else."[29]

Now, a similar pattern was repeating itself. With Washington seeking to step up enforcement of the sanctions called for in the July 2006 UN resolution and showing no interest in face-to-face talks, Pyongyang was getting ready to take the step the United States and the rest of the international community most feared—testing a nuclear bomb.

As tension mounted, so did the frustration in Washington at the limited policy options available to turn the situation around. A military strike had, for all practical purposes, long ago been ruled out. The United States had insufficient intelligence to identify all the North's nuclear sites. The missile launches had shown that Pyongyang had the capability to hit targets in South Korea and Japan, and if the Taepodong worked, possibly the continental United States. Moreover, China, South Korea, and Russia—three critical players in the region—were all vehemently opposed to such a step. At the same time, the financial pressure and talk of intensified sanctions, while clearly causing some pain in Pyongyang, showed little sign of bringing Kim Jong Il's regime to heel.

It was against this backdrop that Washington was the scene of what one senior official described as "trench warfare" in August and September 2006. The combatants were familiar. On the hard-line side stood Robert Joseph, the State Department's under secretary for arms control, UN ambassador John Bolton, Will Tobey and John Rood at the NSC, and the office of Vice President Cheney. But now, Christopher Hill and his State Department allies, increasingly backed by Condoleezza Rice, slowly began to gain the upper hand.

"People were arguing that North Korea is so predictable," said one senior State Department official, "that if we don't engage them, first, we have the missile tests, and then there will be a nuclear test. If we keep on this way, there will be nothing we can do to stop the North Koreans."

One reason for the gradual weakening of the hard-liners' position was the war in Iraq. By the summer of 2006, the war had become a bloody quagmire. Public opposition was growing, the president's popularity ratings were slumping, and polls showed it was a potent issue for Democratic Party candidates running in the fall congressional elections. The Iraqi mess was increasingly discrediting the war's strongest advocates, who were also among the leading supporters of being tough on North Korea, and eroding their clout within the administration.

"I think it is the kind of fallout that comes from Iraq turning into a total disaster," observed Brent Scowcroft, who served as national security adviser in the administration of George H. W. Bush, "and therefore undermining all of the statements in favor of regime change."

Under the circumstances, a less hawkish approach that might offer a way out of the North Korea nuclear deadlock became an increasingly attractive prospect within the administration.

"They need something that smacks of success," observed a senior Pentagon official involved with Asia policy. "Rice's Middle East initiatives have come up completely bust. Iran is a bust. Iraq is Iraq. Hill said, 'Give me some running room and I'll bring you back something.' She sold it to Bush, and off they went."

The internal debate in Washington was also influenced by intense pressure from China and especially South Korea for the United States to show some flexibility in order to get the North to return to the six-party talks. In a series of meetings with Hill, Rice, and other senior officials, South Korea's national security adviser, Song Min-soon (who was an old friend of Hill's from the days when both men served as ambassadors in Poland), led the way.

"The South Koreans would say, 'Wind up Banco Delta Asia,'" recalled one U.S. official involved in the process. "In return, the North Koreans will freeze [the Yongbyon reactor]. Then we will have to give fuel oil." That, the South Koreans argued, was how to jump-start talks they felt that Washington, by making face-to-face dialogue with Pyongyang a reward rather than a diplomatic tool, was largely responsible for undermining.

The Bush administration felt "it was more important not to have bilateral negotiations with North Korea than letting them get away with nuclear weapons," complained one exasperated senior South Korean official. "It was more important to crack down on their illicit activities than stopping them from building a nuclear arsenal."

During a state visit in mid-September, South Korean president Roh Moo-hyun pushed President Bush to end the sanctions and reengage with Pyongyang. But in that session and in other meetings, administration officials stuck to the familiar public line that the BDA sanctions were a law enforcement issue and could not be modified or ended for political reasons. Privately, however, work began on exploring ways to bring the episode to a close. In this process, Hill was backed by State Department counselor Philip Zelikow. Although he had little clout in the bureaucracy, Zelikow had the ear of Condoleezza Rice.

In September 2006, Zelikow drafted some ideas for Rice on how to get out of the BDA situation. First, he recalled in an interview, he argued the United

States should recognize that "the destruction of BDA had achieved its objective." BDA was an "exemplary strike that had already achieved, and was continuing to achieve, the desired informal effect on the DPRK's access to the international financial system."

Second, Zelikow urged that an appropriate way be found for the Macau financial authorities to distribute the impounded BDA funds. And, he urged, these things should be done "in a way that reinforced and restarted our overall diplomatic strategy."

Zelikow's ideas were shared with the South Koreans. While no action was taken, the entire process helped lay the groundwork for what would come later.

Meanwhile, the Chinese—especially Vice Foreign Minister Wu Dawei—were reinforcing what the South Koreans were telling the Bush administration.

"Their goals were the same," said one high-ranking State Department official. "They both thought the BDA business was ridiculous and that the U.S. position was not a good one."


In the days immediately after North Korea's October 3 announcement, the warnings not to conduct a nuclear test came form every quarter. The UN Security Council issued a statement saying "a nuclear test, if carried out by the DPRK, would represent a clear threat to international peace and security and that, should the DPRK ignore calls of the international community, the Security Council will act consistent with its responsibility under the Charter of the United Nations."[30]

In Seoul, President Roh Moo-hyun ordered the South Korean government to send a "grave warning" to Pyongyang about the consequences of a test. And China's UN ambassador, Wang Guangya, declared that "no one is going to protect North Korea" if it went ahead with "bad behavior." Wang continued, "If the North Koreans do have a test, I think that they have to realize they will face serious consequences."[31] Privately, the Chinese were making the same point to Pyongyang.

In Washington, Christopher Hill struggled with a difficult balancing act. As a leading voice for engagement, he found his position within the Bush administration weakened by the North's saber rattling. Almost as if to overcompensate, Hill issued a series of tough public warnings.

"North Korea can have a future or it can have these weapons," he declared. "It can't have both. We are not going to live with a nuclear North Korea. We are not going to accept it."[32] Precisely what it meant for the United States to refuse to "live with" a nuclear North Korea was never spelled out.

At the same time, Bush's top advisers held a series of emergency meetings to discuss how to respond. Vice President Cheney was reportedly adamant that the United States should not agree to any bilateral talks with the North. Some reports quoted hard-line NSC officials as saying that if the North went ahead with a nuclear test, the United States would implement sanctions so tough they would "shut everything down."[33]

The administration also decided to convey a warning directly to North Korea's diplomats at the United Nations. But so rigid was Washington's prohibition against bilateral meetings with the North Koreans that instead of traveling to New York for a face-to-face confrontation, the head of the State Department's Korea Desk, Sung Kim, delivered the warning—on the telephone.

# 17

# THE BOMB

THE HEADS-UP CAME FROM THE CHINESE. ON THE MORNING of Monday, October 9, 2006 (Sunday evening Washington time), North Korean officials informed the Chinese embassy in Pyongyang that a nuclear test was imminent. In Beijing, the Chinese immediately informed the U.S. Embassy, which passed the word to Washington. National Security Adviser Stephen Hadley alerted President Bush. In the White House Situation Room—the 5,000-square-foot complex in the basement of the West Wing, packed with computers, plasma screens, and secure communications facilities—senior administration officials gathered to monitor developments.

Twenty minutes after the alert, at 10:36 A.M. Korea time, seismic monitors detected an explosion deep inside a mountain at the Punggye test site near Kilju City, 385 kilometers northeast of Pyongyang and 130 kilometers from the country's border with Russia. The U.S. Geological Survey reported that twenty seismic stations—from China, Japan, and South Korea to Australia, Ukraine, and Nevada—picked up the shockwave from the blast, which produced a tremor of 4.2 magnitude. Immediately, a U.S. Air Force WC-135 Constant Phoenix atmospheric collection aircraft, equipped with special sensors to collect information from radioactive clouds after tests, was deployed. Other agencies, including the CIA, the Defense Intelligence Agency, the Energy Department, the National Security Agency, and the National Geospatial Intelligence Agency, which studies satellite imagery, also went into action.

All of them were reporting to former CIA operative Joseph DeTrani.

In late 2005, DeTrani—who had functioned as Christopher Hill's deputy in the negotiations which produced the September 19 Declaration—had left his position as special envoy for talks with North Korea to take up a newly created position. Working for Director of National Intelligence John Negroponte, he became the DNI's first "mission manager" for North Korea. His responsibility now was to coordinate all intelligence efforts on the test, issuing twice-daily summaries and briefing the White House, the Pentagon, and the State Department.

Even for a first nuclear test, the blast was unusually small—barely half a kiloton, equivalent to 500 tons of TNT. The initial intelligence reports even questioned whether it had actually been a nuclear explosion. In a matter of days, however, air samples and other technical analysis showed that the explosion had indeed been produced by a nuclear device—plutonium-based, like the much larger (21–23 kiloton) plutonium bomb that the United States had dropped on Nagasaki, Japan, in August 1945. Even if only partially successful, the test showed that North Korean scientists had basically mastered nuclear weapons and design technology, and evidently had enough weapons-grade plutonium to be able to stage a test and have some left over to make other bombs.

Whatever the technical shortcomings of the event, the political fallout was enormous. In an instant, any remaining ambiguity about the North's nuclear capability disappeared. Kim Jong Il's regime had become the world's eighth declared nuclear power, joining the United States, Britain, France, Russia, China, India, and Pakistan. The implications were alarming. The global nuclear nonproliferation regime suffered a serious blow just as tensions over Iran's nuclear ambitions were increasing. Now North Korea—a charter member of Bush's Axis of Evil, with its long history of missile sales and military cooperation with some of the world's most unsavory regimes—was flaunting a nuclear capability that it might be tempted to sell to countries like Iran or Syria, or—even worse—to terrorist groups.

For the Bush administration, the test represented the utter failure of its entire approach to North Korea. During the president's six years in office the United States had used warnings, threats, sanctions, muscle flexing, and half-hearted diplomacy. Just in the past few days, administration officials had repeatedly declared that a test would be "intolerable" and "unacceptable." Yet the United States had been unable to prevent Kim Jong Il from quitting the Non-Proliferation Treaty, evicting international inspectors, restarting the frozen reactor, reprocessing more spent fuel into weapons-grade plutonium, breaking its eight-year moratorium to test missiles—including an ICBM that could conceivably reach the continental United States—and boycotting the six-party talks.

Now, in spite of warnings from almost every quarter, North Korea had defied the international community and conducted a nuclear test.

"What does that communicate to Iran and the rest of world?" asked Harvard University professor Graham Allison, author of a book on nuclear terrorism. "Is it possible to communicate to Kim credibly that if he sells a bomb to Osama bin Laden, that's it?"[1]

Now a President who—for all the administration's tough posturing—had been unwilling to set firm "red lines" finally did so.

"The transfer of nuclear weapons or material by North Korea to states or nonstate entities," though not technical know-how, President Bush said at a press conference twelve hours after the test, "would be considered a grave threat to the United States, and we would hold North Korea fully accountable for the consequences of such action."[2]

But the blast yet again produced the sort of mixed signals that had been the hallmark of the Bush administration's gyrations on North Korea policy for so many years. Laying down his new "red line," the president said the United States "reserves all options to defend our friends and our interests in the region against the threats from North Korea."[3]

At the same time, though, he stressed that "the United States remains committed to diplomacy." To emphasize his point, Bush used the word "diplomacy" eleven times in his comments on the North Korean situation.[4]

John Bolton and other hard-liners responded very differently. To them, the test meant the end of efforts to resolve the issue through negotiations.

"The only solace conservatives found in the North's test," he wrote, "was that, finally, it would be impossible for the EAPeasers [the advocates of engagement in the State Department's Bureau of East Asia and Pacific Affairs] to continue their solicitous approach to the DPRK."[5]

The morning after the test, Bolton—with Condoleezza Rice's authorization—circulated a draft resolution at the UN Security Council outlining tough new measures against North Korea. These included financial and trade sanctions, an arms embargo, a ban on luxury goods, and most important, the authorization of the inspection of cargo entering and leaving the North. Bolton hoped the move would, in effect, constitute UN endorsement for his cherished Proliferation Security Initiative, the effort that began in 2005 to combat the spread of weapons of mass destruction by allowing the United States and its allies to search ships and planes suspected of carrying materials for missiles or nuclear, chemical, and biological weapons.

In Japan, the reaction to the test was even stronger. The specter of Kim Jong Il's regime eventually being able to mount a nuclear warhead on a missile that could reach Tokyo generated widespread alarm. At the UN, Japan's envoy sought to toughen the U.S. resolution by calling for a ban on all North Korean exports and on the movement of North Korean planes or ships. At home, Prime Minister Shinzo Abe, who had been in office less than a month, unilaterally implemented similar measures, banning North Korean imports—Japan was the third-largest importer of North Korean goods, after China and South Korea— and closing Japan's ports to North Korean ships.

For China, the test amounted to a brusque slap in the face from a no-longer compliant "younger brother." Beijing was outraged. Just hours after the test, the Chinese Foreign Ministry issued a strongly worded condemnation, characterizing the North's behavior as "brazen." In Chinese, the word *hanran*—meaning "brazen" or "flagrant"—was normally reserved for denouncing the most offensive behavior of political rivals or enemies. The Chinese statement, however, also called for calm and urged all parties to resolve the issue through "consultation and dialogue."

Nonetheless, an angry President Hu Jintao immediately dispatched Foreign Minister Li Zhaoxing to talk to the North Koreans. Sources familiar with Li's meeting with senior North Korean officials say it was "one of the roughest meetings ever between Chinese and North Koreans." Beijing felt the North had violated a fundamental understanding in their relationship, which was never to conduct a nuclear test without prior consultation.

"Kim had personally told Chinese leaders that he was committed to denuclearization," said one Chinese official. "It was his father's decision. The father's decision was more important than the son's. Kim wanted to express his sincerity in denuclearization by using his father's name. We understood this. But they did the nuclear test. They violated their commitment."

According to one source, Li Zhaoxing told the North Koreans, "You've gone over the line. This is totally unacceptable. You have to promise this won't happen again."

One sign of Beijing's anger came in an encounter at the White House shortly after the test. A delegation from the People's Liberation Army happened to be in Washington on a previously scheduled visit. The highest-ranking Chinese general, who was known to be close to Hu Jintao, was invited to meet privately with National Security Adviser Stephen Hadley. During the meeting, which was never made public, President Bush stopped by. The general told Bush and Hadley that both prior to and after the test, the PLA had asked their North Korean counterparts for information and got no response.

"This Chinese general," according to a senior administration official, "was saying that, 'They're out of control, they're just totally out of control.' And he was saying, 'It's not the same sort of relationship.'"

China was upset not simply because Pyongyang had ignored appeals for restraint. The nuclear test had the potential to fundamentally alter the strategic landscape in Northeast Asia by setting off what China saw as a nightmare scenario—a regional arms race that would prompt Japan, Beijing's leading regional rival, to consider developing its own nuclear capability.

Indeed, Pyongyang's test did trigger calls from some senior Japanese government officials to begin public discussion of this long-taboo topic. Among those urging a national debate on whether Japan should develop its own nuclear weapons were Shoichi Nakagawa, the policy chief of the ruling Liberal Democratic Party and a close friend of Prime Minister Abe, as well as the hawkish foreign minister, Taro Aso.[6] With a large supply of plutonium from its extensive nuclear power program, and boasting a space rocket capability, Japan was widely believed capable of implementing a sophisticated nuclear weapons program in a matter of months.

As the only nation ever to suffer a nuclear attack, the calls struck a sensitive nerve. With his allies having put the issue on the political agenda, Prime Minister Abe moved swiftly to reaffirm Japan's nonnuclear status, and most observers were quick to dismiss the idea as far-fetched. "Japan going nuclear is completely unrealistic because the so-called nuclear allergy due to Hiroshima and Nagasaki is so deeply felt," noted one Japan Defense Agency official. But in the region— especially in South Korea and China, where memories of Japan's militaristic past remained fresh—there was widespread alarm.

For South Korean president Roh Moo-hyun, who had staked his entire reputation on engaging North Korea and had made a strong appeal to Pyongyang not to go ahead, the test was a sharp personal rebuff. An angry Roh immediately called for "stern measures" and indicated he would have to rethink his entire approach toward reconciliation with the North. Seoul immediately announced it would halt humanitarian aid shipments to Pyongyang.

"He had tried so hard to get North Korea to denuclearize," noted one Seoul-based diplomat. "He had drawn a red line, and had said publicly if there was a test it would not be possible to continue with business as usual. So he responded with anger as if he had been personally insulted."

The test fueled intense speculation about Kim Jong Il's motives for taking such a dramatic action. Some analysts argued that Kim needed to placate the military—widely believed to be the most hard-line institution in North Korea—in order to maintain his hold on power. Others noted that the day after the test was the 61st anniversary of the founding of the ruling Korean Workers' Party, and that Kim may have intended to use the test to rally public support and stir nationalistic sentiment. October 9 itself was also the day on which the UN Security Council confirmed the nomination of South Korea's Foreign Minister Ban Ki-moon to succeed Kofi Annan as the U.N.'s new secretary-general, and there was even some speculation the test was in part intended to spoil the South Korean diplomat's big moment.

There is no way to know for sure. In any case, on October 11, North Korea's Foreign Ministry released a statement that linked the test directly to its frustration with the Bush administration, while signaling—as it had done after the missile tests—that it still wanted to deal.

"The DPRK's nuclear test was entirely attributable to the U.S. nuclear threat, sanctions, and pressure," the statement said. Responding to President Bush's new "red line," the statement continued, "The DPRK will never use nuclear weapons first but strictly prohibit any threat of nuclear weapons and nuclear transfer. . . . Although the DPRK conducted the nuclear test due to the United States, it still remains unchanged in its will to denuclearize the peninsula through dialogue and negotiations. The DPRK is ready for both dialogue and confrontation."[7]

But most likely of all, the test was a blunt way of telling Washington "we don't care about your threats or sanctions. If you keep treating us like an enemy, we will keep arming. If you reverse course, so will we."

"The purpose of the missile test," concluded a veteran U.S. intelligence analyst, "was to shock the U.S. into negotiations."

Not apparent in the statement, but clearly evident in Pyongyang's behavior, was a second message. With the test conducted in open defiance of vocal and public Chinese objections, Pyongyang clearly wanted to disabuse the United States of the notion that China would be able to exert leverage to force a change in Pyongyang's behavior.

At the United Nations, there were tense negotiations over the final language of a resolution condemning the nuclear test. As had been the case after the missile tests, China and Russia, despite their alarm at Pyongyang's action, demanded that some of the harshest provisions be softened. The most contentious issues were a clause authorizing all countries to inspect cargo going in and out of North Korea and the invoking of Chapter Seven of the UN Charter. The Chinese and Russians worried that the Chapter Seven provision, which made implementing the sanctions mandatory, could be seen as a justification for the use of force. An irritated John Bolton described their attitude as a "brick wall of opposition."[8]

Forced to compromise, the United States and Japan agreed to drop Tokyo's proposal to ban North Korean aircraft from taking off or landing in other countries. The call for a freeze on North Korean assets linked to the country's missile and nuclear programs was retained, but a reference to freezing assets from other illicit activities—such as counterfeiting, money laundering, and narcotics—was dropped. In addition, a reference to Article 41 of the UN Charter was inserted, permitting only "means not involving the use of force" to implement any of the approved measures. The document's wording was also changed to say that inspections would be "cooperative" with local authorities, and new limits were placed on the kinds of cargo that could be inspected.

Still, when Resolution 1716 passed unanimously on October 15, 2006, it was the toughest international action taken against North Korea since the end of the Korean War. The final version denounced the nuclear test as a "clear threat to international peace and security" and demanded that North Korea end its programs to produce nuclear weapons, ballistic missiles, and other weapons of mass destruction. The resolution called the North's missile trade "illicit" and required all countries to block the sale or transfer of material related to North Korea's nuclear, missile, and unconventional weapons programs, banned North Korea from exporting such weapons, barred Pyongyang from importing luxury goods, and authorized inspections of cargo going into and out of the country.

To some in Washington, especially those in the hard-line camp, the U.N. resolution provided the justification for an escalation of pressure on North Korea. As one senior official recalled, "There were some people who felt—now is the time to really sock it to them."

And there were hopes that if the measures outlined in Resolution 1716 were aggressively implemented, they might trigger not just a change in North Korean policy but the collapse of the Kim Jong Il regime. Even President Bush, at least emotionally, shared such a hope. At one meeting, he exclaimed, "We want him to get rid of his nukes, and if he doesn't get rid of his nukes, we have to get rid of him!"

But the prospect that sanctions might topple Kim Jong Il fueled an ongoing debate in Washington about whether such an outcome, however emotionally satisfying, might make an already worrying situation even more dangerous. Critics of squeezing Pyongyang argued that, ironically, regime change and the subsequent chaos would—by raising the prospect of a internal fight over control of North Korea's nuclear arsenal—increase rather than decrease the possibility that nuclear material or know-how might fall into the hands of other rogue states or terrorist groups.

One such voice was Robin "Sak" Sakoda, who had served as chief of staff for Richard Armitage in the Bush administration's first term. At a Washington think-tank conference shortly after the test, he warned that "too much pressure on North Korea risks making the situation worse than now . . . perhaps collapse, refugees, and no control of North Korea's nukes and missiles. Because of the risk of collapse, there must be caution about how much pressure, how much we can squeeze North Korea."[9]

His views were echoed by a longtime State Department Northeast Asia expert. "The ultimate irony is that, for all the Bolton hype, the scariest scenario you can come up with is a collapse scenario," he said. "That's the moment you have to worry."

Indeed, the nuclear test threw into stark relief the three choices facing the Bush administration—none of them, from the president's perspective, attractive. The first was the use of force to destroy either North Korea's nuclear capability or the regime itself. But with the United States uncertain of the location of key nuclear stockpiles—and any attack almost guaranteed to produce North Korean reprisals that could draw in South Korea, or even China—that choice was, for all practical purposes, off the table.

The second option was stepped-up unilateral sanctions. But North Korea was used to poverty, hunger, and isolation, and with both South Korea and China committed to preventing North Korea from collapsing, it was far from clear that any punitive measures, even those backed by the force of a UN resolution, would have enough support to be effective.

"It became evident that trying to shut all the windows and doors and lock them in a box was not going to change North Korea," noted one American official. "These are tough people, their threshold for pain is so much higher than we could ever fathom."

The third option was real negotiation, with genuine give-and-take in which North Korea would get real benefits—including movement away from enmity to normalization, aid, and ultimately political recognition—in exchange for meaningful steps toward denuclearization. This approach had long been advocated by Christopher Hill, and both Rice and Bush at various points had indicated some support. But administration hard-liners remained adamantly opposed to negotiations, and for the past year, emboldened by North Korea's provocative steps, they had managed to undermine any efforts to move the diplomatic process along.

In the wake of the nuclear test, however, even leading Republicans were calling on the Bush administration to reverse course and agree to hold direct talks with North Korea. Among those urging such a step were Richard Lugar, chairman of the Senate Foreign Relations Committee, and Pennsylvania's Arlen Specter.

"Let's talk to them," Specter urged Bush. "The issue is serious enough with

North Korea, with their having nuclear weapons and the capability to deliver them, that I think we ought to use every alternative, including direct bilateral talks."[10]

"You don't give away anything," said James Baker, who had served as secretary of state in the administration of the president's father. "In my view, it is not appeasement to talk to your enemies."[11]

T he week after the UN resolution was passed, Condoleezza Rice set off for Japan, South Korea, and China. One of her goals was to reaffirm that Japan and South Korea still remained under the U.S. nuclear umbrella—a particularly important point in Tokyo, where such reassurance was critical in order to discourage further talk about Japan's developing its own nuclear capability. But the reassurances did not address the larger question: by failing to deal with North Korea, Washington had put Japan's security in jeopardy.

Rice's larger aim, as she spelled out before her departure, was to push for the aggressive implementation of the UN sanctions. "As North Korea scorns the international community," she said, "we will collectively isolate North Korea from the benefits of participation in that community. North Korea cannot endanger the world and then expect other nations to conduct business as usual in arms or missile parts. It cannot destabilize the international system and then expect to exploit elaborate financial networks built for peaceful commerce. Resolution 1716 points the way. We expect every member of the international community to fully implement all aspects of this resolution."[12]

Rice also talked about the need to "expand defensive measures" against North Korea, and in Japan, she found the Abe government eager to intensify already close military cooperation with the United States.

"As a result of the NK nuclear test, the Japan-U.S. relationship is stronger than ever before," said the U.S. ambassador to Japan, Thomas Schieffer. "The Japan-U.S. alliance is becoming more concrete every day, and much less abstract."

Numerous U.S.-Japanese initiatives in security cooperation received a big boost, especially a joint effort to develop ballistic missile defenses and moves to co-locate American and Japanese air-defense commands.

"Kim Jong Il gave us a wonderful case for increased ballistic missile defense cooperation," noted a State Department official.

A s Rice arrived in South Korea, however, accompanied by Japanese foreign minister Taro Aso, what Washington had hoped would be a demonstration of tripartite solidarity against North Korean nuclear adventurism became instead evidence of the yawning gap between the three ostensible allies. Although

President Roh had swiftly condemned the nuclear test, he resisted pressure from Rice for the aggressive implementation of sanctions.

"The chemistry in their meeting was poor," recalled one official who was there.

Roh was blunt with the secretary of state. "You Americans keep on saying you want this resolved diplomatically," he told her, "but you are always putting up more hurdles." Roh complained specifically about the U.S. unwillingness to resolve the Banco Delta Asia investigation and the fact that Christopher Hill was not being allowed to talk directly to the North Koreans or go to Pyongyang.

Roh was particularly unyielding on a key U.S. demand—that Seoul shut down two projects that had come to symbolize the South Korean president's unwavering commitment to engagement and had also become a vital source of much-needed foreign exchange for Pyongyang. The first was a resort that had been built at North Korea's scenic Mt. Kumgang by the South Korean company Hyundai Asan, which was estimated to provide the North with close to half a billion dollars a year, and the Kaesong economic zone, where North Korean workers manufactured goods for South Korean companies.[13] The South Korean government, however, bluntly told Rice it had no intention of terminating either project or ending its broader contacts with the North Korean regime.

"These [projects] are the last bridge to the North," said one senior South Korean official, "and there was a reluctance to burn all bridges to the North, to put everything on the line to pressure North Korea into abandoning nuclear weapons."

Moreover, concerned that searching North Korean ships risked the danger of clashes between North and South, Roh also rebuffed American requests to join the Proliferation Security Initiative.

"We are closer to the source of the threat," said a South Korean diplomat, "and that makes us more averse to risk-taking. As a front-line state, we're inclined to be more cautious in taking the risks of direct confrontation on the high seas or in our territorial waters with North Korean vessels which are suspected of carrying contraband materials."

Rice was "pissed off," said one senior State Department official. "It was a tough visit."

Although Roh held his ground, the North's test also clearly demonstrated that his conciliatory policies had not prevented Kim Jong Il from either expanding his nuclear arsenal or testing a bomb. Leaders of the opposition Grand National Party (GNP) denounced Roh and demanded he take tougher measures, even though the opposition also acknowledged that engagement in some form would remain the guiding principle of South Korean policy.

Under pressure both at home and from Washington, in late October, several key South Korean figures closely identified with Roh's engagement policy resigned. The most notable casualty was Seoul's point man on North Korean policy, unification minister Lee Jong-seok, a longtime critic of the United States and an advocate of reconciliation with the North at almost any price.

At the same time, with the imminent departure of Foreign Minister Ban Ki-moon to become Kofi Annan's replacement as UN secretary-general, the pragmatic Song Min-soon—the former ambassador and veteran foreign ministry official who had known Hill from their days in Warsaw—was named as the new foreign minister.

By the time Rice arrived in Beijing, it was becoming clear that her effort to enlist Washington's Asian partners in a united front to ratchet up the pressure on North Korea was failing. Even in Japan, for all the anger at the test, cooler heads seemed to be prevailing. Soon after Rice's departure from Tokyo, Defense Minister Fumio Kyuma announced that Japan wanted to give diplomacy more time before making a decision on whether to join in inspections of North Korean ships.

And Rice had to battle a growing perception in the region that the Bush administration was seeking to escalate the crisis. In particular, the talk about interdicting North Korean shipping had raised fears of an Asian version of the 1962 Cuban missile crisis, when President Kennedy had imposed a naval blockade against Cuba. Even as she sought support for tougher sanctions, Rice was forced to emphasize that Washington still hoped for a diplomatic solution. Speaking to reporters before leaving Seoul, she stressed, "We want to leave open the path of negotiation. We don't want the crisis to escalate."[14]

For their part, the Chinese had made clear that, whatever the UN resolution said, they would not participate in the interdiction of vessels going to or from North Korea. Beijing had, however, quietly taken some measures to pressure the North—temporarily cutting off the supply of military spare parts and curbing money transfers from Chinese banks. There were also unconfirmed reports that China had briefly cut off supplies of oil. But when Rice arrived in Beijing, the message she got from Chinese leaders was that, in the words of President Hu Jintao, the United States should show restraint and flexibility to, "prevent the situation from deteriorating or losing control." It was clear that maintaining stability in a sensitive border area remained China's top priority. However angry it might be with Kim Jong Il, Beijing was not going to support any effort to bring the North Korean regime to its knees.

Rice's most important meeting involved China's state councilor Tang Jiaxuan. On the day the Secretary of State arrived in Beijing, Tang was in Pyongyang meeting Kim Jong Il to deliver a personal message from President Hu warning against any further tests and urging the North to return to the six-party talks. Tang was the first foreign official to see Kim since the nuclear test. It was the final stop of a round-the-world trip. Dispatched by President Hu shortly after the nuclear test, Tang, accompanied by Deputy Foreign Minister Wu Dawei, had traveled first to Washington, where he met President Bush and urged him to resume talks with North Korea, and then to Moscow to see Russian president Vladimir Putin.

By the time he arrived in the North Korean capital, Tang was in a position to tell Kim Jong Il not only of the widespread international opposition to the test, but that George W. Bush, as well as Putin and Hu Jintao, wanted to see a diplomatic solution to the crisis.

One key factor influencing the way the Chinese shaped their message to Kim was an encounter between Henry Kissinger and President Hu. By chance, Kissinger had been scheduled to meet the Chinese president in Beijing on October 10, the day after the nuclear test. Given his role in the opening of relations between the United States and China, Kissinger's word carried considerable weight, not just with the Chinese but in much of Asia. In the preceding months, he had become increasingly concerned at the drift toward confrontation on the Korean peninsula. After participating in Track II conversations with the North Koreans earlier in the year in New York, he spoke about the issue with President Bush, for whom—as the Iraq war went bad and the U.S. position in the world eroded—he had become a trusted adviser.

According to a senior official familiar with those discussions, over the summer of 2006, Kissinger's message to Bush was, "You need a negotiating track. You need to work with China, and you need to let your negotiator do his job."

Before meeting Hu, Kissinger had been in touch with National Security Adviser Stephen Hadley, who had given him some talking points backing up the U.S. position as it pursued a sanctions resolution at the UN. But Kissinger also emphasized to Hu what Bush had said during their April 2006 lunch—that the president remained interested in a broader, peaceful resolution of the entire Korean situation—including a peace treaty ending the Korean War and North Korean participation in regional security arrangements—and that this should be conveyed to the North Koreans.

Back in Beijing the day after his meeting with Kim Jong Il, Tang met with Rice. Publicly, all he would say was that his visit to North Korea "had not been in vain." China's official Xinhua News Agency quoted Tang as urging the United States to "take a more active and flexible attitude."

In private, however, Tang had a more encouraging message. If Pyongyang could be assured that the United States was ready to find a way out of the Banco Delta Asia deadlock, Tang told Rice, he was convinced, after talking with Kim Jong Il, that Pyongyang was prepared to return to the six-party talks.

But first, the Americans were going to have to pay a price that they had, for more than a year, been unwilling to pay. George W. Bush was going to have to hold his nose and allow Christopher Hill to have bilateral meetings with his North Korean counterpart Kim Gye Gwan, and this time, negotiate in earnest. The nuclear test had put the ball back in Washington's court. Sanctions alone, President Bush had decided, were not enough.

# 18

# "HOW ARE WE GOING TO GET OUT OF THIS?"

C HRISTOPHER HILL WAS ON A PLANE OVER THE SOUTH PA-
cific heading from Fiji to Sydney when the call came through in
the last week of October 2006. Condoleezza Rice was ordering
him to cut short a scheduled visit to Australia and head to Beijing for a
secret meeting with North Korean envoy Kim Gye Gwan.

The Chinese had brokered the meeting, communicating their proposal to Rice a few days before. If Hill would show up and indicate flexibility on the Banco Delta Asia issue, they hinted, Kim was ready to
declare that Pyongyang would return to the six-party talks.

At the National Security Council in Washington, hard-liners argued
strongly against accepting the invitation. But according to one State Department official, the message from Beijing was that "the way to deal
with the North Koreans was to engage them, as upset as everyone might
be" about the nuclear test. Since it could be presented as a three-way
discussion, not a bilateral negotiation, Rice thought it was worth a try,
and she convinced George W. Bush to override the NSC objections and
authorize the meeting.

Said one of the hard-liners later, "I don't know why she approved
that. It was not welcome more widely in the U.S. government."

For Rice, it was a pivotal moment. She had been interested in resolving
the nuclear standoff diplomatically from the moment she had become secretary of state. Although the reference in her January 2005 confirmation
hearing to North Korea as an "outpost of tyranny" had captured the attention of the always suspicious Pyongyang regime, she had also said in

the same statement that "the time for diplomacy is now." Confronted with continuing pressure from the hard-liners and her own distaste for the North Koreans, in the nearly two years since taking office, she had displayed a willingness both to engage and confront the North Koreans. Christopher Hill described Rice's strategy as a "two-track policy. On the one hand we will squeeze. On the other hand we'll talk."

But the nuclear test changed everything. Although hard-liners had expected a test to be the event which showed that engagement did not work and that increased pressure was the only option, Rice—and Bush—grudgingly reached the opposite conclusion. As David Straub, the former head of the State Department's Korea Desk, observed, "It became the moment where she and Bush had to confront the fact that everything they had been doing in terms of North Korea did not work."

Rice's post-test trip to Asia had underscored this fact. The Chinese and the South Koreans, whose participation was essential if sanctions were to have any chance of forcing a change in North Korean behavior, made clear they were not prepared to implement really tough measures.

"She got the message that, 'If you guys had not been so intransigent,'" said one official involved in Rice's trip, "'this might not have happened. Your refusal to deal with Kim Jong Il has led to this point. You can't attack. You have to address his concerns. He wants to talk to you. You have to talk to him.'"

At the same time, Hill continued to push Rice to give him a chance to negotiate. "He is possibly one of the most tenacious, intractable, and stubborn people I have ever met," observed one colleague. "He was like the energizer bunny," recalled one former official. "He kept saying, 'Give me a little leeway.'"

Despite continuing sniping from the skeptics, "Hill was able to convince Rice" that he could pull off a deal, noted one senior State Department official, and the secretary became an increasingly "stalwart ally."

"I think she realized that the North Korea talks were going nowhere," said another official who dealt with the issue. "Everything was a mess, and here was Chris Hill, who seemed to have somewhat of a workable plan."

For Hill, receiving permission to go to Beijing was the opening he had been looking for. "Basically," he recalled, "the concept was that they would start the talks and that we would agree to address the banking issue."

On October 31, Hill, Kim, and Chinese vice foreign minister Wu Dawei spent seven hours at the Diaoyutai State Guest House. Hill started out meeting privately with Wu, who then hosted a lunch for all three envoys. At the end of the meal, Wu announced he was going, and walked out, leaving Hill and Kim on their own. While Hill's instructions from Rice allowed him to participate in three-way discussions and to explore ideas for getting Pyongyang back to the six-party process, they did not sanction a bilateral. But the U.S. envoy—not for the first time—stretched his instructions. Hill and Kim retreated to a separate room for the kind of face-to-face meeting the North Koreans had been requesting and that Hill had been privately advocating—without success—for nearly a year. Their conversations continued during coffee breaks, and then all three envoys gathered for a formal meeting at the end of the day.

Apart from the fact that he was getting the long-desired one-on-one with Hill—with all that it meant, in North Korean eyes, as an American gesture of respect for North Korea's legitimacy—the central issue for Kim Gye Gwan was, as it had been since the Banco Delta Asia sanctions were announced in September 2005, ending the U.S. financial squeeze. Kim put on the table the ideas his colleague Li Gun had raised with Hill's deputy Kathleen Stephens in New York the previous March, including the formation of a bilateral working group to deal with the BDA issue. And this time, though, instead of the standard U.S. line that the BDA affair was a law enforcement matter in which the State Department was powerless to interfere, Hill signaled a willingness to explore ways to bring the episode to a close.

"They wanted to hear that we would address the issue of the financial measures in the context of the talks," Hill said afterward, "and I said we were prepared to create a mechanism, a working group, to address these financial issues. That is, to discuss these [matters] and for the purpose of resolving them."[1]

The conversations, which Hill described as "businesslike," also covered how to implement the September 19, 2005 joint declaration, and both envoys reiterated their governments' commitment to doing so. To protect himself politically at home, Hill took pains to emphasize that he had held "bilateral discussions," not "negotiations," and that only in the six-party talks would it be possible to test the proposition that Kim Jong Il might really be ready to negotiate an end to his nuclear program. At the end of the day, the Chinese made it official, announcing that the six-party talks would resume, either in November or December.

There was considerable debate about what had prompted the North Koreans to decide to return to the table. The party line in Washington was that pressure from the Chinese, including angry remonstrations from top officials, an unannounced cutoff of military spare parts, and tighter cross-border inspections may have played a role. But the nuclear test also appears to have had an important psychological impact.

"I think the Chinese really did put some heat on them," said Hill. "I think they were shocked by the fact that the Chinese supported the UN Security

Council resolution. And also—they had fired off the weapon . . . so they did have this chest-thumping thing . . . now we are a nuclear power, we can talk."

Kim Gye Gwan himself subsequently made precisely the same point. "We have taken defensive measures against sanctions imposed on us through this nuclear experiment," he told reporters. "As we have attained that position, now we can have talks on an equal basis."[2]

Of equal importance to Pyongyang, by talking face-to-face with Kim and agreeing to a bilateral "mechanism" to address the BDA issue, Hill had, in effect, accepted terms the North Koreans had been putting forward for most of the previous twelve months. This included North Korean envoy Li Gun's visit to New York in March, when he had proposed just such a mechanism, and Kim Gye Gwan's eagerness for bilateral with Hill in Tokyo the following month—overtures the Bush administration rejected and which had led to the nuclear test.

News of Hill's "breakthrough" did not go down well with the hard-liners. As on so many previous occasions, there was sharp criticism that he had offered the North Koreans too much without getting enough in return.

"That was a real miscalculation on his part," said one critic. "People were not happy with that meeting. Any sort of commitments that Chris might have made at that meeting all had to be walked back in future meetings."

Although Rice remained supportive of reviving the diplomatic process, she too was unhappy, largely because Hill had held the bilateral with Kim in defiance of her instructions. Hill reportedly responded by saying that the Chinese had basically walked out and left him alone with Kim. What was he supposed to do—stalk off and insult the North Korean just as the United States was trying to coax Pyongyang back to the talks? An angry Rice was not mollified. She sent a stiff note to Beijing complaining about Wu Dawei's behavior and, in early November, Rice deliberately excluded Hill from a high-level U.S. delegation going to China, Japan, and South Korea to discuss the North Korea issue. Rice asked a trusted aide, Under Secretary for Political Affairs Nicholas Burns, to lead the group, which included prominent hard-liners Robert Joseph and Will Tobey. But Hill remained in Washington.

According to one person familiar with the internal deliberations, "The purpose of those discussions was to talk about implementing sanctions, and that people shouldn't get the impression that we were becoming weak-kneed. The thinking was, we'll eventually get back to diplomacy. But [the North Koreans] have got to feel the pain for a while, in terms of the sanctions and the [United Nations] resolution."

In Beijing, the tougher American position puzzled the Chinese, who had heard Hill strike a very different tone just a few days earlier. In response, they were told the more hard-line posture accurately reflected the views of Secretary Rice and National Security Adviser Stephen Hadley.

Yet again, mixed messages seemed to characterize the administration's approach to North Korea.

While the U.S. delegation—minus Hill—was in Asia, Americans went to the polls. In a historic rebuff to George W. Bush—mostly because of his handling of the war in Iraq—on November 7, 2006, voters handed control of both the Senate and the House of Representatives to the Democrats. Within days, Secretary of Defense Donald Rumsfeld resigned. The influence of Vice President Dick Cheney—already weakened by the indictment of his former chief of staff, Lewis "Scooter" Libby, on charges of lying about his role in the leak of an undercover CIA operative's identity to reporters—was further eroded. In addition, John Bolton, who was UN ambassador as the result of a "recess appointment" in 2005, had clear indications the Senate would not confirm him and chose to step down. A discouraged Robert Joseph, who had succeeded Bolton as under secretary for arms control but had been cut out of the action on North Korea by Hill with Rice's approval, was also planning to resign early in the new year. The right-wing hard-liners who had dominated the Bush administration for so long were in retreat.

For Rice and Hill, the election and the changed balance of power within the administration provided a new opportunity to wrest control of North Korea policy from those who had for so long sought to block real negotiations, and to win support for a new approach from a weakened President Bush. Moreover, with the quagmire in Iraq the principal reason for Bush's unpopularity and the Republicans' electoral defeat, the possibility of a successful agreement on North Korea appeared increasingly attractive to Rice, not only on its own merits but also because it offered what could become one of the few positive foreign policy legacies of the Bush administration.

"The election galvanized the minds of the administration," said a senior congressional staffer. "Time is short. Our days are numbered. We have two years left. We have lost our majorities. [A North Korea deal] is something doable. This is a deliverable."

One other factor also contributed to the administration's change of approach. After the nuclear test, Victor Cha, the director of Asian affairs at the National Security Council, had written a memo to the President arguing that the United States had to try to engage with North Korea to test whether Pyongyang was serious about implementing the denuclearization pledges it had made in the September 2005 joint declaration. Cha, whose article on "hawk engagement" had led to his appointment to the NSC, told Bush that it was important for the president to show he was serious about diplomacy by allowing face-to-face contact with the North Koreans. If Bush did so and the negotiations fell apart, Cha wrote, Bush would be in a better position to enlist the support of the other participants in the six-party process for tougher measures against Pyongyang. Because of his reputation as something of a hard-liner, Cha's views carried weight with the president in a way that a similar memo from the State Department would not have done.

One important sign of the shift in approach came in mid-November, when Bush met South Korean president Roh Moo-hyun on the sidelines of the annual Asia Pacific Economic Cooperation summit in Hanoi, Vietnam. Bush told Roh, whose sometimes strident opposition to Washington's tough line toward Pyongyang had long been a source of tension, that he would be ready to sign a declaration formally ending the Korea War if Kim Jong Il agreed to give up his nuclear weapons. What about a summit meeting to seal such an accord, Roh asked? Bush said he would be willing to meet with Kim once his nuclear weapons were gone. It was an offhand comment—not a serious policy position—but the implication was that Bush, who had never disguised his loathing for Kim and his hope that the "evil" regime would disappear, was open to ending decades of hostility, and perhaps even to a face-to-face meeting. After the summit with Roh, Bush told reporters, "We want the North Korean leaders to hear that if it gives up its weapons—nuclear weapons ambitions—that we would be willing to enter into security arrangements with the North Koreans, as well as move toward new economic incentives for the North Korean people."[3] For Bush, the remarks, however casual, underscored the change in the administration's position.

A t the end of November, Hill returned to Beijing for two days of meetings. Like the session in October, there were both three-way conversations with North Korea's Kim Gye Gwan and Chinese vice foreign minister Wu Dawei, as well as separate bilaterals between Hill and Kim.

Hill began by presenting a list of what the United States wanted from North Korea even before the six-party talks resumed—what he dubbed the "early harvest"—and by spelling out, in greater specificity than any previous U.S. envoy, what Washington was prepared to offer in return.

Hill's draft proposal reportedly included North Korea's halting activities at Yongbyon, allowing IAEA inspections, providing a list of its nuclear facilities, and closing down its nuclear test sites. All these measures were to be completed by 2008. In return, North Korea would receive food and energy aid, a U.S.

pledge to work with North Korea to find a way to end the sanctions against Banco Delta Asia, and the prospect of accelerated efforts to normalize relations with Washington.[4]

The North Koreans listened intently, but Hill and his team were disappointed by Kim Gye Gwan's response.

"He continued to insist on solving the bank issue first," Hill recalled, "before getting anything else done. That meant you were sort of back in the same soup."

From Pyongyang's perspective, the issue was not simply the $25 million dollars in frozen accounts. The U.S. measures against BDA and other sanctions had become a symbol of the "hostile" American policy the North Koreans repeatedly complained about.

"Kim said, 'You ask for action, but only offer words. You need to end your hostile policy,'" noted one American diplomat. "'You treat us as a terrorist state, so you have to change your own laws and regulations to show the U.S. does not have a hostile policy.'"

A frustrated Hill complained to the Chinese, who had brokered the meeting and who had led the United States to expect a more forthcoming attitude from the North Koreans. But Kim Gye Gwan was unyielding.

"We are willing to implement the September 19 [2005] joint statement," he told reporters before leaving Beijing. "But at the current stage, we cannot abandon the nuclear program in a one-sided way."[5]

For Hill, pushing the "early harvest" concept was intended to generate quick progress and show that the diplomatic process was alive and well, something he needed to maintain political support for his efforts in Washington. He left Beijing seriously concerned that his efforts were going nowhere.

On the same day came a new move by the hard-liners. Reporters in Washington were leaked the contents of a list of luxury goods the administration had drawn up which North Korea was to be barred from importing. Altogether, there were more than sixty items, including yachts, motorcycles, large-screen DVD players, iPods, Rolex watches, and cognac. The notion was to deprive Kim Jong Il, whose taste for luxury was well-known, of the power and prestige he derived from being able to import such products and distribute them to members of the ruling elite.

Any luxury item the United States embargoed, however, could be easily obtained elsewhere. The idea that banning iPods and cognac would somehow coerce the Dear Leader into changing his policies seemed laughable to some observers. Jerrold Post, director of the Political Psychology program at George

Washington University, told the *Washington Post* that the curbs on luxury goods
would not end Kim's weapons program "unless they use Hennessy to fuel their
rockets."[6] Much more likely, however, was that the gesture, with its calculated
attempt to publicize Kim's embarrassing eccentricities, would further fuel
Pyongyang's suspicion of American motives and sincerity.

Nonetheless, Pyongyang agreed to send its diplomats to a new official round
of six-party talks beginning in Beijing on December 18, 2006.

In yet another sign of the divisions in Washington, a week before the talks
were due to start, Stuart Levey, the Treasury Department's hard-line under
secretary for terrorism and financial intelligence, gave a speech that signaled the
administration would show no flexibility on the BDA sanctions.

"We must monitor the financial activities of known terrorists and proliferators
and prohibit their access—and that of their support networks—to the financial
system," Levey said. "We must also go beyond simply designating individuals
and entities that have been named by the UN and . . . hold them publicly accountable, isolate them financially and commercially, and ensure that all of their
activities, whether seemingly legitimate or illicit, are shut down."[7]

Levey's unyielding position came as officials at State and Treasury were struggling over the thorny question of just how to handle the BDA issue. From the beginning, the designation of BDA as a suspect entity under section 311 of the USA
Patriot Act had been as much a symbolic gesture as a substantive one. The broader
goal of making financial institutions elsewhere in the world reluctant to do business with North Korea was more important than simply taking a few million dollars out of circulation from an obscure bank in Macau.

"The goal is not to touch real money here," acknowledged a senior administration official. "The goal is to besmirch their reputation so that around the
world people don't want to touch it, because bankers are conservative people,
right? They're not wanting to get involved with companies that get them in
trouble. Once you do this in a banking system, then banks all over the world get
wary of these guys."

In that aim, somewhat to Washington's surprise, the action against BDA had
succeeded. Treasury's designation of BDA as a "primary money-laundering
concern" had set off a global chain reaction, as banks around the world moved
to sever financial links with Pyongyang for fear of becoming targets of U.S.
sanctions themselves.

"The impact that BDA had on North Korea as a whole," said one senior
U.S. official involved with the issue, "exceeded our expectations. It opened our
eyes to the power financial sanctions can have."

The Treasury Department had expected that, once BDA was targeted, the North Koreans would simply withdraw their cash from the bank. What Treasury did not anticipate, however, was that the Macau Monetary Authority would intervene and freeze all the suspect accounts. The decision appears to have been taken partly in response to the run on BDA the day after the Treasury designation was made public in September 2005, partly because the Treasury move cast doubt on the probity of China's banking authorities, and partly because the Macau government, with Beijing's backing, had ambitions to attract investment from American gaming companies in the hope of turning the territory into the "Las Vegas of the East." Any questions about the integrity of the territory's financial system risked jeopardizing Macau's long-term plans, prompting the local government to appoint a three-person committee to manage the bank's affairs while the freeze remained in effect.

The upshot was, that on the question of resolving the specifics of the BDA situation, without Treasury's willing cooperation, Washington had no clear idea of how to proceed.

"We were honestly stuck with a $25 million problem that was quite unsolvable," the same senior official said. "This was money that now becomes a difficulty on principle, because what are you going to do with it when it's unfrozen? It's messy."

Indeed, finding an answer to that question would turn out to be exceptionally complicated. The fifty-two accounts were owned by a variety of individuals, companies, and other entities, and simply having all the account holders withdraw the money in cash was not feasible. Moreover, the North Koreans had few other options to move their money elsewhere because no international banks would touch these now-tainted assets for fear of suffering the same fate as BDA. In what was largely a cash-based economy, North Korea's own financial institutions were either nonexistent or had almost no association with the broader international economy. As a result, direct wire transfers and other modern methods of moving cash between organizations were problematic as well. And the North's shaky credit rating meant it could not borrow money.

Said one senior State Department official, "Treasury had no idea how to undo what it had done."

Further undermining the Bush administration's position was a 128-page confidential audit of BDA by the international accounting firm Ernst & Young, under a commission by the government of Macau. The audit, conducted in the months after the suspect accounts were frozen, raised doubts about one of the claims at the heart of the U.S. case against BDA. In its initial finding, the Treasury

Department had alleged that "senior officials in Banco Delta Asia are working with DPRK officials to accept large deposits of cash, including counterfeit U.S. currency, and agreeing to place that currency into circulation."[8] Ernst & Young, however, said it did not find any evidence to corroborate the U.S. claims.

"From our investigation," the audit concluded, "it is apparent that . . . to a material degree, the bank did not introduce counterfeit U.S. currency notes into circulation over the relevant period."[9]

The audit said the only confirmed counterfeiting case with a North Korea connection was a 1994 episode when BDA staff brought to the attention of Macau and U.S. authorities bogus U.S. bills that had been deposited by North Korea's Zokwang Trading Company. The report from Ernst & Young was, however, hardly a ringing endorsement of the bank. It criticized BDA for lax internal controls, inadequate information technology, failure to conduct sufficient due diligence about its North Korean clients, and insufficient attention to Macau's anti-money-laundering laws. But on the big charges made by the Bush administration, the audit said the evidence just wasn't there.

The conclusion dovetailed with that reached by those in the administration who had been skeptical of the push against BDA all along. "There was nothing they could present to the Macau authorities that could substantiate that these accounts were involved in illicit activities," recalled a former high-ranking State Department official who worked on the issue. "Believe me, particularly after we had seized the accounts and had a chance to go through some of the receipts, if there had been evidence of massive money laundering of, for example, profits from missiles or drugs or any other kind of sales, you could be sure it would all be in the public arena right now."

In fact, as the journal *Japan Focus* chronicled in a detailed examination of Treasury's allegations, virtually all the Bush administration's published documents and official statements on the BDA case were strikingly short of specifics. When it came to concrete evidence, almost every allegation against BDA in the initial Treasury Department finding was ambiguously worded. The key claims of wrongdoing were made using phrases such as "it has been widely reported," "sources showed," or "investigations have revealed."

"None of these charges have been accompanied by conclusive or convincing evidence of wrongdoing," the *Japan Focus* study concluded. "It is a list of allegations, which are by their nature almost impossible to verify since the basic factual information needed to confirm criminality, such as dates, sums of money involved and names of individuals or DPRK entities involved, is absent."[10]

When pressed about these doubts after the issue was finally resolved, Daniel Glaser responded, "The designation of BDA was based not on North Korean counterfeiting but upon our concern that BDA was being used for facilitating a variety of illicit North Korean financial activities."

Glaser referred to the same 1994 counterfeiting case involving North Korea's Zokwang Trading Company mentioned by the Ernst & Young audit. But his point was that when Treasury acted against the bank in 2005, "Zokwang continued to have that same account at BDA. So BDA's reaction [to the 1994 incident] was not, 'Gosh, this is a customer we'd rather not do business with,' but was 'let's not only maintain this account, but in fact adopt a policy within the bank of reduced scrutiny of North Korea–related clients.' . . . The concerns about the bank were systemic anti-money-laundering concerns."

For many of those pushing for financial sanctions against BDA and the Pyongyang regime, however, the absence of any corroboration that Treasury or U.S. intelligence was willing—or able—to make public was not a big problem. Indeed, underpinning the entire effort was a belief that North Korea was so deeply involved in illicit activities—a "Sopranos state," in David Asher's memorable term—that there was no such thing as a legitimate North Korean bank account, business entity, or financial transaction.

As Christopher Hill subsequently acknowledged, "It was a lot of taint by association. Treasury basically had the point of view that if money were passed by or near an entity that had been involved in bad stuff, then the money was tainted."

While the BDA designation was having the intended effect of cutting off North Korea's access to the international financial system, the strategy was ultimately proving counterproductive. As it became increasingly apparent that finding a way out of the BDA deadlock was central to broader progress on the nuclear issue, it had become a huge stumbling block.

A week before Christmas, the six-party talks reconvened in Beijing. From the outset, it was clear Kim Gye Gwan had strict instructions from Pyongyang to discuss only the BDA issue and not even address the nuclear issue. The atmosphere, in the words of one participant, was "stiff."

"They basically said, 'We can't talk about [denuclearization] until we resolve the BDA sanctions,'" recalled one member of Hill's team.

Hill was visibly frustrated. "The purpose of our being here was to discuss the denuclearization of the Korean peninsula," he griped to reporters. "I want to emphasize I'm not here to talk about [Banco Delta Asia]. That's not what I do."[11]

Following up on Hill's promise that the United States would work with the North Koreans to find a way out of the BDA deadlock, a team led by Deputy

Assistant Treasury Secretary Daniel Glaser spent two days meeting with a
North Korean delegation on the sidelines of the six-party talks. In a sign of the
seriousness with which Pyongyang viewed the issue—and its hopes for real
progress—the North Korean group was headed by Oh Gwang Chul, president
of the country's Foreign Trade Bank and a leading financial expert. Educated in
Russia, Oh was a member of a younger generation of North Korean tech-
nocrats. He had spent several years at the Foreign Trade Bank's office in Paris,
and was reportedly believed to be a key figure in the mysterious Bureau 39,
which was responsible for overseeing all of the North's international financial
transactions. In two days of talks at the U.S. and North Korean embassies,
Glaser explained the legal basis for the U.S. actions, and the two men discussed
possible ways to proceed. But they reached no agreement.

Four days before Christmas, the six-party talks recessed. As he prepared to
return to Pyongyang, Kim Gye Gwan said, "The U.S. has been unable to come
to a decision to lift its sanctions and give up its hostile policy against us. The
U.S. is now jointly undertaking dialogue and pressure, carrots and sticks. And
we are standing against them with dialogue and shields. The shield is to improve our deterrent."[12] The implicit threat was that without movement, the
North would stage a second nuclear test. Within days, U.S. intelligence detected renewed activity at the North Korean nuclear test site. "We think they've
put everything in place to conduct a test without any notice or warning," a senior Pentagon official told ABC News.[13]

As the talks recessed, Hill and his colleagues returned to the U.S. Embassy
to take stock. They were discouraged that Kim Gye Gwan had not come
prepared to discuss substantive nuclear issues, but Hill felt they could not let
the process fall apart. He instructed Korea Desk director Sung Kim to contact
the North Korean embassy. That evening, Kim and Victor Cha met with
Pyongyang's UN envoy Kim Myong Gil. They chose what they called the "Little Velvet Lounge" of the Kerry Centre, an office complex far away from the St.
Regis Hotel and its hordes of waiting reporters. Just off the lobby, with furniture
upholstered in velvet, the lounge was a discreet place to meet.

Kim and Cha told the North Korean the United States was serious about
reaching a deal.

"We are interested in continuing the discussion," Kim said. "If you want to
meet bilaterally, we can arrange something."

The discussion ended inconclusively.

The next morning, December 23, 2006, Victor Cha arrived at the Beijing
airport to catch his flight back to Washington. As he was going through the spe-

cial immigration channel for diplomats, he bumped into Kim Gye Gwan, Li Gun, and the rest of the North Korean delegation, who were preparing to board the Air Koryo flight to Pyongyang. With time to kill before their flights departed, Cha and the North Koreans decided to have coffee together.

As they sat down, Cha asked, "How are we going to get out of this? What are we going to do?"

Li Gun said, "Maybe we should do an intersessional bilateral. "But we want to do it outside Beijing. We don't trust the Chinese anymore. We think they are in too much cooperation with you."

Cha thought to himself, *Well, Li has just validated the entire U.S. strategy,* which was to enlist Beijing's help in pressuring Pyongyang.

Li then proposed meeting in Geneva, but Cha said that might be a political problem in Washington because that was where the Clinton administration had negotiated the Agreed Framework. Cha countered with London, and Li in turn suggested Berlin.

"I don't have any instructions," Cha told the North Koreans. "But I promise I will take this back." The North Koreans' flight was then called, and Cha said good-bye.

Before his plane left Beijing, he contacted Hill. Although the two men shared somewhat similar views, and Cha was part of Hill's negotiating team, they had an uneasy relationship, in large part because Hill's relations with the White House—and thus with the NSC—were still rocky. Given the extent to which the NSC had been the source of opposition to Hill's initiatives, not to mention earlier efforts by Powell and Jim Kelly to engage the North Koreans, Hill remained deeply suspicious, although in Cha he appeared to have found something of an ally. Hill liked the idea of a meeting in Berlin, and he agreed to ask for Rice's approval while Cha ran the proposal by National Security Adviser Stephen Hadley, arguing, as he had in his October memo, that this would be an important opportunity to test North Korea's intentions.

The following week, Hill got the go-ahead, and the North Koreans, through their UN mission in New York, sent back a message. Berlin was fine.

In the run-up to the meeting, Hill displayed what had already—and would increasingly—become his trademark operating style. To prevent hard-liners from torpedoing the process, which they had repeatedly done in the past, he simply froze them out. Apart from Rice, Bush, Stephen Hadley, Victor Cha, and a small handful of trusted aides, "nobody else knew about it," said one person who was in the loop. "It was meant to be kept very quiet." The normal interagency procedures for such a meeting—preparing position papers, drafting talking points and circulating them through the bureaucracy—simply didn't happen.

"Chris refused to play nice," observed one of his colleagues. "He was extremely careful about not leaving a paper trail, since every time you called an interagency meeting, everybody would veto things. He just wasn't going to do it. He decided to cut people out."

He was supported by Rice, who in January had told her senior staff that finalizing a nuclear deal with North Korea was one of three issues on which she intended to concentrate during her remaining two years in office. The others were Iran's nuclear program and the Israeli-Palestinian conflict.[14]

To Hill, the Bush administration was still full of people who were opposed to negotiations, and who felt the mere act of speaking with foreigners displayed weakness. So the leading hard-liners—Vice President Cheney's office, the office of the secretary of defense, Robert Joseph, the outgoing under secretary for arms control—were kept in the dark. As one of Hill's aides joked, "They weren't given a vote" on whether Hill should go to Berlin. They only learned of plans for the meeting after the president had already given it his blessing—too late to try to stop it from happening.

Ironically, it was Hill's old boss in the Clinton administration, former UN envoy and Bosnian peace deal negotiator Richard Holbrooke, who provided the cover. Holbrooke was hosting a meeting of the American Assembly, a regular gathering of scholars, government officials, and policy analysts that happened to be convening in Berlin in mid January. Hill arranged for Holbrooke to issue an invitation to speak, giving Hill an excuse to travel without alerting the press or anyone else to what he intended to do.

The symbolism of the meeting with the North Koreans was of enormous importance. It would mark the first time that senior American and North Korean officials would hold a bilateral meeting on their own, not in Beijing with China acting as match-maker or intermediary. Finally, representatives of George W. Bush and Kim Jong Il were sitting down together, on their own, to sort out how to move forward.

On the night of January 16, 2007, Hill and his team hosted Kim Gye Gwan and the North Korean delegation—including the mysterious and always-present interpreter Miss Chae—for dinner. The Americans had booked a private room at the Berlin Hilton and went out of their way to lay out a lavish meal.

"We pulled out all the stops," recalled one member of Hill's team, "because we wanted to demonstrate we were serious and sincere."

After eighteen months of on-and-off encounters, Hill had reached certain conclusions about his North Korean interlocutors. Products of a rigid authoritarian system, they invariably came with strict instructions from Pyongyang and little leeway to deviate from them. But they were neither bizarre nor naïve. They also had a sense of humor, and it was possible to forge a personal connection that could become one of the key building blocks for creating the mutual trust the two sides so obviously lacked.

During the four-hour dinner, copious amounts of liquor were served—something the hard-drinking North Koreans appreciated—and friendly toasts to the future success of their work were exchanged. The symbolism could not have been lost on Kim Gye Gwan and his colleagues, who undoubtedly remembered Jim Kelly's October 2002 visit to Pyongyang, where Kelly had been ordered by the hard-liners not to make a toast or host a banquet. Now, Hill was trying to signal that things had changed.

The next morning, the two delegations met at the American Embassy. Hill began with a long presentation, which he described as his "performance art" style of negotiating.

"We made a good start with the September 19 Declaration [in 2005]," Hill told Kim Gye Gwan. "But you have exploded a nuclear device thinking that what you would get is greater security and leverage to force the world to reckon with. What you have gotten is the exact opposite. China for the first time has voted 'yes' on a resolution to impose sanctions on your regime. The rest of the international community has decided it is too risky that in the face of the U.S. to deal with you and therefore your access to the international financial system is going to be increasingly restricted. You have cut yourself off from a major source of currency in terms of trade and remittances from Japan. You have made it extremely difficult and uncomfortable for the South Koreans to continue their program of economic cooperation. You have also embarrassed the Chinese. You have also got hawks in the U.S. considering extreme responses. And you now have in your possession weapons of mass destruction that if they got into the wrong hands would guarantee an extreme response from the U.S."

As Kim listened intently, Hill continued, "We need to find a way to get you out of the corner that you have gotten yourself into and we're serious about doing so."

Kim's response was civil and level-headed. Happy simply to get this unprecedented bilateral meeting, he did not address any of the specific points Hill made, but also did not try to flaunt North Korea's nuclear status. Instead, he stressed Pyongyang's desire to negotiate on "an equal footing" with the United States and turned the discussion of what the North considered the central bilateral issue: Banco Delta Asia and U.S. financial sanctions.

Reinforcing his earlier promises, Hill stressed to Kim that the Bush administration was committed to resolving the BDA situation.

Kim said that once North Korea got its money back, Pyongyang was ready to move on the nuclear front. Hill pressed for a commitment to shut down and seal the Yongbyon nuclear facility, allow IAEA inspectors to return, and discuss a list of North Korea's nuclear assets. Kim raised the issue of energy assistance and asked for shipments of heavy fuel oil. The two men haggled over the timing and sequence of events. Hill offered oil shipments if the North shut down Yongbyon within forty-five days. Kim proposed ninety days. They agreed to compromise on sixty days, with the precise amount of oil to be determined when the six-party talks reconvened. Suddenly, after months of wrangling and deadlock, in just two days of bilateral meetings, the outline of a deal had come into view.[15]

No formal agreement was prepared, and neither envoy put his signature to any document. However, Hill recalled, "The ideas we went through together were written down" so that both sides were clear about what had been agreed.

Rice, winding up a trip to the Middle East, stopped in Berlin for a briefing on her way back to Washington. Hill told her what had been discussed and gave her a one-page memo summarizing the talks. Rice called National Security Adviser Stephen Hadley and then spoke directly with President Bush to seek his approval. As had been the case in the run-up to the Berlin meeting, the usual interagency process was circumvented; none of the leading hard-liners were informed of what was happening. In a matter of hours, Bush told Rice to give Hill the go-ahead.

Publicly, Hill maintained the fiction that the Berlin meetings were simply "an exchange of ideas." In fact, though, he acknowledged, "Basically, we created a Berlin Agreement." The details still had to be fleshed out at the next round of six-party talks and endorsed by the other four participating nations, but Washington and Pyongyang had, on their own, created the basis for a new deal designed to end the North Korean nuclear program. In his speech to the American Assembly in Berlin, Hill was upbeat, holding out the possibility of a fundamental rapprochement with Pyongyang.

"We look forward," he said, "to establishing a normal relationship with North Korea."[16]

But even though the meeting in Berlin was a breakthrough in terms of forging a positive relationship between Hill and Kim and convincing the North Koreans that the Bush administration was finally serious about a deal, a critical misunderstanding would jeopardize the entire process in the months that followed.

Hill, preoccupied with the nuclear issue, had devoted little time to mastering the details of the BDA case; like the rest of his team, he had not thought through the mechanics of resolving it. He figured that if he and Kim found common ground, the Chinese would be happy to act as facilitators and that getting the money back to the North Koreans would be a straightforward business. That assumption would turn out to be a serious miscalculation.

"So we had this discussion about how to resolve the BDA issue," one member of Hill's team recalled. "Now one of the things about the BDA issue is that we never got into a detailed discussion of what exactly you meant by 'resolving' it. All we said was that we would 'resolve' BDA. And they took away one understanding of it—that what we meant by 'resolve' was that we would immediately drop all the charges and free up their bank accounts . . . that we would simply tell the Macanese to release [the funds]. And we had another understanding of it. What we meant was that we would conclude our investigative process."

At the time, neither side seemed too troubled by the ambiguity over BDA. The fact that they had apparently broken the deadlock was much more important. That evening, the North Koreans hosted a banquet for the Americans at Berlin's China Garden Restaurant. The mood was lighthearted. The North Koreans were gracious hosts, and the alcohol flowed freely. Hill, however, was constantly being called away to the phone. At one point, Rice called, so Hill, making a veiled mocking reference to the Dear Leader, got up and said, "Excuse me, I've got a call from a very senior authority." When he returned, Kim Gye Gwan stood up and said, "I have a call from an even higher authority." Then Kim paused for dramatic effect and declared, "I have to go to the toilet." The table erupted in laughter.

The goodwill would not last long.

# 19

# "WE ARE ALL WAITING FOR YOU"

A S HE FLEW INTO BEIJING ON FEBRUARY 7, 2007, FOR THE next round of six-party talks, Christopher Hill was confident a deal with North Korea was within reach. After the Berlin meeting, he had briefed the Chinese as well as the other participants in the talks. Chinese Vice Foreign Minister Wu Dawei and his advisers were already at work on a draft proposal based largely on the understandings Hill and Kim Gye Gwan had forged the previous month that the North would shut down and seal—but not disable—the Yongbyon reactor and discuss providing a list of its nuclear activities in return for a lifting of the Banco Delta Asia sanctions, supplies of energy, and movement toward better relations.

When the talks convened the next morning at the Diaoyutai State Guest House, the Chinese circulated their draft of an agreement. It would require North Korea to halt operations at the Yongbyon reactor within two months in exchange for an initial shipment of fuel oil. It would also create five working groups to address other issues, including the details of further denuclearization, the U.S. financial sanctions, the eventual normalization of relations by both the United States and Japan, and broader security arrangements for Northeast Asia.

Then Kim Gye Gwan dropped a bombshell—a demand for a huge amount of heavy fuel oil and electricity before the North would agree to take even the first steps toward denuclearization. Unless the North got two million tons of oil (the equivalent of four years of oil shipments under the Agreed Framework) and two million kilowatts of electricity, Kim declared, there would be no deal.

The other participants were stunned, no one more so than Christopher Hill. "We get to Beijing thinking we've got pretty much a set deal," said a member of the U.S. delegation, "and then the North Koreans do something they have often done in the past, which is to attempt to renegotiate. They didn't disavow Berlin, but they said they wanted more."

Kim's ploy was partly a standard North Korean negotiating tactic—staking out a wildly unrealistic bargaining position to test the bottom line of those sitting across the table. But it also reflected Pyongyang's long-standing sense of grievance over the cutoff of Agreed Framework fuel shipments in 2002 and the fact that the promised light-water reactors had never been built. In the North's eyes, that meant being deprived of vast amounts of power critical to reviving its devastated economy.

Hill and Kim held several private meetings, including one that was described as "lengthy and very frank" on Sunday, February 11. Kim was unyielding. Accounts leaked to reporters described him as "unleashing a tirade" against the Americans and "throwing a fit."[1]

"There are moments when he [Kim] is upset, and, boy, you can tell it," said one U.S. official. "He kind of turns a darker shade of purple."[2]

But the specifics of Kim's demands left the Americans perplexed, as he would first insist on the fuel oil, then on the electricity supplies, then both, without being clear about just precisely what he wanted.

"They're so opaque," one American official told reporters, "they never quite say what they really need."[3]

By the end of the weekend, the talks were close to collapse. Hill, in the words of a colleague, was "pulling his hair out because their demands got so ludicrous. The North Koreans were being intractable on the demand for fuel oil, with nothing more to give [on their part]."

All the parties had agreed the round would conclude on Tuesday, February 13, with or without an agreement. With time running out, Hill warned Kim that, unless the North modified its demands, "We are willing to walk away, and if we walk away, you've got nothing."

Kim seemed unmoved. He told Hill that there would clearly be another round of talks, and that the understanding reached in Berlin would remain as a basis for negotiations. But the frustrated Hill played hardball.

"If we don't reach a six-party agreement today," Hill warned, "there is no Berlin. What was agreed at Berlin is off."

Kim suddenly appeared to realize he had pushed too hard, and his approach immediately changed.

"My sense of it," said one American official familiar with the talks, "is that Kim Gye Gwan was faced with having to report to Pyongyang that 'I had a deal on BDA [Banco Delta Asia] but I lost it. I had something and now I've got nothing.'"

With Kim Jong Il's birthday just four days away, on February 16, returning home completely empty-handed and facing the consequences could not have been an appealing prospect for Kim Gye Gwan.

Kim quickly offered to drop his demand to 1.5 million tons of oil—"because we are generous," he told Hill—and then, when the American continued to say "no," Kim came down further.

But the key to breaking the deadlock came from an initiative by South Korea's negotiator Chun Yung-woo, a tough and canny diplomat who had spent time at the IAEA. Meeting privately with Kim Gye Gwan, Chun told the North Korean that if he wanted more fuel oil, Pyongyang would have to agree to do more. The two men mapped out a deal under which North Korea would get 50,000 tons of heavy fuel oil for freezing Yongbyon. But if Kim agreed to disable the reactor and declare all its programs, the North would receive 450,000 tons more in 50,000 ton tranches, plus the equivalent of 500,000 tons of oil in electricity and other assistance, to be delivered as they implemented their side of the bargain.

Hill was having his own meetings with Kim. In Berlin the previous month, the U.S. envoy had pushed for a North Korean commitment to go further than just shutting and sealing Yongbyon, but Kim had refused. But now, Hill too seized on the concept of "more for more."

Hill told Kim that the U.S. was not prepared to provide a huge amount of oil simply for a shut-down of Yongbyon; that would appear too much like Clinton's Agreed Framework. But Hill did say, "We're prepared to do more fuel oil for more denuclearization"—specifically, moving from a simple shutdown to the permanent disabling of Yongbyon.

"It became apparent that what mattered to them was a big number that he would be able to sell back home," said one American official, "but there was some flexibility in how we provided it."

The North Koreans also came under pressure from the other four participants in the talks—the Chinese, the South Koreans, the Japanese, and the Russians—who, in the wake of the Berlin meeting, were convinced the BDA issue had now been dealt with, and it was time for Pyongyang to begin fulfilling the commitment to denuclearize it had made in the September 19, 2005, accord.

"Everybody else's expectations," said one senior U.S. official, "including the Chinese, were, 'If we're going to get past this nuclear test, and have any future to the six-party talks, now that we've got them back at the table, they've really got to take a step in terms of implementing the joint statement.' So the North

Koreans were under tremendous pressure in the February round. I don't think they expected this."

As the haggling dragged on, Hill was on the phone repeatedly with Rice, who became intimately involved in the negotiations, down to the level of approving or rejecting specific words in the text of the proposed document. This time, however, Washington's internal deliberations contrasted sharply to the behind-the-scenes maneuvering that led to the September 19 Declaration in 2005. Then, each draft was submitted to a torturous interagency review in Washington, which provided the hard-liners a chance to raise objections and to try to torpedo Hill's efforts to complete the deal, and worse, write his plenary statement back-tracking partway from what had been agreed. Now, in a situation reflecting the changed balance of power in Washington, Rice was able to bypass the bureau-cracy altogether. Hill dealt with the secretary of state, who dealt directly with the president. The hard-liners were again cut out of the action until after a decision was made. When they found out, they were furious, but with no support from Rice or Bush, they could do little to derail the process.

By the early hours of Tuesday, February 13, however, with the talks due to recess later that day, there was still no agreement. At the last minute, Rice au-thorized Hill to offer what Chun had initially worked out. The North would get 50,000 tons of heavy fuel oil to be delivered as soon as Yongbyon was shut down, without committing the United States to provide it; 450,000 tons of HFO and the equivalent of another 500,000 tons in energy and other assistance were to be supplied after an acceptable declaration of all North Korean nuclear programs, and all existing nuclear facilities had been disabled and were being dismantled. The idea was to avoid "front-loading" all of the North's benefits be-fore Pyongyang had taken concrete steps to disarm—a long-standing adminis-tration complaint about Clinton's Agreed Framework.

In urging Kim not to be greedy and accept the offer, Hill used the symbol of a traditional Korean wine cup, the Gye Young Bae, which is designed so that if just the right amount is poured, one can drink, but if too much is poured, the cup automatically drains.

"We are now faced with a situation where you and I can both drink out of the cup," Hill told Kim, "but if one of us attempts to put too much in that cup, the whole thing will drain, and both of us will go thirsty. It's your choice."

By now it was nearly 3:00 A.M. on February 13. At the Diaoyutai State Guest House, Hill and Wu Dawei were, in the words of one American diplomat, "shuttling from room to room, delegation to delegation, trying to nail down the final language," while each delegation was calling back to their respective capi-tals for final instructions.

Finally, the North Koreans agreed. Later that morning, seventeen months—

and one nuclear test—after the September 19 joint declaration, weary delegates gathered to announce what amounted to an "action plan" to implement the principles agreed in September 2005. North Korea agreed that, within 60 days, it would "shut down and seal for the purpose of eventual abandonment the Yongbyon nuclear facility," readmit inspectors from the International Atomic Energy Agency, and begin discussions on a list of all its nuclear programs. In return, the North would receive 50,000 tons of heavy fuel once it shut down Yongbyon, with the remaining 950,000 tons of HFO or its equivalent to come after the provision of the "complete declaration of all nuclear programs and disablement of all existing nuclear facilities." In addition, the U.S. agreed to "start bilateral talks aimed at resolving bilateral issues and moving toward full diplomatic relations." Among those issues were ending the North's designation as a "state sponsor of terrorism" and removing long-standing sanctions imposed under the Trading With the Enemy Act.[4] Although it was not in the text, in a side meeting Hill assured Kim that Washington would begin discussions on ending the BDA sanctions within thirty days.

As the final session broke up, Kim Gye Gwan approached Hill to say goodbye. Kim clasped Hill in a tight handshake, smiled broadly and said, with real emotion in his voice, "Let's take this all the way to the end!"

In Washington, President Bush hailed the agreement as "the best opportunity to use diplomacy to address North Korea's nuclear programs" and singled out Rice and Hill for special praise.[5] For the President, the deal represented yet another major turnaround. Since taking office, Bush had insisted there would be no bilateral negotiations with a regime he loathed, and that North Korea would never be "rewarded" for bad behavior; the administration's previous stance at the six-party talks had reflected this hard-line view. Washington's demands that Pyongyang disarm first and its refusal to consider economic or diplomatic benefits until the North was well on its way to denuclearization had amounted in many ways to simply negotiating the terms of Kim Jong Il's capitulation.

Now, underscoring the failure of its preference for coercion, threats, sanctions, and talk of pre-emptive strikes, Bush had signed on to a deal whose outline had been established in Hill's unprecedented bilateral with Kim Gye Gwan in Berlin. North Korea would get benefits first—a resolution of the BDA sanctions—before having to take any steps to shut down the Yongbyon facility. For all the linguistic gyrations that had produced the phrase "shut down and seal," Bush had accepted what amounted to a freeze as an initial step—something the North Koreans had been offering and which the United States had consistently rejected since 2003. And Pyongyang would begin to receive heavy fuel oil and other equivalent aid, long before giving up its nuclear arsenal. Moreover, the United States had committed itself to gradual reconciliation by working toward the removal of other sanctions and negotiating the eventual normalization of relations.

Indeed, with the accord bearing striking similarities to the 1994 Agreed Framework, Bush now appeared to be embracing virtually the same deal he had come to office in 2001 rejecting—but with a critical difference: the North's nuclear program was now more advanced. It had seven to ten bombs worth of plutonium and had tested a nuclear device. It was a point many veterans of the Clinton administration were quick to make.

Administration officials, however, took pains to emphasize that the accord was not identical to the Agreed Framework, emphasizing that North Korea had committed not just to freeze but to dismantle its nuclear facilities, that the bulk of the benefits would come only after meaningful progress on denuclearization had been achieved, and that the involvement of all six countries participating in the talks ensured that the United States was not alone in cutting a deal with Pyongyang.

Still, as Democratic senator Joseph Biden—a longtime critic of the president's earlier refusal to engage in meaningful negotiations—noted, the deal in crucial ways, "takes us back to the future."[6]

Not surprisingly, news of the deal triggered a near revolt among the right-wingers who had long been the strongest supporters of Bush's previous tough line toward North Korea. John Bolton, who had just left his post as U.S. ambassador to the UN, led the charge, denouncing the agreement as an abandonment of the basic premises of the president's earlier approach.

"It sends exactly the wrong signal to would-be proliferators around the world," he told one reporter. " 'If we [North Korea] hold out long enough, wear down the State Department negotiators, eventually you get rewards.' "[7]

In his memoir, *Surrender Is Not an Option*, Bolton was even more scathing. "This deal let North Korea escape from the corner where we had put them by Resolution 1718's sanctions and our Treasury Department's aggressive efforts to impose tough economic pressure on the DPRK for its illicit money-laundering. The February 13 agreement is what Powell would have loved to try in 2001 before Bush pulled him back from 'leaning too far forward' on his skis."[8]

An editorial in the *Wall Street Journal* denounced the accord as "faith-based nonproliferation,"[9] while the *National Review*, long a leading right-wing mouthpiece, ran a headline asking, "When Exactly Did Kim Jong Il Become Trustworthy?" and insisted the deal would only give the North Korean leader another opportunity to cheat.[10]

The deal was unquestionably vague on a number of key points. The statement committed the North to the "eventual abandonment" of its nuclear facilities. But Pyongyang's pledge to "discuss a list of all its nuclear programs, including plutonium extracted from used fuel rods," contained no explicit reference to a uranium enrichment effort—the issue that had sparked the crisis in 2002 (and a program that the North Koreans continued to insist did not exist). Nor was there a reference to any existing nuclear weapons, raising doubts about how—or whether—the North would live up to its commitment in the September 2005 joint statement to "abandon all nuclear weapons and existing nuclear programs." It was not only the hard-liners in Washington who suspected Kim Jong Il might be doing little more than playing for time, with no intention ever to abandon his nukes.

On the U.S. side, although Washington had committed itself to the goal of "resolving bilateral issues"—including removing the North from the terrorism list and the Trading With the Enemy Act—the statement issued in Beijing used words such as "start," "begin," and "advance" to describe the process; there was no explicit pledge that the United States would actually implement the specified actions, leaving movement on these matters dependent on progress in other areas.

Clearly, much hard bargaining remained ahead.


The conclusion of the February 13 deal also left Japan as odd man out. While South Korea quickly signaled its intention to accelerate economic and diplomatic engagement with Pyongyang, an irritated Prime Minister Abe refused to join the other participants in providing the aid the North had been promised under the deal. Tokyo's fixation on the fate of the abductees—which its envoy to the talks, Kenichiro Sasae, had raised with Kim Gye Gwan in Beijing, with no effect—remained the key stumbling block. Having built his political career on the abductee issue and his tough stance toward North Korea, Abe was in no mood to offer any conciliatory gestures to Pyongyang. Indeed, so intense were the domestic political pressures, which Abe himself helped generate, that one Japanese scholar told the *New York Times* that the situation was one in which "Japanese diplomacy has, so to speak, been abducted by the abduction issue."[11]

Chris Nelson, editor of a widely respected daily newsletter on U.S. Asia policy, compared the Japanese obsession with the abductees to the American fixation on the fate of its soldiers missing in action in Indochina after the end of the Vietnam War, which for more than two decades crippled the ability of successive governments in Washington to normalize relations with Hanoi. It was far from clear whether Kim Jong Il, having already taken, by his standards, the unprecedented step of admitting to and apologizing for the abductions, would be willing to do much more.

"Both governments are now in a trap," Nelson wrote. "Even if you assume that Kim Jong Il can look sincere on this tragedy, how can Prime Minister Abe or his successors, be satisfied with whatever Pyongyang comes up with? And even if the government of Japan is satisfied, how can it convince the public and the media?"[12]

Japanese officials expressed their intention to address the issue in a bilateral working group set up under the new accord. But Abe's rigid position left Japan—whose brutality during World War II was still bitterly resented throughout the region, especially in Korea—looking morally obtuse, if not downright hypocritical. Moreover, Tokyo now appeared so concerned with the fate of a handful of people that it risked losing sight of the broader goal of getting rid of Kim Jong Il's nuclear weapons.

The Japanese stance also raised the prospect of a split with its four allies in the six-party process—most notably with the United States. Unless they included a resolution of the abductee issue that was acceptable to Japan, U.S. plans to remove North Korea from its list of states sponsoring terrorism would be much more complicated, potentially leaving Washington with the difficult choice of ignoring the top policy priority of a key ally or seeing the entire process unravel.

The Beijing deal nonetheless was a significant breakthrough. It would shut down a reactor that was generating enough plutonium for one new bomb each year and would halt the construction on a far larger reactor that could produce much more nuclear fuel. It would also shut the reprocessing plant that extracted the plutonium from the reactor's spent nuclear fuel. Perhaps most important of all, it would shut and seal a refurbished fuel fabrication plant that would enable the North to make more fuel rods to run through the reactor and reprocessing plant. With the presence of IAEA inspectors on the ground, it would also be harder for the North to remove fissile material from production sites and make it available to other "rogue states" or terrorist groups. Most important, the accord laid out a roadmap with the potential to achieve both Washington's goal of eliminating the North's nuclear program, and Pyongyang's wish for a fundamental shift in its decades-old confrontation with the United States. North Koreans, from Kim Jong Il on down, had long insisted they would not need a nuclear capability if Washington was no longer their enemy. The February 13 deal, by explicitly offering that prospect to Pyongyang, created conditions in which, for the first time, it would be possible to test whether the North actually meant what it had consistently said.

Still, Hill and his colleagues were realistic. "Have the North Koreans made a decision to give up their nuclear weapons program?" mused one U.S. official involved in the negotiations. "I think that's actually not the right question to ask, because it wouldn't make sense for them to have made the decision at this point in the relationship, because the point of the bombs is security. It's not so much a military weapon as a political tool, so it doesn't make sense for them to have made this decision at a point where they are not 100 percent sure where their relationship with us and the rest of the world is going. Maybe another way to think of it is that we are only now beginning to go steady. It is probably not the best time to be talking about grandchildren. It's a little premature."

One of the thorniest issues left unresolved by the February 13 deal was the status of North Korea's uranium effort. Within days of the signing of the accord, Christopher Hill began to signal what appeared to be a significant backtracking from the administration's long-standing assertion that the North was developing a full-blown highly enriched uranium [HEU] program. That belief represented such a serious and immediate threat that it had justified refusing to negotiate, cutting off shipments of fuel, and adopting a more confrontational posture, which were the steps that, in 2002, had spurred Pyongyang to end the freeze begun under the Agreed Framework and stage its nuclear breakout. At the time, President Bush was so sure of the HEU intelligence that in November 2002 he had declared at a press conference, "We discovered that, contrary to an agreement they had with the United States, they're enriching uranium, with a desire of developing a weapon."[13] The intelligence, of course, did not quite say they were enriching uranium, only that they were acquiring the means to do so.

Now, Hill indicated that the United States was much less certain about what the North was up to. In a speech on February 22, 2007, he said, "We have information . . . that North Korea made certain purchases of equipment highly consistent with HEU . . . it's a complex program, it does require more equipment than we know they have purchased, and a variety of techniques we don't know they have worked out. But we need to know why they purchased aluminum tubes from Germany and elsewhere—tubes we know fit the Pakistani-designed centrifuges we know they purchased. If the tubes do not go to an HEU program, fine, we can discuss that later on [in the six-party talks process.]"[14]

Hill's statement contained none of the headstrong language of earlier administration claims. He made no reference to North Korea's so-called admission—the pivotal moment that had triggered the crisis. Instead, he made clear that the only thing the administration knew for certain was that the North had been engaged in the procurement of technology that could have applications to a highly enriched uranium program—indicating there was no reliable intelligence to confirm the existence of an actual HEU production facility. With the administration's intelligence failures in Iraq looming in the background, Hill appeared willing to entertain the possibility that the North Koreans might come up with a plausible alternative explanation for their high-tech shopping spree.

Five days later, Joseph DeTrani, the former CIA operative and onetime member of Hill's negotiating team—and now the North Korea mission manager at the Directorate of National Intelligence—also backed off the earlier assertions. In testimony before the Senate Armed Services Committee, he said that while the Bush administration had "high confidence" that the North Koreans had engaged in a procurement effort, it had only "mid-confidence" that the North would be in a position to enrich much anytime soon.[15] In the jargon of the intelligence community, this appeared to be a significant retreat from the administrations earlier claims that the North was well on its way to being able to manufacture a uranium-based bomb.

Several factors appear to have been at work in these efforts at political fine-tuning. The use of "high," "medium," and "low" confidence in measuring intelligence was a recent development; it was introduced in the past four years to provide a "metric" to judge the degree of interagency consensus on the reliability of an intelligence judgment. The approach had its skeptics. "Most of the time you can't quantify this stuff," observed one former intelligence analyst.

In any case, DeTrani's use of "mid-confidence" referred to the fact that although the original estimate had foretold an operational program to produce enough HEU for at least a bomb a year by mid-decade, it was now 2007 and no compelling evidence had ever turned up of a uranium enrichment facility being built or operated inside North Korea. It also suggested that procurement had slowed, or as one senior intelligence official noted, "We were seeing less and less evidence" of North Korean activity related to uranium.

But there appear to have been clear diplomatic benefits in making these redefinitions of the intelligence assessments public. If the United States were to get to the bottom of what the North had actually done—and thus make it easier for the North Koreans to acknowledge their activities, which was an essential step to a long-term resolution of the entire nuclear crisis—the starting point had to be based on the actual evidence, not the inflated claims from 2002.

According to one person who had participated in the six-party talks, "There never was the suggestion that we could compromise on our judgment that they had a [uranium] program. But the North Koreans seemed to be saying, 'If we do have a program, how do we get past it?' So the issue is—how do we help the North Koreans get to the point where they can admit it and not be embarrassed?"

Embarrassment was not just an issue for the North Koreans. Given the Bush administration's track record on misuse of intelligence on Iraq and Iran, the backtracking on HEU claims set off a firestorm of controversy, with front-page stories and angry editorials in the *Washington Post*, *New York Times*, and other newspapers.

"Once again," thundered a *Post* editorial, "the Bush administration is being accused of exaggerating intelligence to justify an aggressive policy toward a rogue regime, with disastrous results."[16]

But the HEU question, if it was to be addressed, would have to come at a later stage in the process. Before anything else could happen, the United States had to make good on its pledge in the Berlin meeting to resolve the Banco Delta Asia sanctions—an issue that now sparked a bitter internal battle between Christopher Hill and the Treasury Department, and almost torpedoed the entire February 13 deal. Failure to return the $25 million would allow North Korea to keep making more plutonium for nuclear weapons. Yet Treasury's position was, in essence, Hill made the deal; let him implement it.

With Hill pushing to draw a line through the BDA affair, Treasury grudgingly indicated that, having made its point, it would not oppose the idea of separating legitimate from illicit accounts and returning of at least some the long-frozen funds to North Korea. In a background briefing to the *New York Times* months later, Treasury officials said that of the fifty-two frozen BDA accounts, thirty-five—holding about $13 million—were relatively clean. The remaining seventeen—containing about $12 million—were suspect, with Treasury officials contending the money came from counterfeiting, drugs, and other illicit activities.[17] In this briefing, as in virtually all other public statements, the Treasury Department provided no evidence for its assertions. It remains unclear whether the Department's judgment was based on the fact that the account holders had a record of dubious activities or whether Treasury knew of specific transactions that were tainted but did not want to reveal its sources and methods. According to one senior U.S. official involved in the issue, "Our concerns focused on the account holders and their conduct at the bank, not the actual funds themselves."

On March 14, Stuart Levey, the Under Secretary for Terrorism and Financial Intelligence, acknowledged "positive developments" by the Macau authorities to strengthen anti-money-laundering regulations and "safeguard itself from financial crime." But Levey blasted BDA, dismissing the bank's efforts to improve its business practices and ignoring the Ernst & Young audit which said there was no convincing evidence of counterfeiting, and saying, "The deceptive financial practices and grossly inadequate controls within BDA have run too deep for us to ignore. BDA's business practices pose a real threat to banks worldwide, and BDA has no business accessing the U.S. financial system."[18]

The decision appears to have been based only partly on the specifics of the case. "It was sort of an interagency battle [between State and Treasury] at that point," said one official who was involved with the issue. "Treasury found itself in the position where it felt it would be too embarrassing not to come out with a judgment that seemed to reinforce the notion that [BDA was] carrying out illicit activities." At issue was Treasury's post-9/11 authority under Section 311 to go after Iran and others. Moreover, the harsh step was consistent with the hardline views on North Korea long held by Stuart Levey, who had played a key role in trying to isolate the North from the U.S. financial system and had repeatedly argued that all North Korean funds were suspect.

"The North Koreans were apoplectic," said one Western businessman whose plans for projects in North Korea had been stymied by the BDA issue. The North's bad credit rating precluded it from borrowing; it had to conduct foreign trade in cash. "To them it was a fundamental issue—how do you run an economy if you can't have any bank accounts? You can't even sell a case of beer in Singapore because they can't pay for it."

For this reason, the North Koreans were determined not to accept any partial lifting of the BDA freeze, or to take any steps to dismantle their nuclear program until they got all the money back. Pyongyang's position was made clear during a visit by the head of the International Atomic Energy Agency, Mohamed El Baradei. As a gesture of sincerity, the North had issued an invitation to El Baradei just days after the signing of the February 13 deal. He was the first IAEA official to visit the country since the expulsion of the nuclear inspectors at the end of 2002. By coincidence, El Baradei was in Pyongyang as the Treasury Department announced its permanent designation of BDA. Officials told the IAEA chief they remained "committed" to the deal. Unless the sanctions were lifted and the money returned, however, they warned that the Yongbyon reactor would continue to operate.[19]

The next round of six-party talks convened in Beijing the following week. State and Treasury were still battling. Concerned about the deadlock and the possible damage to U.S.-China relations—especially to a U.S.-China strategic dialogue spearheaded by Treasury Secretary Hank Paulson—Condoleezza Rice prevailed on Paulson to instruct his staff that all of the North Korean money could be returned. But no guidance was given as to the specifics of how that should be done.

Arriving in Beijing ahead of the six-party session, Hill met privately with Kim Gye Gwan to work out an arrangement. The Treasury Department was concerned that the released funds not go back to the so-called bad actors—the original North Korean account holders suspected of illicit activities. Treasury had pressed Hill to insist the North agree to a "tracking regime"—a mechanism whereby the North Koreans would have to account to the United States for how released money was used. The North Koreans, not surprisingly, were not receptive. Instead, Kim pledged that the funds would be used only for "humanitarian activities." The understanding would in fact allow the North Koreans to do whatever they wanted, but it saved face, and, in the broader context of resolving the BDA impasse so the nuclear deal could proceed, Hill felt it was an acceptable compromise.

On the evening of Sunday, March 17, Deputy Assistant Treasury Secretary Daniel Glaser, Treasury's point man for the BDA issue, flew into Beijing. The next morning, he and Hill were scheduled to hold a joint news conference to announce that Washington had no objection to the money being returned to the North Koreans. Late that night, Glaser's and Hill's teams met at the St. Regis Hotel to go over talking points for the upcoming media event. Despite the agreement that Hill had reached with Kim Gye Gwan, Glaser was under intense pressure from his boss, Stuart Levey, the Treasury Department's hard-line under secretary. Levey was insisting that Glaser push Hill to go back to the North Koreans and renegotiate the understanding to include the "tracking regime." Hill said the deal was as good as he was going to get, and that both Condoleezza Rice and Treasury Secretary Hank Paulson had signed off on returning the money. But Levey and Glaser persisted. The differences led to a bitter argument between the Treasury and State officials that lasted most of the night, with Glaser and aides to Hill exchanging shouts and insults that reverberated through the corridors of Beijing's luxurious St. Regis Hotel.

Hill's staff "basically bullied the crap out of Treasury," said one official familiar with what happened, "corralling Glaser in his hotel room at two o'clock in the morning, just yelling and badgering him until he was emotionally rattled."

"It was not a pretty moment," one eyewitness recalled.

The next morning, at the Diaoyutai State Guest House, Glaser issued a statement, saying, "The DPRK has proposed the transfer of the roughly $25 million frozen in BDA into an account held by North Korea's Foreign Trade Bank at the Bank of China in Beijing. North Korea has pledged . . . that these funds will be used solely for the betterment of the North Korean people, including for humanitarian and educational purposes. We believe this resolves the issue of the DPRK-related frozen funds."[20]

For an always skeptical Pyongyang, however, a promise was not good enough. In its view, Washington had reneged on past promises. As the six-party talks got under way, Kim Gye Gwan made clear that Pyongyang needed to see the cash before it would halt any nuclear activities. Kim then refused to even discuss nuclear matters, boycotting the plenary session and throwing the entire round into disarray.

After four days, the talks broke up with no progress—and the $25 million still sitting in the Banco Delta Asia in Macau.

Having agreed to allow North Korea to retrieve the funds, in the weeks that followed, the State Department tried to get Chinese, South Korean, and even American banks to accept the BDA money. All refused for fear of being tainted by money-laundering charges.

By late spring, the usually optimistic Hill was close to despair—feeling alarmed that a historic opportunity to resolve the North Korean nuclear crisis might be slipping away as well as increasingly frustrated by his inability to find a way forward. There seemed no way to solve the problem, but he continued to press Rice on the matter. "I kept saying, 'For Christ's sake, we're getting them to shut down their reactor by giving them their own money,'" he recalled. "'Why is that such a bad deal?'"

Condoleezza Rice again went to Treasury Secretary Hank Paulson and President Bush, pressing them for what Hill had called a "strategic decision" to resolve the matter regardless of the logistical difficulties. But until a bank could be found to handle the money, the situation remained at an impasse.

Finally, in May, an obscure Russian bank called Far East Commercial Bank, based in Khabarovsk, emerged as a possible savior. The North Koreans had given the bank's name to the Americans as a possible option shortly after the decision had been made to return the money. With no other options, the U.S. ambassador in Moscow, William J. Burns, was authorized to ask the Russians for help. The Russians told him that if the United States would provide assurances their banks would not face any negative consequences under U.S. anti-money-laundering regulations, Moscow would handle the final transfer. Complex negotiations ensued. The Russians hired a Washington law firm to represent them in talks with Treasury and State Department officials. Eventually, they agreed on acceptable wording for the assurance. However, for greater security, the Russian Foreign Ministry demanded that the document be transmitted in the form of a formal diplomatic note from the State Department. Treasury and State both agreed. At the end of the first week in June, President Bush reportedly discussed the broad outlines with Russian President Vladimir Putin at the G8 summit in Germany,[21] and the long-running drama moved toward resolution.

A week later, on June 14, with the blessing of the Treasury Department, BDA moved $23 million dollars to the Macau Monetary Authority, which then wired the funds to the Federal Reserve Bank of New York on June 14. Two million dollars remained in Macau due to legal disputes. The money was transferred to the Russian central bank, which deposited it at the North Korean Foreign Trade Bank account at the Far East Commercial Bank. Why Treasury would prefer the due diligence exercised by a bank in the wild east of Russia and not a reputable U.S. bank was never clear.

Although a huge obstacle to movement on the nuclear front was resolved, the entire episode left Washington in a sour mood.

"In the end, we laundered the money for them," sighed one senior official who supported the move, "by washing it through the Federal Reserve."

Some members of Congress were furious. Representative Ileana Ros-Lehtinen, the ranking Republican on the House Foreign Affairs Committee, demanded an investigation by the General Accounting Office into whether the BDA transfer had been legal. Nothing came of her demand, but it was a reflection of the weak political support in Washington for any gestures that could be portrayed as "rewarding" North Korea.

Still, once the transfer was under way, the North Koreans acted quickly, as promised. On June 16, an invitation was issued for a delegation from the IAEA to visit Yongbyon and discuss suspending operations at the reactor.

That same week, Christopher Hill was on an Asian tour, spending much of his time consulting with Chinese, Japanese, and South Korean officials about restarting the six-party talks. He was in Mongolia when he unexpectedly received an invitation to visit North Korea from Kim Gye Gwan. The invitation was relayed by North Korean diplomats to the U.S. embassy in Beijing; it was a sign that with the BDA issue nearing resolution, Pyongyang, again as promised, was ready to reengage on the nuclear issue.

Hill had long wanted to visit the North, but his earlier efforts had been repeatedly thwarted. This time, in keeping with what had become his standard operating procedure, he bypassed the interagency process to prevent conservative critics from stopping him. Instead, he called Rice and argued that with the BDA affair settled, the trip offered a chance to jump-start the diplomatic process. It would a good time to go in and take the temperature personally, he said, arguing that "if you are going to negotiate with somebody, you need to know where they are coming from, literally as well as figuratively." Rice spoke to Bush, who gave his approval. It all happened quickly, and Hill took only the four colleagues who were already traveling with him. Officials from the Pentagon and other agencies who would normally be on such a trip were frozen out.

"It was all very hush-hush," said one official who worked on the Washington end of the logistics. "There was a lot of grumbling [from other agencies] because they felt they should be there as well."

The grumbling increased when Rice, on very short notice, called Defense Secretary Robert Gates to tell him that Hill needed a military aircraft to transport his team to Pyongyang.

"The Pentagon freaked out about it," recalled one knowledgeable official. "They tried their damn best to prevent it, but what were they going to do? Gates had said, 'Do it.' "

Still, given the divisions in Washington, Hill was taking a huge risk. "He's raising the stakes, his personal stake," said one official working on Korean issues at the time. "If the North Koreans don't follow through, he's gone way out on a limb, and that branch is pretty shaky."

But the move was part of a pattern that had come to characterize Hill's behavior. He was, as one sympathetic official said, a "Lone Ranger" but also a highly skilled operator—"the rare career Foreign Service officer," said one colleague, "who behaves with the confidence and political savvy of a political appointee." Within the administration, he was pursuing a strategy of "marginalizing everybody." The logic of freezing out those who for years had obstructed progress on resolving the North Korea issue had an obvious appeal for someone so ambitious.

In relation to the North Koreans, Hill believed it was essential to show, through his personal actions, that the shift in U.S. policy was genuine and that he was a trustworthy interlocutor.

That required what one longtime North Korea hand described as "a certain amount of personal courage in his willingness to be flexible and to communicate with the North in a way that a level of trust is built in the negotiations. It is a risky business."

But Rice and Bush appeared ready to let him take the risks. As a State Department official observed, the president and Rice "basically said, 'OK, fine. If Chris Hill thinks he can do it, let him do it. If he succeeds, we get the credit. If he fails, then he takes the blame for it and we hang him out to dry.'"

Still, so acute were the internal tensions in Washington that Hill was instructed to remain on the ground in Pyongyang no more than twenty-four hours. One official involved with the arrangements said, they were told "that they needed to get in, get the business done, and get out."

It was, in the words of a former colleague, a "high-wire act without a net." But Hill was undeterred. On June 21, he arrived, in a driving rain, on a small U.S. Air Force jet at Pyongyang's virtually deserted airport. He was the most senior U.S. official to visit the North Korean capital since Jim Kelly's trip in October 2002, which had sparked the crisis Hill was now seeking to resolve.

Standing on the tarmac to greet him, holding an umbrella, was Li Gun, North Korea's deputy nuclear negotiator. Smiling broadly, Li extended his hand.

"We are all waiting for you," he said.

Almost immediately after arriving, Kim Gye Gwan offered to take Hill to Yongbyon. For the secretive North Koreans, it was a significant gesture of goodwill. But it put Hill in an awkward position. As he huddled with his aides, Korea Desk director Sung Kim urged that Hill say "no." The North Koreans had not yet begun the process of disablement, and the BDA issue was still in its final stages. The optics were not good, Sung Kim told Hill. The picture in the newspapers would be Chris Hill observing Yongbyon in operation, not observing a shut-down. Hill agreed and declined the invitation.

Kim Gye Gwan seemed disappointed, and then suggested Hill meet the head of North Korea's Department of Atomic Energy. The Americans were dubious, convinced all they would get would be standard North Korean rhetoric. This offer too was declined.

Instead, apart from a brief courtesy call on Foreign Minister Pak Ui Chun, Hill spent most of his time with Kim Gye Gwan. By now, the two men were more or less comfortable with each other, and the discussions were wide-ranging, covering everything from the six-party talks and immediate questions like shutting down the Yongbyon reactor to broader issues such as permanent security arrangements in Northeast Asia and the normalization of relations between Washington and Pyongyang. Hill came away convinced that once the North Koreans got their money back, they would indeed move on disabling Yongbyon.

Unlike on many other occasions, on this visit, Hill followed his instructions not to stay more than twenty-four hours. Just twenty-one hours after landing, he flew out of Pyongyang.

Two days later, the Macau funds were wired to the North Korean account at the Far East Commercial bank in Khabarovsk. The next day, a four-member team from the International Atomic Energy Agency landed in Pyongyang to visit Yongbyon.

Less than a month later, on July 18, the IAEA announced that the reactor had been shut down.

# 20

# "DEAR MR. CHAIRMAN"

ROBERT CARLIN COULD HARDLY BELIEVE WHERE HE WAS. The veteran U.S. intelligence analyst—who had spent nearly twenty years studying North Korea at the CIA and another decade doing the same thing for the State Department's Bureau of Intelligence and Research (INR) before quitting the government in disgust after the Axis of Evil speech in 2002—was standing inside the Yongbyon nuclear facility. It was late summer of 2007, and Carlin was part of a group organized by Stanford University professor John Lewis, a frequent visitor to North Korea. The delegation also included Siegfried Hecker, former head of the Los Alamos Nuclear Laboratory, and another North Korea hand from the American intelligence community—John Merrill, who still studied the country for INR.

The last time Hecker and Lewis had been to Yongbyon was in January 2004. The North Koreans had showed them the complex, and even let Hecker hold a container of plutonium to prove they did indeed have a nuclear "deterrent." Ironically, this time the group had been taken to Yongbyon because the North Koreans wanted to demonstrate that they were moving to shut the facility down. Inspectors from the IAEA had already been back at Yongbyon for several weeks, putting seals on machinery and mounting surveillance cameras on the walls. From the moment the Americans arrived at the main gate of the complex, the change in the political atmosphere that had produced such openness became evident. One of the Americans had left his passport in his room at the Koryo Hotel in Pyongyang; in security-conscious North Korea, not having the right piece of paper would in the past have virtually guaranteed that permission to visit would be denied. Now, though, he simply showed his U.S. driver's license to the tough-looking, rifle-toting North Korean guards. They waved him through.

Carlin took in the scene at the nuclear complex that had consumed so much of his analytical energy for so many years. It was dark, run-down, and decrepit. There were puddles of water on the floors and mold on the walls. To Carlin, it looked like it was being held together by sheer will. As they were briefed by the staff, it became clear to Carlin that the employees of Yongbyon knew their time was almost up—that a political decision had already been made to cease operations. Nonetheless, the presence of the Americans—especially people with an intelligence background—still made them uneasy. In a conversation with one engineer, Hecker, one of the world's leading nuclear authorities, asked a particularly detailed and sensitive technical question. Carlin saw the engineer's eyes dart to the chief of the complex, seeking guidance on whether to respond. Ever so slightly, the chief nodded, and the engineer began to talk.

The incident highlighted a trend toward openness that was becoming increasingly evident in North Korea in the last half of 2007, not in the country's oppressive political system, but in its economy, in daily life, and, most notably, in the interaction between foreigners and ordinary North Koreans.

"The lines you are not supposed to cross have been redrawn," Carlin observed.

The increasing number of foreign visitors—Carlin included—remarked on the many signs of change. On the once-empty streets of Pyongyang, more and more motorcycles were visible, suggesting official tolerance for a means of transport that gave citizens in a tightly controlled society greater mobility. Carlin, who had made numerous trips to Pyongyang, was struck by the number of well-dressed women and especially by his first sighting of a North Korean in blue jeans.

More telephone kiosks were evident on street corners, often with lines of people waiting to use them, and more people were using mobile phones—another sign of a slight easing of social controls on internal communications. Small shops and vendors were visible, and officially sanctioned free markets offered goods ranging from food to clothing to electrical appliances and tools. Visitors reported a clear sense of greater economic possibility emerging, with a greater receptivity both to foreign business and the profit motive.

One member of Carlin's group was taken by a Polish diplomat to what had been a safe house for North Korea's intelligence service. Located in the hills above the enormous Arch of Triumph (bigger than the one in Paris), the safe house had been converted into a for-profit restaurant and guesthouse open to foreigners—a joint venture between the North Koreans and a pro-Pyongyang

Korean citizen of Japan. The Americans were convinced that the food was as high quality as the surveillance equipment monitoring their conversation in the building.

At another privately run restaurant, Carlin was amazed to see that the waitresses, after serving the food, sat in a back room listening to a tape recording of Italian opera.

These were not the only hints of greater openness to dealings with foreigners. Carlin's group, led by Stanford University professor Lewis, wanted to discuss the possibility of starting educational exchanges—hosting a small group of North Korean students in California, sending Stanford professors to Pyongyang, and eventually establishing a formal exchange program. The implications of such exchanges were potentially eye-opening—exposing members of the North Korean elite to life outside their own bleak, impoverished, and sealed society, possibly acting as a catalyst for change inside the country. Despite some official skepticism, the group was surprised to find their proposal getting a positive response. At the education ministry, an initially skeptical official eventually asked how many students he might send to Palo Alto. The Americans said three or four.

"How about eight or ten?" the North Korean replied.

A group composed of U.S. congressional staffers visited North Korea later in the fall of 2007. They were invited to meet English-language students at the Pyongyang Foreign Language University. Officials there asked for help in acquiring English-language books and teaching materials. The U.S. group, which included people who had previously visited the country, also found themselves allowed to walk unaccompanied through the streets and to interact easily with local residents—the sort of unsupervised contact that had previously been strictly forbidden. At a museum devoted to the ideology of Kim Il Sung, the visitors got into a discussion with a guide about the origins of the Korean War. They rejected their guide's standard explanation that the war was the fault of the "American imperialists," countering that Americans were taught it was Kim who started the conflict. The guide politely said, "Well, we disagree." The mere fact that a civilized exchange could be held on such a sensitive topic was a sign of an easing of the previously oppressive atmosphere.

In another move full of symbolism, in December 2007, the New York Philharmonic accepted a North Korean invitation to perform in Pyongyang in early 2008. The breakthrough was the latest in a long series of American orchestras playing important diplomatic roles. In 1956, at the height of the Cold War, the Boston Symphony became the first American orchestra to perform in the Soviet Union, and in 1973, the Philadelphia Orchestra made a historic trip to China, a follow-up to ping-pong diplomacy and Richard Nixon's path-breaking trip to

Beijing a year earlier. The New York Philharmonic's visit was finalized after complex negotiations requiring the personal involvement of Kim Gye Gwan. Surprisingly, the North Koreans accepted the orchestra's conditions that foreign journalists cover the concert, that it be broadcast live throughout North Korea and that the orchestra be allowed to play "The Star-Spangled Banner."

"We haven't even had ping-pong diplomacy with these people," said Christopher Hill, who encouraged the orchestra to go. "It would signal that North Korea is beginning to come out of its shell, which everyone understands is a long-term process. It does represent a shift in how they view us, and it's the sort of shift that can be helpful as we go forward in nuclear weapons negotiations."[1]

There were many possible explanations for these trends. Kim Jong Il had clearly been interested in tinkering with economic reforms for some time, which was underscored by his visits to and complimentary comments about Shanghai, Shenzhen, and other centers of China's economic transformation. In late 2007, the focus shifted to Vietnam, another Communist country experimenting with economic reforms. In October, Prime Minister Kim Yong Il, who was in charge of economic policy, visited Vietnam. His visit followed a trip to Pyongyang earlier that month by Vietnam's Communist Party secretary Nong Duc Manh. It was the first such visit by a high-ranking Vietnamese official in fifty years, and the North Koreans rolled out the red carpet, mobilizing huge crowds to welcome him. Forgotten was Vietnam's role in allowing North Korean refugees to pass through from China en route to South Korea. Indeed, given the tensions between Beijing and Pyongyang, Kim Jong Il appeared increasingly interested in Vietnam's experience as a possible model for reform in North Korea.

The two countries had much in common. Both had been divided by the Cold War and fought bloody wars with the United States. As small Communist states, both had struggled with years of American sanctions and other pressures. But now, Vietnam had emerged from isolation, establishing diplomatic relations with Washington and embarking on a program of market-oriented reforms that had helped to attract foreign investment and jump-start an impoverished, war-ravaged economy. As the North Korean prime minister visited ports and industrial sites, it was clear the North believed it might have much to learn from the Vietnamese experience.

As one Western diplomat based in Pyongyang observed, "North Korea is looking at how the Vietnamese did it. The idea of how to introduce economic change without political change is now at the forefront."

Perhaps an even greater catalyst for change had been pressure from below for greater tolerance of individual economic activity, fueled by the famine of the 1990s and the failure of the state-run economy to meet people's basic needs for food and fuel. These social forces propelled the government to legitimize free-market behavior to allow people to survive.

"The government can't provide anymore, so people have to find a way to make ends meet," observed one aid worker, who had been visiting the country since the mid-1990s. "Now, every family is trying to have someone in trading, because that means access to foreign currency."

Growing trade and contact with China and South Korea were also contributing to change. In addition to refugees who by the thousands had fled to the People's Republic, growing numbers of North Korean migrants were now moving back and forth across the border as smugglers or casual laborers—their passage eased by bribery and indifference among the North Korean border security forces. Once they are in China, as Russian scholar Andrei Lankov noted in a penetrating essay in *Asian Policy*, many younger North Koreans are exposed to the Internet, which is readily available in shops in most Chinese towns, Chinese citizens of Korean ethnicity, as well as South Korean businessmen, tourists, missionaries, and to activists seeking to help North Koreans flee or undermine Kim Jong Il's rule.

When they return home, these North Koreans have been bringing back stories of Chinese and South Korean prosperity, as well as radios, cell phones able to operate on the Northern side of the frontier through the Chinese mobile network, VCR machines, and videos of South Korean soap operas and pop culture, which are becoming increasingly popular inside North Korea.[2] Above all, they bring home new ways of thinking.


One other contributing factor to the cracks in the North's long-standing siege mentality was progress on the diplomatic front. While the regime remained deeply suspicious of the United States—out of a combination of genuine conviction, bitter experience, and the utility of having an external enemy to justify tight internal controls and the harshness of daily existence—gradually, some of the suspicion appeared to be easing. The notion that the United States was not going to attack them began to seep into the thinking of North Korean officials.

Christopher Hill was convinced that his style of doing business—defying hard-line pressure in Washington to show that the Bush administration really wanted better relations and taking political risks to address North Korean concerns—had contributed to the changed atmosphere.

"I like to think the way we've negotiated this thing" has made a difference, he said. "We've really shown sincerity—and, frankly, a little imagination."

Hill was also confident that he was gradually building up a relationship of trust with Kim Gye Gwan.

"The atmospherics are very good," said one American official involved in the diplomacy. "Compared to a year ago—or, more dramatically, two years ago—it's like night and day. There is some real dialogue and give-and-take that takes place."

"It's a good negotiating relationship," Hill said. "I think Kim sees me as someone who wants to try to reach a deal. Perhaps most importantly, he realizes I have access [to Secretary of State Rice and, through her, to President Bush]."

For their part, the Americans were heartened to learn that Kim Gye Gwan had been rewarded by the Dear Leader for his role in the recent months of diplomacy. U.S. visitors to Pyongyang learned that Kim had been provided a new residence in what was known as "Grace Village," an exclusive area of Pyongyang with housing for the ruling elite. Kim Jong Il had also given his nuclear negotiator a new Mercedes. And in early October, when South Korea's president Roh Moohyun visited Pyongyang for a summit with Kim Jong Il, came the clearest evidence that Kim Gye Gwan had his own high-level access. The Dear Leader asked Kim, rather than a higher-ranking official, to brief the South Korean leader on the North's view of the six-party process.

The positive tone was reinforced by a series of developments on the nuclear front in the fall of 2007. In the beginning of September, Hill and Kim Gye Gwan met in Geneva. (By now the Bush administration no longer seemed bothered that the Swiss city had been the place where the Clinton administration had negotiated the Agreed Framework thirteen years before.) In a replay of their encounter in Berlin nine months earlier, they put together the basics for what was called the "Second Phase" of implementing the September 19, 2005, joint declaration.

"It was essentially the Berlin model," said one U.S. official familiar with the meeting, "trying to get an understanding beforehand so when we go into a six-party meeting, we will walk out with a product."

As before, Hill also kept his agenda for the talks closely held, again circumventing the normal interagency process that had been such an obstacle to engagement in previous years. The other players in the six-party talks were also kept in the dark until the Geneva meetings concluded.

Later in the month, all six parties gathered again in Beijing to ratify what Kim and Hill had worked out. The new deal, made public on October 3, committed the North to complete the disablement of the three key components of the Yongbyon complex—the five-megawatt reactor, the plutonium reprocessing plant, and the nuclear fuel rod fabrication facility—by December 31, 2007. Kim

Gye Gwan also agreed that Pyongyang would "provide a complete and correct declaration of all its nuclear programs" by the same date and pledged that North Korea would not "transfer nuclear materials, technology or know-how"[3] to other parties or countries.

Already, work had begun on disabling Yongbyon. It had not been easy, with the United States and North Korea initially far apart even on how to define the term "disablement." In 2007 late summer, it had taken what Hill called "tough negotiations" at a meeting of a six-party working group in Shenyang, China, to bridge the gap. The Americans came with a series of papers, which they had first shared with the other participants in the six-party process, spelling out a list of measures designed to ensure that, once the facilities were shut down, they could not be easily reopened.

"[The North Koreans] wanted us to do less," Hill acknowledged. "We wanted them to do more."[4]

But once an understanding was reached, with IAEA inspectors already on the scene, U.S., Chinese, and Russian nuclear experts began to visit Yongbyon. They were eventually shown designs of the facility and held detailed discussions with North Korean engineers about how to disable it. The process was complex, involving the cutting of drive chains on some equipment, disassembly of machinery, and disposing of fuel rods currently in the reactor containing weapons-grade plutonium for more bombs. The main problem was that the cooling pond was unusable for storing the spent fuel without a time-consuming effort to clean it. The fuel rods could not be canned as they were in 1995. They would have to be reprocessed. Despite technical headaches, however, the process continued to move ahead, and the North Koreans proved surprisingly cooperative.

"[The visiting experts] were shown drawings and plans that no U.S. officials or IAEA officials had ever seen before," said one American official involved in the diplomacy. "We asked if we could take photographs and they said 'no.' They then came back with a compromise that they would give us a photographer to accompany us, which they did."

Hill said the goal was to move "in a seamless continuum [from disabling] toward dismantlement, that is toward taking these facilities apart and making sure they are irreversible—that they're never used again for the purpose that they were used for before."[5]

The declaration was a much tougher issue. Pyongyang had pledged to provide a "complete and correct" accounting of all its nuclear programs as the next necessary step to ending them. For Hill, that meant not only full disclosure of the amount of fissile material that had been produced, but also coming clean about the issue that had sparked the crisis five years before—the North's uranium program, the existence of which Pyongyang had, since 2002, regularly denied. The North had agreed in the February 2007 joint statement to "discuss with other parties a list of all its nuclear programs . . . that would be abandoned." The language in the diplomatic deal contained no specifics, one of the points that critics of Hill's efforts regularly cited. Thus there was concern on the American side that the North might dissemble, delay, play games, or offer half truths—and that any declaration, in Hill's words, would not "pass the laugh test." Without a credible document indicating that North Korea was serious, it would be impossible for Washington to take Pyongyang off the U.S. list of state sponsors of terrorism or lift sanctions under the Trading With the Enemy Act. And that scenario would risk the collapse of the entire diplomatic process. So Hill preferred to extend discussions rather than accept a list that would turn out to be partial.

As one of Hill's colleagues acknowledged, "The declaration is going to be very tricky and difficult."

The two sides began fencing over how to bring the information the United States wanted into the open. Neither side knew exactly what the other had.

"They want it to be a situation in which we confront them with evidence and they provide an explanation," said one American official familiar with the negotiations. "And of course what we want is for them to come clean on what they've done and then we match it up with what we have."

Still, there were some signs of movement. From categorical denials of any uranium enrichment effort, Kim Gye Gwan began to acknowledge that the North had tried to procure aluminum tubes and other components. Confronting Kim with specific information acquired by U.S. intelligence, Hill pressed for detailed answers about particular transactions. Kim insisted the tubes were not for a uranium program, but for launching rockets.

"We're asking them questions," said Hill, "they're giving us some answers. It's beyond, 'We don't have any of the material you say we have.' But they're not 'fessing up yet to an enrichment program. But they've admitted buying some of the things. They tried to show us they were buying them for conventional purposes."

But the North Korean explanation defied credibility. "Their story didn't add up," said one U.S. official. "They were lying."

Hill and his colleagues realized it would take time and more negotiations before the North Koreans would come clean—if they were in fact prepared to do so.

"In terms of locations and confirmation of the numbers of the weapons, that's going to be an end-game issue," said one senior official. "If you look at it objectively, it simply wouldn't make sense for them to disclose all of that information at this point."


The negotiations over the declaration cut to the heart of the biggest question in the entire crisis: Was Kim Jong Il, in the end, ready to make the strategic decision to trade away his nuclear capability? Despite all the harbingers of change, did Pyongyang have the political will to consummate the kind of diplomatic deal with Washington that it had maintained for years it was seeking—denuclearization in return for political reconciliation in the form of normalized relations and massive economic aid—and cope with the potentially destabilizing consequences of North Korea's rigid system being drawn into greater contact with the rest of the world?

Ultimately, the answer depended on internal dynamics in North Korea which outsiders, no matter how closely they followed the situation, could only dimly grasp. The indications of internal economic change and signs of greater external contact did not make the inner workings of North Korea's system or decision-making process any less opaque.

Although the cult of Kim Jong Il was as all-pervasive as ever, many analysts believed North Korea's ruling elite was sharply divided over what to do.

"Kim Jong Il may be a dictator," observed one longtime U.S.-government North Korea watcher, "but he's still got politics. He still has constituencies he needs to placate."

On one side were hard-liners in the military and security apparatus who were skeptical of the prospects of reaching an accommodation with the United States and who argued that nuclear weapons were essential to the regime's long-term security. The hard-liners also had institutional interests to protect, including the enormous investment in nuclear-related personnel and resources dating back decades as well as the party's role in directing the economy and the *songun* "military first" doctrine that gave the armed forces primacy over the party in North Korean society. The transformation of the United States from an enemy to a potential partner could jeopardize the military's clout. On the other side were pragmatists who favored a nuclear deal in the hope of reviving the economy and ending North Korea's crippling isolation. Such possibilities resonated in a younger generation with no memory of North Korea's economic success in the 1960s and '70s (in the early 1970s the North's economy was considered equal to or even stronger than that of the South), and whose experience with their own society in the past two decades had been one of decline, deprivation, and crisis.

Kim Jong Il was widely thought to lean toward the pragmatists, but he remained dependent on the military to maintain his grip on power. It was not a co-incidence that throughout the fall of 2007, almost all of his public appearances reported in the state-run Korean Central News Agency involved visits to military units. Christopher Hill felt that the incessant references to Kim in state propaganda and by government officials as the "Great General"—especially given the fact that, unlike his father, he had no meaningful record as a real soldier—highlighted not his control of, but his dependency on, the armed forces.

And, at the age of sixty-five and considering the persistent reports of health problems, Kim had another consideration: Would any of his children inherit the leadership of North Korea after his death? Kim was already well behind his father's timetable. Kim Il Sung was only sixty-one when he designated Kim Jong Il as his heir in 1971. The younger Kim had had more than twenty years to hold a series of leading positions, enabling him to gain experience and build up his power base, before his father died in 1994. But now, with three sons from two different women, neither of whom he married, Kim Jong Il has no obvious successor, certainly not one who has been groomed for years to assume the leadership.

The eldest son is Kim Jong Nam, now in his late thirties, whose mother, a movie actress, attracted Kim Jong Il's attention in the 1960s when he was spending time at film studios in Pyongyang. But Jong Nam's chances of inheriting his father's mantle were damaged after he was detained in 2001 at Tokyo's international airport while trying to enter Japan on a fake Dominican Republic passport, telling the authorities that he was planning to visit Tokyo Disneyland.

Following this public embarrassment, he was exiled to Beijing for several years. In addition, his mother fell out of favor with Kim Jong Il and went into exile in Moscow, where she died in 2003.

The other two sons—both now in their late twenties—are Kim Jong Chol and Kim Jong Un. Their mother, Ko Yong Hee, a dancer at the country's most prestigious song and dance troupe, met Kim Il Sung when the group performed at one of his parties in the 1970s. Little was known about either son. The older, Jong Chol, has reportedly studied in either France or Switzerland, and is said to be polite but to have an "effeminate" manner that his father disapproves of. The younger, Jong Un, possesses a "glaring ferocity," according to a Japanese chef who has traveled frequently to Pyongyang to cook for the Dear Leader.[6] It was not clear which son Kim Jong Il prefers, and as of early 2008, none of them has emerged as a credible successor.

For Kim, concerned about the survival of his family and his regime, the succession problem was becoming increasingly urgent. U.S.-government North Korea watchers speculated that the Dear Leader felt growing pressure to resolve the nuclear question so that whoever succeeded him would inherit a country confident that it would not be attacked and able to offer the next generation brighter economic prospects than the current one. It was less likely for any of his sons, inexperienced as they were, to succeed him if tensions remained high and North Korea remained insecure, both politically and economically.

"If he wants a smooth succession," noted one North Korea analyst, "he has to create a situation which the elite and most of the masses can support. The trajectory they were on was a trajectory that would have guaranteed him an increasingly impoverished, isolated country, and that's not the kind of country that a leader can hope to transfer peacefully to his successor."

The question, however, remained: In the final analysis, would Kim Jong Il—and the North Korean military—conclude the regime was safer with a nuclear deal or a nuclear bomb?

The front-page article in the London Sunday *Times* read like the opening passage of a spy thriller.

"It was just after midnight when the 69th Squadron of Israeli F-15Is crossed the Syrian coast-line. On the ground, Syria's formidable air defenses went dead. An audacious raid on a Syrian target fifty miles from the Iraqi border was under way. At a rendezvous point on the ground, an air force commando team was waiting to direct their laser beams at the target for the approaching jets. The team had arrived a day earlier, taking up position near a large underground depot. Soon the bunkers were in flames."[7]

For ten days, the purpose of the Israeli raid into Syria on September 6, 2007, remained cloaked in secrecy. Then, slowly, came a trickle of leaks with a stunning claim—Israel had targeted a Syrian nuclear project that was apparently being undertaken with help from North Korea. But the details remained sketchy. Israel imposed severe censorship to ensure its media revealed nothing of the raid. In Washington, too, the news was closely held on the orders of National Security Adviser Stephen Hadley. Curiously, even the Syrians remained tight-lipped.

With virtually no officials talking for the record, the information that did emerge—usually from unnamed "intelligence sources"—described the target as a facility in a remote desert area near the Euphrates River. Leaks to the *New York Times* said it was a "partly constructed nuclear reactor apparently modeled on one North Korea has used to create its stockpile of nuclear weapons fuel."[8] But it was not clear just what the North Koreans may have provided the Syrians. Press speculation included the possibility of diagrams, equipment, technical support, and the presence of North Korean experts, but not fissile material. There was no way to be certain, although the extreme secrecy surrounding the episode, especially in Washington, suggested that the leaks about some kind of North Korean connection did indeed have substance.

Indeed, even before the raid, enduring hard-line suspicions about North Korea triggered a new push by conservatives in the administration to torpedo the effort by Rice and Hill to pursue a diplomatic solution to the nuclear issue. As part of an administration debate in the summer of 2007 over whether an Israeli attack would be justified, Vice President Cheney and other hard-liners reportedly urged that the entire U.S. approach to negotiating with Pyongyang should be reconsidered, and that the decision to provide the North with shipments of fuel oil, as agreed in the February 13 deal, be reversed. In contrast, Condoleezza Rice and Defense Secretary Robert Gates urged caution, arguing that the Syrian facility appeared to be years away from completion and warning of the possible diplomatic fallout.[9]

The debate surfaced in an op-ed by John Bolton in the *Asian Wall Street Journal* on August 31, the eve of Hill's talks with Kim Gye Gwan in Geneva. "We need to learn the details of North Korean nuclear cooperation with other countries. We know that both Iran and Syria have long cooperated with North Korea on ballistic missile programs, and the prospect of cooperation on nuclear matters in not far-fetched. Whether and to what extent Iran, Syria or others might be 'safe havens' for North Korea's nuclear weapons development, or may have already benefited from it must be made clear."[10]

The arguments intensified after news of the raid became public, with Bolton in the lead. "I think the [the incident] shows right there that North Korea has no intention whatever of seriously complying with its commitment to give up nuclear weapons," he said. "And I think it gives the president a real opportunity to repudiate the deal and go back to putting pressure on North Korea, which is the only thing that ever gets their attention."[11]

If, as appears to have been the case, North Korea really was helping the Syrians, one intriguing question—apart from just what Pyongyang was providing—was the timing. Some weeks after the Israeli attack, satellite photos released by a commercial company, Virginia-based GeoEye, showed that construction at the site was under way in 2003.[12] In terms of possible North Korean involvement, the timing may not have been a coincidence as 2003 was a year when tension between the United States and North Korea had boiled over; there was the collapse of the Agreed Framework, Washington's refusal to negotiate, the restarting of the Yongbyon reactor to make more weapons-grade plutonium, the toppling of Saddam Hussein, and talk by some senior administration officials about the desirability of regime change in North Korea. Given Pyongyang's penchant for "tit-for-tat" behavior, providing some nuclear help (short of fissile material) to another country on George W. Bush's "bad guy" list at that particular time would have had a certain logic. As scholar Leon Sigal put it in unscholarly plain English, "When we fuck with them, they fuck with us."

But unlike the muscular and bellicose tone Bush had adopted toward North Korea in previous years, this time, the president and Condoleezza Rice appeared determined not to let the Syrian incident derail ongoing diplomatic efforts with Pyongyang. Despite what he was told about the Syria–North Korea connection, Bush allowed Hill to hold a bilateral meeting with Kim Gye Gwan in Geneva just days before the Israeli raid, and signed off on the "Second Phase" deal agreed at the six-party talks in October, even as the storm of controversy over the Syrian incident continued to swirl.

"The reason we have the six-party process, and the reason we have put together a number of pretty serious countries in this process, is to make sure that the North Koreans get out of the nuclear business," Hill said. "At the end of all this, we would expect to have a pretty clear idea of, you know, whether they have engaged in proliferation in other countries."[13]

Privately, Hill was scathing in his criticism of his hard-line adversaries. He saw them as people sitting in the cheap seats continually sniping at him but offering no credible alternative to negotiations.

But pressure from skeptical congressional conservatives complicated the administration's diplomatic efforts. In late October, Representative Ileana Ros-Lehtinen, the ranking Republican on the House Foreign Affairs Committee, published an opinion article denouncing the administration for its secrecy over the Syrian episode and its conciliatory approach to Pyongyang. Rice then held what was described as a "tense" meeting with Ros-Lehtinen, and the next day, Christopher Hill was pressed repeatedly by angry legislators over why the administration was not more forthcoming about whether North Korea had really provided nuclear help to Syria.

The reason for the reticence seems to have been a request by Israel not to reveal the details of its attack. Israel had been holding highly secret talks with Syria and hoped to continue them, even after the attack. Hill was deliberately vague and evasive, but he used language that left many observers even more convinced that there was some truth to the allegation.

"I am not in a position to discuss intelligence matters," he told the legislators. "I am not in a position to confirm or not."

As Washington insider Chris Nelson of the *Nelson Report* noted, "Given the critical importance of being able to assure the Congress of North Korea's trustworthiness, and the President's personal commitment to a successful 6-party process . . . [and] asked repeatedly . . . with every possible incentive to calm Congressional fears on a potentially critical point, [Hill] didn't."[14]

The implication—which no one in the administration was publicly acknowledging—was that the claims of a Syrian–North Korean connection indeed had some credibility, which could create a backlash that could jeopardize a still delicate and uncertain diplomatic process. Hill and his supporters were convinced there was no alternative but continued engagement with Pyongyang. In their view, sanctions and other pressures had not forced the North to abandon its nuclear program and seemed unlikely to have any meaningful impact as "punishment" for a relationship with Syria begun several years before—and which, with the Israeli destruction of the suspect site, had no lasting effect on U.S. security. Indeed, administration officials did brief some members of Congress, telling them that whatever assistance North Korea once provided had ended, and prompting the two leading senators on the Foreign Relations Committee, Democrat Joseph Biden and Republican Richard Lugar, to authorize aides to say they had heard nothing to convince them the United States should end its policy of negotiating with Pyongyang. The upshot was a conscious decision to say as little as possible about the episode.

Pressure from Capitol Hill was only one of the problems facing the U.S. negotiator. In late October, Thomas Schieffer, the American ambassador to Japan, sent a private cable to President Bush complaining that Hill had left the embassy in the dark about his diplomatic dealings with Pyongyang. The cable was highly unusual. Normally, ambassadors report to the secretary of state. But Schieffer was a longtime personal friend of the president and had been a coinvestor when Bush purchased the Texas Rangers baseball team in 1989. His use of the private channel was a reflection of the extent of his frustration. And he was not alone.

"In the process of pursuing his 'Lone Ranger' policy," noted one former State Department official, "Hill has overreached . . . and started to use up his bureaucratic capital in Washington. Despite the weakening of the neocons, he has created new adversaries in Congress and elsewhere in the administration."

In his cable, Schieffer warned that Hill's commitment to remove North Korea from a U.S. list of states sponsoring terrorism risked harming relations with Japan. The government in Tokyo continued to insist that North Korea account for the Japanese abductees before being taken off the terrorism list. Indeed, the Japanese parliament had passed a resolution to that effect.

"The Japanese are really unhappy with Hill and with Bush," observed a onetime senior State Department Northeast Asia expert. "All this stuff is moving forward. The Japanese feel they are being betrayed. The feeling is extremely strong up and down the bureaucracy."

The only restraining factor was that Yasuo Fukuda, who had replaced the hard-line Shinzo Abe as Prime Minister in the summer of 2007, was a moderate pragmatist looking to find a way out of the abductee impasse. Knowing that Abe had been told in March of Washington's intention to delist Pyongyang, Fukuda did not reopen the issue when he met Bush in November. While maintaining the demand for a full accounting, Fukuda's administration signaled that it might modify the Japanese position to make it easier for Pyongyang to take at least some steps to bring the controversial issue to closure. But the Japanese remained very uneasy with the way Hill was handling the negotiations and concerned about the impact on relations with Washington if the North was taken off the terrorism list too quickly.

Back in Washington, Hill also had few fans at the Pentagon. When the hard-line Donald Rumsfeld had been the secretary of defense, the Pentagon had been a major player on North Korea policy, with DOD staffers—usually supporters of a tough line against Pyongyang—attached to all the earlier U.S. delegations to the six-party talks. Even though Rumsfeld's successor, Robert Gates, was a moderate whose views on Korea were closer to Rice's than to his predecessor, Hill kept the Pentagon—including the U.S. military commander in South Korea—out of the loop.

Watching from the sidelines, even a longtime proponent of engagement like Chuck Kartman, who had been the Clinton administration's point man on North Korea, was concerned.

Hill's style of operating was "not the kind of pattern that can be sustained," Kartman observed. Kartman had spoken with Hill when he was offered the job of assistant secretary, and Kartman urged Hill to "build up an interagency consensus." Instead, Hill had taken exactly the opposite approach. "Without an interagency consensus," Kartman said, "the policy process is not working. It is dysfunctional, and you can end up having your legs cut out from under you."

Given the efforts by the hard-line "cabal"—a memorable term first used by Colin Powell's former chief of staff, Lawrence Wilkerson—it was understandable that Hill felt he had no choice but to circumvent the bureaucracy to restart and sustain the diplomatic process. But if diplomatic progress was to be translated into new policy, the administration would eventually require the cooperation of Congress, the Pentagon, the Energy Department, the intelligence community, and other key agencies who had been effectively frozen out of the action. Their antipathy toward Hill raised the prospect of problems down the road, especially when it came time to implement agreements he had negotiated with the North Koreans.

Still, Hill continued to have the support of the two people who counted most—the president and the secretary of state.

"Chris Hill is communicating directly with the secretary and the president and [they] have made clear the direction they want to go," observed a well-placed administration official. "It would be unusual if not just outright foolish for the rest of the bureaucracy to attempt to upend something the president and the secretary have made clear they want."

Nevertheless, the upsurge of criticism and the Syrian controversy led the administration to raise the bar. Hill was instructed to tell the North Koreans that the declaration had to include not only the amount of plutonium they had produced, but also the full details of their uranium program, their alleged transfer of nuclear technology and materials to other countries such as Syria, and the actual status of their nuclear weapons. With an already difficult task suddenly much harder, Chris Hill decided it was time for President Bush to make an overture directly to Kim Jong Il.

In the history of North Korean diplomacy, most of the important breakthroughs had come with the personal involvement of Kim Jong Il or his father Kim Il Sung. It was the elder Kim's meeting with former president Jimmy Carter in 1994 that paved the way for the Agreed Framework. And it had been the Dear Leader's own participation that was critical to the North–South summit in June 2000, to Madeleine Albright's visit in October of that year, and to Japanese prime minister Koizumi's summit meetings in Pyongyang in 2002 and 2004.

While Hill had established a cordial working relationship with Kim Gye Gwan, Kim Jong Il remained one step removed from the process: His name was constantly invoked by North Korean officials without anyone in the Bush administration having an opportunity to deal with him face to face.

As one former senior State Department official noted, "This is a guy who is obviously in charge and prepared to do some unconventional things. If you want a deal with North Korea on matters of deep sensitivity and vital interest, we will have to engage with him."

Of course, Kim's aloofness was hardly the only reason for the lack of contact. George W. Bush had not been shy in proclaiming his "loathing" for a man he described as a "tyrant" and a "pygmy." Now, Hill set out to convince his bosses that the circumstances required a direct personal communication from the President to the Dear Leader. The logic was straightforward. What Kim had sought from the United States—almost more than anything else—was recognition and respect as the head of a sovereign state. Since the North Korean system portrayed Kim as an almost god-like figure, Bush's numerous denunciations of Kim and refusal to grant him legitimacy had become a source of anger and resentment. If the United States expected Kim to take the necessary steps to get rid of his nuclear program, the symbolic impact of a respectful letter from Bush could be enormous.

Hill's idea was to take a letter from Bush to Kim and try to deliver it in person in Pyongyang. The letter would lay out a broad vision for future cooperation, including the lifting of sanctions, the normalization of relations, and the creation of permanent security arrangements for Northeast Asia. But it would also insist that progress would be impossible unless North Korea fulfilled its commitment to complete the dismantling of the Yongbyon reactor and fully declare its nuclear programs.

Hill pitched the idea to Rice, arguing that it offered the best chance for him to see Kim Jong Il and to convince the North Koreans that the shift in the Bush administration's attitude from confrontation to cooperation was genuine. The initial response was skepticism, so Hill offered a fall-back position—sending personal letters from Bush not just to Kim Jong Il but to also the leaders of the five other nations in the six-party process. He commissioned Yuri Kim, a talented young Korean-American diplomat who was one of his key North Korea specialists, to quickly write five individual letters. The drafts were delivered to Rice within hours.

Over the 2007 Thanksgiving weekend holiday, Rice tried to convince Bush of the benefits of communicating directly with Kim. Early the following week, Hill left Washington for Asia and a planned stop in Pyongyang, still unsure if he would have the letter to deliver. It was not until the night of Friday, November 30—with Hill due in Pyongyang the following Monday—that National Security Adviser Stephen Hadley agreed to the final wording. Bush finally signed the letter early Saturday morning, and Yuri Kim picked it up at the White House on her way to the airport to join Hill.

With the letter now complete, Yuri Kim's colleague, Korea Desk director Sung Kim—now in Seoul with Hill and preparing to leave for Pyongyang—telephoned North Korea's UN representative, Kim Myong Gil.

"Ambassador Hill is bringing a signed letter from President Bush," he told the North Korean. "This is very important development, and you should take it very seriously."

Over the phone, the American diplomat felt his North Korean counterpart was initially almost speechless. Kim Myong Gil then said he would report the news immediately to Pyongyang.

Sung Kim also dropped the first hint that Hill wanted to see the Dear Leader, saying that the United States hoped a meeting could be arranged so the letter could be presented in "an appropriate manner."

The North Korean was noncommittal. But the surprise of such a letter coming from the man responsible for the phrase Axis of Evil was genuine. In a follow-up phone conversation, Kim Myong Gil asked Sung Kim for reassurance. "You really have a letter from President Bush?" he queried. "An original, signed letter?"

It was bitterly cold in Pyongyang. Hill and his colleagues were housed in the Paekhawan Guest House, which was usually used for high-level visitors. In his first meeting with Kim Gye Gwan, Hill made a direct pitch to deliver the letter to Kim Jong Il, saying it was the American custom to deliver such important letters personally. Kim was evasive, replying that Kim Jong Il did not normally meet foreigners.

Hill pointed out that he was staying at the very guesthouse where Kim had greeted Madeleine Albright seven years before. Then the North Koreans offered another excuse. Kim Jong Il was out of Pyongyang inspecting military units. Hill got the message. Not only was he too junior in rank for the Dear Leader, the Americans sensed that North Korean officials, having not yet seen the text of the letter, might well have been worried about its substance and tone. That alone would make them reluctant to push their boss to receive Hill. Instead, they suggested Hill give the document to Foreign Minister Pak Ui Chun.

Hill agreed, and on December 5, in the grim and unheated North Korean Foreign Ministry building, he handed the letter to a solemn but visibly pleased Foreign Minister Pak.

The letter began "Dear Mr. Chairman," and in Yuri Kim's respectful and almost cordial language, the document raised the possibility of normalized relations if Kim fully disclosed and dismantled his nuclear programs. In the only part of the text the White House made public, the letter said, "I want to emphasize that the declaration must be complete and accurate if we are to continue our progress."

The White House, concerned about criticism from conservatives, downplayed the letter. But Bush's personal commitment to fully normalize relations with a nonnuclear North Korea was a 180-degree turn from his previous position. It also put the ball squarely back in the North Korean court.

"Hill was working to disarm the arguments and excuses of the North Koreans," observed one knowledgeable Republican congressional staffer. "One by one, he was addressing the excuses in the minds of the North Koreans that would prevent them from changing their focus . . . or he was calling their bluff."

The North Koreans appeared genuinely pleased with the letter. One indication was that the moment Hill left the country, they made the news public. It was only a two-line announcement in the official Korean Central News Agency.

But it spoke volumes about the North's reaction. For someone KCNA had denounced in 2005 as a "hooligan, half-baked man and a philistine," the statement used Bush's full title—"the President of the United States of America"—a reference not to the man but to the prestige of the office. It was a signal that the relationship was improving and the regime wanted its people to know that. A week later, North Korean diplomats at the United Nations passed on to Washington a positive verbal response from Kim, with no specifics, but a message that if the United States lived up to its commitments, Kim would live up to his.

But the goodwill generated by the letter didn't make Hill's talks with Kim Gye Gwan on the status of the declaration any easier.

"It's becoming an honesty test," said one U.S. official involved in the process, "and the North Koreans have never been very strong in that regard."

With less than a month before the December 31, 2007, deadline for the North to provide a "complete and correct" list of all its nuclear activities—including how much plutonium and how many warheads had been produced, the status of the uranium effort, and what, if anything, the North had done to help the nuclear programs of Syria or other countries—Kim Gye Gwan did not even have a draft to share. Instead, he produced what the Americans called "reference materials"—precursors of a first draft.

It quickly became clear to Hill the materials were neither complete nor correct, and would cause huge problems in Washington if it was as far as Pyongyang was prepared to go. Sitting with Kim, Hill went through the information point by point, noting the absence of crucial details and other big holes and pushing the North Koreans to do more.

On uranium, Kim continued to stick with his claim that the aluminum tubes and other items the North was acknowledging had been intended for rockets, not a nuclear program. None of the Americans took the claim seriously. And while Kim insisted the North did not now have an enrichment program, he was not forthcoming about other past activities, such as the centrifuges supplied by A. Q. Khan.

Kim Gye Gwan said there were some nuclear materials and facilities, such as isotopes for medical use and laboratories at Kim Il Sung University, that were for peaceful purposes and which the North did not intend to give up.

"We can decide later if such items are subject to dismantlement," Hill replied. "But it has to be on the list."

And Hill pointed out some other glaring omissions, such as the absence of a reference to the North's nuclear test site.

There was also the issue of the actual number of nuclear weapons. When asked, Kim Gye Gwan replied, "We're still technically at war with you. It would be inappropriate for us to discuss weapons with an enemy state."

But from Hill's perspective, an accurate declaration on the amount of plutonium the North had produced would probably suffice, since U.S. scientists
would be able to use that figure to determine the number of weapons.

Hill ended the meeting by pushing the North to move forward.

"A famous artist can sell an unfinished painting for a lot of money," he told
Kim. "A diplomat can't sell an unfinished work for anything."

Hill had no illusions. He realized how hard it would be for the North to produce a credible list, and even if that hurdle could be overcome, the challenges
would only become more difficult. The deals negotiated in Beijing in February
and October only spelled out a road map to disablement and a declaration. The
next steps would involve dismantling all nuclear facilities and, eventually, taking
all fissile material, including warheads, out of the country. A verification process
to assure the United States and the international community that the North was
not hiding bombs or facilities would also be required.

Even if additional progress was made, Hill was hardly alone in harboring
doubts that the North Korean military would ever give up its precious nuclear
weapons. It was clear another new set of negotiations would be required, with a
much more complicated and ambitious agenda. The outcome of these talks
would likely include the establishment of full diplomatic relations between the
United States and North Korea—including the opening of embassies, an end to
sanctions, and an ever-greater package of compensation for the North, which
could mean having to deal with Pyongyang's long-standing demand for light-
water reactors and the creation of a lasting peace mechanism on the Korean
peninsula to replace a war-time armistice. Without such steps, it was hard to
imagine such a closed and paranoid state actually abandoning what its military
and top leaders saw as the most important guarantee of their security.

But Hill and his colleagues came away from their meetings with cautious
hope, convinced that, for all the frustrations, they had finally begun a real discussion with Kim Gye Gwan on the issue, and that, in his own way, the North
Korean envoy was trying to find a way forward. Indeed, a look back at the past
year revealed a surprising pattern of North Korean cooperation.

"The entire process since [the] February 13 [deal] has been a test," noted
one American official. "On February 13, the question was: Will they actually
let the International Atomic Energy Agency back in? The answer is 'yes.' Will
they actually shut down and seal Yongbyon? The answer we found is 'yes.'
Will they discuss a list? 'Yes.' So now [with the contents of a declaration] we
have a new test. It's a higher threshold. But so far, with disablement, the answer again has turned out to be 'yes.'"

And it was not the first time the North Koreans had proved so agreeable. In
the 1990s, after the signing of the Agreed Framework, the North Koreans

proved surprisingly cooperative on a host of issues. In a paper written after he
left government, former CIA analyst Bob Carlin documented a series of issues
where negotiations between Washington and Pyongyang produced agreement,
and the North Koreans honored what they had agreed to. These included: what
model would be used for the construction of the light-water reactors promised
under the Agreed Framework; monitoring of the supplies of heavy fuel oil delivered under the same deal; arrangements for canning and secure storage of
spent fuel rods after the Yongbyon facility was frozen; allowing the U.S. military
to search for the remains of Americans missing in action from the Korean War;
resolving U.S. suspicions about the underground site at Kumchangri in 1998;
and a 1999 moratorium on missile tests.[15]

"At every step, there's always a huge challenge," said another official
involved in the process. "It's just part of dealing with North Korea. But so far,
they're actually doing what they said they would."

And for all the dangers, uncertainties, and frustrations, Hill did have one
undeniable achievement: the Yongbyon nuclear facility had been shut down,
disabled, and was no longer producing plutonium for future nuclear bombs.
With fissile material previously manufactured there now stored in some secret
hiding place, critics complained that shutting Yongbyon was a bit like closing
the barn door after the horse had escaped. But, both in practical and symbolic
terms, it represented an important step forward, and Hill now felt the time was
right to see for himself.

The five cars in Hill's convoy were the only vehicles on the road to Yongbyon. For mile after mile, they passed barren fields and rocky hills, eliciting
blank stares from the few people they passed. The Americans waved out the
window. Occasionally a small child would wave back. Other youngsters, seeing
the line of Mercedes, bowed.

The North Koreans were hospitable and professional, and gave Hill a full
tour of the drab and decaying complex, which struck one of his colleagues as
more resembling a dungeon more than a scientific facility. They were even
shown thousands of fresh fuel rods. *Thank God we stopped them when we did*,
Hill thought to himself. Under the October agreement, these fuel rods would
be dismantled.

As Bob Carlin and his group had found during their visit to the complex
four months earlier, the staff at Yongbyon seemed resigned to their fate. Many
of them had invested their entire lives in the nuclear program, and they were
clearly worried about what would happen to them.

"Please remember our livelihood," they pleaded with Hill. "Please remember
that you can't just forget about us after it is shut down."

With Yongbyon so decrepit to begin with, and with enough plutonium already hidden away for several bombs, disabling the plant was a relatively easy step for the Pyongyang regime. It was in such bad shape that it would not have been able to operate much longer in any case. Getting a credible declaration and securing the actual fissile material were much tougher challenges. But after so many ups and downs, Hill was heartened by what he saw. The North Koreans weren't going to be making any more bombs at Yongbyon.

The irony was that it had taken nearly seven years to return to virtually the same situation that had existed when George W. Bush won the presidency. The big difference was that North Korea, instead of having a few kilograms of weapons-grade plutonium, now possessed enough nuclear fuel for as many as ten bombs. And with its nuclear test in October 2006, Kim Jong Il's regime had become a full-fledged nuclear power—a much more dangerous situation than the one Bush had inherited from his predecessor, and one much harder to reverse.

Hill believed there were two major lessons from this bitter experience. One was the importance of drawing North Korea into a multilateral process. Pyongyang was undertaking obligations not only to its longtime enemy—the United States—but to its immediate neighbors. Despite its isolation, North Korea already had a complex web of political, economic, and interpersonal relationships with these countries. That fact increased the stimulus for the North to be cooperative.

But a multilateral diplomatic strategy was not enough. Unquestionably, the Bush administration's refusal for more than five years to engage in serious bilateral talks with North Korea—despite Pyongyang's repeated appeals—had been a central factor fueling the nuclear crisis. The refusal to show respect, the personal insults about Kim Jong Il, and the macho talk about regime change— such as Dick Cheney's famous words, "We don't negotiate with evil. We defeat it"—reflected the arrogance, cultural insensitivity, and ideological blinders that the hard-liners had brought to the administration.

Now, finally, the administration was serious about a negotiated deal. Many others were trying to convey the same message, including Henry Kissinger. At a Track II meeting late in 2007, the venerable statesman told North Korean officials that George W. Bush, despite his past track record, offered them their best chance for concluding an agreement and having it implemented. Waiting for a Democrat to become president in 2009, the North Koreans were warned, would not ensure better terms. Indeed, a new Democratic president, trying to wind down the war in Iraq, might well feel unable to be as conciliatory toward North Korea as Bush. And key Republicans in Congress who—despite the public complaints from hard-liners like John Bolton—were grudgingly going along with the president's engagement policy, would have no incentive to show restraint in denouncing a Democrat pursuing similar policies.

At the start of 2008, North Korea's long-term intentions remained unclear. It was entirely possible that Kim Jong Il himself had not made up his mind—that he was allowing events to play out one step at a time, and would only come to a final decision on whether to abandon his nuclear weapons after seeing what was ultimately being offered in return and deciding whether such steps would actually be implemented.

In the meantime, though, it was also becoming clear that ending the nuclear program was about more than simply shutting one facility or agreeing on a list of nuclear materials and equipment. Ultimately, it was about changing the mind-set of the people—and the leadership—in two countries that had been enemies for more than half a century.

At the end of his day in Yongbyon, Hill and his colleagues met Ri Je Son, the director-general of the General Department of Atomic Energy. Ri's rank was equivalent to a government minister. In his mid-fifties, he was confident, polished, and well-dressed. His demeanor made it clear that he was less than enthusiastic about giving up the nuclear program.

As he talked with Hill, he pointed to his own head. "Changing the relationship with the United States involves reversing fifty years of what we have been taught and what we think," he said. "But we are trying."

Hill thought to himself, *The same thing could be said about the American side.*

By the time the U.S. envoy left Yongbyon, night had fallen and the temperature was well below freezing. Just outside the complex where North Korea had produced the nuclear weapons that had brought the two countries to a dangerous confrontation, Hill's Mercedes bumped along a dirt road. It was pitch black, there wasn't a single light to be seen in any direction. Occasionally, Hill's car passed figures moving like phantoms in the dark, bundled against the bitter cold, some pushing carts, others bicycles, still others trudging slowly by the side of the road. North Korea had defied the United States—and China, Japan, Russia, South Korea, and the United Nations Security Council. It had withstood years of sanctions and isolation, survived the collapse of almost all its Communist allies, the death of its founding father, and a devastating famine to make itself a nuclear power. But its citizens had paid a terrible price, victims of both their own government and the U.S. effort to undermine it—and, unless a final deal was sealed, would continue to do so.

# POSTSCRIPT

CHRISTOPHER HILL WAS FRUSTRATED, ANGRY, AND MORE THAN a little bitter. Four months after delivering President Bush's personal letter to Kim Jong II in Pyongyang and inspecting the work to disable the Yongbyon nuclear facility, he was under more political pressure than at any time since the diplomatic breakthroughs of late 2006 and early 2007.

Privately, Hill complained to friends that negotiating with the North Koreans was often less fraught than dealing with the hard-liners in Vice President Cheney's office and elsewhere in the administration.

The source of Hill's frustration was a move, supported by Cheney; his ally, CIA director Gen. Michael Hayden; and other hard-line opponents of a negotiated deal with North Korea, to go public with information— which the administration had acquired nearly a year earlier from Israel— about Pyongyang's nuclear connection with Syria. In late April 2008, the intelligence community was authorized to conduct a series of classified briefings for members of Congress. Within hours, the information, including photographs taken by Israeli agents, was leaked to the media. The thrust of the briefings, and the administration's "spin" which accompanied it, was that North Korea had been helping Syria to build a nuclear reactor similar to the one at Yongbyon, and that the facility was close to completion before it was destroyed in an Israeli air strike on September 6, 2007. To buttress the case, administration officials showed reporters a photograph of a man identified as a senior official from Yongbyon with the director of Syria's nuclear agency.

The disclosures—officially explained as necessary to secure congressional support for further denuclearization negotiations—sparked a storm of protest. Much of it targeted Hill, and came from those in Congress and the media opposed to, or skeptical of his dealings with, the North Koreans and angry that the administration had withheld the intelligence on Syria for so long. Some lawmakers warned that they would block funding for any deal, and conservative Republican senator Sam Brownback placed a hold on the nomination of Hill's deputy, Kathleen Stephens, to become the next U.S. ambassador to South Korea.

An aide to Brownback told the *Washington Post* that "people are very mad, very angry" about any deal with "a regime that has repeatedly demonstrated that its word is indistinguishable from a lie."[1] And stoking that anger, Hill believed, was precisely what Cheney and other hard-liners were trying to do, with the goal of generating political pressure on President Bush to pull back from the accord Hill had been seeking to negotiate.

Throughout the winter and spring of 2008, Hill and his North Korean counterpart Kim Gye Gwan had struggled to find common ground on a key element of the agreement reached the previous October—Pyongyang's commitment to provide a "complete and correct declaration of all its nuclear programs. In return, the United States was to remove the North from Washington's list of states sponsoring terrorism and end sanctions under the Trading With the Enemy Act.

Of the three components of the declaration—North Korea's plutonium program, its efforts to acquire a uranium enrichment capability, and its nuclear cooperation with Syria—Kim had been relatively forthcoming on plutonium, although many details remained to be verified. He had also revealed critically important information that the thousands of aluminum tubes North Korea was known to have acquired had not been used to make centrifuges—presumably because the North had not been able to acquire the other critical components it needed. But on the other two issues, he had stonewalled, refusing to acknowledge that the North had received centrifuges or other uranium know-how from Pakistan's A. Q. Khan, and flatly denying any nuclear relationship with Syria. Hill continued to push, on one occasion showing Kim the photo of a man believed to be a North Korean nuclear official with the head of the Syrian nuclear agency and saying, "Mr. Kim, this is a problem."

There appeared to be several reasons for the North's reluctance to come clean. One was the sheer discomfort and loss of face involved in acknowledging activities that Kim Jong Il's regime had consistently denied. Another was apparently rooted in the North's previous experience with "confession diplomacy"— Kim Jong Il's 2002 admission to Japanese prime minister Koizumi that Pyongyang's agents had kidnapped Japanese civilians. Kim had believed that taking the unprecedented step of admitting past wrongdoing would pave the way to a rapprochement with Japan. Instead, the admission sparked a furious reaction in Japan, and, six years later, continued to be the major stumbling block to improved relations.

North Korean officials, still deeply distrustful of the United States, bluntly told American visitors in early 2008 that they feared a similar reaction in the United States if they made the full disclosure required by the October 3 agreement. A private message to Kim Gye Gwan from Condoleezza Rice, delivered by former Secretary of Defense William Perry during a trip to Pyongyang in late February, promising confidentiality did not ease the North Koreans' suspicions.

Convinced that Pyongyang would not agree to a public confession and fearful that the deadlock could jeopardize the entire process of disabling the plutonium facilities and obtaining an accurate declaration of the North's plutonium program, in late winter of 2008, Hill held a series of meetings with Kim Gye Gwan, first in Geneva and then in Singapore. The result was an agreement that the North would supply a full declaration of its plutonium program, but the Syria and uranium issues would be finessed with a confidential side letter. In that document, the United States would lay out what it knew and Pyongyang would "acknowledge the U.S. conclusions," not contest them, and "take serious note of U.S. concerns."

For Hill, the logic of this apparent concession was clear. With the Syrian reactor destroyed by Israel, whatever the North had done there was a matter of history, not a current security threat. As for uranium, while Pyongyang had unquestionably made an effort, there was no credible evidence that the North had actually acquired the capacity to manufacture highly enriched uranium for a bomb. Although the agreement he had negotiated with Kim was hardly perfect, Hill believed it would allow the process to move ahead and focus on the clear and present danger—North Korea's stock of weapons-grade plutonium.

"The real issue," said one former senior State Department Korea expert, "is getting an accurate fix on the amount of plutonium they produced and getting rid of it."

But as word of the proposed deal reached Washington, the pushback was immediate. John Bolton, writing in the *Wall Street Journal,* declared that Hill had agreed "to accept on faith, literally, North Korean assertions that it has not engaged in significant uranium enrichment, and that it has not proliferated nuclear technology or materials to countries like Syria and Iran," and had left the Bush administration's policy toward North Korea's nuclear weapons program looking "like something out of Bill Clinton's or Jimmy Carter's playbook."[2]

Not all the criticism, however, came from the hard-liners. Even many longtime supporters of negotiations were convinced that Hill, in his eagerness to reach a deal, had given away too much. "The concern I have," said Jack Pritchard, who had resigned in 2003 to protest the administration's refusal to engage North Korea, "is a North Korean acknowledgement of U.S. concerns does not appear to translate into a complete and correct declaration of their activities. It doesn't, on the surface, satisfy the requirement of completeness. It is the United States that is presenting the information; it is not North Korea presenting the information."[3]

The controversy over the proposed deal produced an opening, and Hill's adversaries seized it to roll out the intelligence on Pyongyang's Syrian connection. But the intelligence briefing raised as many questions as it answered. While the evidence that Pyongyang was helping Damascus build a nuclear plant appeared compelling, the released material contained no evidence of plans to fabricate fuel rods and no information as to how the Syrians would obtain the uranium necessary to fuel the plant. There were no signs of a reprocessing facility, and, despite all the public fanfare, the officials who conducted the briefing acknowledged that U.S. intelligence had only "low confidence" the site was actually going to be used for a weapons program.

With memories of the political manipulation of intelligence in Iraq still fresh, an editorial in the *New York Times* asked, "Is it another example of this administration insisting that information be withheld for national security reasons—until there is a political reason to release it?"[4]

In any case, though, the revelations left Hill politically damaged, further eroding his credibility with the Congress and raising new doubts about the level of backing he retained from Secretary of State Rice and President Bush. The man both admirers and critics had dubbed the "Lone Ranger" for the way he had circumvented the bureaucracy to achieve his goals was increasingly on the defensive. Weary of the endless internal battles, angry at being portrayed as "soft" on North Korea, in his darker moments, he mused about resigning or at least threatening to do so if Rice didn't give him her full support.

As the Bush administration entered its final months, the internal battle for control of North Korea policy, which began within days of the president taking office in 2001, showed no sign of ending.

# A NOTE ON SOURCES

MELTDOWN IS BASED IN PART ON MY OWN EXPERIENCES AS A journalist covering many of the key events recounted here— from the 1994 nuclear crisis to the six-party talks to my numerous trips to North Korea. But in seeking to reconstruct the inside story of North Korea's nuclear breakout, I have relied primarily on hundreds of interviews with key participants in Washington, Seoul, Beijing, Tokyo, and elsewhere. Some people spoke on the record, and when they are quoted, unless otherwise footnoted, the quote comes from my interviews. Other interviews were conducted on background, which allowed me to use the information but not identify the source by name. Many people were interviewed multiple times. Some interviewees asked that I not reveal that I had spoken with them, and I have honored those requests. I have also relied on documents, including memos, personal notes, transcripts of congressional hearings and press conferences, chronologies, and the extensive coverage of my journalistic colleagues who were also following the North Korea story.

Thoughts or feelings attributed to a particular person have been obtained from that person, someone the person spoke to, or from the written record. When I have quoted private conversations, the information came from one of the participants, a witness, or someone who was told about the conversation in its immediate aftermath. Whenever possible, I have sought to corroborate my accounts with multiple sources.

Although I made repeated requests, North Korean officials declined to speak with me for this book. In seeking to understand and document

Pyongyang's thinking, I have relied partly on my own travels there, and the conversations I was able to have with the late President Kim Il Sung, Vice Foreign Minister Kim Gye Gwan, and other officials, as well as the invaluable recollections and insights of a small number of people with extensive North Korea experience: diplomats and aid workers in Pyongyang, present and former U.S. and South Korean officials who have visited regularly and held extensive discussions with the North Koreans, and scholars and others involved in Track II meetings with North Korean diplomats.

With its bombast and overheated rhetoric, North Korea's state-run media is often dismissed as meaningless propaganda and all too often not taken seriously by journalists and others following the situation. During my research, however, I spent many hours poring over Pyongyang's official pronouncements. It became increasingly clear that stripped of the verbiage, they were also a valuable tool to understanding the thinking of the North Korean regime.

## INTERVIEWS

Takeshi Akahori
David Albright
Madeleine Albright
Richard Armitage
David Asher
Jeffrey Bader
Jeffrey Baron
Peter Beck
Sandy Berger
John Bolton
Richard Boucher
Stephen Bradner
Michael Breen
Peter Brookes
Raymond Burghardt
Robert Carlin
Fred Carriere
Victor Cha
Sheena Chestnut
Woosuk Kenneth Choi
Richard Christenson
Warren Christopher
Chun Yung-woo
Chung Dong-young
Maureen Cormack
Nigel Cowie

Gerald Curtis
Joseph DeTrani
Joseph Donovan
Chuck Downs
Robert Duajarric
Robert Einhorn
Richard Falkenrath
William Fallon
Thomas Fargo
Evelyn Farkas
Scott Feeney
Douglas Feith
Michael Finnegan
Mark Fitzpatrick
Gordon Flake
James Foster
Aaron Friedberg
David Frum
Robert Gallucci
Bonnie Glaser
Daniel Glaser
Michael Green
Raymond Greene
Donald Gregg
Mark Groombridge
Dennis Halpin

Han Sung-joo
Siegfried Hecker
Christopher Hill
James Hoare
Thomas Hubbard
Balbina Hwang
Hyun Hong-choo
Hajime Izumi
Frank Jannuzi
Neil Joeck
Robert Joseph
Arnold Kanter
Charles "Chuck" Kartman
Ryozo Kato
James Kelly
James Kelman
Kil Jeong-woo
Kim Dae-joong
Kim Dae-jung
Kim See-hang
Kim Sook
Stephen Kim
Yuri Kim
Andrea Koppel
Joseph Kruzich
Elise Labot

James Laney
Leon LaPorte
Richard Lawless
Lee Kyeum-ryung
Lee Yong-joon
John Lewis
Kenneth Lieberthal
Lim Sung-nam
Stephen Linton
Keith Luse
Kevin Madden
Robert Manning
Alexandre Mansourov
Bradley Martin
David Maxwell
John McLaughlin
John Merrill
W. Michael Meserve
Narushige Michishata
James Minnich
Jami Misick
Mark Mohr
Anthony Namkung
Chris Nelson
Don Oberdorfer

Masao Okonogi
William Overholt
Park Chan-bong
Park Guen-hye
Michael Pillsbury
Ricardo Pinto
Colin Powell
Charles "Jack" Pritchard
Kenneth Quinones
Mitchell Reiss
Scott Rembrandt
Evans Revere
Alan Romberg
John Rood
Robert Ross
Stapleton Roy
Rexon Ryu
Akitaka Saiki
Gary Samore
Stephen Sargeant
Yukio Satoh
Thomas Schieffer
Suzanne Scholte
Randy Schriver
Brent Scowcroft

Wendy Sherman
Sahoku Shiga
Leon Sigal
Barbara Slavin
Robin Sokoda
David Straub
Sung Kim
Hitoshi Tanaka
Lynn Turk
Alexander Vershbow
Steve Vickers
Wi Sung-lac
Dennis Wilder
Lawrence Wilkerson
John Wolf
Jon Wolfsthal
Tadamichi Yamamoto
Yang Sung-chul
Stephen Yates
Yoon Young-kwan
Joseph Yun
Philip Zelikow
Kathi Zellweger

# NOTES

## 1. "WITHOUT YOU THERE IS NO US"

1. Mike Chinoy, *China Live: People Power and the Television Revolution* (Boulder, CO: Rowman & Littlefield, 1999), 331.
2. Ibid.
3. International Institute for Strategic Studies, *North Korea's Weapons Programmes: A Net Assessment* (New York: Palgrave Macmillan, 2004).
4. Don Oberdorfer, *The Two Koreas* (New York: Perseus Books, 1997), 324.
5. David Albright, *Solving the North Korean Nuclear Puzzle.* Nov. 24, 2002. http://www.isis-online.org/publications/dprk/book/prologue.html
6. National Security Archive. http://www.gwu.edu/~nsarchiv/NSAEBB/NSA EBB25/index.htm
7. "Review of United States Policy Toward North Korea: Findings and Recommendations," Unclassified Report by Dr. William J. Perry, U.S. North Korea Policy Coordinator and Special Adviser to the President and the Secretary of State, Washington, DC, Oct. 12, 1999.
8. The People's Korea. http://www1.korea-np.co.jp/pk/144th_issue/2000072502.htm
9. Roy memo, Jun. 16, 2005. Declassified in National Security Archive. http://www.gwu.edu/~nsarchiv/NSAEBB/NSAEBB164/EBB%20Doc%2016.pdf

## 2. SO CLOSE . . .

1. Daniel Poneman, Joel Wit, and Robert Gallucci, *Going Critical: The First North Korean Nuclear Crisis* (Washington, DC: Brookings Institution Press, 2004), 374.
2. U.S.-DPRK Communiqué, U.S. State Department, Oct. 12, 2000.

3.  Ibid.

4.  Madeleine Albright, *Madame Secretary* (New York: Miramax Books, 2003), 462.

5.  Ibid., 461.

6.  Ibid., 463.

7.  Ibid.

8.  Ibid.

9.  Konstantin Pulikovsky, *Orient Express: Across Russia With Kim Jong Il,* (Moscow: Gordetz, 2002). Translation provided by *Christian Science Monitor,* March 14, 2003. Additional segments translated by the Jamestown Foundation. http://www.jamestown.org/publications_details.php?volume_id=398&issue_id=2915&article_id=23573)

10.  Albright, *Madame Secretary,* 465.

11.  State Department Paper, Talking Point for S/Ivanov Telephone Call, Tuesday, 10/29/00 [document incorrectly dates telephone call in August], ca. Oct. 23, 2000. Source: State Department FOIA release. http://www.gwu.edu/~nsarchiv/NSAEBB/NSAEBB164/

12.  John Nichols, *The Nation*, Apr. 14, 2005.

13.  "John Bolton: The Iron Hand in the State Department's Velvet Glove," *Wall Street Journal,* Jul. 19, 2002.

14.  *Rodong Sinmin,* Nov. 7, 2000.

15.  Bob Woodward, *State of Denial*, (New York: Simon & Schuster, 2006), 14.

16.  Karen DeYoung, *Soldier: The Life of Colin Powell* (New York: Alfred A. Knopf, 2006), 286.

17.  Ibid., 179.

18.  James Mann, *Rise of the Vulcans: The History of Bush's War Cabinet* (New York: Penguin Books, 2004), 97.

19.  Ibid., 250.

20.  Ibid., 721.

21.  Condoleezza Rice, "Campaign 2000: Promoting the National Interest," (*Foreign Affairs,* Jan.-Feb. 2000). http://www.foreignaffairs.org/20000101faessay5-p50/condoleezza-rice/campaign-2000-promoting-the-national-interest.html

22.  Ibid.

23.  Albright, *Madame Secretary*, 182.

24.  Interviews with Sherman, Einhorn, Pritchard, Kartman, Powell.

25.  David Sanger, "Clinton Scraps North Korea Trip, Saying Time's Short for Deal," *New York Times*, Dec. 29, 2000. http://select.nytimes.com/search/restricted/article?res=F00715FF3D5F0C7A8EDDAB0994D8404482

26.  Albright, *Madame Secretary*, 470.

## 3. REGIME CHANGE

1.  "NK Official Calls for US to Continue Engagement," *Chosun Ilbo*, Feb. 6, 2001.

2.  Charles L. Pritchard, *Failed Diplomacy: The Tragic Story of How North Korea Got the Bomb,* (Washington, DC: Brookings Institution Press, 2007), 50.

3.  *International Herald Tribune*, Jan. 8, 2001. David Ignatius. http://www.iht.com/cgi-bin/generic.cgi?template=articleprint.tmplh&ArticleId=658

4.  "Kim, Bush Agree to Meet Soon to Discuss N. Korean Issues," *Korea Herald,* Jan. 26, 2001.

5. Patrick Tyler, "South Korea Takes Russia's Side in Dispute Over U.S. Missile Defense Plan," *New York Times*, Feb. 27, 2001.

6. Donald Kirk, "South Korea Now Pulls Back From Russia on Missile Shield," *New York Times*, Mar. 2, 2001.

7. Karen DeYoung, *Soldier: The Life of Colin Powell* (New York: Alfred A. Knopf, 2006), 290.

8. David Sanger, "Korean to Visit Bush, but They Could Be at Odds," *New York Times*, Mar. 7, 2001.

9. Ibid.

10. Steven Mufson, "Bush to Pick Up Clinton Talks on N. Korean Missiles," *Washington Post,* Mar. 7, 2001.

11. White House, Office of the Press Secretary, Remarks by Secretary of State Colin Powell to the Pool, Mar. 7, 2001.

12. David Sanger, "Bush Tells Seoul Talks With North Won't Resume Now," *New York Times*, Mar. 8, 2001.

13. Bob Woodward, *Bush at War* (New York: Simon & Schuster, 2002), 340.

14. Transcript of Press Briefing: Presidents Bush, Kim Dae-jung, Mar. 7, 2001, http://seoul.usembassy.gov/030701_2.html

15. CNN interview, May 14, 2001. http://transcripts.cnn.com/TRANSCRIPTS/0105/14/se.01.html

16. Interviews with several participants in the Policy Review process.

17. Jane Perlez, "Fatherly Advice to the President on North Korea," *New York Times*, Jun. 10, 2001.

18. Charles L. Pritchard, "U.S. Policy toward the Democratic People's Republic of Korea," Testimony of the special envoy for negotiations with the DPRK and U.S. representative to KEDO before the Subcommittee on East Asia and the Pacific, House Committee on International Relations, Jul. 26 2001.

19. All comments by Frank Jannuzi are from interviews conducted in October 2006, when he was the Hitachi International Affairs Fellow of the Council on Foreign Relations, Tokyo, Japan.

20. John Bolton, *Surrender Is Not an Option*, (New York: Threshold Editions, 2007), 103.

21. Pritchard, *Failed Diplomacy*, 4.

22. Ibid.

## 4. "AXIS OF EVIL"

1. KCNA, Sept. 12, 2001.

2. KCNA, Nov. 3, 2001.

3. Congressional Research Service, "North-South Korean Relations: A Chronology of Events, 2000–2001," Jan. 9, 2002.

4. http://www.washingtonpost.com/wp-srv/onpolitics/transcripts/bush_112601.html

5. Nuclear Posture Review Submitted to Congress on Dec. 31, 2001.

6. Ibid.

7. "Rumors of War," *Newsweek,* Feb. 19, 2007.

8. http://www.whitehouse.gov/news/releases/2002/01/20020129-11.html

9. John Bolton, *Surrender Is Not an Option* (New York: Threshold Editions, 2007), 104.

10. Bush speech at Dorasan, Feb. 20, 2002.

11. White House Press briefing, Mar. 20, 2002. http://www.whitehouse.gov/news/releases/ 2002/03/20020320-16.html

## 5. THE "SCRUB"

1. Christopher Clary, unpublished thesis, Naval Postgraduate School, 2003.

2. "Beyond the Axis of Evil: Additional Threats from Weapons of Mass Destruction," by The Honorable John R. Bolton, Heritage Lecture #743, May 6, 2002.

3. "German Officials Identify Former DPRK Diplomat as 'Ringleader' in WMD Export Deal," *Der Spiegel*, Sept. 22, 2003; "Germany Stops Freighter With Nuclear Weapons-Grade Material for N. Korea," *Der Spiegel*, Apr. 26, 2003.

4. Joby Warrick, "N. Korea Shops Stealthily for Nuclear Arms Gear," *Washington Post*, Aug. 15, 2003.

5. Gordon Corera, *Shopping for Bombs: Nuclear Proliferation, Global Insecurity, and the Rise and Fall of the A. Q. Khan Network* (New York: Oxford University Press, 2006), 87.

6. Interview with Benazir Bhutto, *New Perspectives Quarterly* (spring 2004). "Concerning North Korea, the army and scientists came to me in 1993 and asked me to go to North Korea, which I did, to negotiate the exchange of nuclear delivery technology for cold cash."

7. Joseph S. Bermudez, DPRK-Pakistan Ghauri Missile Cooperation, GlobalSecurity.org, May 21, 1998. http://www.globalsecurity.org/wmd/library/news/pakistan/1998/ghauri2.htm

8. George Tenet, *At the Center of the Storm* (New York: HarperCollins, 2007), 283.

9. Paul Watson and Mubashir Zaidi, "Death of N. Korean Woman Offers Clues to Pakistani Nuclear Deals," *Los Angels Times*, Mar. 1, 2004.

10. Tenet, p. 284.

11. Colin Powell, Remarks at Asia Society Annual Dinner, Jun. 10, 2002. http://www.state .gov/secretary/former/powell/remarks/2002/10983.htm

12. John Bolton, *Surrender Is Not an Option* (New York: Threshold Editions, 2007), 107.

13. Ibid., 108.

14. Bob Woodward, *Bush at War* (New York: Simon & Schuster, 2002), 340.

15. Remarks by President Bush and Prime Minister Koizumi in Joint Press Conference, Feb. 18, 2002. http://www.whitehouse.gov/news/releases/2002/02/20020218.html

16. Thomas Hubbard, Testimony before Senate Foreign Relations Committee regarding John Bolton's nomination to be U.S. Ambassador to the United Nations, Apr. 28, 2005.

17. Bolton, *Surrender Is Not an Option*, 111.

## 6. HIGH-LEVEL MEETINGS

1. KCNA, Feb. 7, 1997.

2. KCNA, U.S. State Under Secretary's Anti-DPRK Remarks Under Fire," Aug. 31, 2002.

3. Dr. C. Kenneth Quinones, "North Korea Nuclear Talks: The View from Pyongyang," *Arms Control Today* (October 2004).

4. Letter from Leon Sigal to James Kelly, Sept. 11, 2002.

5.  *Times of India*, Jan. 30, 2001.

6.  KCNA, "Kim Jong Il's answers to questions raised by president of Kyodo News Service," Sept. 14, 2001. http://www.kcna.co.jp/item/2002/200209/news09/14.htm

7.  "Japan-DPRK Pyongyang Declaration," Sept. 17, 2002. http://www.armscontrol.org/pdf/200209_Pyongyang_Declaration.pdf

8.  Charles L. Pritchard, *Failed Diplomacy: The Tragic Story of How North Korea Got the Bomb* (Washington, DC: Brookings Institution Press, 2007), 33–34.

9.  Frank S. Jannuzi, "North Korea: Back to the Brink," in *George W. Bush and Asia: A Midterm Assessment*, (Woodrow Wilson Center for International Scholars, 2003).

10. Pritchard, *Failed Diplomacy*, 36.

11. Ibid.

12. Ibid., 37.

13. Korean Central News Agency, "Conclusion of Non-Aggression Treaty between DPRK and U.S. Called For," Oct. 25, 2002. The tone of his comments was reflected in a North Korean Foreign Ministry statement released by the official Korean Central News Agency later in October, which a number of well-informed sources with access to North Korean thinking say accurately reflects much of what Kang told Kelly.

    "The DPRK recently received a special envoy of the U.S. President in the hope that this might help fundamentally solve the hostile relations with the U.S. and settle outstanding issues on an equal footing. Regretfully, the Pyongyang visit of the special envoy convinced the DPRK that the hostile attempt of the Bush administration to stifle the DPRK by force and backpedal the positive development of the situation in the Korean Peninsula and the rest of Northeast Asia has gone to the extremes. Producing no evidence, he asserted that the DPRK has been actively engaged in the enriched uranium program in pursuit of possessing nuclear weapons in violation of the DPRK-U.S. agreed framework. He even intimidated the DPRK side by saying that there would be no dialogue with the U.S. unless the DPRK halts it, and the DPRK-Japan, and north-south relations would be jeopardized. The U.S. attitude was so unilateral and high-handed that the DPRK was stunned by it. The Bush administration listed the DPRK as part of the "axis of evil" and a target of the U.S. preemptive nuclear strikes. This was a clear declaration of a war against the DPRK as it totally nullified the DPRK-U.S. joint statement and agreed framework."

14. Pritchard, *Failed Diplomacy*, 38.

15. KCNA, Oct. 25, 2002.

16. Pritchard, *Failed Diplomacy*, 38.

17. Ibid.

18. KCNA, Oct. 25, 2008. The North Korean Foreign Ministry's October 25 statement is again useful here in offering a clear summary of Kang's position.

    "The DPRK considers that it is a reasonable and realistic solution to the nuclear issue to conclude a nonaggression treaty between the DPRK and the U.S. if the grave situation of the Korean Peninsula is to be bridged over. If the U.S. legally assures the DPRK of nonaggression, including the nonuse of nuclear weapons against it by concluding such treaty, the DPRK will be ready to clear the former of its security concerns."

## 7. THE FOUR-LETTER WORD

1. KCNA, "Spokesman for D.P.R.K. Foreign Ministry on D.P.R.K. Visit of Special Envoy of U.S. President," Oct. 7, 2002.
2. http://www.whitehouse.gov/news/releases/2002/10/20021007-8.html
3. State Department Press Statement, Richard Boucher, Spokesman, Oct. 16, 2002.
4. Peter Slevin and Glenn Kessler, "Bush Plans Diplomacy on N. Korea's Arms Effort," *Washington Post,* Oct. 18, 2002.
5. *Asahi Shimbun,* "Undeterred, Koizumi to Push North Korea Ties," Oct. 19, 2002.
6. Agence France-Presse, "South Korea Seeks Talks With North on Nuclear Crisis," Oct. 17, 2002.
7. AFP, "South Korean Leader Says No to Sanctions Against North Korea," Oct. 23, 2002.
8. David Sanger, "U.S. to Withdraw from Arms Accord with North Korea," *New York Times,* Oct. 20, 2002.
9. Karen DeYoung, "U.S. Might Try to Salvage Part of N. Korean Accord," *Washington Post*, Oct. 25, 2002.
10. Mike Allen and Karen DeYoung, "Bush Seeks China's Aid to Oppose North Korea: Jiang's Statement Not as Forceful as U.S. Hoped," *Washington Post,* Oct. 26, 2002.
11. White House, Office of the Press Secretary, "Joint US-ROK-Japan Statement," Oct. 26, 2002.
12. Text of Kim Jong Il's message provided to the author by Don Oberdorfer.
13. Transcript: Douglas Feith news conference, U.S. and Japan Discuss North Korea, Security Issues, Nov. 8, 2002. http://seoul.usembassy.gov/8_nov_02.html
14. Ibid.

## 8. MELTDOWN

1. Mike Allen, "CIA's Cash Toppled Taliban: New Book Details Bush Advisers' Doubts and Rivalries," *Washington Post*, Nov. 16, 2002.
2. Korean Central News Agency, "DPRK Foreign Ministry Spokesman on U.S. Decision to Stop Supplying Heavy Oil," Nov. 22, 2002.
3. KCNA, "U.S. Denounced for Ditching International Agreement," Nov. 25, 2002.
4. Mike Allen and Barton Gellman, "Preemptive Strikes Part of U.S. Strategic Doctrine," *Washington Post,* Dec. 11, 2002.
5. National Security Presidential Directive/NPSD 23. http://www.fas.org/irp/offdocs/nspd/nspd-23.htm
6. KCNA, "Operation and Building of Nuclear Facilities to be Resumed Immediately," Dec. 12, 2002.

7. Charles L. Pritchard, *Failed Diplomacy: The Tragic Story of How North Korea Got the Bomb,* (Washington, DC: Brookings Institution Press, 2007), 43.

8. KCNA, "Operation and Building of Nuclear Facilities to be Resumed Immediately," Dec. 12, 2002.

9. Gary Samore, "North Korea's Nuclear Weapons Program: A Net Assessment," International Institute for Strategic Studies. London, Jan. 2004

10. "US Hawk Warns Not to Rule Out Military Options," *Chosun Ilbo,* Dec. 18, 2002.

11. KCNA, "DPRK Government Decides to Order IAEA Inspectors Out of DPRK," Dec. 27, 2002.

12. "The United States, North Korea, and the End of the Agreed Framework," *Naval War College Review*, Mar. 26, 2003, 55.

13. Transcript, *Meet the Press,* Dec. 29, 2002.

14. Bill Richardson with Michael Ruby, *Between Worlds: The Making of an American Life* (New York: G. P. Putnam's Sons, 2005), 297–98.

15. Steven R. Weisman, "North Korean Talks? U.S. Weighs the Possible Price," *New York Times*, Jan. 13, 2003.

16. Leigh Strope, "North Korea Ready to Negotiate with U.S." The Associated Press, Jan. 12, 2003.

17. "President Discusses Iraq, North Korea with reporters," White House, Office the Press Secretary, Dec. 31, 2002.

18. http://people-press.org/reports/pdf/165.pdf

19. James Brooke, "South Korea Criticizes U.S. Plan for Exerting Pressure on North," *New York Times*, Dec. 30, 2002.

20. Nicholas Kralev, "N. Korea to Restart Nuke Reactor, *The Washington Times*, Dec. 13, 2002.

21. *Asahi Shimbun*, "Koizumi, Bush Talk on North Korea, Iraq," Jan. 27, 2003.

22. KCNA, "Kim Jong Il Inspects KPA Unit," Jan. 31, 2003.

## 9. WAR GAMES

1. George Bush, State of the Union, White House transcript, Jan. 28, 2003. http://www.whitehouse.gov/news/releases/2003/01/20030128-19.html

2. CNN.com, "Tenet: North Korea has Ballistic Missile Capable of Hitting U.S.," Feb. 12, 2003. http://www.cnn.com/2003/WORLD/asiapcf/east/02/12/us.nkorea/

3. David Sanger, "U.S. Sending Two Dozen Bombers in Easy Reach of North Koreans," *New York Times*, Mar. 5, 2003.

4. Guy Dinmore, "Heed Lessons of Iraq, U.S. Tells Iran, Syria, and North Korea," *Financial Times,* Apr. 10, 2003.

5. Steven R. Weisman, "Pre-Emption: Idea with a Lineage Whose Time Has Come," *New York Times*, Mar. 23, 2003.

6. Transcript, North Korea Interview, BBC News, Feb. 6, 2003.

7. Nayan Chanda, "China's Mediation Effort Backfires on North Korea," YaleGlobal Online, Apr. 28, 2003.

8. Keith Bradsher, "North Korea Says a U.S. Attack Could Lead to a Nuclear War," *New York Times,* Mar. 3, 2003.

9.   Andrew Scobell, "China and North Korea: From Comrades-in-Arms to Allies at Arms Length," Strategic Studies Institute, U.S. Army War College: Carlisle, PA, 2004, 27.

10.  Karen DeYoung, *Soldier: The Life of Colin Powell*, (New York: Alfred A. Knopf, 2006), 474.

11.  Charles L. Pritchard, *Failed Diplomacy: The Tragic Story of How North Korea Got the Bomb*, (Washington, DC: Brookings Institution, 2007), 62.

12.  "Bush Vows to let Japan, S. Korea Join N. Korea Talks," Kyodo, Apr. 17, 2003.

13.  David E. Sanger, "Bush Takes No-Budge Stand in Talks with North Korea," *New York Times*, Apr. 17, 2003.

14.  David E. Sanger, "Administration Divided Over North Korea," *New York Times*, Apr. 21, 2003.

15.  Ibid.

16.  KCNA, "Spokesman for DPRK Foreign Ministry on Expected DPRK-U.S. Talks," Apr. 18, 2003.

17.  Glenn Kessler and Doug Struck, "N. Korean Statements Jeopardize New Talks," *Washington Post,* Apr. 19, 2003.

18.  Joseph Kahn, "North Korea May be Angering its Only Ally," *New York Times*, Apr. 26, 2003.

19.  KCNA, "Foreign Ministry Spokesman Accuses U.S of Derailing Denuclearization Process," Apr. 30, 2003.

## 10. "READ MY STATEMENT"

1.   Joby Warrick, "North Korea Shops Stealthily for Nuclear Arms Gear; Front Companies Step Up Efforts in European Market," *Washington Post,* Aug. 15, 2003.

2.   Transcript, "Remarks by the President to the People of Poland," Krakow, Poland, May 31, 2003.

3.   Joseph Curl, "U.S. Keeps Preemption Doctrine Open," *Washington Times,* May 13, 2003.

4.   Gordon Fairclough and Karen Elliot House, "South Korean President Roh Counsels Patience with North," *Wall Street Journal,* May 13, 2003.

5.   Hearing Transcript, Senate Foreign Relations Committee, Feb. 4, 2003.

6.   David E. Sanger, "U.S. Sees Quick Start of North Korea Nuclear Site," *New York Times*, Mar. 1, 2003.

7.   *Oriental Economist*, "Bombing on North Korea" (March 2003).

8.   David E. Sanger, "Bush and New President of South Korea Are Vague on North Korea Strategy," *New York Times*, May 15, 2003.

9.   KCNA, "U.S. Warned of Catastrophic Consequences of Its Blockade Operation Against DPRK," Jun. 17, 2003.

10.  "Hu Jintao Writes to Kim Jong Il to Open Door to Six-Party Talks, *Hong Kong Economic Journal*, Aug. 28, 2003 (translated by BBC Monitoring Service).

11.  Karen DeYoung, *Soldier: The Life of Colin Powell* (New York: Alfred A. Knopf, 2006), 475.

12.  Charles L. Pritchard, *Failed Diplomacy: The Tragic Story of How North Korea Got the Bomb* (Washington, DC: Brookings Institution, 2007), 85.

13. "Chinese Special Envoy Shuttles Between U.S. & DPRK: Commentary," *Peoples's Daily,* Jul. 21, 2003.

14. Pritchard, *Failed Diplomacy,* 85.

15. Glenn Kessler, "Proposals to N. Korea Weighed," *Washington Post,* Jul. 22, 2003.

16. "NK Hellish Nightmare: U.S. Official," Reuters, Aug. 1, 2003.

17. Interview with Ambassador Thomas Hubbard with Regard to the Bolton Nomination, Senate Foreign Relations Committee, Apr. 28, 2005.

18. Ibid.

19. Ibid.

20. Christopher Marquis, "Top U.S. Expert on North Korea Steps Down," *New York Times,* Aug. 26, 2003.

21. KCNA, "Keynote Speeches Made at Six-Way Talks," Aug. 29, 2003.

22. Fred Kaplan, "Rolling Blunder: How the Bush Administration Let North Korea Get Nukes," *Washington Monthly,* (May 2004).

23. Ibid.

24. John Pomfret, "N. Korea Nuclear Talks End with Agreement to Meet Again," *Washington Post,* Aug. 30, 2003.

25. "China Blames America for Failure of Talks," *Washington Times,* Sept. 2, 2003.

26. Joseph Kahn, "U.S. Stand Could Stall Korea Talks, Chinese Say," *New York Times,* Sept. 3, 2003.

27. John Pomfret and Anthony Faiola, "U.S. Flexibility Sought on N. Korea," *Washington Post,* Sept. 4, 2003.

28. "Bush Says He's Open to Security Assurances for North Korea," Reuters, Oct. 19, 2003.

29. David E. Sanger, "Bush taking New Approach on Negotiations with North Korea," *New York Times,* Oct. 19, 2003.

30. KCNA, "DPRK to Continue Increasing Its Nuclear Deterrent Force," Oct. 2, 2003.

31. Ibid., "Spokesman for DPRK Foreign Ministry on U.S. Rumour over Nuclear Issue," Oct. 16, 2003.

32. Bill Gertz, "N. Korea Retests 100-mile-range Cruise Missile," *Washington Times,* Oct. 21, 2003.

33. KCNA, "U.S. Shameful Behavior under Fire," Oct. 21, 2003.

34. Ibid. "Spokesman for DPRK Foreign Ministry."

35. KCNA, "U.S. Urged to reciprocate DPRK's Good Faith," Nov. 4, 2003.

## 11. "WE DON'T NEGOTIATE WITH EVIL WE DEFEAT IT."

1. "Interview of Ms. DeSutter With Regard to the Bolton Nomination," Transcript, Senate Foreign Relations Committee, May 5, 2005.

2. Karen DeYoung, *Soldier: The Life of Colin Powell* (New York: Alfred A Knopf, 2006), 499.

3. Glenn Kessler, "Impact From the Shadows: Cheney Wields Power With Few Fingerprints," *Washington Post,* Oct. 5, 2004.

4. Barbara Slavin, "N. Korea OKs U.S. Visit to Complex," *USA Today,* Jan. 2, 2004.

5. Transcript, Seigfried Hecker testimony, Senate Committee on Foreign Relations Hearing on Visit to the Yongbyon Nuclear Scientific Research Center in North Korea, Jan. 21, 2004.

6. Ibid.

7. Ibid.

8. Ralph Cossa, "Washington-Seoul: Tough Times Ahead?" *The Japan Times*, Jan. 21, 2004. http://search.japantimes.co.jp/cgi-bin/eo20040121rc.html

9. Glenn Kessler, "U.S. Will Stand Firm on N. Korea," *Washington Post*, Feb. 16, 2004.

10. George Crile, *Charlie Wilson's War* (New York: Grove Press, 2003), 268.

11. James Kelly, Testimony Before the Senate Foreign Relations Committee, Mar. 2, 2004. http://www.state.gov/p/eap/rls/rm/2004/30093.htm

12. Karen DeYoung, *Soldier*, 499.

13. Ibid.

14. Glenn Kessler, "Bush Signals Patience on North Korea Is Waning: Directive Sent to Team at Talks in Beijing," *Washington Post,* Mar. 4, 2004.

15. Daniel Sneider, "Dangerous Deadlock," *San Jose Mercury*, Kyodo Mar. 18, 2004.

16. Choe Sang-hun, "S. Korean Chief Seeks Less U.S. Reliance," The Associated Press, Mar. 1, 2004.

17. Joseph Kahn, "Cheney Urges China to Press North Korea on A-Bombs," *New York Times*, Apr. 15, 2004.

18. Doyle McManus, "Cheney Makes Clear U.S. Is Not Willing to Bend on North Korea," *Los Angeles Times,* Apr. 16, 2004.

19. KCNA, "DPRK Foreign Ministry Spokesman Blasts Cheney's Anti-DPRK Remarks," Apr. 18, 2004.

20. Selig Harrison, "Riding a Tiger in North Korea," *Newsweek*, May 17, 2004.

21. Ibid. "Inside North Korea: Leaders Open to Ending Nuclear Crisis," *Financial Times*, May 4, 2004.

22. "N. Korea's Kim Told Koizumi He Is Eager for Talks With U.S.," Kyodo, Jun. 22, 2004.

23. David Pilling, "N. Korea 'Ready to Abandon Nuclear Arms'—Koizumi," *Financial Times*, Jun. 8, 2004.

24. "Bush: Kim Jong Il Is a Liar," *Dong-A Ilbo*, Jun. 16, 2004.

## 12. "SOME GOOD, SOME BAD, SOME UGLY"

1. John Kerry, "New Strategies to Meet New Threats," speech in West Palm Beach, FL., Jun. 1, 2004.

2. Yoichi Funabashi, *The Peninsula Question: A Chronicle of the Second Korean Nuclear Crisis*, (Washington, DC: Brookings Institution Press, 2007), 361–67.

3. Senate Foreign Relations Committee, Hearings: "Dealing with North Korea's Nuclear Program," Prepared Statement of James Kelly, Assistant Secretary of State for Asian and Pacific Affairs, Jul. 15, 2004.

4. Philip P. Pan and Glenn Kessler, "U.S. Revises Proposal at North Korea Nuclear Talks: Fuel Aid, Security Statement Possible During 3-Month Test," *Washington Post,* Jun. 24, 2004.

5. Senate Foreign Relations Committee, Hearings: "Dealing with North Korea's Nuclear Program," Kelly.

6. Ibid.

7. KCNA, "DPRK Foreign Ministry Spokesman on Six-Party Talks," Jun. 28, 2004.

8. Senate Foreign Relations Committee, Hearings: "Dealing with North Korea's Nuclear Program," Kelly.

9.   David L. Asher, "The North Korean Criminal State, Its Ties to Organized Crime, and the Possibility of WMD Proliferation," Remarks to the Counter-Proliferation Strategy Group, Woodrow Wilson Center, Oct. 21. 2005.

10.  Anthony Failoa, "As Tensions Subside Between Two Koreas, U.S. Strives to Adjust," *Washington Post*, Jul. 25, 2004.

11.  KCNA, "KCNA Terms Bush Fascist Tyrant," Aug. 24, 2004.

12.  White House Transcript, "President's Remarks at Ask President Bush Event," Aug. 18, 2004.

13.  Transcript of nationally televised debate on PBS, Sept. 30, 2004.

14.  KCNA, "U.S. 'North Korea Human Rights Act Failed,'" Oct. 4, 2004.

15.  KCNA, "Spokesman for DPRK FM on Prospect of Resumption of Six-party Talks," Nov. 13, 2004.

## 13. "WE HAVE MANUFACTURED NUKES"

1.   The White House, official transcript, Inaugural Address, Jan. 20, 2005.

2.   The White House, official transcript, State of the Union Address, Feb. 2, 2005.

3.   Transcript, "Opening Statement by Dr. Condoleezza Rice," Senate Foreign Relations Committee, Jan. 18, 2005.

4.   David E. Sanger and William J. Broad, "Tests Said to Tie Deal on Uranium to North Korea," *New York Times*, Feb. 2, 2005.

5.   Ibid.

6.   Glenn Kessler and Dafna Linzer, "Nuclear Evidence Could Point to Pakistan," *Washington Post*, Feb. 3, 2005.

7.   Sanger and Broad, "Tests Said to Tie Deal on Uranium to North Korea."

8.   Kessler and Linzer, "Nuclear Evidence Could Point to Pakistan."

9.   Dafna Linzer, "U.S. Misled Allies About Nuclear Export: North Korea Sent Material To Pakistan, Not to Libya," *Washington Post*, Mar. 20, 2005.

10.  KCNA, "DPRK FM on Its Stand to Suspend Its Participation in Six-Party Talks for Indefinite Period," Feb. 10, 2005.

11.  Secretary of State Condoleezza Rice, "Remarks at Sophia University," Mar. 19, 2005.

12.  U.S. State Department transcript, "Condoleezza Rice, Interview with James Rosen of Fox News," Apr. 21, 2005.

13.  White House, Office of the Press Secretary, Press Conference by President Bush, Apr. 28, 2005.

14.  KCNA, "FM Spokesman Slams Bush's Vituperation against DPRK's Supreme Headquarters," Apr. 30, 2005.

15.  KCNA, "U.S. VP's Vituperation against DPRK's Supreme Headquarters Rebuked," Jun. 2, 2005.

16.  Selig Harrison, Center for International Policy, Apr. 21, 2005.

17.  KCNA, "Spokesman for DPRK Foreign Ministry Assails Rice's Reckless Remarks," Apr. 25, 2005.

18.  David E. Sanger and William J. Broad, "U.S. Cites Signs of Korean Preparations for Nuclear Test," *New York Times,* May 6, 2005.

19.  Ibid.

20. Choe Sang-hun, "Epithets Increase Tension Over Korea," *International Herald Tribune*, May 31, 2005.

21. Joseph Kahn, "China Says U.S. Impeded North Korea Arms Talks," *New York Times*, May 13, 2005.

22. Glenn Kessler, *The Confidante: Condoleezza Rice and the Creation of the Bush Legacy* (New York: St. Martin's Press, 2007), 77.

23. KCNA, "Spokesman of DPRK FM on Contacts Between Heads of DPRK and U.S. Dels," Jul. 9, 2005.

## 14. THE SEPTEMBER 19 DECLARATION

1. "Joint Declaration on the Denuclearization of the Korean Peninsula," Feb. 19, 1992.

2. Glenn Kessler, *The Confidante: Condoleezza Rice and the Creation of the Bush Legacy* (New York: St. Martin's Press, 2007), 259.

3. "How to Keep Talking," *Time* Magazine, Sept. 26, 2005.

4. The full text of the September 19 Declaration reads as follows:

> Joint Statement of the Fourth Round of the Six-Party Talks
> Beijing 19 September 2005
> The Fourth Round of the Six-Party Talks was held in Beijing, China, among the People's Republic of China, the Democratic People's Republic of Korea, Japan, the Republic of Korea, the Russian Federation, and the United States of America from July 26th to August 7th, and from September 13th to 19th, 2005.
> Mr. Wu Dawei, Vice Minister of Foreign Affairs of the PRC, Mr. Kim Gye Gwan, Vice Minister of Foreign Affairs of the DPRK; Mr. Kenichiro Sasae, Director-General for Asian and Oceanian Affairs, Ministry of Foreign Affairs of Japan; Mr. Song Min-soon, Deputy Minister of Foreign Affairs and Trade of the ROK; Mr. Alexandr Alekseyev, Deputy Minister of Foreign Affairs of the Russian Federation; and Mr. Christopher Hill, Assistant Secretary of State for East Asian and Pacific Affairs of the United States attended the talks as heads of their respective delegations. Vice Foreign Minister Wu Dawei chaired the talks.
> For the cause of peace and stability on the Korean Peninsula and in Northeast Asia at large, the Six Parties held, in the spirit of mutual respect and equality, serious and practical talks concerning the denuclearization of the Korean Peninsula on the basis of the common understanding of the previous three rounds of talks, and agreed, in this context, to the following:
>
> > 1. The Six Parties unanimously reaffirmed that the goal of the Six-Party Talks is the verifiable denuclearization of the Korean Peninsula in a peaceful manner.
> > The DPRK committed to abandoning all nuclear weapons and existing nuclear programs and returning, at an early date, to the Treaty on the Non-Proliferation of Nuclear Weapons and to IAEA safeguards.
> > The United States affirmed that it has no nuclear weapons on the Korean Peninsula and has no intention to attack or invade the DPRK with

nuclear or conventional weapons.

The ROK reaffirmed its commitment not to receive or deploy nuclear weapons in accordance with the 1992 Joint Declaration of the Denuclearization of the Korean Peninsula, while affirming that there exist no nuclear weapons within its territory.

The 1992 Joint Declaration of the Denuclearization of the Korean Peninsula should be observed and implemented.

The DPRK stated that it has the right to peaceful uses of nuclear energy. The other parties expressed their respect and agreed to discuss, at an appropriate time, the subject of the provision of light water reactor to the DPRK.

2. The Six Parties undertook, in their relations, to abide by the purposes and principles of the Charter of the United Nations and recognized norms of international relations.

The DPRK and the United States undertook to respect each other's sovereignty, exist peacefully together, and take steps to normalize their relations subject to their respective bilateral policies.

The DPRK and Japan undertook to take steps to normalize their relations in accordance with the Pyongyang Declaration, on the basis of the settlement of unfortunate past and the outstanding issues of concern.

3. The Six Parties undertook to promote economic cooperation in the fields of energy, trade and investment, bilaterally and/or multilaterally. China, Japan, ROK, Russia and the US stated their willingness to provide energy assistance to the DPRK.

The ROK reaffirmed its proposal of July 12th 2005 concerning the provision of 2 million kilowatts of electric power to the DPRK.

4. The Six Parties committed to joint efforts for lasting peace and stability in Northeast Asia.

The directly related parties will negotiate a permanent peace regime on the Korean Peninsula at an appropriate separate forum.

The Six Parties agreed to explore ways and means for promoting security cooperation in Northeast Asia.

5. The Six Parties agreed to take coordinated steps to implement the aforementioned consensus in a phased manner in line with the principle of "commitment for commitment, action for action."

The Six Parties agreed to hold the Fifth Round of the Six-Party Talks in Beijing in early November 2005 at a date to be determined through consultations.

5. "Statement of Assistant Secretary of State Christopher R. Hill at the Closing Plenary of the Fourth Round of Six-Party Talks," Sept. 19, 2006.

## 15. ILLICIT ACTIVITIES

1. Bruce Townsend, Remarks to the International Association of Financial Crimes Investigators, Sept. 2, 2004, Chicago, Ill. Cited in Sheena Chestnut, "The Sopranos State?

North Korean Involvement in Criminal Activity and Implications for International Security," Center for International Security and Cooperation, Stanford University, May 20, 2005.

2. Sheena Chestnut, "The Sopranos State? North Korean Involvement in Criminal Activity and Implications for International Security," Center for International Security and Cooperation, Stanford University, May 20, 2005, 154–55.

3. A detailed list of various press accounts about Bureau 39 can be found in Congressional Research Service, "Drug Trafficking and North Korea: Issues for U.S. Policy," Dec. 5, 2003, 11.

4. Donald Greenlees and David Lague, "The Money Trail That Linked North Korea to Macao," New York Times, Apr. 11, 2007.

5. Indictment. United States District Court for the Central District of California, June 2005 Grand Jury, United States of America, Plaintiff, v. Chao Tung Wu, Paul Tak Cheung Yeung, Chen Chiang Lu, Thi Hong Lan, Defendants.

6. Ibid.

7. Ibid.

8. Greenlees and Lague, "The Money Trail That Linked North Korea to Macao."

9. Department of Treasury, "Treasury Designates Banco Delta Asia as Primary Money Laundering Concern under USA PATRIOT Act," Sept. 15. 2005.

10. Ibid.

11. Dana Millbank, "A Hard-Nosed Litigator Becomes Bush's Policy Point Man," Washington Post, Apr. 30, 2002.

12. Joel Brinkley, "China Says North Korea Talks Will Resume Tuesday," New York Times, Sept. 9, 2005.

13. "N. Korea Demands End to U.S. Financial Sanctions," Chosun.com, Nov. 11, 2005.

14. Lee Chi-dong, "Nuclear Talks Turn Sour After Pyongyang's Accusation of Washington," Yonhap News, Nov. 10, 2005.

15. KCNA, "DPRK Foreign Ministry Spokesman Urges U.S. to Lift Financial Sanctions Against it," Dec. 2, 2005.

16. Glenn Kessler, "Semantic Dispute Cancels N. Korea Treasury Meeting," Washington Post, Dec. 1, 2005.

17. "Pocketbook Policing," Newsweek, Apr. 10, 2006.

18. David L. Asher, "The North Korean Criminal State, Its Ties to Organized Crime, and the Possibility of WMD Proliferation," Remarks at the Woodrow Wilson Center, Oct. 21, 2005.

19. Nigel Cowie, "U.S. Financial Allegations—What they Mean," Nautilus Institute, Policy Forum Online, May 6, 2006.

20. KCNA, "DPRK Foreign Ministry Spokesman Urges U.S. to Lift Financial Sanctions," Feb. 28, 2006.

21. Henry A. Kissinger, "A Test for Nuclear Diplomacy," Washington Post, May 16, 2006.

22. "Hill Snubs N. Korea's Chief Nuclear Negotiator," English.chosun.com, Apr. 12, 2006.

23. "N. Korea's Nuke Negotiator Digs in After Snub from U.S." Chosun Ilbo, Apr. 13, 2006.

24. "DPRK Threatens to Boost Nuclear Arsenal," Reuters, Apr. 13, 2006.

## 16. GOING BALLISTIC

1. White House, Office of the Press Secretary, Press Conference in Chicago, Jul. 7, 2006.
2. http://www.ifpa.org/pdf/fences.pdf, 44.
3. C. P. Vick, May, June, July 2006 *Build-up to the Taepodong-2c/3 Satellite Launch Attempt,* Global Security.org, Oct. 7, 2006. http://www.globalsecurity.org/wmd/library/news/dprk/2006/060710-nkir2627.htm
4. KCNA, "DPRK Foreign Ministry: DPRK's Stand on Six-Party Talks Reclarified," Jun. 1, 2006.
5. Reuters, "N. Korea Said to Seek talks Over Missile," Jun. 21, 2006.
6. William J. Perry and Ashton B. Carter, "If Necessary, Strike and Destroy: North Korea Cannot Be Allowed to Test This Missile," *Washington Post,* Jun. 22, 2006.
7. Charles L. Pritchard, "No, Don't Blow It Up," *Washington Post,* Jun. 23, 2006.
8. USINFO.State.gov, Jun. 29, 2006.
9. Michael Hirsh, Melinda Liu, and George Wehfritz, "We Are a Nuclear Power," *Newsweek,* Oct. 17, 2006.
10. U.S. Embassy Transcript, "Ambassador Schieffer Comments on North Korean Missile Launches," Jul. 5, 2006.
11. http://english.chosun.com/w21data/html/news/200607/200607060024.html
12. Norimitsu Onishi and Joseph Kahn, "North Korea's Neighbors Condemn Missile tests but Differ on What To Do," *New York Times,* Jul. 5, 2006.
13. John Bolton, *Surrender Is Not An Option,* (New York: Threshold Editions, 2007), 291.
14. Michael A. Fletcher, "Bush Rejects Solo Talks With North Korea," *Washington Post,* Jul. 8, 2006.
15. Helene Cooper and Warren Hoge, "U.S. Seeks Strong Measures to Warn North Koreans," *New York Times,* Jul. 5, 2006.
16. Bolton, *Surrender Is Not An Option,* 295.
17. Ibid., 297.
18. "China Pressures North Korea to Return to Talks," The Associated Press, Jul. 11, 2006.
19. Bolton, *Surrender Is Not An Option,* 294.
20. "Hu Says China Opposes Any Action That May Worsen Korean Peninsula Situation," Xinhua News Agency, Jul. 12, 2006.
21. KCNA, "DPRK Foreign Ministry Spokesman on Its Missile Launches," Jul. 6, 2006.
22. USINFO@State.gov. "New Draft Resolution on North Korea Not Strong Enough, U.S. Says," Jul. 13, 2006.
23. Warren Hoge, "U.N. Council, in Weakened Resolution, Demands End to North Korean Missile program," *New York Times,* Jul. 16, 2006. See also text, UN Security Council Resolution 1695. http://www.un.org/News/Press/docs/2006/sc8778.doc.htm
24. USINFO@State.gov, "U.N. Security Council Demands North Korea End Missile Program," Jul. 15, 2006.
25. Bolton, *Surrender Is Not An Option,* 302.
26. KCNA, "DPRK Foreign Ministry Refutes 'Resolution of UN Security Council,' " Jul. 16, 2006.
27. KCNA, "DPRK Foreign Ministry Clarifies Stand on New Measure to Bolster War Deterrent," Oct. 3, 2006.

28. ABCNews.com, "North Korea Appears to be Preparing for Nuclear Test," Aug. 17, 2006. http://abcnews.go.com/International/Story?id=2326083&page=1

29. *The Nelson Report*, Oct. 3, 2006.

30. United Nations Security Council, Statement by the President of the Security Council, S/PRST/2006/41, Oct. 6, 2006.

31. "South Korean President Warns Against North Korea Nuclear Test," The Associated Press, Oct. 5, 2006.

32. Dafna Linzer, "U.S. Won't Accept a Nuclear North Korea," *Washington Post*, Oct. 5, 2006.

33. *The Nelson Report,* Oct. 5, 2006.

## 17. THE BOMB

1. David E. Sanger, "The North Korean Challenge: A Strategic Jolt," *New York Times*, Oct. 10, 2006.

2. The White House, "President Bush's Statement on North Korea Nuclear Test," Oct. 9, 2006.

3. Ibid.

4. Ibid.

5. John Bolton, *Surrender Is Not An Option* (New York: Threshold Editions, 2007), 303.

6. David Pilling, "Abe Fails to Quell Calls for Debate on Going Nuclear," *Financial Times*, Nov. 9, 2006.

7. http://www.kcna.co.jp/calendar-e/frame.htm

8. Bolton, *Surrender Is Not An Option*, 308.

9. *The Nelson Report,* Oct. 23, 2006.

10. Transcript, *Fox News Sunday,* Oct. 22, 2006.

11. ABC News, *This Week with George Stephanopolous,* Oct. 8, 2006.

12. U.S. State Department Transcript, Rice Briefing on Upcoming Trip to Asia, Oct. 16, 2006.

13. *Joong Ang Daily*, Oct. 18, 2006.

14. Glenn Kessler, "Rice: China Gave N. Korea 'A Strong Message,'" *Washington Post*, Oct. 20, 2006.

## 18. "HOW ARE WE GOING TO GET OUT OF THIS?"

1. Transcript, Christopher Hill Press Conference at U.S. Embassy, Beijing, China, Oct. 31, 2006. http://seoul.usembassy.gov/420_103106_1.html

2. "North Korea, U.S. Demand Compromise But Appear Not to Budge Ahead of Nuclear Talks," *International Herald Tribune*/The Associated Press, Dec. 16, 2006.

3. White House Transcript, "President Bush Meets With President Roh of the Republic of Korea," Nov. 18, 2006.

4. Lee Jo-hee, "News focus: Doubts Surround Success of Nuke Talks," *Korea Herald*, Dec. 12, 2006.

5. "N. Korean Delegate Rules Out Unilateral Nuke Abandonment," Kyodo, Nov. 30, 2006.

6. Elizabeth Williamson, "Hitting Kim Jong Il Right in the Cognac," *Washington Post*, Nov. 30, 2006.

7. U.S. Treasury Department, Prepared Remarks of Stuart Levey, Under Secretary for Terrorism and Financial Intelligence, Before the US-MENA Private Sector Dialogue on Combating Money Laundering and Terrorist Financing, Dec. 11, 2006.

8. Department of Treasury, "Treasury Designates Banco Delta Asia as Primary Money Laundering Concern under USA PATRIOT Act," Sept. 15, 2005.

9. Confidential report of Banco Delta Asia, Ernst & Young, Dec. 16, 2005 (leaked to McClatchey Newspapers and posted on the Internet).

10. John McGlynn, "Financial Sanctions and North Korea: In Search of the Evidence of Currency Counterfeiting and Money Laundering," *Japan Focus*, Jul. 7, 2007. http://japanfocus.org/products/details/2463

11. Edward Cody, "N. Korea Balks at Weapons Discussion," *Washington Post*, Dec. 22, 2006.

12. "North Korea Talks End With No Deal," Reuters, Dec. 22, 2006.

13. Jonathan Karl, "North Korea Prepping Nuclear Weapons Test, Defense Officials Tell ABC News," ABC-TV, Jan. 4, 2007.

14. Glenn Kessler, *The Confidante: Condoleezza Rice and the Creation of the Bush Legacy* (New York: St. Martin's Press, 2007), 238.

15. Jim Yardley, "Private talks Held in Berlin Spurred Sides to Reach a Deal," *New York Times*, Feb. 14, 2007.

16. Transcript, Christopher Hill speech to the American Assembly, Berlin, Jan. 17, 2007. http://seoul.usembassy.gov/420_011707_3.html

## 19. "WE ARE ALL WAITING FOR YOU"

1. Jim Yardley, "Seed of North Korean Nuclear Deal was Planted in Berlin," *New York Times*, Feb. 14, 2007.

2. Chris Buckley, "N. Korea Deal Born as Storm in a Tea Cup," Reuters, Feb. 14, 2007.

3. Ibid.

4. "Text of the Joint Agreement on North Korea's Nuclear Disarmament," as provided by the Chinese Foreign Ministry, Feb. 13, 2007.

5. White House Transcript, "Statement by President Bush on Six-Party Talks," Feb. 13, 2007.

6. Helene Cooper and Jim Yardley, "Pact With North Korea Draws Fire From a Wide Range of Critics in U.S.," *New York Times*, Feb. 14, 2007.

7. James Sterngold, "How Deal on Korea Nuclear Program Was Cut: Bush, Kim Jong Il Both Gave Ground to Permit a Pact," *San Francisco Chronicle*, Feb. 14, 2007.

8. John Bolton, *Surrender Is Not an Option*, (New York: Threshold Editions, 2007), 311.

9. "Faith-Based Non-proliferation, *Wall Street Journal*, Feb. 14, 2007.

10. "Agreeing to the Same Framework," *National Review*, Feb. 14, 2007.

11. Norimitsu Onishi, "Japan Maintains Hardline Stance Toward North Korea," *New York Times*, Feb. 14, 2007.

12. *The Nelson Report,* Feb. 21, 2007.

13. Glenn Kessler, "New Doubts on Nuclear Efforts by North Korea," *Washington Post,* Mar. 1, 2007.

14. Transcript, "Update on the Six-Party Talks With Christopher R. Hill," The Brookings Institution, Center for Northeast Asian Policy Studies, Feb. 22, 2007.

15. Transcript, Hearing of the Senate Armed Services Coimmittee, "Current and Future Worldwide Threats to the National Security of the United States," Feb. 27, 2007.

16. Editorial, "Another Intelligence Twist," *Washington Post*, Mar. 2, 2007.

17. Steven R. Weisman, "The Ripples of Punishing One Bank," *New York Times*, Jul. 3, 2007.

18. Treasury Department, "Prepared Remarks of Stuart Levey, Under Secretary for Terrorism and Financial Intelligence," Mar. 14, 2007.

19. Anne Penketh, "North Korea Visit 'Cleared the Air,' Says U.N. Nuclear Chief," *The Independent*, Mar. 15, 2007.

20. U.S. Treasury Department, "Statement by DAS Glaser on the Disposition of DPRK-Related Funds Frozen at Banco Delta Asia," Mar. 19, 2007.

21. Steven R. Weisman, "The Ripples of Punishing One Bank," *New York Times*, Jul. 3, 2007.

## 20. "DR. MR. CHAIRMAN"

1. Daniel Wakin, "Philharmonic Agrees to Play in North Korea," *New York Times*, Dec. 10, 2007.

2. Andrei Lankov, "The Natural Death of North Korean Stalinism," *Asia Policy*, Jan. 2006.

3. U.S. Department of State, "Six-Party Talks—Second-Phase Actions for the Implementation of the September 2005 Joint Statement," Oct. 3, 2007.

4. Transcript, Assistant Secretary of State Christopher Hill Press Conference," Tokyo, Japan, Nov. 3, 2007. http://tokyo.usembassy.gov/e/p/tp-20071103-71.html

5. Ibid.

6. Bradley K. Martin, *Under the Loving Care of the Fatherly Leader* (New York: St. Martin's Press, 2004), 700.

7. Uzi Mahnaimi, Sarah Baxter, and Michael Sheridan, "Israel 'Blew Apart Syrian Nuclear Cache,'" *Sunday Times* (London), Sept. 16, 2007.

8. David E. Sanger and Mark Mazzetti, "Israel Struck Syrian Nuclear Project, Analysts Say," *New York Times*, Oct. 14, 2007.

9. Ibid.

10. John R. Bolton, "Pyongyang's Upper Hand," *Asian Wall Street Journal,* Aug. 31, 2007.

11. Jim Brown, "John Bolton Blasts Bush, Rice for Policy of 'Rewarding Proliferators,'" OneNewsNow.com, Oct. 29, 2007.

12. William J. Broad and Mark Mazzetti, "Yet Another Photo of Site in Syria, Yet More Questions," *New York Times*, Oct. 27, 2007.

13. Glenn Kessler, "Syria-N. Korea Reports Won't Stop Talks" *Washington Post*, Sept. 15, 2007.

14. *The Nelson Report,* Oct. 25, 2007.

15. Robert Carlin, *The Korea Yearbook, 2007* (Leidens: Konniklijke Brill NV, 2007).

## POSTSCRIPT

1. Glenn Kessler and Robin Wright, "Accusing N. Korea May Stall Nuclear Pact," *Washington Post*, Apr. 26, 2008.

2. John R. Bolton, "Bush's North Korea Capitulation," *Wall Street Journal*, Apr. 15, 2008.

3. Arshad Mohammed, "U.S. Lays Out Way to Break North Korea Nuclear Deadlock," Reuters, Apr. 11, 2008.

4. "North Korea Redux," *New York Times* editorial, Apr. 25, 2008.

# SELECT
# BIBLIOGRAPHY

Madeleine Albright, *Madam Secretary,* Miramax Books, New York, 2003.

John Bolton, *Surrender Is Not an Option: Defending America at the United Nations and Abroad,* Threshold Editions, New York, 2007.

Michael Breen, *Kim Jong Il, North Korea's Dear Leader,* John Wiley & Sons, Singapore, 2004.

Bill Clinton, *My Life,* Random House, New York, 2004.

Gordon Corera, *Shopping for Bombs: Nuclear Proliferation, Global Insecurity, and the Rise and Fall of the A. Q. Khan Network,* Oxford University Press, Oxford, 2006.

Karen DeYoung, *Soldier: The Life of Colin Powell,* Alfred A. Knopf, New York, 2006.

Chuck Downs, *Over the Line: North Korea's Negotiating Strategy,* The AEI Press, Washington, 1999.

Selig Harrison, *Korean Endgame: A Strategy for Reunification and U.S. Disengagement,* Princeton University Press, Princeton, 2002.

Helen-Louise Hunter, *Kim Il-song's North Korea,* Praeger, Westport, CT, 1999.

Kang Chol Hwan, *The Aquariums of Pyongyang: Ten Years in the North Korean Gulag,* Basic Books, New York, 2001.

Glenn Kessler, *The Confidante: Condoleezza Rice and the Creation of the Bush Legacy,* St. Martin's Press, New York, 2007.

Adrian Levy and Catherine Scott-Clark, *Deception: Pakistan, the United States and the Secret Trade in Nuclear Weapons,* Walker & Company, New York, 2007.

James Mann, *Rise of the Vulcans: The History of Bush's War Cabinet,* Penguin Books, New York, 2004.

Bradley K. Martin, *Under the Loving Care of the Fatherly Leader,* St. Martin's Press, New York, 2004.

Marcus Noland, *Avoiding the Apocalypse: The Future of the Two Koreas,* Institute for International Economics, Washington, DC, 2000.

Don Oberdorfer, *The Two Koreas,* Basic Books, New York, 1997.

Daniel Poneman, Joel S, Wit, and Robert Gallucci, *Going Critical: The First North Korean Nuclear Crisis,* Brookings Institution Press, Washington, DC, 2004.

Charles L. Pritchard, *Failed Diplomacy,* Brookings Institution Press, Washington, DC, 2007.

Leon V. Sigal, *Disarming Strangers: Nuclear Diplomacy with North Korea,* Princeton University Press, Princeton, 1998.

Hazel Smith, *Hungry for Peace: International Security, Humanitarian Assistance and Social Change in North Korea,* United States Institute for Peace, Washington, DC, 2005.

Ron Suskind, *The One Per Cent Doctrine: Deep Inside America's Pursuit of Its Enemies Since 9/11,* Simon & Schuster, New York, 2006.

Bob Woodward, *State of Denial,* Simon & Schuster, New York, 2006.

Yoichi Funabashi, *The Peninsula Question: A Chronicle of the Second Korean Nuclear Crisis,* Brookings Institution Press, Washington, DC, 2007.

# INDEX